The Borders of Integration

OHIO UNIVERSITY PRESS POLISH AND POLISH-AMERICAN STUDIES SERIES

Series Editor: John J. Bukowczyk

Framing the Polish Home: Postwar Cultural Constructions of Hearth, Nation, and Self, edited by Bożena Shallcross

Traitors and True Poles: Narrating a Polish-American Identity, 1880–1939, by Karen Majewski

Auschwitz, Poland, and the Politics of Commemoration, 1945–1979, by Jonathan Huener

The Exile Mission: The Polish Political Diaspora and Polish Americans, 1939–1956, by Anna D. Jaroszyńska-Kirchmann

The Grasinski Girls: The Choices They Had and the Choices They Made, by Mary Patrice Erdmans

Testaments: Two Novellas of Emigration and Exile, by Danuta Mostwin

The Clash of Moral Nations: Cultural Politics in Piłsudski's Poland, 1926–1935, by Eva Plach

Holy Week: A Novel of the Warsaw Ghetto Uprising, by Jerzy Andrzejewski

The Law of the Looking Glass: Cinema in Poland, 1896–1939, by Sheila Skaff

Rome's Most Faithful Daughter: The Catholic Church and Independent Poland, 1914–1939, by Neal Pease

The Origins of Modern Polish Democracy, edited by M. B. B. Biskupski, James S. Pula, and Piotr J. Wróbel

The Borders of Integration: Polish Migrants in Germany and the United States, 1870–1924, by Brian McCook

The Borders of Integration

*Polish Migrants in Germany
and the United States, 1870–1924*

Brian McCook

OHIO UNIVERSITY PRESS

ATHENS

Ohio University Press, Athens, Ohio 45701
www.ohioswallow.com
© 2011 by Ohio University Press

To obtain permission to quote, reprint, or otherwise reproduce or distribute material
from Ohio University Press publications, please contact our rights and permissions
department at (740) 593-1154 or (740) 593-4536 (fax).

Printed in the United States of America
Ohio University Press books are printed on acid-free paper ⊗ ™

18 17 16 15 14 13 12 11   5 4 3 2 1

Library of Congress Cataloging-in-Publication Data
McCook, Brian Joseph, 1973–
  The borders of integration : Polish migrants in Germany and the United States, 1870–
1924 / Brian McCook.
    p. cm. — (Ohio University Press Polish and Polish-American studies series)
  Includes bibliographical references and index.
  ISBN 978-0-8214-1925-0 (hardcover : acid-free paper) — ISBN 978-0-8214-1926-7
(pbk. : acid-free paper) — ISBN 978-0-8214-4351-4 (electronic)
  1. Poles—Cultural assimilation—Germany—Ruhr River Valley—History. 2. Polish
Americans—Cultural assimilation—Pennsylvania—History. 3. Immigrants—
Germany—Ruhr River Valley—History. 4. Immigrants—Pennsylvania—History.
5. Coal miners—Germany—Ruhr River Valley—History. 6. Coal miners—
Pennsylvania—History. 7. Community life—Germany—Ruhr River Valley—History.
8. Community life—Pennsylvania—History. 9. Ruhr River Valley (Germany)—Ethnic
relations. 10. Pennsylvania—Ethnic relations. I. Title.
  DD801.R8M35 2011
  304.8'4355043809034—dc22
                            2010050771

Publication of books in the Polish and Polish-American Studies Series has been made possible in part by the generous support of the following sponsors:

Polish American Historical Association,
New Britain, Connecticut

Stanislaus A. Blejwas Endowed Chair in Polish
and Polish American Studies,
Central Connecticut State University,
New Britain, Connecticut

The Polish Institute of Arts and Sciences of America, Inc.,
New York, New York

The Piast Institute: An Institute for Polish
and Polish American Affairs,
Detroit, Michigan

Thomas Duszak,
Harrisburg, Pennsylvania

Contents

Illustrations

Młody Polak w Niemczech (Young Pole in Germany), a ZPwN magazine
   for teenagers

A blessing ceremony led by ZPwN president Father Bolesław Domański

The leadership of the ZPwN in 1937

A 1923 steamship advertisement

The 1936 ZPwN meeting held in Bochum, Germany

Tables

Series Editor's Preface

In the late nineteenth century and the early twentieth, the lands of partitioned Poland bled off "surplus" population that migrated in search of bread and work. Over three hundred thousand Poles found their way to the coal mines of the Ruhr; 160,000, to the collieries of northeastern Pennsylvania. Given the similarities of their principal industry and their immigrant populations, these two sites offer up a nearly perfect opportunity to investigate how different social structures, governmental policies, and political systems affected the process of immigrant incorporation.

The Borders of Integration: Polish Migrants in Germany and the United States, 1870–1924, Brian McCook's study of Poles in Germany's Ruhr region and in northeastern Pennsylvania, is a model of how comparative history can highlight factors and conditions that have helped produce widely varying historical outcomes. "Cast as an internal 'other' against which German and American national identities became defined," McCook writes, "Poles experienced significant levels of discrimination; their presence both in the workplace and larger society was increasingly deemed undesirable, even dangerous, by large segments of the general public and the state." Yet, after fifty or so years at their respective destinations, Polish migrants achieved different levels of social integration, different organization patterns, and different types of identity. In the best transnational fashion, *The Borders of Integration*, winner of the Polish American Historical Association's Stanley A. Kulczycki Prize, thus illuminates the respective histories of two classic migration stories, hitherto usually treated separately in the historical literature. But McCook's pioneering research also holds profound implications for current debates involving the incorporation of contemporary immigrants into today's host societies.

Publication of the Ohio University Press Polish and Polish-American Studies Series marks a milestone in the maturation of the Polish studies field and stands as a fitting tribute to the scholars and organizations whose efforts have brought it to fruition. Supported by a series advisory board of accomplished Polonists and Polish-Americanists, the Polish and Polish-American

Studies Series has been made possible through generous financial assistance from the Polish American Historical Association and that organization's Stanley Kulczycki Publication Fund, the Stanislaus A. Blejwas Endowed Chair in Polish and Polish American Studies at Central Connecticut State University, and the Kosciuszko Foundation, and through institutional support from Wayne State University and Ohio University Press. The series has benefited from the warm encouragement of many persons, including Gillian Berchowitz, M. B. B. Biskupski, the late Stanislaus A. Blejwas, Thomas Duszak, Mary Erdmans, Thaddeus Gromada, Anna Jaroszyńska-Kirchmann, James S. Pula, Thaddeus Radzilowski, and David Sanders. The moral and material support from all of these institutions and individuals is gratefully acknowledged.

John J. Bukowczyk

Acknowledgments

There are many persons and institutions I wish to thank for making this comparative study of Polish migrants possible. For financial support during the research, writing, and production of this volume, I am indebted to the German Chancellor Scholars Program of the Alexander von Humboldt Foundation; the German Historical Institute (Washington, D.C.); the Kosciuszko Foundation; the Social Science Research Council's Berlin Program for German and European Studies; the Institute for European History at the University of Mainz; the Mellon Foundation; the School of Cultural Studies at Leeds Metropolitan University; the University of California at Berkeley, especially the Center for German and European Studies, the Center for Slavic and East European Studies, the Institute of International Studies, the Phi Beta Kappa Society, and the Berkeley History Department. While conducting research in Germany, I was fortunate to be affiliated and work with Klaus Bade and Jochen Oltmer at the Institute for Migration and Intercultural Studies in Osnabrück and Klaus Tenfelde at the Institute of Social Movements in Bochum. I also thank the professional and helpful staff at the State Archives in Münster, the Main State Archive in Düsseldorf, and the City Archives of Bochum, Gelsenkirchen, and Oberhausen, respectively. In Poland, I am indebted to the German Historical Institute in Warsaw, which generously opened its library to me, and to the archivists at the Poznań City and State Archives. In the United States, I cannot thank enough the personnel at the Pennsylvania State Archives in Harrisburg, the Historical Society of Pennsylvania in Philadelphia, the Catholic University Archives in Washington, D.C., the Polish National Catholic Church, the Anthracite Mining Museum, and the Public Library in Scranton.

A number of conferences, workshops, and forums helped me refine and focus my ideas. I presented papers at the German Historical Institute in Washington, D.C.; the Woodrow Wilson Center Junior Scholars Training Seminar in East European Studies; the American Historical Association/Polish American Historical Association meetings in Chicago, Washington, D.C., and Philadelphia; the Trans-Atlantic Summer Institute in German

Studies; the European Social Science History Conference meetings in Amsterdam and Lisbon; the Social Science History Conference in Minnesota; the Social History Society meeting in Warwick; the Central European University in Budapest; the Ruhr-University Bochum; the University of Glamorgan (Wales); the University of Swansea; the University of Mainz; the University of Münster; the University of Osnabrück; the University of Salzburg; the University of Cologne; and De Montfort University (Leicester). From these papers, I have published the following articles relating to the Polish experience in the Ruhr and/or northeastern Pennsylvania: "Divided Hearts: The Struggle between National Identity and Confessional Loyalty among Polish Catholics in the Ruhr, 1904–1914," *Polish Review* 47, no. 1 (2002): 67–95; "The Struggle for Polish Autonomy and the Question of Integration in the Ruhr and Northeastern Pennsylvania, 1880–1914," in *Towards a Comparative History of Coalfield Societies,* ed. Stefan Berger (Aldershot, UK: Ashgate, 2005), 177–90; "Migration, Citizenship, and Polish Integration in the Ruhr Valley and Northeastern Pennsylvania, 1870–1924," *Bulletin of the German Historical Institute* 38, no. 1 (2006): 119–34; "Becoming Transnational: Continental and Transatlantic Polish Migration and Return Migration, 1870–1924," in *Relations among Internal, Continental, and Transatlantic Migration,* ed. Annemarie Steidl, Josef Ehmer, Stan Nadel, and Hermann Zeitlhofer (Göttingen: Vandenhoeck and Ruprecht Unipress, 2009), 151–71. I thank the journals and publishers listed for their permission to include material from these articles in this volume.

Over the course of research and writing, I am beholden to many. First and foremost, I thank John Connelly, Kim Voss, and the sadly passed Gerald Feldman and Reginald Zelnik. I also express my gratitude to numerous other colleagues and friends for their help, advice, and comments: Klaus Bade, Stefan Berger, Thomas Duszak, Shane Ewen, David Frick, Gordon Johnston, Leighton James, Bernd Klesmann, Burkhard Olschowsky, Jochen Oltmer, James Spohrer, Valentina-Maria Stefanski, Annemarie Steidl, Klaus Tenfelde, Pien Versteegh, Joseph Wieczerzak, and many others. The professional support provided by the Ohio University Press Polish and Polish-American Studies series has been invaluable. The three anonymous reviewers offered stimulating and helpful advice, and the book is much the better thanks to their efforts. Sincere thanks to John Bukowczyk, the series editor, and the production team at Ohio University Press, including Gillian Berchowitz, editorial director; Nancy Basmajian, managing editor; Beth Pratt, production manager; Jean Cunningham, marketing manager;

and Teresa Jesionowski, copyeditor. Claudia Walters, geographer in the Department of Social Sciences at the University of Michigan at Dearborn prepared the maps. Not to be forgotten is the support provided along the way by my parents Brian and Mari McCook, my extended family, and my partner Allyn Pazienza, whose patience and advice through the years has been invaluable.

Brian McCook

Abbreviations

Alter Verband	Verband zur Wahrung und Förderung der bergmännischen Interessen im Rheinland und Westfalen—Union for the Protection and Promotion of Miners' Interests in Rhineland and Westphalia (Germany)
AOH	Ancient Order of Hibernians
DL&W	Delaware, Lackawanna, & Western Railroad
Gewerkverein	Gewerkverein christlicher Bergarbeiter—Christian Miners' Union (Germany)
IWW	Industrial Workers of the World
NCF	National Civic Federation
NPR	Narodowa Partia Robotnicza—National Workers' Party (Germany/Poland)
NSR	Narodowe Stronnictwo Robotników—National Party of Workers (Germany)
P&R	Philadephia & Reading Railroad
PFA	Związek Sokołów Polskich—Polish Falcons Alliance (USA)
PNA	Związek Narodowy Polski w Stanach Zjednoczonych Północnej Ameryki—Polish National Alliance in the United States of North America
PNCC	Polsko Narodowego Katolickiego Kościoła—Polish National Catholic Church (USA/Poland)
PNU	Polsko-Narodowa Spójnia—Polish National Union (USA)
PPS	Polska Partia Socjalistyczna—Polish Socialist Party (Germany/Poland)

PRCU	Zjednoczenie Polskie-Rzymsko-Katolickie—Polish Roman Catholic Union (USA)
PWA	Związek Polek—Polish Women's Alliance (USA)
Sokół (sg.), Sokoły (pl.)	Falcon(s)—gymnastic association(s) for Polish young men
SPD	Sozialdemokratische Partei Deutschlands
UMW	United Mine Workers of America
WBA	Workingmen's Benevolent Association
ZPwN	Związek Polaków w Niemczech—Union of Poles in Germany
ZZP	Zjednoczenie Zawadowe Polski—Polish Trade Union (Germany/Poland)

Guide to Pronunciation

The following key provides a guide to the pronunciation of Polish words and names.

a is pronounced as in father
c as ts, as in cats
ch as guttural h, as in German Bach
cz as hard ch, as in church
g (always hard), as in get
i as ee, as in meet
j as y, as in yellow
rz as hard zh, as in French jardin
sz as hard sh, as in ship
szcz as hard shch, as in fresh cheese
u as oo, as in boot
w as v, as in vat
ć as soft ch, as in cheap
ś as soft sh, as in sheep
ż as hard zh, as in French jardin
ź as soft zh, as in seizure
ó as oo, as in boot
ą as a nasal, as in French on
ę as a nasal, as in French en
ł as w, as in way
ń as ny, as in canyon

The accent in Polish words almost always falls on the penultimate syllable.

Partitioned Poland in the late nineteenth century

The Ruhr industrial region

The anthracite regions of northeastern Pennsylvania

Migration and Citizenship in a Globalizing World

EXPERTS HAVE LABELED THE last few decades the "age of migration."[1] Indeed, according to the United Nations, the total number of international migrants, defined as those living in a country different from the one in which they were born, more than doubled between 1970 and 2009 and stands at 200 million persons.[2] In Europe and North America, the arrival of large numbers of immigrants since the 1960s has generated significant controversy. In the twenty-first century, the twin issues of migration and integration present governments and societies on both sides of the Atlantic with pressing political, social, and security challenges. Fundamental questions are being asked regarding the value of immigration and the desirability of integrating newcomers into the national community. Do immigrants contribute to the common good or, given their "foreign ways," undermine national cultures and drain the public purse? In what ways does state policy promote or hinder integration? How can immigrants empower themselves in a culturally foreign environment? Why do certain immigrant groups appear to be permanently locked into a "ghettoized" underclass status while others, at least outwardly, provide a "model" of seamless adaptation into Western society?

Finding answers to such questions is difficult. However, there are important antecedents in the history of both Europe and the United States that can aid in illuminating contemporary debates. During the late nineteenth and early twentieth centuries, industrialization and the consolidation of the modern nation-state launched a first global "age of migration" that lasted into the early 1920s. By the beginning of the twentieth century, immigration in the United States reached levels that have been surpassed only in the last few years.[3] Meanwhile, during the same period, many countries of Western Europe were also affected by large inflows of "foreign" populations, a development that foreshadowed the movements of later generations of postwar immigrants. The arrival and settlement of large numbers of migrants during the late nineteenth and early twentieth centuries produced significant social tensions whose historical legacy continues to inform present social attitudes and government policies toward immigration.[4]

My study seeks to better understand this earlier wave of migration and its long-term effects on European and American societies by examining migrant Polish integration patterns in the Ruhr Valley of Germany and northeastern Pennsylvania. Approximately 300,000 Poles migrated to the Ruhr and 160,000 settled in northeastern Pennsylvania between 1870 and 1914. The origins, outlooks, occupational employment, and community organization patterns of Poles in both regions were in many ways similar. Poles arriving in each region were largely unskilled and hailed from predominately agricultural backgrounds. They entered two major industrial environments where Polish men worked overwhelmingly in the coal-mining industry. On settlement, Poles relied on the Catholic Church and numerous associations to help bind the ethnic community together. Most also remained in frequent contact with the homeland. Nevertheless, the development of these two Polish communities did diverge in reaction to experiences within the political, economic, and cultural environment of their host societies. After World War I, this divergence was reflected by dramatically different integration trajectories. The vast majority of Poles in northeastern Pennsylvania opted by the mid-1920s to accommodate themselves to American society, although full integration would remain another generation away. By contrast, two-thirds of the Polish community in the Ruhr immigrated to France or returned to Poland. The third of the community that remained subsequently integrated comparatively quickly into German society during the interwar period. By exploring why these differing adaptation patterns emerged, I seek to broaden our understanding of the role of government, the marketplace, and civil society in defining identities of citizenship and belonging within democratic states as well as the efforts of excluded actors to redefine the parameters of inclusion, or what I term "the borders of integration," over time.

Examining the historical Polish migrant experience is particularly useful for illuminating debates regarding issues of globalization and mass migration. Historically, Poles were one of the first ethnic groups whose migration occurred within the context of a rising global economy, the solidification of the democratic nation-state, and the emergence of modern mass cultures. In Germany, Poles constituted the largest ethnic minority during the late nineteenth and early twentieth centuries, while in the United States they constituted one of the largest groups of "new" migrants arriving between 1870 and 1914. In both countries, Poles were an internal "other"; similar in many respects to colonial subjects, the contact between these migrants and their German or American "hosts" served to solidify national understandings of self on both sides of the ethnic divide. In this regard, it is essential to emphasize that Poles were active agents in this process of identity formation, contesting attempts to impose an identity "from above" by developing their own counterhegemonic identity "from below." To be Polish in the Ruhr and northeastern Pennsylvania meant not only fulfilling "objective" criteria based on heritage, language, and Catholicism; subjective factors were equally important. Being Polish meant subscribing to a general historical mythos grounded not just in ethnicity, but also in shared experiences derived from the migratory process, an existence as members of an industrial underclass, and for Polish male mine workers, the idea of being producers, protectors of the family, and bedrocks of the social order. Overall, the Polish acculturation process was complex and offers important insights into current debates about migration and integration.

Defining Integration: Transatlantic Considerations

The field of migration studies has experienced important transformations over the last two decades, both in the United States, *the* immigrant society, and in Europe. Most notably, there is a growing recognition that the two major schools of thought about migration inadequately account for the diverse ways migrant populations actually integrate into Western societies.[5] The traditional Chicago School "assimilationist" models of immigrant incorporation stressed the absorption of immigrants into a singular core national community, and the contrasting "reactive ethnicity" approaches emphasized the maintenance of difference within a pluralistic and multiethnic society. In place of these paradigms, a "neo-assimilationist" model has gained ascendancy. This model defines assimilation as a process in which immigrants become similar in some, though not necessarily all, respects to a reference population that itself is in a constant state of change. Such a conceptual definition, which my book embraces, stresses that there are multiple modalities of assimilation, as well as nonassimilation, which are not predetermined and which change over time and place. In discussing the varied aspects of Polish incorporation in the Ruhr and northeastern Pennsylvania, I prefer the term *integration* because it emphasizes an ongoing, multidimensional process that is not predetermined and does not result in sameness in the way assimilation has been traditionally interpreted. This is especially true in Europe, where the two concepts are readily seen as synonymous with each other.[6]

In the United States, there is growing consensus that integration is a process, not just an end, involving multilayered cultural and socioeconomic negotiations between immigrants and their receiving societies; such attitudes in Europe are less prominent. The primary cause for this disparity can be found in the continued reticence of many European countries to acknowledge that they are countries of immigration, and historical ones at that. Since the 1970s, government policies across Europe have focused on ways to limit the inflow of migrants, particularly from non-European regions. Yet these policies have largely failed due to a lack of political will to recognize immigration as a historical phenomenon and the role migration has played in the development of their own national identities.[7] In Germany, the issue of immigration is at the forefront of contemporary politics. However, as Ulrich Herbert once noted, debates over "foreign" workers and the desirability of their integration into German society continue to be discussed "without any sense of history," betraying a rich, if troubled, past of foreign labor that dates to the beginnings of the modern German state.[8] Indeed, governmental claims and popular perceptions that Germany "ist kein Einwanderungsland" (is no land of immigration) are only now slowly beginning to change in the wake of the new reforms in citizenship law that were passed in 1999 and 2005 as well as recognition that over 14 percent of the present German population was not born within the country's present borders.[9] A similar situation prevails in France. The rise (and fall) of Le Pen in 2002, the building of a Museum of Immigration, the 2005 riots, and the restrictions on and continuing debates over wearing religious garb—all have brought new public attention to the immigrant question, sparking heated debates over the meaning of French republican values of inclusion. However, as Gérard Noiriel argued in the 1990s, although one in five persons in France has a grandparent of immigrant origin, "the role played by immigration in the constitution of collective memory of the French remains completely repressed in their national identity."[10]

Academics have not been immune from this inability to acknowledge the reality of immigration. Though European migration scholarship still lags behind that of the United States, important inroads have been made. Pioneers such as Noiriel in France, Klaus Bade and Dirk Hoerder in Germany, Colin Holmes in Britain, and many others have made notable strides in broadening our understanding of both historical and contemporary migration within Europe.[11] A special note should also be accorded to Polish scholars, who have maintained an active engagement in understanding the effects of migration and return migration since the 1930s.[12] However, Bade's prediction in 1980 that the German experience of hiring *Gastarbeiter* (guest-workers) and the formation of permanent minority communities would encourage a "new interest in the historical development of transnational migration" has yet to fully come to fruition.[13] One clear reason for this is the sense that historical migration offers few lessons for dealing with the supposedly qualitatively different migrants of today, a belief that is shared by many on both sides of the Atlantic.

Old versus New Migration

Although migration scholars across disciplines have worked together to significantly refine views of integration, this cooperation belies a key division within the field. Specifically, a contentious debate exists among historians and social scientists over whether parallels can be drawn between the mass migrations of the late nineteenth and early twentieth centuries and those since the 1960s. In its basic outline, various sociologists and others studying contemporary migration argue that there are qualitative differences between the experiences of white European migrants a hundred years ago and predominately Asian, African, and Latin American migrants today, and that the disparities preclude any useful comparison between the two migration waves.[14] In particular, "discontinuity scholars" contend that present-day migrants suffer from racial discrimination on a par with African Americans and have less opportunity for occupational and social mobility due to a split labor market that segments many migrants into low-wage service-sector positions. Further, post-1960s immigrants are more likely to possess transnational networks marked by frequent migration and remigration. This "recycling" constantly infuses fresh blood into immigrant ethnic communities, encouraging continued affinity to the homeland while inhibiting identification with American or European society. Assimilation, if it occurs, is highly segmented and stands in stark contrast to the integration patterns of earlier white ethnic Europeans.[15] Alejandro Portes and Rubén Rumbaut have best summarized this argument by noting that "contemporary immigration features a bewildering variety of origins, return patterns and modes of adaptation . . . although pre–World War I European immigration was by no means homogenous, the differences . . . pale by comparison with the current diversity."[16]

In response, other historians and sociologists argue that discontinuity proponents all too readily assume the seamless assimilation of earlier migrants while overemphasizing the limited integration prospects of contemporary migrants, largely because of race.[17] Yet, as whiteness studies that emerged in the 1990s argue, racial categories in the past were fluid and open to renegotiation, just as they are today.[18] Further, many contemporary discontinuity proponents appear to fall into the trap of meekly accepting Chicago School notions of assimilation for nineteenth- and early twentieth-century migrants. Little attention is paid to the fact that many, if not all, earlier migrants "transplanted" elements of their ethnic culture from the homeland and were subjected to multigenerational occupational segmentation.[19] European migrant groups from this earlier period, especially Italians, Poles, and Slovaks, exhibited high levels of circularity in their migration patterns, maintained transnational ties, and were often engaged in homeland politics.[20]

The points raised by discontinuity studies are important. Exact parallels between past and present can never be drawn. Poles in the Ruhr were Prussian citizens and possessed rights that most present-day migrants to that country do not have. Moreover, the lack of physical differences such as skin color gave Poles a potential advantage, by no means inconsequential, in their ability to integrate. Nevertheless, Poles in both regions experienced occupational segmentation well into the second and even third generations. They were cast as an "other," categorized in racialized terms, and exposed to widespread discrimination and ridicule. Poles were targets of organized "Germanization" or "Americanization" campaigns designed to destroy their ethnic culture and inhibit their participation in the body politic. Overall, the Polish experience was different, but not altogether dissimilar, from that of contemporary migrants. Reacting to the various threats to their economic, political, and cultural interests, Poles mobilized to defend their rights within their adopted communities. They joined trade unions, participated in elections, and organized countless ethnic institutions. While politically active in American and German life, Poles also endeavored to maintain strong bonds with the homeland. Remittances, the continuous exchange of information through letters and newspapers, and frequent patterns of return migration all ensured that connections to people and places in Poland remained durable. This existence of living between two worlds is highly analogous to the situation faced by many contemporary immigrants, making the Polish experience especially valuable for shedding light on the nature of immigrant transnationalism.

Transnationalism and Migrant Identity

In recent years, transnationalism has acquired increasing saliency as a conceptual tool for understanding migrant acculturation and outlook. Since the 1990s, scholars such as Nina Glick Schiller, Alejandro Portes, Peter Smith, Luis Guarnizo, and Peter Kivisto have contributed to developing this concept, and Thomas Faist provides the most fully elaborated definition of transnationalism as it pertains to migrants.[21] For Faist, transnationalism involves the creation by migrants of a distinct social space crossing traditional nation-state borders in which migrants maintain complex political, economic, and cultural networks linking them to their country of origin. Living between two (or more) worlds, migrants construct a hybrid identity based on mutual affinities to their homeland and adopted society in the emigration; while not fully part of either, migrants are actively engaged in both.[22] Key factors that influence the development of transnational social spaces include the existence of advanced transportation and communication technologies, troubled nation-state formation, contentious minority policies in the country of origin, socioeconomic discrimination within sending or receiving societies, and political opportunities to promote multicultural rights within the countries of immigration.[23]

This general definition provides a useful starting point for discussion. However, many elements of transnationalism remain nebulous; scholars in various disciplines often talk past each other; and the need for more empirical studies into this issue is great.[24] Numerous questions remain unresolved. What types of migrants can be considered transnational? Do transnational identities promote or hinder integration? Is transnationalism solely a recent phenomenon? Or can the concept be applied historically? What role does the state play in fostering transnationalism? Finally, what are the limits of transnational social spaces?

In considering these questions, my study argues that by the late nineteenth century, global levels of mobility and communication were sufficiently high to enable the emergence of transnational social spaces not only among mobile elites such as businessmen and intellectuals but also certain ethnic migrant labor groups as well.[25] For instance, steamship companies engaged in periodic fare wars, similar to airlines today, that could bring down the cost of a one-way passage in steerage on "the Atlantic highway" from approximately thirty-five dollars ($870 in 2009) to as little as ten dollars ($250); this latter sum represented a little more than a week's wages for the average Polish mineworker in northeastern Pennsylvania.[26] The transnational identities created within these newly emerging immigrant social spaces could, depending on the circumstances, aid the integration process, since they did not automatically prevent migrants from developing close affinities with their host societies.[27] In the case of Poles, my study finds that the transnational social space created by immigrants in northeastern Pennsylvania was better able to promote integration over the long term than that which existed in the Ruhr. This development highlights another key aspect to transnationalism, namely any attempt at analysis must account for the role played by sovereign states in determining the parameters of immigrant transnational social spaces.[28]

To better illustrate these points, a brief synopsis of the migrant memoir of Walek, which helped ignite my interest in undertaking this comparative study, is illuminating.

> In 1872, Walek was born into a Polish farming family living along the German-Russian frontier in the Prussian province of Posen (Poznań), and at the age of sixteen left his village to work in Saxony. By 1892, unemployment forced Walek to move elsewhere, and, after returning home briefly, he decided to seek his fortune in America, settling in 1893 in Scranton, the industrial center of the coal-producing regions of northeastern Pennsylvania. In Scranton, Walek was able to find work as both a miner and an ironworker and saved money to send home to relatives. Outside of work, Walek was active in the local Polish ethnic community, joining several Polish associations, campaigning for Polish candidates in elections, and agitating for Polish rights within the local Catholic Church.
>
> Recession in Scranton forced Walek to leave by 1895 and return home to Poznań. Within a few weeks of returning, he decided to leave for the Ruhr Valley and once there, found work as a miner and steelworker. In the workplace, Walek was a popular figure. He was physically strong, spoke German, and willingly defended the rights of fellow male workers, be they Polish or German. Outside of work, Walek participated in the vibrant ethnic life of the Polish community, joining a variety of Polish ethnic organizations, participating in political activities, and promoting demands for better spiritual care from local Catholic bishops.

Eventually, Walek married a woman from the homeland and by 1906 returned home with enough money to buy land. Upon returning, Walek found that his experiences abroad aroused suspicion. Local village leaders, particularly priests, were generally upset by returning Poles' penchant for challenging their traditional authority, leading priests to warn compatriots about the corrupt ways of these westernized Poles. For his part, Walek defended the rights of returnees to make their voices heard, noting that returning migrants possessed broader, more modern outlooks than those who had stayed in the village all of their life. He himself soon became active in local political affairs well into the 1920s.[29]

As one can see from this vignette, Walek existed for many years in a social space that was not fully Polish, American, or German and moved through all three worlds due to the existence of extensive ethnic networks. While in northeastern Pennsylvania and in the Ruhr, he maintained physical and economic links to the homeland and engaged in political and cultural activities designed to preserve and promote ethnic identity. Confrontation and collaboration with inhabitants of the local community nevertheless brought Walek closer to his host society by drawing him out of a homogeneous subculture and into the public sphere where, as a politically engaged actor, he defended his ethnic, class, religious, and gendered interests.

In pursuing a multifaceted political engagement, Walek adopted forms and practices familiar to natives within the host society that over time made him appear less "foreign," such as participation in clubs and elections as well as petitioning the Catholic Church. Such activity also changed Walek's identity, as can be seen when on his return to Poland he felt himself to possess a more modern, superior outlook than those who had never migrated. He defended other returnees from the attacks of traditional authority figures and became active in politics, something that would have been unheard of in earlier years given Walek's heritage and previous social standing. Overall, Walek's life story highlights how transnational identities can aid the integration process by encouraging greater immigrant participation in local community life. By themselves, however, such identities are insufficient for promoting full integration. Walek eventually did return to the homeland. This is because transnational social spaces are historically contingent; their existence is primarily dependent on the willingness of sovereign democratic states and societies to tolerate them. The identities formed therein, by their nature, lack stability.[30] Consequently, a key to determining whether migrants are able to integrate is the extent to which they can use transnational social spaces to mobilize and attain permanent identities grounded in broadly conceived understandings of citizenship.

Citizenship and Immigrant Integration

T. H. Marshall, the proverbial grandfather of citizenship studies, provides a useful starting point for considering issues of citizenship and Polish integration in the Ruhr and northeastern Pennsylvania. In 1950 Marshall defined citizenship as "a status that is bestowed on those who are full members of the community. All who possess the status are equal with respect to the rights and duties with which the status is endowed."[31] The "rights" of citizenship included a trinity of civil, political, and social protections. Civil rights were defined as guarantees of liberty provided most generally by the courts, including the right to free assembly. Political rights encompassed the right to participate in the exercise of political power, that is, to vote and be represented in a democratic assembly. These civil and political rights are intimately tied to the state. Social rights, however, were conceived along the lines of what today we would label fundamental human rights. These included the rights necessary to live as a "civilized being," such as the right to education and free association, a degree of economic welfare, and security derived from inclusion within a shared cultural community.[32] Reinhard Bendix has written in a similar vein.[33] By explicitly emphasizing the community, as opposed to the state, scholars such as Marshall and Bendix encourage us to conceive of citizenship in broad terms, including types of citizenship grounded not only in national but also in local, industrial, gendered, transnational, and other forms of collective belonging.[34] My examination embraces this approach, emphasizing that Poles fought for and gained multiple forms of citizenship within the societies of both the Ruhr and northeastern Pennsylvania.

Marshall's critics are correct in pointing out that citizenship is as much about exclusion as inclusion, since each redefinition of citizenship rights brings with it new duties and expectations as well as new designations conferring differing degrees of insider and outsider status. As a result, identities of citizenship become more, not less, bounded, contributing to the emergence of a "citizenship continuum" of full, partial, and noncitizens within which the divides of ethnicity, race, and gender matter enormously.[35] As gender scholars have shown, discourses on citizenship have been constructed, since the French Revolution, to exclude women from becoming full citizens by limiting their ability to enter the public sphere on the basis of their role as protectors of the home and progenitors of the nation.[36] Even more apparent has been the historical utilization of citizenship as a tool of exclusion in relation to immigrants and ethnic minorities, producing egregious examples of discrimination in all Western societies.

Since the 1970s, the language and practice of citizenship have changed. A traditional emphasis on assimilation within a closed national community has given way to a discourse accentuating multiculturalism, equality of cultures, and, above all, the rights of ethnic minority groups to self-representation. However, such apparent advances in the treatment of immigrants can prove a double-edged sword, unintentionally reinforcing exclusionary tendencies and limiting the basis on which immigrants can participate in the larger body politic as full citizens. Legally, this can be seen in the growth of various semicitizenship or "denizenship" categories within European and American jurisprudence that grant migrants certain legal and social protections while continuing to deny them significant political rights.[37] In general, the discourse of multiculturalism poses the danger of essentializing newcomer difference, especially when it privileges certain "traditional" authorities and customs within a given migrant community as being representative of the whole. This can lead to the suppression of alternate voices and individual rights within the migrant group while serving to undermine a sense of commonality, based on shared values and experiences, between migrants and members of the host society.[38]

Altogether, the process of becoming "full," or at least fuller, citizens involves a complex renegotiation of the boundaries of inclusion and exclusion as well as a balance between group and individual rights.[39] This comparative examination of the experience of migrant Poles elaborates on this view by stressing what Jürgen Habermas has described as the power of "self-transformation." Specifically, Polish integration was dependent on Polish willingness to engage in social conflicts within the boundaries of civil society, defined broadly as that sphere which is public, political, and independent of the state, not only as members of a group, but also as individuals. Over time, this "exchange with the other" produced by conflict could gradually help integrate Poles politically as participatory citizens in their adopted communities.[40] At the same time, the extent to which Poles could become active as citizens in the public sphere was heavily influenced by the state and the socioeconomic environment within which they lived.

Challenging Existing Frameworks of Citizenship

In the United States, scholars have made notable strides since the 1960s in highlighting the difficulties immigrants and minorities faced in attempting to acculturate and become citizens within society. Nevertheless, the melting-pot myth still enjoys widespread acceptance both in American popular culture and parts of the academy.[41] Meanwhile, the horrors of National Socialism in Germany have too often overshadowed an effective understanding of that country's rich, if troubled, multicultural past. In particular, the esteem accorded to the *Sonderweg* (special path) thesis, which posits that Nazism is rooted in conservative, authoritarian, and illiberal German "traditions" dating to at least the late nineteenth century, has encouraged a widespread view of Germany as a historically ethnocultural, or worse "racial," nation closed to non-German integration.[42] By conducting this comparative study, I seek to move beyond simple representations, if not caricatures, of German and American societies and provide a more in-depth, nuanced account of why immigrant acculturation differed between these two multiethnic states. Important to understand are the varied ways Poles could become citizens, in the broad Marshallian sense of the word, within the receiving societies in which they lived.

By far the most influential book framing recent discussions of citizenship in Europe and the United States remains Rogers Brubaker's *Citizenship and Nationhood in France and Germany,* in which the inclusive French territorial *jus soli* tradition of citizenship is contrasted with the historically exclusive German *jus sanguinis* model based on bloodline descent within a closed ethnocultural community. Penetrating and insightful, Brubaker's analysis is significant for helping us understand how formulations of modern citizenship law were influenced by historic self-understandings of the nation that became crystallized under the increasing pressure of nationalism and immigration in the late nineteenth century.

There are weaknesses to Brubaker's book. The emphasis on the role of nationhood traditions is deterministic. On the one hand, Brubaker adopts a neo-Sonderweg approach emphasizing the historically nonintegrationist and ethnically exclusive character of German society, evidenced most notably by the passage of the infamous 1913 Citizenship Law that first codified the *jus sanguinis* citizenship regime that has existed in Germany for nearly a century.[43] However, as many German historians such as Dieter Gosewinkel argue, it is vital to remember that an "ethno-cultural conception of German citizenship was not determined by a specific conception of the nation, but rather managed to assert itself because of political decisions" made within a specific historical context.[44] In essence, political circumstance, not tradition, dictates the nature of citizenship regimes. This point was borne out by the 1999 and 2005 reforms to German citizenship law that introduced elements of *jus soli*, reversing decades-old policies regarding immigrant naturalization. Although Brubaker could not have predicted them, these changes highlight the fact that self-understandings of the nation in Germany are less ingrained than one might suppose.[45]

On the other hand, Brubaker generally views France, and by extension other Atlantic rim democracies such as Great Britain and the United States where territorial citizenship traditions exist, as models of inclusion par excellence, failing to adequately recognize that ethnocultural and even "racialist" thinking managed to assert itself for long periods in the citizenship policies of these countries. In the case of the United States, the most obvious examples of the desire to preserve citizenship as a right strictly reserved for white, Anglo-Saxon Americans were the various immigration restriction acts, ranging from the Chinese Exclusion Act of 1882 to the National Origins Act of 1924.[46] Overall, the endurance of *jus soli* citizenship policies among the Atlantic rim democracies was never and is currently not an inevitable certainty.[47]

A second limitation is the inadequate analysis of the experience of two and a half million Poles, as well as other minority groups in Germany, who as Prussian subjects always possessed German citizenship and continued to do so even after 1913. Brubaker, as others before him, is correct to point out that the relationship between Poles and Germans in Imperial Germany was marked by ethnic conflicts and a "struggle for land" in the Prussian eastern provinces of Posen, West and East Prussia, and the district of Upper Silesia.[48] The Prussian state took an active part in this conflict, enacting *Polenpolitik* measures (anti-Polish political legislation) that among other things restricted expressions of Polish culture in public, banned the use of Polish in schools, and limited the ability of Poles to acquire land in the eastern provinces. Polish activities were also subject to constant police supervision. However, precisely because Poles were citizens, they possessed important political and civil rights, which they actively exercised. Poles voted and were represented in local, regional, and national assemblies. Within these various bodies, Poles made numerous alliances with German political parties, most notably the Catholic Center Party and Social Democrats. They were also often able to make successful use of the German courts to protect their interests, much to the repeated dismay of German nationalists. This contrasts with the state of affairs in the United States where African Americans and others were denied fundamental civil and political rights despite the provisions of the Fourteenth and Fifteenth Amendments. Minority policy in Wilhelmine Germany was repugnant; yet, for the period it was not anomalous, especially given the exclusionary policies that existed in other Western countries.

In German society, the position of Poles was never predetermined. Even in the nationalist political climate of the late Wilhelmine period, integration on the local level was occurring. My examination of the Polish migrant population in the Ruhr, which by 1914 constituted approximately 15 percent of the total number of Prussian Poles in the Empire, emphasizes precisely this point.[49]

Finally, the third drawback to Brubaker's analysis is that the focus on the legal statutes and administrative attitudes toward immigration neglects the diverse ways immigrants actually became citizens in the communities in which they lived. As Yasemin Soysal observed in her analysis of post-1945 immigrants, exclusionary citizenship laws do not necessarily preclude immigrants from attaining a level of social integration in their host society, a point borne out, albeit in a much different context, by my research.[50] As Prussian citizens, Poles in the Ruhr possessed significantly more civil, political, and economic rights than the often unnaturalized Polish immigrants of northeastern Pennsylvania. Polish integration nonetheless proved more extensive in the latter region. This highlights the need to move beyond the "thin" analysis of citizenship as a legal status grounded exclusively in the relationship of the individual or group to the state in favor of a "thick" investigation that explores the contestation of citizenship between and among groups within society.[51] Clearly, the state matters since it most often helps define the parameters of citizenship by enacting and enforcing laws regarding civil and voting rights, economic liberties, and, since the rise of the welfare state, levels of social entitlements. However, citizenship is multidimensional. In the case of Poles, levels of integration were ultimately dependent on the extent to which they could actively fight for their rights within the public spheres of their host societies and stake claims to various forms of social and cultural citizenship.

Poles in the Ruhr and Northeastern Pennsylvania

Among scholars who have examined the individual Polish communities in the Ruhr and northeastern Pennsylvania, disagreement exists over levels of

Polish integration, with two general schools of thought competing to explain the Polish relationship with the surrounding community. The first emphasizes how competing ethnic antagonisms, driven by nationalist sentiment, economic competition, and cultural difference, limited integration prospects over the long term. As a consequence, Polish communities remained, on the whole, segregated within German and American societies, forming distinct subcultures, or parallel societies, that were isolated from the mainstream. The second argues that although Poles faced significant obstacles to their integration, many did become integral members of the societies in which they lived by embracing a hybrid identity that, as one historian noted, both "united [Poles] with and separated them from" their German or American neighbors. In essence, the majority of Poles were well socialized within their adopted environments, at least before World War I.[52] Such interpretive differences reinforce the usefulness of a comparative study for better fleshing out the changes in Polish identity and levels of integration over time.

In building on earlier analyses, I focus on investigating how multilayered Polish identities developed as a result of inter- and intraethnic conflicts in the workplace and local society, where disputes over wages and jobs, religious and associational activity, family and citizens' rights continually reformulated Polish outlooks. I also explore how lived experiences in Poland and the imagined concept of "homeland" within the two migrant communities affected Polish workers' attitudes within their host society. Drawing from a rich array of historical materials available from archives and libraries in Germany, Poland, and the United States, I argue that integration was dependent on Poles engaging in social conflicts within the boundaries of civil society, first as members of a group and then as individuals. Group conflict brought Poles out of an initially homogeneous subculture and encouraged them to engage in a multidimensional form of politics in order to defend varied interests based not only on ethnicity but also on class, religion, gender, transnational sensibilities, and ideas of citizenship. In pursuing a multifaceted political engagement, Poles adopted native forms and practices, which over time began to change the discursive construction of the "Pole" within the native mind-set, making them appear less "foreign." Such politics also transformed Polish identities, contributing to greater self-reflection and conflict over goals and desires within the ethnic group. The subsequent decline in ethnic unity, together with changes in native attitudes, eventually enabled Poles to become, as individuals, more equal and active citizens within their adopted societies. In the Ruhr and northeastern Pennsylvania, the emergence and resolution of specific conflicts within civil society did create a basis for integrating at least part of the Polish ethnic community in both regions. This is an important finding given the continued tendency to view pre-1945 German society as essentially "racialist" and closed to minority inclusion. Nevertheless, differences in the organization of industry and markets, the levels of government intervention in economic and cultural matters, and the strength of civil society meant that the ability of Polish immigrants to integrate was, over the long term, comparatively greater in northeastern Pennsylvania than in the Ruhr.

1 ılı Migration and Settlement

Building Polish Communities in the Ruhr and
Northeastern Pennsylvania

MORE THAN 10 PERCENT of the population of partitioned Poland left for North America or Western Europe during the late nineteenth and early twentieth centuries; many migrated to the Ruhr and northeastern Pennsylvania.[1] Between 1870 and 1890, 31,629 Poles settled in the Ruhr, and 15,142 arrived in northeastern Pennsylvania.[2] From the 1890s onward, the size of Polish communities in each region grew exponentially, and by 1914, the Polish presence was substantial. In the Ruhr, 297,322 Poles were living in this region along with 159,743 Masurians, a Slavic ethnic group from southern areas of East Prussia (present-day northeast Poland) who spoke a dialect of Polish; combined they represented 9.4 percent of the total population.[3] Meanwhile, approximately 160,000 Poles, constituting 13.8 percent of the total population, worked and lived in northeastern Pennsylvania.[4] Why did Poles migrate? To what extent did homeland origins influence immigrant outlook? What was the topographical, social, and cultural terrain of areas in which Poles came to live? How did informal and formal institutional support mechanisms within the ethnic community aid Poles in building vibrant ethnic communities? This chapter addresses these questions in order to understand Polish community development in each region.

Causes for Polish Migration

Migration to the Ruhr and northeastern Pennsylvania was driven by a variety of causes. Classic economic push-and-pull factors associated with modernization played one important role. Over the course of the nineteenth century, the growth in population in Polish lands led to a decrease in sustainable farms within the agricultural sector, contributing to the creation of a large, landless labor pool that drove down wages. The lack of significant industrialization, with the notable exception of Upper Silesia, limited the ability of nearby urban centers to absorb the excess population. From the 1870s onward, domestic agriculture was also in crisis due to foreign competition and government policies that favored larger agricultural estates over small farms. As a consequence of these demographic and economic developments, growing numbers were pressed to migrate, both overseas to North America and to parts of Western Europe. Added to these push factors was the pull generated by industrial growth in countries such as Germany and the United States, where labor shortages and high wages attracted many. In the Ruhr and northeastern Pennsylvania, demand for coal drove an ever-increasing need for workers. By the early 1880s, traditional sources of labor in both regions were becoming exhausted and employers sought to attract "foreign" workers in order to ensure the continued expansion of the industry. Beginning in the 1870s, operators either directly, or indirectly through agents, began recruiting Poles, especially those from Upper Silesia with mining experience. This practice of recruitment soon expanded to include the predominately agricultural regions of Poland. By the late 1880s, the role of employers in driving migration receded in importance as more informal networks between early and later Polish migrants became established, spreading news of the opportunities to be found in Western Europe and the United States.[5]

Migration westward was also spurred by political struggles in Polish lands, which at the time were partitioned by Prussia, Austria, and Russia. In both the Prussian- and Russian-controlled areas of Poland, extensive efforts were made from the 1860s onward to restrict Polish culture and contain nationalist sentiment. In Austrian-controlled Galicia, Poles enjoyed much greater freedom of expression and thought, though here too the government did take steps to guard against the political threat of peasant populism.[6] Such attacks and restrictions on Polish culture factored prominently into the decision of small numbers of middle-class national agitators and priests to migrate west, including to the Ruhr and northeastern Pennsylvania, where they could organize Polish immigrants for the nationalist cause and hinder their assimilation into German or American society.

For Polish peasants, most of whom lacked a national consciousness prior to migrating, the policies of the partitioning powers also influenced the decision to leave, though indirectly. In Russian-controlled Polish lands, younger Poles chose to go abroad in order to escape service in the armies of the tsar. Whereas only a few Russian Poles found refuge in the Ruhr, usually illegally, thousands left for the United States every year, many of whom settled in the anthracite fields of northeastern Pennsylvania, especially after the mid-1890s.[7] Meanwhile in the eastern Prussian provinces, Poles left because the Prussian government's Germanization campaign, which sought to buy Polish agricultural land for colonization by Germans, significantly increased land speculation and prices; increasingly it became impossible for people of ordinary means to buy land.[8] Andrzej Pietrzak, a Polish miner in Oberhausen, noted in 1906 that "in order to feed our families we had to leave our homeland and move to the [Ruhr] because the *Hakatists* [German nationalists] have ensured that the earth and soil in our homeland will be bought out."[9] This statement emphasizes a great irony in German history. Namely, policies implemented to Germanize Polish areas of eastern Prussia helped instead to Polonize parts of the German heartland.

In addition to economic and political considerations, Polish migration was facilitated by other factors. Over the course of the nineteenth century, literacy rates among Poles increased, widespread print media provided Poles with greater knowledge about opportunities in the wider world, and transportation networks improved vastly, particularly with the growth of German rail and steamship lines during the second half of the nineteenth century.[10] Polish peasant society was also increasingly mobile. Many Poles had prior migration experiences, as there existed a tradition of seasonal agricultural migration across the borders separating Prussia, Austria, and Russia. Exchanges between cities and countryside occurred regularly. Such regional migration went far in preparing would-be migrants for more distant trips. As Thomas and Znaniecki noted in their seminal study, the seasonal migration of Poles to Saxony to work as agricultural laborers was "often the first step preparing the individual psychologically and economically for the idea of transoceanic emigration." The same holds true for migration to western Germany.[11] In addition, for many young Poles who were coming of age, the prospect of becoming more independent by going abroad was exciting.[12]

Extensive ethnic networks connecting migrants with their kin in the homeland also encouraged migration. After early migrants left, most remained in contact with relatives and friends in Poland through letters, continuous financial remittances, and return visits. The constant communication meant that with each successive year, the dangers associated with long distance migration, including potential dislocation and isolation, diminished while the apparent rewards increased. As Poles created "little Polands" in the Ruhr and northeastern Pennsylvania, they urged relatives and friends to join them. The memoir provided by the Polish immigrant Jan Ziołkowski aptly illuminates the role played by ethnic networks in driving the migration phenomenon. In 1903, Jan's father, a peasant from the Małopolska region near Kraków, arrived in the United States and settled in Hazleton, Pennsylvania. Three years later Jan joined his father, finding work in mining. Finally, at the end of 1907, enough money was saved to bring Jan's mother and his three siblings.[13] In this pattern, whole communities of Poles migrated from partitioned Poland to the Ruhr and northeastern Pennsylvania. All told, the rise in "chain migration" proved increasingly responsible for sustaining the high level of Polish migration to the Ruhr and northeastern Pennsylvania in the decades prior to World War I.[14]

Finally, in understanding the motivations behind the Polish decision to leave, it is essential to bear in mind that most Poles who chose to migrate never had the intention of permanently settling abroad. The majority of Poles migrated *za chlebem* (for bread); in other words, they left for the opportunity to earn money and gain livelihoods that one day would hopefully enable them to return home and buy land. Well into the early 1920s, exchanges between the Polish homeland and the Ruhr and northeastern Pennsylvania were frequent; the east-west migration flow of Poles is best characterized as circular, not linear. As Prussian citizens, Poles in the Ruhr were unimpeded by national boundaries, and as a consequence Poles migrated repeatedly between the Ruhr and the eastern Prussian provinces. Poles in northeastern Pennsylvania likewise made frequent trips home. Scholars estimate that at least 35 percent of Polish immigrants to the United States returned to Poland prior to World War I. Although a majority of Poles who migrated to the United States and a sizable minority of Poles in the Ruhr eventually abandoned the dream of returning to Poland, all Polish migrants followed political and social developments in Poland with keen interest and sought to influence developments there.[15]

The Character of Polish Migration

Polish migration to the Ruhr and northeastern Pennsylvania between the 1870s and early 1890s was quite similar. During the 1870s, the majority of early Polish migrants to each region tended to come from traditional coal-mining areas in Upper Silesia.[16] However, a divergence occurred in Polish migration patterns by the 1890s. In the Ruhr, the immigration restrictions placed on non-Prussian Poles after 1885 meant that subsequent Polish migrants came almost exclusively from the provinces of eastern Prussia.[17] The regional origins of these migrants also changed. In the two decades before World War I, Polish workers increasingly arrived from agricultural areas of Posen and East Prussia, as opposed to industrial Upper Silesia.[18] In northeastern Pennsylvania, the 1890s brought a different type of transformation. The numbers of Poles arriving from Prussia rapidly decreased, a direct result of industrial growth in the Ruhr combined with the 1893 economic crisis in the United States, and the majority of migrants now began arriving from Galicia (Austria) and the Congress Kingdom (Russia).[19]

The differences in the character of Polish movement to the Ruhr and northeastern Pennsylvania raise two important and related questions. First, did the internal migration to the Ruhr, in contrast to the overseas migration to northeastern Pennsylvania, create a qualitative disparity in the way the migration experience was perceived by Poles? Simply answered, no it did not. Although political borders influenced the choice of destination, the migration experience itself was perceived quite similarly. Regardless of whether Poles went to the Ruhr or northeastern Pennsylvania, they were aware that they were crossing clear cultural boundaries and entering urban, industrial environments that qualitatively differed from agricultural life in the homeland. In the Ruhr, Poles often described themselves as living *na obczyznie* (in a foreign milieu). Similarly, in northeastern Pennsylvania, there was a clear belief that Poles were forced to go into overseas exile *za chlebem,* for the bread necessary to survive.

Second, did the fact that Poles in the Ruhr came almost exclusively from eastern Prussia, while those in northeastern Pennsylvania arrived from all three partitions, predetermine the disparities that would later emerge between each community? On the whole, premigration origins were of less importance than might be assumed; while there was significant political mobilization in Polish lands during the nineteenth century, especially among the nobility, clergy, and burgeoning middle class, the majority of migrants to the Ruhr and northeastern Pennsylvania were peasants possessing similar cultural identities grounded in Catholicism and local village life.[20] It was in the emigration that most Poles hailing from peasant backgrounds first began to develop a strong Polish national identity. The migratory process exposed many peasants who previously possessed local or, at most, regional identities to the "other" and forced these migrants for the first time to surmount

particularistic loyalties and embrace a larger national consciousness. Freed
from a society dominated by the *szlachta* (nobility) and clerics in the homeland, the national awareness that arose in the emigration was decidedly
different from traditional Polish nationalism; the experience of living as
low status industrial workers in vastly different cultural milieus as well
as the greater exposure to more modern democratic forms and practices
combined to broaden Polish outlook. Stanisław Wachowiak, a Polish activist in the Ruhr, noted in 1916 that "when the migration [of Poles] began,
a political awareness among the lower classes in the homeland was quite
small. The majority vegetated there without at all being concerned with
political matters. The migrants were completely un-schooled politically.
The changed environment, the active trade-union life, the presence of ethnic associations, all of this forced Polish workers in the West to politically
orient themselves."[21] Wachowiak's analysis highlights how greater Polish
engagement in the political life of the Ruhr and in northeastern Pennsylvania caused multifaceted identities to arise over time. This is not to say that
the Polish homeland no longer mattered to Poles. In fact, issues concerning
Poland and the "Polish nation" assumed greater relevance in the emigration, where dreams of an eventual national resurrection led the majority of
Polish men and women to embrace a positivist program emphasizing the
need to preserve and promote ethnic community strength. Great importance was placed on maintaining Polish religious practices, creating ethnic
associations, and educating the children in national traditions and language.

Migrant Poles further sought to influence societal developments in
Poland both before and after World War I.[22] In this regard, the examples
of the Zjednoczenie Zawodowe Polski (ZZP—Polish Trade Union), established by Polish miners in the Ruhr in 1902, and the Polish National
Catholic Church (PNCC), founded in northeastern Pennsylvania in 1896,
are noteworthy. From its base in the Ruhr, the ZZP grew to become not
only the third-largest coal-miners union in all of Germany, but it also
embarked on organizing Polish workers in the homeland prior to World
War I. After 1918, the ZZP become the largest trade union in early interwar Poland and spawned the emergence of the Narodowa Partia Robotnicza (National Workers' Party—NPR), which held twenty-eight seats in
the first postwar Polish Sejm (Parliament).[23] The PNCC was a schismatic
movement that broke away from the Roman Catholic Church as a result
of disputes between immigrant Poles and the Irish-dominated church hierarchy in America. Initially embracing an ideology that stressed the role of

working-class immigrant Poles in rebuilding the Polish nation, the PNCC organized support from across the United States for Józef Piłsudski and his followers in Poland prior to World War I. After the war, the PNCC established parishes throughout Poland in an attempt to build a National Church free from Rome. Although it never fulfilled this goal, more than seventy PNCC churches were founded in the interwar period.[24] Overall, the ZZP and PNCC highlight the remarkable vitality, independence, and dynamism of Polish community institutions that arose in the emigration as well as their desire to influence politics in the homeland.

The Geographical, Social, and Cultural Terrain

The Ruhr Valley comprises approximately 1,300 square miles. North to south the region lies between the Lippe and Ruhr rivers. It extends east to west from the city of Witten, near Dortmund, to Duisburg along the banks of the Rhine. From 1871 to 1945, three different districts known as *Regierungsbezirke,* governed sections of the Ruhr. Regierungsbezirk is a unique German administrative designation that falls between the size of a county and a province/state. The largest part of the Ruhr fell under the Regierungsbezirk Arnsberg and included the city and land *Kreise* (subdistricts) of Bochum, Dortmund, and Gelsenkirchen. The northernmost section of the Ruhr, around the city of Recklinghausen, belonged to the Regierungsbezirk Münster. Both the Regierungsbezirk Arnsberg and Regierungsbezirk Münster were administrative districts within the province of Westphalia. The third administrative district, controlling cities and land Kreise from Essen to Duisburg, was the Regierungsbezirk Düsseldorf, which was part of the Rhineland province.

The coal-producing counties of northeastern Pennsylvania encompass a territory of approximately 1,700 square miles. Though the region is comparable in size to the Ruhr, it is geologically more mountainous, with elevations ranging from 600 to 1,600 feet. The primary mining areas, roughly 500 square miles, were divided into three distinct geological fields. The southern field, stretched from southwest to northeast across Dauphin, Schuylkill, and Carbon counties, with Pottsville forming this field's hub. The middle field contained two distinct subfields spanning Northumberland, Columbia, northern Schuylkill, southern Luzerne, and northern Carbon counties. The larger, western-middle field extended from Shamokin in the west to Mahanoy City in the east. The smaller, eastern-middle field was centered on the cities of Hazleton and Lattimer. During the late nineteenth century, the southern and western-middle coalfields were grouped together in what was called the Schuylkill field, and the eastern-middle field was known as the Lehigh field. The geographically separated northern, or Wyoming, field was the richest in terms of coal deposits, running from southwest to northeast and comprising Luzerne and Lackawanna counties. The Wyoming field was densest in population, containing within it the major cities of Scranton and Wilkes-Barre.[25]

From the midcentury onward a dramatic transformation in the landscape of the Ruhr and northeastern Pennsylvania occurred because of the ever-increasing demand for coal. Urbanization levels and population rose rapidly. In the Ruhr, towns such as Essen, Bochum, and Dortmund, which in 1849 had a combined population under 25,000, quickly grew into large cities. By 1910, Essen's population approached 300,000, while Dortmund and Bochum reached 215,000 and 136,000, respectively. More than 4.6 million persons lived in the region as a whole. Though less urbanized, population growth in northeastern Pennsylvania was also dramatic. In 1850, the population stood at 209,000. By 1910, this figure exceeded 1.16 million, with Scranton and Wilkes-Barre boasting 130,000 and 67,000 inhabitants, respectively.[26]

As the population in each region increased, so too did the degree of social stratification. The most privileged group in both regions was, not surprisingly, the small numbers of German and American industrialists and company directors who exercised significant sway over local economies. Secondary elites comprised high-ranking government officials, doctors, lawyers, and other professionals who formed the bulk of the upper middle class. The middle class included small business owners, shopkeepers, tradesmen, teachers, and local administrative officials. The vast majority of the population, approximately 90 percent, was working-class and dependent on industrial wage labor for survival. Polish migrants fell solidly into this latter social category.[27]

When working-class Poles arrived in the Ruhr and northeastern Pennsylvania, they encountered a variety of other ethnic migrants.[28] In the Ruhr, hundreds of thousands of Germans and Masurians from the eastern provinces of Prussia arrived from the late 1860s onward. In addition, several thousand Belgian and Dutch workers, along with hundreds of Poles from Austrian Galicia and Russian Poland, German-speaking Austrians, Czechs, Slovaks, Hungarians, Russians, Croats, Slovenes, Romanians, and Italians also found employment in the coalfields. Within a European context, the diversity was impressive, highlighted by the fact that over twenty different languages and idioms were spoken in the Ruhr by 1914.[29] Ethnic diversity was greater in northeastern Pennsylvania. From the 1830s to the 1860s, the bulk of the mine labor force was made up of English, Welsh, Irish, and German migrants and these "old" migrants and their American-born children constituted the core of the "native" workforce of the region. After the American Civil War, the continued demand for laborers spurred the immigration of Germans and Poles from eastern Prussia during the 1870s and 1880s as well as Galician and Russian Poles, Ukrainians, Lithuanians, Slovaks, and Italians from the 1890s onward. By 1914, twenty-seven different nationalities worked and lived in the anthracite region.[30]

The differing lengths of settlement and diversity among migrant workers led to the establishment of distinct ethnic hierarchies. In the Ruhr, Germans with local or regional roots had the most status, followed by Germans from the Prussian East and the small number of western Europeans. In northeastern Pennsylvania, the English and Welsh occupied the highest rung on the ethnic ladder followed by German Catholic immigrants. The Irish occupied a middle position due to their Catholicism and largely peasant backgrounds. In both regions, recently arriving Poles, along with other eastern Europeans, generally possessed the lowest social standing, at least until other immigrants from southern Europe began to arrive at the turn of the twentieth century. As a consequence, Poles suffered from significant discrimination due to their "foreign" habits, language, and peasant backgrounds. In either region, being called a "Pollack" was never a term of endearment, and the stereotypical "Polish joke" was (and today remains) popular.

Ethnic divides were complemented by those of confession. In the Ruhr, the population was evenly divided between Protestants and Catholics. Catholics generally predominated in the western areas of the Ruhr that were part of the Regierungsbezirk Düsseldorf and Regierungsbezirk Münster, whereas Lutheran Protestants were in the majority within the Regierungsbezirk Arnsberg. However, many towns were evenly divided between Catholics and Lutherans. In addition, there were small numbers of Protestants of other denominations as well as Jews. Although there was a general decline in sectarian strife after the turn of the century, the divide between Catholics and Protestants remained stark well into the 1920s. At the local level, Catholics were colloquially referred to as the "blacks" whereas Protestants were known as the "blues," due to voters' respective political affiliation with either the Center Party or the largely Protestant

National Liberal Party.[31] In northeastern Pennsylvania, religious tensions between Protestants and Catholics were similarly fierce. Before the large influx of immigrants in the mid-nineteenth century, this region was overwhelmingly Protestant. The arrival of Irish and German Catholics, together with the later migration of large numbers of Catholic ethnics from eastern and southern Europe, transformed the religious balance. By the turn of the twentieth century the majority of the population was Catholic. In addition there was a small Jewish population. The rapid growth in the number of Catholics encouraged a rise in anti-Catholicism during the 1880s and 1890s, driven by native Protestant fears of Catholic immigration.[32]

Polish Lifeworlds in the Emigration

Homeland origins, religious affiliation, and industrial expansion based on the geological location of coal—all influenced early Polish settlement patterns. In the Ruhr, Poles who arrived from the 1870s to mid-1890s settled predominately within the present-day outskirts of Gelsenkirchen, Bottrop, Recklinghausen, Herne, and Bochum. During the late nineteenth century, this north-central Ruhr region was transformed, as Christoph Klessmann noted, from a once largely agricultural area, into an "'American-style' industrial environment."[33] Poles were drawn in large numbers to this area because of the growth in new, large-scale coal-mining operations that employed more than a thousand men and paid above average wages. By the turn of the twentieth century, nineteen of these mines became known as *Polenzechen* (Polish mines) because over one half of the workforce came from the four eastern provinces of Prussia.[34] To attract and retain a loyal labor force, mine companies often sent agents to directly recruit labor from specific villages or regions in eastern Prussia. Some employers, such as Emil Kirdorf and August Thyssen, hired only those workers who shared their respective Protestant or Catholic faith, believing that shared religious belief would limit worker militancy in their mines. As a consequence of such recruitment practices, areas around Bottrop became centers of Polish Catholic settlement from Upper Silesia, while Polish and Masurian Protestants from East and West Prussia populated regions around Gelsenkirchen. Catholic Poles from Posen and West Prussia were more scattered but tended to settle in areas around Herne, Recklinghausen, and Oberhausen.[35]

Polish settlement grew more diffuse beginning in the 1890s, driven by the expansion of the Ruhr coal industry, the high fluctuation in employment levels in mining, expanding transportation networks, and the ability of Poles to find employment in other industries such as steel and chemicals. Though still traceable, Polish settlement areas became less defined by regional origins, confession, or attachment to a specific mine colony. By 1914, Poles were present in every sizable community between Düsseldorf and Hamm, settlement patterns that brought Poles into greater contact with the institutions and people of their host society while also giving impetus for the formation and centralization of larger, region-wide Polish ethnic organizations that could bind the ethnic community together.[36]

Poles arriving in northeastern Pennsylvania initially settled predominately in the Schuylkill field where the coal industry was most established. Early Polish settlements were founded in the 1860s and 1870s in Shamokin, Shenandoah, Mt. Carmel, and Nanticoke, the latter of which soon became known as the most Polish city in America based on the density of Poles per square mile.[37] Although less pronounced than in the Ruhr, regional origins in the homeland also influenced where Poles lived. In Nanticoke, most Poles were initially of Upper Silesian origin, while those in Shenandoah arrived from the northeast region of Russian Poland. With more Poles entering the region during the 1880s and 1890s, Polish settlement spread. Soon every major city in the region and most hamlets had a sizable Polish community. From the 1890s onward, the direction of settlement shifted as the Wyoming field surpassed the Schuylkill field in attracting Polish migrants. By 1900, 12,350 and 24,770 Poles were settled in the Schuylkill and Wyoming fields, respectively.[38] In the Wyoming field, major areas of settlement were, in addition to Nanticoke, the cities of Scranton, Wilkes-Barre, Dickson City, and Pittston. Between 1880 and 1900, the Lehigh field also experienced increased growth in Polish population with significant communities becoming established in Hazleton and Lattimer. As in the Ruhr, ongoing industrialization throughout the region created a dense network of transportation links that increased levels of Polish mobility and contact with local society, while also serving to foster a larger sense of Polish community. This was especially true in the Wyoming field, where urbanization rates were high and Polish organizational strength most advanced.

Wherever Poles settled, they faced enormous challenges. As Poles, Catholics, and workers, these migrants were a triple minority subject to severe discrimination. In order to combat and overcome inequality and navigate the terrain of the Ruhr and northeastern Pennsylvania, Poles relied heavily on the support provided by both informal and formal institutions encompassing their everyday lifeworld. Informal institutions included the immediate family as well as the boardinghouse and saloon. As Polish communities grew, formal institutions arose that promoted the long-term socialization of Poles into their host societies. Among the most important of these were the local Catholic parish, ethnic associations, newspapers, banking institutions and small businesses, and independent trade unions.

The Polish Family

Single young men or married men who left their wives in the homeland dominated the first wave of Polish migration to the Ruhr and northeastern Pennsylvania. From the 1870s until the turn of the century, approximately 70 percent of Slavic immigrants to each region were male.[39] Polish men continued to outnumber women until after World War I, though the gender gap eased as many who originally intended to return to Poland after working for a few years decided to permanently settle and subsequently sent for wives from the homeland. By 1910, the ratio of Polish women to men in the Ruhr stood at 76:100 compared to 64:100 in northeastern Pennsylvania.[40] On entering matrimony, Polish males were generally in their mid- to late-twenties whereas females were in their early twenties. In the Ruhr town of Bottrop the average age of marriage for Polish men was twenty-five years of age, and for women it was twenty-two. In the northeastern Pennsylvania cities of Shenandoah and Mahanoy City, average marriage age was twenty-seven for males and twenty-three for females. Nearly every Polish male was married by the time he reached thirty years of age.[41] Rates of interethnic marriage between Poles and other ethnic groups in both regions were negligible.[42] The number of children born to married Polish couples varied between the two regions. Couples in the Ruhr had on average two to three children, while in northeastern Pennsylvania the average was four to five, a difference due likely to the higher costs associated with maintaining children in the Ruhr.[43]

Within each Polish household, divisions of labor were strict. Men worked in the mines or in other industries such as steel in the Ruhr or the railroads in northeastern Pennsylvania. Married women worked almost without exception in the home, where they managed the household and the family budget, raised the children, and added to the family income by selling garden produce, assuming odd jobs such as washing clothes, and caring for boarders.[44] In the Ruhr, enforced truancy laws meant that children went to state schools until the age of fourteen, and in those schools the language of instruction was exclusively German.[45] In northeastern Pennsylvania, Polish children generally did not attend school beyond the age of twelve, and many left earlier. Truancy enforcement was infrequent, and as the superintendent of schools in Dunmore noted at the turn of the century, "Girls and boys whose ages range from 9 to 12 years, are employed in the mills, factories and breakers, and this with the consent of the parents." In local public schools, the language of instruction was English. However, many Polish children attended parochial schools where they could often be taught in both English and Polish, depending on the subject.[46]

Polish schoolchildren in both regions suffered under the prejudices of their day. Hazing in the classroom by both teachers and other pupils was often a problem, particularly for those who spoke little German or English.[47] Further, school administrators often assumed that Polish children were less intelligent than native children. The 1911 Senate Immigration Commission study of schoolchildren in Scranton found that "the degree of retardation among children of native parents . . . is considerably below that of children of foreign born parents . . . it will be noted that Italians and Poles have a very high percentage of retardation."[48] Although the lower levels of reported achievement were directly related to the language barrier Polish children faced, the perception that Poles were less intelligent meant that little effort was expended to aid these children in reaching appropriate grade levels. Instead, the general attitude among educators in both the Ruhr and northeastern Pennsylvania was to move Poles out of the school system as quickly as possible. It was exceedingly rare for Polish children to obtain secondary education. Some Polish organizations created fellowships to support a few promising students; however, education costs were high, and most parents expected their children to enter the workforce as soon as possible in order to contribute to the family income.[49] On leaving school, boys overwhelmingly entered mine work. Girls and young unmarried women, restricted in both regions from working underground in the mines, found employment as domestic servants, seamstresses, or in light industries such as textiles.[50]

Families lived in close quarters, and within Polish settlements, the types of housing available varied. On average, 40 percent of the workforce in the northern Ruhr region, where the majority of Poles lived, resided in company housing by 1914. In the Ruhr as a whole, this figure stood at 35 percent.[51] In northeastern Pennsylvania, only the Lehigh field around Hazleton exhibited similar levels of workers living in company housing, a development due mostly to the paternalism of certain employers such as Eckley B. Coxe. On the whole, 35 percent of workers in the Lehigh field lived in company housing, whereas in Schuylkill and Wyoming fields these figures stood much lower, at 10 percent each.[52] The general quality of company housing stock available differed considerably in each region. In the Ruhr, planned-out *Arbeiterkolonien* (workers' colonies) of stone and brick houses were common. A typical Polish family residing within such a colony lived in a semidetached building within which were four apartments with separate entrances. Within each apartment there were three or four rooms.[53] By contrast, company housing in northeastern Pennsylvania was much poorer. Most houses were uninsulated and made with cheap wood planks; as one contemporary observer noted, "some [houses] . . . are built of hemlock boards with weather strips nailed over crevices. No plastering, no ceiling and no wall-paper are furnished . . . this is over 50 per cent of the company housing stock in Luzerne, Schuylkill and Northumberland counties and some of the remaining 50 per cent is worse, classified officially as shanties. These are the types of houses populated by s[c]lavs."[54] In both regions, Polish homes often had small garden plots and/or animal stalls for raising additional supplies of food to meet the family's needs.[55]

The shortage and poor condition of company housing in northeastern Pennsylvania meant that most Poles rented privately built homes that were often located within highly segregated ethnic enclaves of a given city or mine settlement.[56] By contrast, in the Ruhr, the mine colonies were significantly more integrated, with Germans and Poles living side-by-side as well as under the same roof.[57] The lack of company housing in northeastern Pennsylvania also promoted significantly higher levels of home ownership. On average, approximately 13 percent of the Polish population in northeastern Pennsylvania owned their own homes, and in certain areas north of Scranton this figure stood at close to 43 percent.[58] By contrast, less than 2 percent of Poles in the Ruhr owned their own homes.[59] This difference is important when considering the variances in Polish integration patterns between each region. In general, greater levels of integrated housing in the Ruhr contributed initially to aiding Polish adaptation to their environment, a development borne out by higher levels of Polish activism in ethnic associations and politics between 1880 and 1900. The higher rate of home ownership in northeastern Pennsylvania nevertheless made Poles more physically and financially bound to that region over the long term.

The Boardinghouse

In order to help make ends meet, many Polish households in both the Ruhr and northeastern Pennsylvania took in boarders. The large number of single male workers and the tight housing market encouraged the development of an elaborate boardinghouse system in both regions. On arriving in the Ruhr, single men either chose to live in mine company dormitories or opted for private bed and board accommodation. The number of boarders a family took in varied, often depending on mine company regulations. Three to four was typical, and five or six not uncommon.[60] In 1902, approximately 18.5 percent of the total Polish-speaking male migrant population in the Regierungsbezirke of Münster and Arnsberg lived in a boardinghouse. By 1912, this figure still stood at approximately 10 percent.[61] In northeastern Pennsylvania, the general lack of company housing made the boardinghouse system indispensable. During the first decade of the twentieth century, 46 percent of Polish households took in boarders, and Poles had the highest number of boarders per home of all ethnic groups in the region. On average, there were 3.13 boarders for every Polish household, compared to 2.45 for all other foreign-born workers.[62]

As might be expected, the close living spaces, particularly the presence of single, young males in the midst of a family environment, did cause problems. In the Ruhr, police records detail various fights among boarders or illicit liaisons between boarders and miners' wives and daughters that ultimately led authorities to regulate boarding practices from 1892 onward.[63] The repeated warnings of moral decay due to the boardinghouse system were also widespread in northeastern Pennsylvania. Terence Powderly, the head of the Knights of Labor and later general commissioner of immigration, testified before the 1888 Ford Congressional committee investigating labor law violations in the coalfields of Pennsylvania that he witnessed firsthand one house in which there were 105 Eastern Europeans living together in decrepit conditions.[64] However, unlike in the Ruhr, local government generally refused to intervene in such matters.[65]

Despite overcrowding, the boardinghouse system was a durable institution, especially in northeastern Pennsylvania. For families, the extra income that boarders provided to the household was significant. Many young men themselves preferred the family-style accommodations over the crowded and authoritarian company dormitory. Further, the extensive boardinghouse system eased initial migrant dislocation. By facilitating contact with other

Poles, the boardinghouse enabled countless fellow ethnics to learn about job opportunities and associations of interest, hear news from the homeland, and generally become more mobile in their adopted societies. All told, the boardinghouse contributed significantly to the establishment of stable, close-knit ethnic communities in both regions.

The Saloon

Similar to the boardinghouse, the local saloon (or public house) also played a central role in early community development. Since the onset of industrialization, the saloon has been much maligned in the popular imagination. Middle-class reformers, government officials, and union officials in both the Ruhr and northeastern Pennsylvania decried the increase in crime and poverty, and the decrease in morality and worker productivity that the presence of the saloon in a given community was thought to cause.[66] For many years, historians often accepted such prejudicial views of the saloon at face value and only recently has this institution of working-class life been better studied.[67]

Yet despite the historical prejudices, the saloon was more than simply a place to have a drink. It was the salon of the lower class, providing Poles a forum where they could meet to discuss the issues of the day, exchange information, learn about jobs, hold ethnic association meetings, and engage in politics or union activities. In addition, the saloon also served as an informal financial institution, especially in the early years of migration. Saloonkeepers often provided or arranged for loans and helped with the transfer of monies to the homeland.[68] The significance of the saloon in everyday life is best borne out by the comment of one observer in northeastern Pennsylvania, who wryly noted that the saloon "secures the patronage of 80 per cent of the adult male population [and] is better patronized than the church, the theatre, the dancing class, or technical instruction and general culture."[69] Notably, the saloon was not solely a man's domain. Polish women, albeit in smaller numbers, regularly socialized with their men, especially on Sunday when the mines in both regions were closed. Moreover, by going to the saloon and partaking in the public life of the community, Polish women were in many ways more emancipated than their German or American counterparts, who generally left the saloon to their men.[70]

The Catholic Parish

At the center of almost every Polish settlement within the Ruhr or northeastern Pennsylvania stood the local Catholic parish, a familiar symbol of

continuity connecting past and present existences. Aside from satisfying religious needs, the local parish provided an important point of orientation that
helped Poles integrate into the life of the ethnic community and larger society. The establishment of Polish Catholic traditions in both the Ruhr and
northeastern Pennsylvania was not without difficulty. In both regions, Poles
confronted a native Catholic Church hierarchy that had little experience with
or respect for Polish Catholic traditions. Attempts of the hierarchy to use the
church as an instrument of Germanization or Americanization met with resistance by Poles who sought to preserve their religious traditions. For Poles, the
perceived inability, even unwillingness, of the native hierarchy to adequately
provide for their spiritual needs caused significant levels of animosity to
emerge. As a result, Poles agitated for reforms from both within and outside of
the formal structures of the Catholic Church from the 1890s onward. Despite
tensions, Polish allegiance to the Catholic faith, though not necessarily to the
institution of the church itself, remained strong, and the local parish provided
an essential base on which ethnic associational culture developed.

Ethnic Associations

From the 1870s to the early 1890s, the earliest Polish ethnic associations
were affiliated with the Catholic Church and included men's and women's
rosary societies, choral clubs, women's associations, youth associations,
and Polish-Catholic Worker Associations. Between the 1890s and World
War I, the Polish associational movement grew rapidly. By 1912, there was
in both regions approximately one ethnic association for every three hundred Poles.[71] As the associational movement expanded in the decades prior
to World War I, it also became progressively independent of the Catholic
Church and more intently focused on national concerns. New types of secular
associations were established that were increasingly diverse in outlook and
quite politically active. Regardless of orientation, most Polish associations
served to maintain and strengthen Polish national identity in the face of
Germanization and Americanization campaigns by promoting celebrations
of Polish culture, organizing lectures and courses on Polish language and
history, establishing lending libraries, and keeping Poles informed of ongoing political developments in the homeland. Although Polish associations,
as generally ethnic-exclusive institutions, did promote a degree of separa-
tion from native society in both the Ruhr and northeastern Pennsylvania,
they also served as essential vehicles that contributed to long-term Polish
integration. By lessening the economic, political, and cultural dislocation of

Poles, the various associations that arose in both regions ensured community stability and provided an organizational foundation on which greater Polish activism within their host societies could occur.

Ethnic Press

Polish community development was further strengthened by the emergence of a vibrant ethnic press, which in both regions agitated for Polish rights both within the Ruhr and northeastern Pennsylvania as well as within the homeland. In the Ruhr, the earliest Polish newspaper was the *Wiarus Polski* (Old Polish Soldier), which after its founding in 1890 became the most influential Polish mouthpiece in the Ruhr.[72] The *Narodowiec* (Nationalist), a rival newspaper founded in 1909, eventually challenged the dominance of the *Wiarus Polski*, especially among working-class Poles.[73] In addition to these newspapers, other ethnic broadsheets from the region included the ZZP's *Głos Górnika* (The Miners' Voice), the German Social Democratic Party (SPD) supported *Gazeta Robotnicza* (Workers' Gazette), an array of small Catholic weeklies, and various interest publications, including advice and humor magazines. Poles also widely read newspapers from Polish regions of eastern Prussia including the *Gazeta Grudziądzka, Dziennik Polski, Gazeta Toruńska, Gwiazda, Pielgrzym, Postęp, Praca, Przyjaciel,* and *Przyjaciel Ludu*.[74] In northeastern Pennsylvania, the local Polish press was not as extensively developed. The most important local newspaper was *Straż* (The Guard), founded in 1897 in Scranton by the schismatic priest Francziszek Hodur and the political activist Stanisław Dangel. Until the early 1920s, *Straż* was the mouthpiece of the schismatic Polish National Catholic Church movement and generally had socialist and nationalist leanings.[75] By 1903, a rival emerged in the form of the *Górnik*, later *Górnik Pensylwanski* (Pennsylvania Miner), a conservative, Roman Catholic paper founded in Wilkes-Barre with the active support of the local Scranton Diocese.[76] Many Poles also read the *United Mine Workers Journal*, which at the turn of the century began publishing part of the paper in Polish and other Slavic languages. Further, Poles subscribed to newspapers from outside the region. The most influential in this regard were *Zgoda, Naród Polski, Kurjer Polski, Ameryka-Echo, Robotnik, Dziennik Ludowy, Gwiazda,* and *Czas*.[77]

Ethnic Banks and Small Businesses

Polish community security in the Ruhr and northeastern Pennsylvania was solidified by the growth of ethnic banking institutions. When Poles first arrived in each region, there were few financial institutions available to them. In general, Poles tended to send their savings directly back to the homeland.[78] When loans were needed, many Poles turned, first and foremost, to the informal "banks" run by local saloonkeepers, which usually charged high rates of interest. However, after the turn of the twentieth century, Poles also began to place their savings directly into ethnic banking institutions.[79] The volume of savings deposits that Poles placed by the eve of World War I was large. Polish deposits at the local branch office of the *Bank Przemysłowców* (Industrial Bank) Gelsenkirchen for year-end 1913 stood at 15,459,813 Reichmarks or about $3.8 million; meanwhile in 1908, Poles deposited approximately $290,000 in Shenandoah, a sum that represented 15 percent of bank deposits in that city.[80] The growth of Polish savings in each region was important since it made credit available for Poles to acquire property as well as open small businesses, thereby enabling the rise of an indigenous, entrepreneurial middle class. As the police president in Bochum noted in 1913, "The tendency of Poles [in the Ruhr] to utilize their savings to return and settle in the East has declined. Among the Poles in the West there is here now a clear desire, with the help of savings, to open Polish businesses or learn a trade in order to rise into the ranks of the middle class." Similarly, the U.S. Senate Immigration Commission found that Polish ownership of homes and businesses in northeastern Pennsylvania was increasing and that this development contributed to the "Americanization" of these immigrants.[81] The growth in the number of Polish entrepreneurs was impressive, although in actual numbers it was still a small group. In the Ruhr, there were 2,073 Polish businesses by 1913. These included food and provision stores; tailor, shoemaker, and barber shops; saloons; bakeries; and masonry, painting, and plumbing businesses.[82] In northeastern Pennsylvania, similar types of businesses arose. Although figures are unavailable for the region as a whole, it is clear that in the more urbanized areas of Pennsylvania, the number of independent businessmen was high and exceeded that of the Ruhr. In Shenandoah, for example, approximately 19 percent of Polish families were engaged in some type of business enterprise, most notably saloons and provision stores.[83]

Trade Unions

Trade unions were first able to gain a permanent foothold in both the Ruhr and northeastern Pennsylvania during the 1890s. In this decade, however, union organizations in both regions initially neglected Polish workers, arguing that Poles threatened the economic livelihood of native workers and were, given their foreign ways, fundamentally unable to be organized. This initial animosity on the part of native unions led to conflicts between native and Polish workers, especially during the late 1890s, and to a subsequent divergence in Polish workers' organizational patterns. In the Ruhr, tensions with native unions led Poles to create their own ethnic trade union, the aforementioned ZZP, in 1902. Instead of creating their own union, Polish workers in northeastern Pennsylvania focused from the turn of the century onward on gaining greater control within the United Mine Workers of America (UMW). Although the paths chosen in unionizing differed, the overall protections offered to Poles by union organizations such as the ZZP and UMW were significant. After the turn of the century, Poles utilized these bodies not only to redress specific economic inequalities but also to redefine their status within the working-class milieu in which they lived. In the decade prior to World War I, Polish workers were, thanks to their fervent participation in unions, eventually able to gain the greater respect of native workers and integrate themselves more fully into local society.

Assessing the Landscapes

Polish migration to both the Ruhr and northeastern Pennsylvania between 1870 and 1914 was driven largely by economic need and was sustained by the "chain migration" phenomenon. On settling in the Ruhr and northeastern Pennsylvania, Poles entered regions undergoing dramatic social, political, and cultural change. In the wake of rapid industrialization and urbanization, a diverse populace arose. Within such environments, the position of Poles was precarious. A triple minority, Polish migrants faced widespread discrimination. In order to better navigate the local terrain, Poles relied on an array of informal and formal networks. Between the Ruhr and northeastern Pennsylvania, there were important differences in community development patterns. In northeastern Pennsylvania, the ratio of men to women and average family size was greater, children had two to three years less schooling, and the boardinghouse system was significantly more developed, accommodating nearly one-half of the incoming migrant population. The most marked contrast occurred in housing patterns. Poles in the Ruhr were not nearly as "ghettoized" into ethnic enclaves as they were in northeastern Pennsylvania, thus enabling an initially broader Polish participation in societal life. At the same time, Poles in northeastern Pennsylvania acquired greater amounts of local property, a development that bound them more closely to the region over the long term. This difference cannot simply be explained by Polish peasant land hunger. Instead, the variations in levels of home ownership were also due to the disparities in the availability and quality of company housing, property costs, the affordability of land, and in the tax structure between Germany and the United States. Differences in family size and education levels occurred as a consequence of dissimilarities in wages and the enforcement of laws mandating when children should be allowed to work. Overall, it was the unique political, social, and cultural environments of the Ruhr and northeastern Pennsylvania, as opposed to premigration origins, that would prove determinative of the differences in integration patterns within each region.

2 ılı The Face of Mining

The Coal Industry in the Ruhr and Northeastern Pennsylvania

BETWEEN 1870 AND 1914, the demand for coal to power the ongoing industrialization of Germany and the United States caused the mine industries of both the Ruhr and northeastern Pennsylvania to expand dramatically. Annual coal production in the Ruhr increased in this period nearly tenfold, from 12 million to 110 million tons, with most of this fuel going to fire the blast furnaces that enabled the German steel industry to become the largest in Europe. The increase in coal production in northeastern Pennsylvania was also impressive, rising from 14 million to more than 91 million tons; the coal mined provided the energy supplying the majority of eastern railroads, various other industries, and nearly the entire home-heating market in the eastern United States.[1] Since the mechanization of the coal industry in each region was not widespread until after World War I, the expansion of production was contingent on the employment of an ever-increasing number of laborers, including thousands of Poles. In the Ruhr, the overall number of workers employed in the mining industry rose from 51,000 in 1870 to approximately 400,000 in 1914. Similarly, employment in northeastern Pennsylvania rose in the same period from 35,000 to more than 180,000.[2] Coal in both regions was king, and Poles, in particular, were becoming this king's indispensable servants.

The sizable contribution of Polish-speaking migrants to the success of the mining industry cannot be overstated. In the early years of migration, nearly 90 percent of Poles were employed in the mines in both the Ruhr and northeastern Pennsylvania. This percentage decreased after the turn of the century, though mining remained the leading type of employment for Poles. Overall, approximately 25 percent of mine workers in each region were of Polish origin by 1914.[3] This chapter analyzes the similarities and differences in the coal industries, paying specific attention to employer and working-class organization; the division of labor and ethnic stratification in the workplace; coal markets, wages, and income as well as levels of corporate welfare; government policy and public attitudes to the mine industry; and strike patterns.

Employer and Working-Class Organization

As output and employment in the mining industry expanded, mineownership in both regions became increasingly concentrated. In the Ruhr, the consolidation of industry was facilitated by the disengagement of the Prussian government from direct regulation of production, marketing, and labor oversight of the mines during the middle of the nineteenth century. Among the various laws enacted after 1850, the most important was the Allgemeine Berggesetz (General Mining Law) of 1865, which acknowledged mineowners' rights to independence from the state in economic affairs. Although some general oversight of the mining industry remained, most notably in the form of the Bergämter (State Mining Offices) that oversaw the enforcement of various workplace regulations, deregulation encouraged the investment of substantial amounts of capital, and the industry was soon dominated by large privately held corporations or joint-stock companies. As the historian S. H. F. Hickey notes, "Whereas in 1885 only seven companies owned more than one mine, by 1910 a mere nine firms were producing around two-thirds of the Ruhr's total output." In addition, many steel companies in the Ruhr such as Krupp also owned their own mines in order to vertically integrate resources.[4]

The increasing centralization of the German coal industry led to the establishment of employer associations and ultimately a coal syndicate. In 1858, the first employer association, known as the Bergbau Verein (Mine Owners' Association) was founded in Dortmund in order to support employers' attempts to increase worker productivity. This organization quickly enlisted all the major producers in the Ruhr and eventually received formal recognition as the industry's representative body by the government in 1893. Other employer organizations gradually developed, such as the Ausstandssicherungsverband (Strike Insurance Association) in 1890, designed to offer companies strike relief provided they did not negotiate with workers during strikes, and the Zechen Verband (Mine Association), a federation formed in 1908 to coordinate employers' industrial relations policies. Finally, the Kohlen-Syndikat (Coal Syndicate) highlighted the full extent to which the coal industry became consolidated. Founded in 1893 under the tutelage of Emil Kirdorf, the Kohlen-Syndikat controlled over 90 percent of the coal market and assigned members production quotas, set coal prices, and required members to use the organization as their collective selling agent.[5]

Though the consolidation of the coal industry followed a different path, the result in northeastern Pennsylvania was similar. Beginning in the 1850s and 1860s, increasing production costs and falling output prices forced small producers out of the coal market. Eastern railroads soon assumed a dominant position in the anthracite fields, facilitated by a compliant Pennsylvania legislature. In the late 1860s and early 1870s, laws were passed that allowed railroads to expand their landholdings throughout the region and provided for the joint ownership of railroad and mining facilities. Although the state maintained some oversight over the industry through the establishment of a Mine Inspector's Office in 1869 (later known as the Pennsylvania Department of Mines), the independence of this government agency was dubious given the fact that many mine inspectors, when not in government employ, worked for the railroads that owned the mines.[6]

With the withdrawal of barriers to greater consolidation in anthracite mining, the first employer association was established in 1872, though this combination lasted only four years due to cheating on prices and production quotas by individual members. Other failed attempts to manage competition through employer associations followed in 1878, 1880, 1884, and 1886. The industry nevertheless continued to consolidate, and by the turn of the century seven large railroads companies, increasingly tied to each other through interlocking directorates and backed primarily by the banking interests of J. P. Morgan, controlled 75 percent of the region's anthracite coal production and 84 percent of the coal reserves. By 1907, after the last major independents were forced out because of the railroads' monopoly on shipping coal, this rose to 91 and 96 percent, respectively.[7] The growing Morgan presence in Pennsylvania anthracite allowed the industry to form a "community of interest," a coal trust in all but name only, that led to rationalized production and pricing practices. In 1898, permanent production quotas were assigned and brought an end to the overproduction of the 1880s and early 1890s. These quotas remained in effect until World War I and enabled employers to fix the market price of coal. As table 1 (see appendix) highlights, between 1903 and 1912 the wholesale price for a ton of coal held steady at $4.30 a short ton. For employers, the consolidation of the industry also brought the added benefit of strengthening their hand over workers and unions.

To defend their interests against employers, workers in both regions turned to organizing local worker associations and industrial unions. For Ruhr workers, the deregulation of mining in the 1860s proved traumatic and brought to an end the special corporate status mine workers previously enjoyed under the Prussian government.[8] The earliest worker organizations in the Ruhr were local *Knappenvereine,* mutual-aid societies that could be either secular or religious. These Knappenvereine emerged from past corporatist traditions within mining and concerned themselves with protecting the interests of workers in matters involving the Knappschaft, a state-mandated pension system jointly administered by employers and workers' representatives.[9] Other independent workers' associations affiliated with a specific local Catholic or Lutheran parish also were established during the 1870s and 1880s. For newly arriving immigrants such as Poles, these associations were particularly significant. Unlike the Knappenvereine, where Poles initially had no voice, the Polish Catholic worker associations provided an important vehicle through which Poles could collectively come together and articulate their beliefs and concerns. Over the long term, the establishment of both the Knappenvereine and other types of worker associations was important. As Klaus Tenfelde notes, they served "as institutions in which patterns of regulated communal life were learned and the rituals of democratic assembly and organization could be internalized."[10] The worker associations also provided the base for the three main miners' unions that were built starting in 1889 with the establishment of the socialist Alter Verband (Verband zur Wahrung und Förderung der bergmännischen Interessen im Rheinland und Westfalen—Union for the Protection and Promotion of Miners' Interests in Rhineland and Westphalia), followed by the Gewerkverein christlicher Bergarbeiter (Christian Miners' Union) in 1894 and the Polish miners' ZZP union in 1902.[11]

Northeastern Pennsylvania had a longer tradition of independent unionism, though most worker organizations were weak and their life span short from the mid- to late nineteenth century. The first significant union to appear in the region was the Workingmen's Benevolent Association (WBA). Founded in 1869, the WBA successfully organized skilled miners and gained a modicum of recognition from mine operators until a six-month strike led to the collapse of the union in 1875.[12] Early difficulties in unionization increased the importance of informal worker associations that, as in the Ruhr, often broke along religious and ethnic lines. In the 1860s and 1870s, local chapters of the Ancient Order of Hibernians (AOH), an Irish-Catholic association, arose to become hotbeds of informal labor activism. A few AOH members were members of the infamous "Molly Maguires," a secretive group of militants engaged in a concerted campaign of violence against employers, law enforcement officials, and certain targeted workers in the Schuylkill field.[13] In subsequent decades, worker associations became more moderate, particularly as the Catholic Church hierarchy condemned any working-class activism that could lead to violence. Nonetheless, although no informal worker societies ever reached the same degree of radicalism as the Mollies, ethnoreligious associations provided many newly arriving workers, including Poles, their first exposure to new forms of organization and worker mobilization. Renewed efforts at organizing workers were made in the late 1870s and 1880s when the Knights of Labor, under Scranton native Terence Powderly, and the rival Miners' and Laborers' Amalgamated Association began organizing primarily skilled miners in the region. However, the failure of the 1887–88 strike, owing in part to the inability of workers across all three anthracite fields to unite, brought both organizations to an end. An effective union organization would not appear until 1894, when the United Mine Workers of America (UMW), a national union that first arose in the bituminous coal industry, began organizing anthracite men along industrial union lines. Initially, the UMW's foray into the anthracite fields met with little success. After 1897, the UMW was able to overcome the initial skepticism of many anthracite mine workers and by 1900 establish a dominant presence in northeastern Pennsylvania.[14]

The Division of Labor in the Workplace

In the late 1890s, Alfred Krupp declared to his workers, "I await and demand the full trust [of my workers], reject any attempt [by them] to make unjust demands, and will, as in the past, take any justified request [of workers] under consideration. I also propose that it would be in the interests of those not happy with this . . . to leave my establishment, in order to make place for others who understand that in my house, on my property, I am and will remain master." This statement exemplifies what is best described as a "Herr im Haus" (master of the house) paternalism under which mines in both the Ruhr and northeastern Pennsylvania operated.[15] For employers in both regions, the growth in the workers' movement, as well as attempts by government to regulate the workplace and intervene in labor conflicts, threatened to undermine the inalienable rights of property and the individual "freedom of contract" between worker and employer. In the view of the owners, only they should be able to determine workplace rules and regulations since they were the most capable defenders of the existing social order, an order threatened with collapse at the hands of labor activists, socialists, anarchists, and others. George Baer, the president of the Philadelphia and Reading Coal and Iron Company, best summarized this attitude in 1902 when he declared that "the rights and interests of the laboring man will be protected and cared for—not by the labor agitators, but by the Christian men to whom God in his infinite wisdom has given the control of the property interests of the country."[16] Naturally, employees in both regions viewed the attitudes of employers less benevolently. As one worker in the Ruhr observed, the employers believed only in one mantra, namely, "We dictate and you better listen!"[17]

Within the mine complex, employers strove to put their views into practice, though direct control of miners within the mine shaft was difficult due to the nature of the industry. Foremen reporting directly to the mine manager supervised most workers, yet dark, dirty environmental conditions, the high labor turnover, and the diffusion of work sites within a given mine shaft made close supervision difficult.[18] Coercive measures were nevertheless adopted to ensure workers' submission to the authority of the employer. In both regions, extensive spy systems and blacklists were maintained in order to root out unproductive or politically active workers. Ruhr employers enhanced their control even further when they introduced the much despised *Arbeitsnachweis* in 1910, a small pocket-sized notebook that chronicled past employment history. If a miner wished to change employers, he needed to produce this book showing satisfactory work in his prior position before being hired at a new colliery.[19]

Workers within the mining operations of each region in the pre–World War I period can be divided into two types of labor. The first category comprised "company men." These were the unskilled and skilled workers paid an hourly wage. Unskilled wage labor included those occupations involved in transporting and sorting coal, such as haulers, brakemen, mule drivers, and slate pickers. Young men and juveniles held many of these positions. In the Ruhr, children as young as fourteen worked in the mines, though they were not allowed underground until reaching age sixteen. In northeastern Pennsylvania, children often began to work aboveground at age twelve and below ground at age fourteen, though instances exist of children as young as six employed underground. The skilled wage labor subset included engineers, machinists, carpenters, and the pumpmen who ensured that the mine was able to maintain operations. A minority of miners in both regions were also employed as company men.[20]

A second category of worker was the independent, skilled miner and his team of assistants. The miner hewed the coal, provided training and supervision to his team, and negotiated wages directly with the mine foreman based on a piece-rate system. Under this system, a miner and a foreman would contractually agree on a price to be paid for a wagon of coal, a ton of coal, or length of a coal seam mined, taking into account the geological conditions of the mine face. Miners' assistants, normally persons in their late teens or early twenties, were responsible for helping to mine the coal, maintain the mine chamber, and load the coal into carts for transport to the surface. The length of the apprenticeship for miners' assistants varied. At minimum, mines in the Ruhr required miners' assistants to serve a one-year apprenticeship, while Pennsylvania coal mines required two years. The assistants' wages, a percentage of the monthly or bimonthly earnings of the team, were most often paid to him directly by the miner. This meant that the miner was not only a worker but also an employer, a situation that could lead to significant tensions between miners and their assistants.[21] Despite such divisions, miners and their workers were unified in what they considered unfair practices utilized to depress wages, including the frequent practice in both regions of company check weighmen docking weekly earnings based on their subjective determinations that some wagons were insufficiently loaded with coal.[22]

Divides between skilled and unskilled, contract and wage labor, older and younger workers, were also emphasized by obvious ethnic divisions. Workforces in both regions were diverse, and the wave patterns of migration led to ethnic stratification and the persistence of ethnic hierarchies within the workplace well into the 1920s. Cultural conceptions of race were chiefly responsible for the persistence of these labor market inequalities. To those acquainted with whiteness studies, it should come as no surprise that many German- and English-speaking workers propagated racially framed identities that conferred a higher social status on the "Anglo-Saxon" or "Teutonic" worker vis-à-vis the "racially subordinate, ignorant" eastern

European.[23] In the Ruhr, the most common term of derision for Poles was "Pollack," while in northeastern Pennsylvania, "Polack" along with the terms "Hunks," "Hunkies," and "Huns" were widely used. The latter derived from the word Hungarian, but were collectively assigned to represent all workers from eastern Europe to create an image of them as a dangerous horde. In 1899, the socialist newspaper *Arbeiter Zeitung* described Polish workers who went on strike earlier in the year as "horses gone wild" and, in a backhanded compliment, later noted that "we are familiar with the Polish worker and know that even they are open to reason." In describing the Slavic workforce in northeastern Pennsylvania, John Mitchell, president of the United Mine Workers of America, claimed in 1900 that "these miners . . . remind me very much of a drove of cattle, ready to stampede when the least expected. In our meetings they are so impressionable that they are swayed from one side to the other in accordance with the force or eloquence of the speaker." As we will see in the later chapters, this "cultural split" in the labor market began to subside after Poles and other "new" migrants proved themselves to be both capable miners and effective labor agitators. Nevertheless, a racialist outlook persisted that continued to assume that eastern and southern European laborers were ill-equipped to handle the less physical, knowledge-based professions within the mines; an attitude that, as one contemporary observer of the time noted, only served to reinforce the notion that "Poles are an unintelligent people."[24]

Coal Markets, Wages, Employer Welfare, and Standards of Living

The coal industry in both the Ruhr and northeastern Pennsylvania relied almost exclusively on domestic market earnings to achieve profitability, though the types of coal available in each region as well as the size of coal deposits relative to the entire coal industry in each country produced differences in production and marketing strategies. Anthracite coal is a fuel with a high carbon content that produces little black smoke and soot when burned, making it ideal for domestic heating purposes. Bituminous coal, with lesser carbon content, burns dirtier but was cheaper than anthracite, making it well suited for use in heavy industry.[25] The Ruhr basin, which by 1913 accounted for 52 percent of the total coal reserves in Germany and produced over 60 percent of the coal for the country, possessed both forms of coal, although more bituminous than anthracite. The variety in coal types as well as the size of deposits in the Ruhr relative to the entire national industry enabled producers to dominate both the domestic industrial and consumer coal markets, creating a steady year-round demand for coal.[26]

By contrast, northeastern Pennsylvania contained exclusively anthracite coal deposits. In the industrial market, the region was just one of many sources of coal, and industrial grades of anthracite were often sold at a loss because of stiff competition from the vastly larger bituminous coal industry. However, northeastern Pennsylvania had one significant market advantage; the region possessed over 99 percent of the total American deposits for anthracite coal. As a consequence, producers focused on earning profits in the lucrative domestic home-heating market, where consumers preferred anthracite to bituminous. This market, however, was seasonal. Demand was high in winter and low in summer. On the whole, the seasonal market for anthracite and the year-round market for Ruhr coal produced significant differences in the number of days worked. As table 1 (see appendix) indicates, in the period between 1901 and 1914 mines in the Ruhr operated on average around 310 days a year, whereas in Pennsylvania the average was just 209 days.[27]

The difference in number of days worked was also reinforced by the wage structure of each region. In the Ruhr, mine companies determined wages independent of the selling price of coal. By contrast, throughout most of the pre–World War I period, wages in northeastern Pennsylvania were often based on a sliding scale that tied a miner's (and his assistants') compensation directly to the market price of coal.[28] From the mid-1870s until the turn of the century, this scale did not have a base minimum and during periods of overproduction such as the 1890s, wages were consequently depressed. Beginning in 1903, a base minimum was adopted, tied to high fixed prices for anthracite coal after the turn of the century, which caused average wages to be more than double what they were in the Ruhr. Workers' pay in Pennsylvania averaged $2.40 a day, while those in the Ruhr earned $1.14 between 1903 and 1913, as highlighted in table 1 (see appendix). For northeastern Pennsylvania workers, there was a downside to the higher wages they earned. Namely, employers intensified production during the periods when the collieries were in operation, since the faster yearly market demands could be met, the lower their labor costs per ton of coal mined. An examination of production differentials, provided in table 1 (see appendix), shows that after the turn of the century average yearly coal production per man in northeastern Pennsylvania was 484 tons versus 255 tons in the Ruhr.

On a daily basis this translated into an average of 2.24 tons versus 0.82 tons of coal mined, respectively.

Lower daily wage rates paid in the Ruhr were due to specific conditions in the German coal market. Approximately 58 percent of the total market price for coal in the Ruhr was consumed by wages after the turn of the century; for Pennsylvania this figure was significantly lower. German employers also faced higher rates of taxation. Ruhr producers were keen to maintain low wages; yet the demands of year-round production also necessitated ensuring a stable labor supply. As a consequence German employers provided greater social welfare benefits to workers, which contrasted with northeastern Pennsylvania where levels of corporate welfarism were much lower.[29] Such welfare in the Ruhr was evident, first and foremost, in the Knappschaft, the state-mandated insurance organization that provided medical, accident, death, and pension benefits to mineworkers and their families. These benefits were significant for the era as was the fact that workers had some voice in their management. On average, workers contributed approximately 3.5 percent of their yearly salaries to the Knappschaft. For this contribution, workers would receive approximately half their full-time salary if they became infirm or were otherwise unable to work.[30] In northeastern Pennsylvania, an encompassing social welfare program such as the Knappschaft did not exist. In fact, any type of compulsory program requiring employers to contribute to an insurance fund was unconstitutional in this era. Consequently, workers relied heavily on ethnically and religiously based worker associations. Although certain individual coal companies did voluntarily offer their employees some rudimentary death and disability benefits, a development that indeed set the anthracite coal apart from many other industries, they never reached the levels accorded workers in the Ruhr.[31]

In addition to pension and insurance funds, the amount of subsidized company housing provided was substantially higher in the Ruhr, particularly in newer areas where Poles settled.[32] Workplace conditions were also generally of a higher standard. From the 1890s onward, Ruhr mines boasted of on-site changing rooms and baths to increase miners' comfort while at work. Such facilities in northeastern Pennsylvania did not become widespread, despite an 1891 law mandating them, until after World War I.[33] Steps were also taken in the Ruhr to increase mine safety, especially by improving ventilation systems. Interestingly, for this investment in safety, the accident rate in mines in the Ruhr was only slightly better than in northeastern Pennsylvania. In the ten-year period between 1891 and 1900, the average number of fatalities per 1,000 employers working in Ruhr coal mines was 2.73, while in the Pennsylvania anthracite fields it was 3.1.[34]

Overall, the corporate welfare provided by employers in the Ruhr was superior and reflected producers' desire to ensure stability in the workforce while holding the line on wages. For Ruhr miners, the various nonwage benefits they received were welcome because they provided a sense of security, though the total package of social protections naturally came with a price; namely, it gave employers greater leverage and control over their employees. Any worker who became too outspoken risked losing his home and potentially even his pension benefits.[35] Although efforts to control workers' behavior were also made in northeastern Pennsylvania, mine companies possessed fewer tools of coercion.

The disparities in intensity of the work regime, wages, and levels of welfare naturally raise the question: Did workers in northeastern Pennsylvania or those in the Ruhr have an overall higher standard of living and quality of life? Finding a conclusive answer to this question is difficult, and opinion among observers of the time was split. In 1914, *Coal Age* magazine, an American industry trade journal, ran a series of articles highlighting how working conditions and levels of worker satisfaction were comparatively better in Ruhr mines than in the United States. In response to these articles, James Roderick, chief of the Department of Mines in Pennsylvania, defended the organization and practices of the Pennsylvania mine industry, claiming that

> [t]he Pennsylvania miner . . . has a much preferable position to that of his fellow laborer in foreign fields, not only as a wage earner, but as a citizen. . . . His pay is higher, he has less harsh discipline, his opportunities for advancement—for getting out of a rut—are infinitely greater. The doorboy of today may hope to be the foreman or superintendent of the future. The home surroundings that heretofore have been undesirable and unattractive are daily becoming more pleasant. Comfortable houses with modern conveniences, gardens in which the family may find healthy and remunerative recreation in spare hours, neat front yards, public playgrounds, increasing educational facilities, all these and many more advantages are his and tend to elevate and refine his social condition, and make his life easier, happier and in every way more desirable.[36]

Roderick's rather rosy assessment does not entirely accord with the reality of workers' lives in Pennsylvania's anthracite region. Although daily rates of pay were substantially higher for miners in northeastern Pennsylvania than in the Ruhr, there was a narrower gap in the annual income of workers.

As table 1 (see appendix) shows, in the period between 1903 and 1913, mine workers in the Ruhr earned on average $354.98 a year compared to $521.41 for anthracite workers in Pennsylvania. The main reason for this was the effect of part-year employment in northeastern Pennsylvania, which as a Pennsylvania State Senate Investigating Committee noted in 1897, made it "utterly impossible for any moderate sized family to more than exist, let alone enjoy the comforts which every American workingman desires and deserves."[37] Although the number of working days in Pennsylvania did increase over the subsequent decade, they never approached the steady year-round employment available in the Ruhr.

The actual disparity in annual income was also less because the cost of living in northeastern Pennsylvania was higher than in the Ruhr. Unlike miners in the Ruhr, anthracite miners in Pennsylvania usually had to pay for all of their own equipment, including tools and blasting powder, and generally did not receive free or subsidized monthly allotments of coal.[38] The greater isolation of certain mining communities in northeastern Pennsylvania, most noticeable in the middle anthracite field (Lehigh region), also meant that these workers often were forced to buy foodstuffs and other goods in a more expensive company store, where prices exceeding 30 percent over retail were common.[39] Peter Roberts, a sociologist and progressive reformer, estimated in 1904 that the annual expenses of a mine family in Pennsylvania totaled $655.88, whereas in Germany the cost of living for a similar family was only $461.73. Other commentators have claimed a lower basic subsistence level, noting that in the early twentieth century a family could survive on a budget of $460 in northeastern Pennsylvania and $358 in the Ruhr.[40] In examining these yearly income requirements, it becomes immediately apparent that workers in both regions often struggled to make ends meet.

Cultural Attitudes and the Roles of Government

Differences in cultural attitudes toward cartels and trusts as well as varying levels of government intervention in Germany and the United States also led to differences in how the workplace experience unfolded. In Germany, the formation of cartels became a standard business practice in many large industries, a development that met with societal acceptance across class lines because of the supposed order that cartels imposed on the chaos of the free market. Leading labor leaders such as Heinrich Imbusch and Otto Hue welcomed the order the Kohlen-Syndikat imposed. Imbusch once claimed that "without [the Kohlen-Syndikat] it would not have been possible to hold back foreign competition, bring new areas into production, and maintain continually good prices."[41] Some attempts to defy the market dominance of the Kohlen-Syndikat were made. Most notably, the German government reestablished a presence in the mining industry after the turn of the century by opening four state-owned mines and acquiring shares of some publicly held mining firms. However, this challenge proved ephemeral. By 1912, even the government sold its excess coal through the powerful Kohlen-Syndikat.[42] By contrast, the informal anthracite trust was met with outspoken criticism in the United States. Although government often turned a blind eye to many anticompetitive business combinations in the Roosevelt era, the late Gilded Age and Progressive era was a period when trust-busting sentiment became widespread. Populists and later Progressives argued that trusts were antithetical to Smithian notions of free commerce and fairness to the small producer as well as the consumer. Attempts by anthracite producers to limit supply raised the ire of consumers and risked government intervention. In fact, responding to consumer clamor, the government in 1906 began proceedings against the anthracite operators under the auspices of the Interstate Commerce and Sherman Anti-Trust Acts, actions that continued until 1916.[43]

Levels of direct government intervention in labor matters also varied. During the late nineteenth century, various groups from across the political spectrum sought to reconcile workers' interests with the rights of capital. Bismarck's social reforms of the 1880s constitute one well-known example of such interventionism. Another was Kaiser Wilhelm II's action during the 1889 Ruhr Strike, when he met with striking workers and pressured employers to compromise with them. Within the Reichstag, or national parliament, both the Sozialdemokratische Partei Deutschlands (SPD) and Center Party regularly spoke about the rights of workers and the duties of employers. The conservative bureaucracy, wanting to ensure order and social stability, often was a moderating influence in labor relations, with the Bergämter active in guarding against exploitative labor practices.[44] German government involvement in labor matters contrasted with that in the United States, where legislative, executive, and judicial branches of government were heavily weighted in favor of employers at the local, state, and federal levels. Perhaps the most egregious example of direct government support and collusion with business came in the form of the dreaded Pennsylvania Coal and Iron Police, a private security force created by employers and invested with full law enforcement powers by the state legislature.[45]

With the turn of the century, a marked shift occurred in governmental attitudes and responses to labor problems. In Germany, the state acted less as a conciliator and more as an enforcer of employers' interests. Although the government attempted to mediate the 1905 Ruhr Strike, seven years later, in the 1912 strike, it used military interventions to protect the rights of capital. When the SPD became the largest party in the Reichstag in 1912, it proved ineffective in passing legislation that would have significantly aided miners.[46] Meanwhile, in northeastern Pennsylvania, the 1902 Anthracite Strike brought about a sea change in government policy. Having initially maintained a hands-off approach to the labor dispute, the federal government eventually intervened and essentially forced a collective bargaining regime on employers. This unprecedented step anticipated the Wagner Act by more than three decades, strengthened the power of the UMW, and stabilized industrial relations to the extent that no large-scale labor dispute occurred in the anthracite region for another twenty years.[47]

Strike Patterns and Working-class Demands

The dangerous work regime, the struggle for incomes that exceeded mere subsistence levels, and the coercive power of employers encouraged workers in both the Ruhr and northeastern Pennsylvania to organize and defend their interests. In the Ruhr, workers' dissatisfaction with their condition led to the outbreak of significant strikes in 1889, 1899, 1905, and 1912, and mine workers in northeastern Pennsylvania engaged in large-scale work stoppages in 1887–1888, 1897, 1900, and 1902. Not all of these strikes engendered worker solidarity. The 1897 Lattimer Strike in northeastern Pennsylvania and the 1899 Herne Strike in the Ruhr were primarily ethnic strikes led by Polish and other eastern European laborers. However, the level of interethnic class solidarity during the other major strikes was high.

Due to the structural conditions of each region, workers' claims against employers during strike actions varied. A comparison of the demands made during the 1902 Anthracite Strike and the 1905 Ruhr Strike, the largest strikes in each region, reveals subtle differences. In both regions workers pushed for an increase in wages, a reduction in hours, the institution of independent check weighmen, and the recognition of workers' unions by employers. Key differences were that the demands of workers in northeastern

Pennsylvania centered first and foremost on wages and hours whereas Ruhr workers focused less on wages and more on hours and several nonmaterial interests, such as the desire for "humane treatment."[48] This difference in emphasis reflects in part the larger influence employers exercised over Ruhr workers' lives, in contrast to the relationship based primarily on wages that existed between workers and producers in northeastern Pennsylvania. As table 1 (see appendix) highlights, labor economics also help explain the differing tendencies in strike demands. The fact that labor costs in the Ruhr comprised a significant percentage of the market price of coal meant that workers were unlikely to obtain significant wage concessions; if they did it was only when markets were expanding. Demands emphasizing nonmaterial compensation that could remain in place during periods of economic downturn were sensible. In northeastern Pennsylvania, employers had significantly more ability, particularly after the turn of the century, to support increased wages, either by passing costs onto consumers or by absorbing such increases themselves.

Aside from workers' demands, another notable difference between strike actions in the Ruhr and in northeastern Pennsylvania was their respective length. The 1905 Ruhr Strike lasted approximately one month, whereas the 1902 Anthracite Strike lasted five and a half months. Other strikes in the Ruhr were much shorter, whereas in anthracite Pennsylvania they were multimonth affairs.[49] There were several reasons for this disparity. First, the risk of losing company-provided benefits such as housing certainly put a brake on the enthusiasm for a protracted labor conflict among workers in the Ruhr. The general lack of such a benefit in northeastern Pennsylvania left employers without this powerful coercive tool. Second, the seasonality of employment in northeastern Pennsylvania conditioned workers to lengthy periods without work and to either living off savings or seeking work elsewhere in periods when mines were idle. Third, the duration of strikes in the Ruhr was shorter because of German state intervention and the more limited financial resources that the Alter Verband, Gewerkverein, and ZZP had to draw on when compared to those of the UMW. Fourth, the fact that the demands of miners in northeastern Pennsylvania were less complicated and directly focused on wages also aided in generating support across diverse groups of workers. Finally, the fragmented nature of union organization in the Ruhr made coordination more difficult and infighting between the various unions common. Although the various Ruhr unions established a committee known as the Siebenerkommission (Commission of Seven) to coordinate trade union policy in 1905, this institution proved largely ineffectual and fell apart within a few years.[50] Factionalism re-emerged and became clearly exposed in the failed 1912 Ruhr Strike when the Gewerkverein refused to join the other miners' unions in a work stoppage.

The Structural Organization of the Coalfields

The coal industry in both the Ruhr and northeastern Pennsylvania exhibited significant similarities by the end of the nineteenth century. Coal employers were organized into a syndicate or trust in order to better control production levels and market prices for coal, a rationalization of industry that also enabled employers to exercise greater control over the workplace regime and strengthened their hand against burgeoning labor opposition. The dangers of the mines, the struggle for incomes that exceeded mere subsistence levels, and the coercive power of employers both within and outside the workplace encouraged a strong sense of injustice among all workers. In order to redress this inequality, coal workers embraced democratic forms of organization, eventually establishing permanent trade unions to protect and promote their economic interests. The nature of workers' self-organization, however, was dissimilar. In the Ruhr, organized labor was fragmented along various ethnic, religious, and political lines, divisions that made unified collective action more difficult than in northeastern Pennsylvania where one dominant union arose. When strikes did occur, they were longer and more successful in northeastern Pennsylvania after the turn of the century than in the Ruhr. There were other important structural variations between each region. Of great magnitude were disparities in markets and wages, which caused differentials in yearly employment, production practices, levels of social welfare benefits, and income available to workers. Further, social attitudes toward employer consolidation and levels of government interference in business affairs also exhibited noteworthy disparities. Taken together, these structural variations are important because they influenced the decisions Poles could make on a daily basis within the workplace as well as levels of interethnic class solidarity over the long term.

3 ılı Breaking Barriers

Polish Entry into the Mines

THE MAJORITY OF POLES who migrated to the Ruhr and northeastern Pennsylvania were young males in their teens and twenties. These men had little prior exposure to mining, but they were attracted to the industry because barriers to employment were low, the occupational structure was flat, and wages and hours were better than those of many other forms of employment. As Jósef Lipinski, a Polish migrant living in Scranton, wrote in a letter home: "A man does not have to work as hard as he did in the old country; and he can live better and earn more money here. . . . I work in a coal mine . . . deep. I work very deep underground—several hundred łokieć [elbow lengths, i.e., feet] from seven in the morning until two, and sometimes three in the afternoon. I earn two dollars and ten cents."[1] Lipinski's emphasis on depth reflects the odd feeling a new mine worker had in working in claustrophobic, near pitch-black darkness, where the work was dangerous and backbreaking. Conditions alternated from stiflingly hot to bone-chillingly cold. Damp and rats were ubiquitous, though the latter were welcome because they acted as an early warning system in cases of danger. Dangers from falling rock, misfired charges, and methane gas were everywhere. Poles above ground fared little better. Workers on the coal breaker were strictly supervised, and the workday was three to four hours longer than that of underground workers. Corporal punishment was common. Many endured this harsh, autocratic regimen because of their dream of returning to Poland with sufficient earnings to purchase farmland. As one migrant to Scranton claimed, "There was the same intention . . . [get] the money and . . . go home."[2] Others sacrificed themselves in order to build a new life in northeastern Pennsylvania or the Ruhr. Although reasons for migration varied, the initial workplace challenges facing Poles in each region were similar.

The Growth of a Polish Workforce

In the Ruhr and northeastern Pennsylvania, the attitude of native workers toward Poles during the 1870s and early 1880s is best characterized as indifferent. Although instances of open hostility can be found, the limited size of Polish communities and their settlement in isolated areas meant that the overall Polish presence drew limited attention.[3] If acknowledged, the emerging Polish influx was more often than not welcomed because of the economic benefits their labor provided. Employers cautioned that Poles had a predilection for "schnapps" that could make them "wild and uncontrollable," but they also characterized these workers as "energetic, willing, . . . flexible," and possessing superior physical strength. For native miners, the unskilled Polish workers were not yet a significant threat to their position within the labor market, and as independent contractors, they used Polish labor to their advantage. In northeastern Pennsylvania, the *Pottsville Republican* reported that "instead of employing laborers at the regular wage . . . miners would employ a big Slav or Hun cheaply, increasing his own pay check quite an amount. His boasting of the 'snap' caused others to do the same."[4]

Poles were not ones to play fools gladly, and the early perception by natives that these newcomers were naive, tractable, and exploitable employees was soon refuted by Polish actions to gain greater equality in the workplace. By the late 1880s, Poles were a growing and increasingly militant force to be reckoned with in the coalfields, as can be seen by Polish willingness to participate in strikes. From September 1887 to March 1888, the majority of Poles in northeastern Pennsylvania joined in a strike by 32,000 mine workers in the Schuylkill and Lehigh fields. This show of support for the strike caught many by surprise because they expected Poles to act as strikebreakers. The *Freeland Progress* incredulously reported that "one of the most significant features of this strike is the fact that the Poles and Hunks, heretofore a class on which the English speaking workmen could not depend on to stand by them in a strike, are entering this one with as much determination as any other class."[5] In May 1889, a major strike broke out in the Ruhr. Among the 80,000 workers who supported the strike were "thousands of Poles in Westphalia," who, as Bismarck claimed in a speech before the German parliament, "posed a danger to the maintenance of civil order." Bismarck's concerns were exaggerated. In fact, officials from districts where Polish settlement was high generally reported that Poles carried out their protests in a peaceful manner. The alarms raised at the highest levels of the German government about Polish miners nevertheless highlight a fundamental and growing concern over their prominence as political actors in industrial disputes.[6]

The 1890s brought new challenges for all workers in the Ruhr and northeastern Pennsylvania. Both regions suffered from economic downturns that increased interethnic tensions as skilled native workers feared labor competition from the growing number of Poles. Between 1890 and 1900, the Polish population in the Ruhr rose 300 percent, while in northeastern Pennsylvania it increased 210 percent; unofficially, this latter figure was most likely higher. By 1900, Poles, Germans, Masurians, and other migrants from the Prussian eastern provinces accounted for approximately 34 percent of the workforce in the Ruhr. In northeastern Pennsylvania, the impact of "new" immigrant labor was even more dramatic. By 1901, Slavic and Italian labor comprised 68.5 percent of the mining workforce.[7]

The Polish labor influx changed previously ambivalent attitudes among established workers. In Pennsylvania, attacks on Poles grew intense. In 1895, union representatives argued that Poles were depressing wages and subsequently persuaded the Pennsylvania legislature to pass a resolution favoring immigration restriction. A similar resolution was passed again two years later. In the Ruhr, the Gewerkverein became outspoken against Poles, arguing in 1898 that "the arrival of foreign workers" has enabled employers to "depress the wages of workers." Despite the strike solidarity shown by Poles in 1889, the Alter Verband similarly complained that Poles were being imported in order to "punch the class-conscious Westphalian worker in the face" and replace him with an "undemanding and unenlightened worker . . . satisfied with lower wages and who would never think to strike."[8] Unions also agitated against Polish mine employment because of workplace safety concerns. The concern about the inability of many Poles to speak English or German with sufficient fluency, as well as the worry that Poles were being promoted to positions as miners too quickly, rose to new heights during the 1890s, especially in 1896, when each region was beset by major mining disasters blamed on Poles.[9]

Fears that Poles were depressing wages and endangered their fellow workers led to the passage of new restrictions designed to limit the Polish presence in the workforce. Under intense lobbying from John Fahy, the district president of the UMW in the anthracite region, the Pennsylvania legislature in 1897 revised miner certification rules to require mine workers to "answer intelligently and correctly at least twelve questions in the

English language" and produce, in person, a certified miner who would attest under oath to the applicant's fulfillment of the two-year minimum assistantship. Certification fees were also raised; a worker applying for a mine certificate was now forced to forfeit a minimum of two- to three-days' worth of wages simply for the privilege of taking the test. In the same 1897 legislative session an additional bill was passed that imposed a head tax on foreign employment in the anthracite mines. Any operator who employed an unnaturalized foreign-born male was henceforth required to pay a tax of three cents per day on such an individual, with violators subject to fines of $1,000 per offense. Employers complied with the law by deducting the tax directly from a foreign worker's wages. Eventually the tax was declared illegal by the courts, but not before it became a major factor contributing to the outbreak of the Lattimer Strike later that year.[10]

In the Ruhr, the push for greater regulation of Polish labor increased in 1897, spurred by the government's fear that left unchecked a Polish "state within a state" would emerge in the Ruhr. As a consequence, the Ministry of Trade and Industry carried the Germanization campaign westward by mandating that all mines post their rules and regulations only in German and that knowledge of German be made a condition of employment in the mines. Unions, eager to show their loyalty to the government, supported the government by arguing that safety concerns necessitated greater government regulation of miners. As Otto Hue declared at a General Assembly of the Alter Verband, "The workers who do not know German are . . . a danger for the whole workforce." In January 1899, the government issued the Bergpolizeiverordnung (Mining Police Order) requiring that foreign language workers demonstrate an ability to understand verbal instructions in German prior to being employed in the mines; heads of mine teams speak, read, and write German; and employers compile lists and certify the competency of their foreign workers. Violators of these rules faced a 300-mark fine and the possibility of imprisonment. In supporting the Bergpolizeiverordnung, native unions gave little concern to the protests of their Polish members. Reflecting on the impending changes to the competency regulations, the head of the Gewerkverein commented: "The Poles will have to accommodate themselves to existing conditions, whether they want to or not."[11]

The native animosity exhibited toward Poles during the 1890s raises the question: Was the widespread perception that Poles depressed wages and increased safety risks in fact accurate? When viewed over the course of the decade, arguments that Poles lowered wages are incorrect. Poles at the mine shaft knew the going wage rates and demanded equal pay for equal work. The Alter Verband admitted such when it noted in 1897 that "already the past has shown that the 'undemanding' foreign workers are not unable to recognize their class situation" much to the displeasure of employers. Meanwhile, in northeastern Pennsylvania, a former miner recalled, "It was hard for the older people, [but] when they got pushed too hard they would speak back." Emily Balch, a Wellesley economics professor in the early twentieth century, argued that "the earnings of the rough, manly labor of the country have not in general been pushed back" by the influx of Poles.[12]

On the surface, the contention that Poles contributed to an increase in accidents appears more sustainable. Statistics from 1902 show that for every hundred workers in the Ruhr, the accident rate of eastern migrant labor was 17.7 versus 12.1 for locals. In northeastern Pennsylvania, Poles accounted for 26 percent of the fatal accidents that occurred between 1892 and 1905, higher than their average representation within the general mine workforce.[13] Yet as John Kulczycki has noted with reference to the Ruhr, statistics for the period are often incomplete, and depending on year and survey cited, one can find periods when the rate of accidents among Poles was less than average. Further, the state, employers, and native workers all bear some responsibility for Polish accidents in the mines. In the Ruhr, authorities refused to post safety regulations and warning signs in Polish. Though mines in northeastern Pennsylvania did print mine regulations and signs in Polish, as well as many other eastern and southern European languages, safety provisions were not well enforced, and production regimes were intense. Most significantly, in both regions, Poles were likely to be assigned by native foremen and miners to the most dangerous and least profitable positions on the mine face.[14]

The widespread fear held by native workers and their unions that Poles threatened wages and safety was a significant factor in accounting for the rise in efforts to circumscribe Polish employment in the mines during the late 1890s. Compounding native animosity in this period was a rising ethnonationalism on both sides of the Atlantic, a development that colored all debates surrounding the Polish presence in mining. Stereotypes of the dangerous, unintelligent "Pollack" or "Hunkie" were common. In Pennsylvania, working-class representatives who pushed for immigration restrictions in the legislature during 1895, many of whom were ethnically Irish, declared that "we recognize in the constant influx of an ignorant and vicious class of immigrant a great and growing evil highly injurious to American workingmen and dangerous to American institutions."[15]

In the Ruhr, Dr. Adolph Wagner, a prominent professor from Humboldt University, spoke before a Gewerkverein general assembly in January 1897, declaring that the "German people were far more advanced than any other cultural nation," and German workers thought about "their economic and social situation on a deeper and more serious level" than others workers. Although Poles were not directly named, the aspersions cast on Polish labor were clear. For the Alter Verband, appeals to nationalism were subtler given the official internationalism still underpinning German socialism. Yet in a period that saw the lifting of the Sozialistengesetz (Anti-Socialist Law), the Alter Verband was intent on brandishing its credentials as a sober-minded bargaining partner and upholder of the social order. In a March 1897 speech, Otto Hue declared that the union's interests were those of the *Vaterland*. In proving its nationalist credentials, the Alter Verband highlighted the danger of Polish labor and how these newcomers would "sooner or later revolt with elemental violence" unless taken under the paternalistic guidance of the union and lifted up to the same cultural level of the enlightened, class-conscious German worker.[16]

The nationalist rhetoric exhibited by representative authorities of the native working classes reflected wider assumptions among native workers regarding Polish cultural traits and values. In northeastern Pennsylvania, such attitudes were particularly evident in the minstrel shows of the era, which were a major form of entertainment among the region's working class, particularly with the Irish. In the popular minstrel ballad "He Wouldn't Load the Lumps," the following excerpt reveals Irish miners' attitudes toward Poles and other eastern Europeans, collectively referred to as "Huns,"[17] as well as the generally violent atmosphere of mining communities in this period.

> On the eighth day of November I was huntin' with a gun,
> Just above Laurel Run, for it was there I seen the fun.
> Standing at a pay car was a miner and a Hun,
> And the miner had the mon' but he wouldn't pay the Hun.
> Paddy sez, "Now John, you got all you're gonna get."
> The Hun he sez, "You son-of-a-gun, I'm get em two shifts yet."
> Paddy sez, "You'll get it, but you'll get it in the neck."
> And with that he plunked the Hun and he laid him in a lump.
> "All right, Paddy, I'm tomorra fixin' squire."
> "I don't care," sez Paddy, "if you go and fetch the Mayor."
> And with that I seen a Hun go flying through the air.

> Listen to me while I speak:
> At the Huns' there is a wake,
> And his funeral is tomorrow.
> He received a nasty thump
> And they'll bury him in sorrow,
> 'Cause he wouldn't load the lumps.[18]

Popular conceptions of Poles in the Ruhr also incorporated stereotypes and images of violence. One "poem" published in a Center Party paper in Essen referred to Polish parliamentarians as Poles who "drink the dregs of Hungarian wine" and continued:

> The Polish question, for example, that will resolve itself all at once,
> Nowadays, one shuts down assemblies as soon as Polish
>   speeches appear;
> This is wrong. Much better let all the people huff and puff,
> Surround them with soldiers, so that none can get away.[19]

Overall, such characterizations of Poles served a highly functional purpose. The ostracizing of Poles provided a psychological reward and a coping mechanism for many who were otherwise likewise dispossessed within American and German society.

The increasing nationalism of native unions and workers did not sit well with Poles. Polish membership in the UMW was almost nonexistent by the end of 1896; in the Ruhr, Polish membership in the Gewerkverein and the Alter Verband declined precipitously by the turn of the century.[20] Despite native xenophobia, Poles nevertheless were determined to demand greater rights and equality within the workplace. Denied the solidarity of native workers, Poles turned inward, relying on their own ethnic communities and institutions to provide a base of support. The resolve of Poles to persevere in a hostile workplace environment is best illustrated by Polish actions during the 1897 Lattimer Strike in northeastern Pennsylvania and the 1899 Herne Strike in the Ruhr.

The Lattimer Strike of 1897

In the summer of 1897, Polish discontent with working conditions was reaching a boiling point. Recently passed revisions to the miner certification process threatened the ability of younger Poles to move up in the mines, and the proposed head tax on foreign workers would cut into already meager earnings. In early August, small strikes began occurring at collieries in Luzerne County. By mid-August, Gomer Jones, a new mine superintendent at the Honeybrook colliery of the Lehigh Wilkes-Barre Coal Company near Hazleton, stoked the fires of Polish resentment when he arbitrarily announced that mule drivers, an occupation dominated by young Poles and other new immigrants, would have to work an extra one to two hours a day for the same wages. Upset, these workers walked off and began picketing the colliery. Jones, angered by this challenge to his authority, attempted to break up the strike action with an axe handle, but after striking one mineworker, he was quickly overwhelmed and beaten. The incident sent a shock wave throughout the local community, and within one day 3,000 workers from six mines refused to return to work until Jones was fired, wages increased, and the new policy regarding mule drivers rescinded. The strike movement that started at Honeybrook soon spread to engulf the entire Hazleton region. On August 21, the tax on foreign workers went into effect, spurring workers at other mines to go on strike demanding an increase in wages. By the beginning of September, over 10,000 workers were engaged in the work stoppage.[21]

The most remarkable aspect of the strike action was that it was led almost exclusively by Poles, Slovaks, and other "new" immigrants. After initially joining with the protesting mule drivers at Honeybrook, native workers reached accords with employers and returned to work within a few days. Immigrant mineworkers, however, refused to be persuaded by employer promises to address grievances or by the appearance of the Pennsylvania Coal and Iron Police. Organizing a temporary strike committee, new immigrants demanded a 15 percent increase in wages, the right to pay their own physician, an end to the company store system and, in the light of the tax on foreigners, the same wages as "Americans." In order to realize their agenda, the immigrants organized a concerted campaign of marches across the region that eventually caused most of the mine operations in the Hazleton area to shut down by early September.[22]

The actions of the strikers caused widespread hysteria within the region. A contemporary observer commented that the strikers "all live in patches and are exceedingly clannish. Nearly all carry some kind of weapon." In describing the effectiveness of the marches, a police informant noted on September 8 that when rumors reached West Hazleton that marchers were coming, "all the English speaking [went] hiding away in the woods, or else left for some other place for the night. They were afraid to stay home, as the foreigners had announced their intention that they must go along with them." Of particular shock to the public was the fact that Polish and other eastern European women also actively joined in supporting the strikes. A front-page *New York Times* article, titled "Amazon War Threatened," described how at the Audenried mine "about 100 men reported for work" only to be confronted by "a band of women that swooped down upon them with an armament of sticks and stones" causing them to "promptly quit work." Overall, the actions of immigrant labor in support of the strike led the *Hazleton Daily Standard* to remark, with a sense of foreboding, that unless some type of settlement was reached soon, "the whole Lehigh region will be plunged into one of the most threatening conditions ever experienced in the history of Pennsylvania coal mining."[23]

The effectiveness of the marches in shutting down the mines, together with growing public pressure, caused the coal companies to prod local authorities to take more decisive action to end the strike. On September 6, Luzerne County sheriff James Martin began posting notices declaring that a state of riot existed and confronted marchers, telling them that their protests were illegal. He also deputized and armed eighty-seven local residents with Winchester rifles to aid in controlling workers' protests. Many of these deputies were sons of mine managers who were home from college. Over the next few days, Martin traversed the county chasing after striking workers. On September 10, tensions came to a head. That morning approximately 350 unarmed marchers, carrying an American flag in front of them, set out from West Hazleton to shut down the Calvin Pardee and Co. operations in Lattimer, a small town to the northeast of Hazleton. Martin confronted the strikers that morning, making one arrest, seizing the flag, and reading the strikers the riot act. Ignoring the sheriff's order to disperse, the marchers pressed on and later that afternoon approached the outskirts of Lattimer.

In the meantime, Martin had sent orders for all of his deputies to assemble at Lattimer in order to head off the marchers. By three that afternoon, the two sides stood face to face. Martin angrily confronted the head of the strikers' column, waved his pistol, and again ordered the strikers to disperse. A scuffle ensued when Martin tried to arrest another striker and sheriff's deputies opened fire, killing nineteen (fourteen Poles, four Slovaks, and one Lithuanian) and wounding thirty-eight. After learning of the violence, the Pennsylvania governor immediately sent the state militia into the region to restore order. The strike would collapse within the following two weeks.[24] Yet, the reverberations from what later came to be known as the Lattimer Massacre were far-reaching.

Most remarkable in the wake of the strike was the public outrage over the actions of Sheriff Martin and his men. Telegrams and letters from around the country and wider world flooded the governor's office in sympathy for the affected strikers.[25] On the local level, while the Scranton-based *Diocesan Record* commented that Poles and Slovaks were "the scum of Europe," who brought "terror to the hearts and the hearths of the better elements of the community," local opinion largely sided with the victims. The *Carbondale Herald* ran an opinion piece that described the sheriff's deputies as persons who "belong to a class of lazy loafers . . . found in every town and ready to do any kind of low, mean, despicable trick to earn or secure a few dollars. They never had character to lose, hence have nothing to fear [from a trial] now." In fact, the deputies along with Sheriff Martin had much to fear. Public pressure over the massacre led to the indictment of Martin and sixty-eight of his deputies on charges of murder. Though the defendants, as predicted by the *Herald,* were acquitted the following March, the fact that the defendants were even put on trial given their social standing in the community sent a signal that even lowly immigrant Poles had rights that needed to be respected.[26]

Polish reaction to the massacre was bitter, though not vengeful. While Polish newspapers such as *Straż* argued that no American paper portrayed the Poles in a positive light, they also cautioned Poles that the oppression suffered in northeastern Pennsylvania was much less than the suffering endured by Poles in the homeland. Generally, Poles were most concerned with the need to obtain "justice [for] the whole Slovak and Polish nation." To ensure this, they worked with other eastern European ethnics to organize a "prosecution committee" that provided evidence against the defendants in the Martin trial.[27] Poles also established a relief committee to aid the families of the victims of the massacre. Overseen by the Reverend Richard Aust, a German Upper-Silesian who pastored to Poles in Hazleton, the committee raised upwards of $9,100 (equivalent to nearly $200,000 in 2009) for those families.[28]

In addition to mobilizing the ethnic community, Poles also became significantly more active in native organizations, most notably the UMW. Organizers for the union had come to realize that any successful union in the region would have to incorporate the growing numbers of eastern and southern European laborers who dominated the workforce of the region. Consequently after the 1897 Lattimer Strike, the UMW shifted course and promoted the inclusion of Polish and other eastern European workers. As the new president of the UMW John Mitchell (1898–1908) exclaimed, "The coal . . . isn't Slavish or Polish or Irish coal, it's coal."[29] The subsequent drive to recruit Poles was a success. Poles joined the union in record numbers, and overall membership rose rapidly. Whereas at the end of 1897 the UMW had a total membership of around 200, this figure stood at 9,000 at the end of 1899. By 1901, membership grew to 78,437. Nevertheless, a great irony of Polish history in this region is that the union which pushed for stricter certification requirements and the tax on foreigners, which then led to the Lattimer Massacre, was chosen by Poles as the best vehicle through which to protect their interests.[30]

The increased willingness of Poles to join the UMW after 1897 was driven by a desire to utilize the union as a means to further their interests. The union offered Poles an outlet to ensure that their workplace concerns were represented as well as an opportunity to gain greater social standing within the community. Although the UMW initially planned to organize all Poles into national locals, most Poles, as one organizer noted in a meeting in Nanticoke, opted "in favor . . . of going with the English speaking class and it was done."[31] Polish confidence was also enhanced by the ability of Poles to rise to senior positions of significance in the UMW and the pride taken in out-organizing native workers. The rapprochement between the UMW and the Polish community after the Lattimer Massacre was solidified in 1899 when Poles living in and around the city of Nanticoke began an eight-month-long strike that ended in success with the help of the UMW locals, a triumph that subsequently led to large increases in Polish UMW membership.[32]

The Herne Strike of 1899

Although the debates in the Ruhr over the language ordinances that eventually became law in early 1899 limited interethnic solidarity, a bigger blow came later that year when predominantly young Polish workers in and around the town of Herne went on strike during late June. General dissatisfaction with wages in the Herne region had been growing over the preceding years, particularly among younger workers. Between 1895 and 1898, average wages for unskilled workers rose only 8 to 9 percent while those for skilled miners increased approximately 15 percent. By 1898, earnings for the unskilled were less than three marks a day, a wage below the minimum estimated necessary by German unions for a decent standard of living. In the years leading up to the Herne Strike, both the Alter Verband and the Gewerkverein attempted to take advantage of the discontent among workers by passing resolutions demanding a 10 percent increase in wages, but to no avail.[33]

A more immediate cause of the strike was the obligatory increase in payments that haulers and other unskilled workers had to make to the Knappschaft pension fund. Starting in April 1899, younger unskilled workers, who earned on average between 2 and 2.80 marks a shift, were required to contribute 80 pfennige (20 cents) a week to the pension fund, whereas previously they contributed only 1.50 marks (38 cents) per month. For younger workers this increase was a bitter pill to swallow, especially since the Knappschaft dues of skilled workers, who earned significantly more income, were lowered to the same weekly assessment of 80 pfennige. At first many younger workers, particularly Poles, were unaware of the increase in their pension dues since no effort was made to inform them aside from posted notices written in German. The fact that little protest was registered from younger workers during the third week of May, the first pay period for which the new rates went into effect, led skilled workers, unions, and employers to believe that everyone understood and accepted the new rates. However, some employers neglected to deduct the obligatory increase in dues from wages in May, which meant that when deductions were made in June, the minimum deduction, because May was five weeks long, would be 4 marks ($1.00) and could be as high as 7.20 marks ($1.80). While such sums might appear paltry, for unskilled Polish laborers eager to save money the deductions in June represented two to three days' worth of wages. Consequently, when younger workers at the Von der Heydt mine received their pay on Friday, June 23, they immediately agitated for a 20 pfennige per shift increase in their wages, a demand that management denied. With this refusal, sixty-nine younger workers, mostly Poles, walked off the job. By the following day, the strike movement spread to the Shamrock, Julia, and Friedrich der Grosse mines and embraced six hundred to seven hundred workers.[34]

The strike movement likely would have remained small if not for the subsequent actions of local authorities. On Sunday, June 25, a public meeting was called in Herne for the late afternoon to discuss the work stoppage. The lead speaker was to be Sylwester Szczotkowski, an Alter Verband activist and member of the Polish Socialist Party (PPS), an affiliate party of the SPD, who planned to persuade striking workers to remain calm and return to work. By the start of the meeting some four hundred to five hundred workers were present, many of whom were unable to fit into the overflowing meeting hall. As Szczotkowski rose to speak, however, the police officer overseeing the meeting decided that the overcrowded conditions posed a threat to public safety and ordered the meeting disbanded. The gathered assembly reacted to this order with anger but slowly began to withdraw. Nevertheless, outside the meeting hall, clashes between milling workers and police occurred, with police firing blanks and arresting sixteen workers.[35]

In the aftermath of this first confrontation, the situation soon grew out of control. Through the night of June 25, groups of workers angrily gathered in pubs along the Bahnhofstrasse (the main street) to discuss the actions of the police. The following day, the strike spread to include other mines and more than a thousand workers. Incidents were reported of one worker being shot and roving gangs of mineworkers terrorizing the colonies and assaulting workers who chose not to strike. Government officials and the press were particularly taken aback by the actions of Polish women, who in addition to cheering on striking workers, carried baskets of rocks to aid them in their battles with the police.[36] The unrest that affected the Herne region culminated on Tuesday, June 27. During the day, four thousand workers failed to report for work. Later that afternoon, five hundred to six hundred workers were gathered on the main street when a group of strikers confronted police. Accounts of the scene vary, but most agree that workers began pelting a group of policemen with stones. Other mounted officers soon rode to their aid, and in the confusion police opened fire, killing four and wounding at least seven, most of whom were Poles.[37]

In the aftermath of what came to be known as the "Battle of Bahnhofstrasse," the military was called in to restore order. However, before troops arrived late on the evening of June 28, working-class outrage over the violence of the day before reached a peak. The strike grew to include as many as seven thousand workers, and renewed instances of strikers confronting the police occurred. Because Thursday, June 29, was a Catholic holiday, strike activity halted, a pause that proved decisive for calming passions. On that day, the *Wiarus Polski,* the largest Polish-language paper in the Ruhr, warned those Poles not at work to remain home and preserve peace and order because the "enemies of Poles" were using the disturbances to discredit them. The break in strike activity also gave troops stationed in and around Herne time to organize and ensure that no further public protests would occur. Although the strike continued on Friday and Saturday, and even encompassed mines previously untouched by the events at Herne, the overall scope of the strike movement declined. Almost all workers had returned to work by Monday, July 3. The strike ended in failure.[38]

The repercussions of the strike were significant. At least 141 workers were fired in the immediate aftermath of the strike. A further 121 were tried for strike activities and subsequently sentenced to a cumulative total of 37 years in prison.[39] Even more important was the effect that the strike had on native perceptions of Poles in the region. When the strike first began, the strike was simply seen as a movement among young, inexperienced workers who misunderstood the changes in the Knappschaft and were generally dissatisfied with their wages. Official reports make no mention of a specifically "Polish" strike.[40] Government views changed quickly after the Sunday disturbances, revealing a growing obsession that the Herne Strike, referred to after June 27 as a Polish *Krawalle* (riot), was part of a larger conspiracy linking the Social Democrats and the Polish national movement. Completely neglected was the fact that Germans and Masurians also took part in the strike, albeit to a lesser degree.[41] Complementing the concerns of government officials were Conservative and National Liberal newspapers, which openly railed against the Polish "putsch" in Herne and warned their upper- and middle-class readers of growing threats posed by Poles to the region's social stability.[42]

German working-class rhetoric often mirrored the reaction of the authorities and the upper classes. Caught off guard by the outbreak of the Herne strike, the Gewerkverein and Alter Verband were quick to defend themselves against any charges of aiding Poles and sought to use the strike to their own advantage. August Brust, head of the Gewerkverein, called the strike in Herne a "childish prank" and endorsed both the actions of the police and the view that socialist agitation lay behind the movement. Brust further berated employers for bringing uneducated laborers into the Ruhr where they were treated as "machines." The Alter Verband and the SPD proved even more vociferous in their criticism. Contesting the accusations that they supported Poles, both the Alter Verband and the SPD embraced an anti-Polish rhetoric that in many respects surpassed the vituperative tone of the National Liberals and Conservatives. Poles were characterized as "alcoholics," fundamentally "unorganizable," and naturally "prone to violence" because they existed on an "intellectually lower" plane than German workers. The socialists then shifted blame for the strike onto employers who favored Polish over German workers and the Center Party, which "under the cover of religion riles the Poles up against the efforts of the class-conscious workforce, all to the advantage of the capitalists."[43]

Poles naturally viewed the attacks of both the Alter Verband and the Gewerkverein as unfair and unwarranted. As the *Wiarus Polski* highlighted in its coverage of the strike, while accepting that the strike was an uncoordinated, ill-timed affair, it also revealed the pent-up anger of a section of the workforce whose wage increases were not keeping pace with the cost of living or the rates paid to skilled miners. The *Wiarus Polski* further criticized the German misrepresentation of the strike as solely a "Polish uprising," arguing that many Germans took part and the strike had a Polish "character" for the simple fact that large numbers of Poles worked in the Herne region.[44] In the weeks and months after the Herne Strike, Polish resentment grew. Polish leaders in the Ruhr began discussing the possibility of creating a distinct trade union to serve their interests. By 1902, these deliberations led to the formation of the Zjednoczenie Zawodowe Polskie (ZZP), which would become the foremost agent through which Poles subsequently improved their political clout and social status within Ruhr society.[45]

Polish Working-Class Formation

The appearance of thousands of Polish laborers in the coalfields of the Ruhr and northeastern Pennsylvania from the 1870s onward brought about a dramatic transformation in workforce demographics and labor relations. The perceived economic threat posed by Poles to native workers contributed to a breakdown in interethnic worker solidarity. More important than economics in driving native xenophobia were the cultural misconceptions about Poles, driven by the rising tide of nationalism on both sides of the Atlantic that informed the outlooks of many within the working class of each region. Native union rhetoric during the 1890s incorporated stereotypes of the intellectually inferior, impressionable Polish worker who depressed wages and was a danger to his fellow workers, sentiments reinforced within working-class popular culture. Anti-Polish hysteria led to the passage of language and miner certification ordinances and, in northeastern Pennsylvania, a tax on foreign employment. Although ostensibly passed in the name of mine safety, the goal of the various regulations was to restrict Polish access to and advancement within the labor market of each region.

Within this hostile atmosphere, Poles persevered by banding together to seek greater equality. This can be observed during the 1897 Lattimer and

1899 Herne strikes, where Poles adapted established models of labor organization, utilizing speeches and parades to generate support for their struggle for higher wages and recognition as workingmen. As Poles and other eastern European workers marched along the road to Lattimer, behind the American flag, they were sending a clear message regarding the dignity of labor and the right of ethnic workers to be accorded the same treatment as natives. No comparable image exists of Polish workers in the Ruhr; nor could there be, given the attitude of the Prussian state toward Poles. Nevertheless, the fact that Poles there were willing to directly challenge the status quo, even following bloodshed, indicates that the Herne strike was also about redefining the social boundaries of inclusion and exclusion. The most notable difference between the two strikes was the fact that as a result of the Lattimer strike the boundaries shifted to favor the inclusion of Polish workers; in the Ruhr, such a shift would be delayed until after a strike in 1905.

4 ılı Becoming Mining Men

Polish Integration within the Workforce

IN THE AFTERMATH OF workplace struggles during the 1890s, Polish workers recognized the power of collective action and the inadequacy of existing ethnic institutions for promoting social equality. From the turn of the century onward, Poles began joining unions in large numbers, a development that significantly aided integration by making them political actors within the bounds of civil society. The important role of unions in aiding integration was commented on by Emily Balch in her 1910 treatise *Our Slavic Fellow Citizens*, where she noted that the adaptation of Poles in Pennsylvania to "union life" highlighted the maturing of "a political sense (in the best meaning of the word political) with which the Slav has not been commonly credited" and taught Poles "a nobler, more intelligible and more practical lesson in democratic self-government than most ward politics."[1] Though Balch's language conveys some of the prejudices of her time, her analysis highlights how unions acted as instruments of socialization through which Poles could articulate their interests and become familiar with the democratic practices of their host societies. This chapter explores the long-term effects trade unionism and mobilization in labor disputes had on levels of Polish integration and acceptance within German and American working-class milieus.

In both the Ruhr and northeastern Pennsylvania, Poles were eager to join unions; however, their patterns of organization differed. The majority of Poles in the Ruhr, instead of joining existing German unions, mobilized to form the independent Zjednoczenie Zawodowe Polskie (ZZP) trade union in 1902. By contrast, Poles in northeastern Pennsylvania embraced the dominant coal miners' union in the United States, the United Mine Workers of America (UMW). The immediate cause for this disparity was the different outcomes of the 1897 Lattimer and the 1899 Herne strikes. Other factors were also important. In the Ruhr, the formation of the ZZP provided a legal means to create a strong, culturally autonomous organization through which Poles could maintain their community in a period when the Prussian bureaucracy was intent on restricting Polish activities. The existing factionalism of the union movement and the penchant for the Alter Verband and the Gewerkverein to spend more time fighting each other than employers also put off Poles. As Bartholomaeus Wilkowski, a Polish miner who lived in Gelsenkirchen-Rotthausen, noted during an organizational meeting of the ZZP in 1902, "Poles . . . also have the duty to organize. Each man should join the [ZZP] union organization and not let himself be led astray. . . . The Polish working-class must not belong to . . . unions, which . . . wage a mutual war against each other."[2] In northeastern Pennsylvania, union development during the 1890s was practically nonexistent. Joining the UMW offered a tremendous opportunity for Poles to wield influence within a still-nascent organization and enhance their status within local society. This was especially true under the post-Lattimer leadership of John Mitchell, who publicly welcomed Poles into the union.[3] Regardless of the ways Poles unionized, membership in unions brought strength and allowed Poles to begin to forge bonds with other workers across ethnic lines. Moreover, with the help of their unions, Polish workers were at the forefront in challenging their employers for better wages, hours, and working conditions. This can especially be seen in Polish actions and attitudes during major strikes in each region between 1900 and 1905.

Poles, the UMW, and the Strikes of 1900 and 1902

In northeastern Pennsylvania, Poles began joining the UMW beginning in 1898. Under John Mitchell, the UMW adopted a new course and actively began recruiting Poles and other "new" immigrants, an exceptional development given that most other unions at the time refused to organize them. The UMW's decision was necessary and pragmatic. By the turn of the century, the majority of mine workers in northeastern Pennsylvania hailed from eastern and southern Europe, and if the UMW wanted to be effective, those immigrants needed to be organized.[4] The impact of Poles on the growth of the UMW in northeastern Pennsylvania was impressive. In early 1897 the UMW had approximately 200 members organized in the entire anthracite region. By the great 1902 strike, it boasted a membership of 78,437 divided into three separate districts: District 1 (Wyoming field),

District 7 (Lehigh field), and District 9 (Schuylkill field).[5] Although membership figures were not broken down by nationality, the sizable and growing Polish presence in the union and the eagerness of Poles to organize is borne out by numerous accounts of UMW officials. District 9 UMW president John Fahy, who earlier had pushed for the head tax on immigrant workers, claimed that new immigrants were the most receptive to the union's message, while native workers appeared apathetic. Frank Gwisedoskey, a Polish UMW organizer, also highlighted the organizational disparity between Poles and native workers, noting that if "the English-speaking and Americans join, as do . . . the Slavish . . . we would have a union . . . so strong that we could immediately demand better treatment."[6] Gwisedoskey's and other Polish organizers' efforts soon helped to advance the presence of Poles in local and district positions of leadership. Paul Pulaski, a prominent UMW activist and American-born son of Polish immigrants, became vice president of UMW District 9 in late 1899, serving in this capacity for several years. After 1900, two Polish immigrants, Adam Ryszkiewicz and Anton Schlosser, were appointed vice presidents of UMW Districts 1 and 7, respectively.[7] Although overall Polish representation in the leadership of the UMW remained low, the rise of certain individual Poles to positions of prominence as well as the activist efforts of the rank and file testified to the desire of Poles to organize. It also began to alter perceptions of the Polish immigrants within organized labor, though only after the strikes of 1900 and 1902 did attitudes fundamentally change.

By the turn of the century, the anthracite coal industry was experiencing new growth after a decade marked by economic distress. Between 1897 and 1899, production rose from approximately 47 to 54 million tons, an increase of 15 percent. The organization of industry was finally consolidated into an unofficial trust by the banking interests of J. P. Morgan.[8] Despite growth and industry stabilization, workers saw precious little improvement in their condition. The main source of dissatisfaction centered on wages. Although earnings were slowly rising, there was a widespread belief that employers kept pay rates artificially low through various illegitimate practices. Miners complained about nonuniform sizes of mine cars, the piece-rate paid for such cars, and excessive dockage for cars deemed insufficiently loaded with coal. Where wages were determined by ton of coal mined, arguments arose over employers' decision to arbitrarily increase the size of the "miner's ton" from 3,000 pounds (which yielded a legal ton of 2,240 pounds) to 3,300, even 4,000 pounds. Miners in the Lehigh and Schuylkill anthracite fields wanted the abolishment of the sliding scale, which many rightfully saw as the main cause for declining wages during the 1890s.[9]

Younger laborers, the majority from eastern Europe, had even greater cause for complaint as their wages were decreasing. In 1900, breaker boys in certain mines saw earnings decline by nearly 30 percent. Mule drivers' and haulers' wages fell by nearly 10 percent, and miners' assistants saw decreases of 4 percent.[10] Those in the latter group were also aggrieved because they were at the mercy of miners for a fair accounting and payment of wages for work performed. Since there was no requirement that miners show to their laborers the actual income they earned (or that a given mine company keep such records), there existed a clear temptation to cheat or otherwise underpay assistants, since the assistants had little recourse other than to quit and find employment with another miner.[11] As a whole, discontent among miners' laborers was so widespread that one commentator of the time noted that "had there not been a strike [in 1900] led by miners against operators, there probably soon have been a strike led by laborers against miners."[12] In addition to wages, there were other grievances. Miners railed against the unwillingness of mining companies to compensate for "dead work" such as timbering and the exorbitant prices charged for the blasting powder they were obligated to purchase from their employer. Men directly employed by the company as well as miners' laborers complained of having to work ten hours or more a day. All workers were upset with the price-gouging practices of company stores, the requirement that mine workers utilize the company doctor, and the attempts to intimidate workers to keep them from joining the UMW.[13]

By late summer 1900, mounting tensions between workers and employers came to a head when a UMW convention in Hazleton passed resolutions demanding a standardization of the miner's ton at 2,240 pounds, greater uniformity in the size of coal cars, the abolition of the company store system, a reduction in the price of powder, and the abolition of the sliding scale. Acknowledging the lower wages earned by younger workers, the convention also resolved that workers earning less than $1.50 a day be accorded a 20 percent increase in wages. Those earning between $1.50 and $1.74, or above $1.75, should be given a 15 and 10 percent increase, respectively. Anthracite operators were given until September 10 to comply with these various resolutions or face a general strike. Operators were not long in formulating their reply. Disputing most of the mine workers' claims, they categorically refused to negotiate, a response that left the UMW leadership with the critical decision of whether to risk calling a general strike. The leadership was reticent. There was worry about the discipline of Slavic workers and their willingness to "stick" to a protracted dispute, a fear that led Mitchell to secretly meet with heads of the railroads in New York to work out a compromise.[14]

Rebuffed by the operators, the UMW finally declared a strike on September 17, couching its appeal to workers in the language of citizenship and masculinity. On the pages of the *United Mine Workers Journal* (*UMWJ*), the union warned members that "strikes between labor and capital are like wars between nations: they bring hardships, privations and want . . . yet when innumerable wrongs have been heaped upon a people . . . they would be false to themselves, their families and their fellow men if they fail to resist further encroachment upon their rights." To mine workers, these rights comprised not just legal rights, but broader rights based on social citizenship and masculinity. Referring to employers, the *UMWJ* declared that "standing on their legal rights is far from being enough. They are supposed to be civilized Christian and American citizens as well as mineowners. Yet their attitude indicates that they forget all their obligations to the community." Further the *UMWJ* castigated "the mineowners" because they "decline to recognize the miners as men, with men's rights."[15]

The ensuing labor conflict proved to be one of the largest strikes in America, pitting 142,000 mine workers against the best-organized business trust in the United States. The decision to strike was met with near uniform acceptance by mine workers in the Wyoming anthracite field. In the less urbanized Lehigh and Schuylkill fields, responses to the strike were initially more varied due to ethnic, religious, and local animosities. The discord soon contributed to the outbreak of violence. On September 21, Poles and Lithuanians from the "Rocks" section of Shenandoah marched on the Indian Ridge colliery determined to shut the mine. At four in the afternoon, a contingent of mostly English, Irish, and American workingmen left the gates of the mine under the armed escort of a sheriff's posse. As reported by the Associated Press, within minutes a melee ensued.

> Workmen . . . walked up the middle of East Center street, and reached the Lehigh Valley Railroad station. Here was gathered a large crowd of Poles, Slavs and Hungarians—men, women and children—who lined both sides of the street. A shot rang out from a saloon. This was followed by a shower of stones. Many of the crowd had picked up sticks and stones and were acting in a threatening manner. Seeing this . . . the sheriff commanded [his men] to fire. The order was obeyed, with terrible results.[16]

When the smoked cleared, a Polish miner and a bystander were killed; seven other strikers, all eastern Europeans, were wounded. In addition, several strikebreakers had been assaulted by furious strikers and severely beaten. That night the governor of Pennsylvania, William Stone, ordered state militia into Shenandoah to restore order. Despite the presence of military forces in the region, disturbances continued and in subsequent days spread to Mahanoy City, Hazleton, Mt. Carmel, Minersville, and Pottsville, with eastern European laborers cited as the main cause.[17]

The most significant act of violence occurred toward the end of the strike, led not by striking miners, but by their wives and daughters. As the strike progressed into October, tensions at collieries owned by the Coxe Brothers & Company near Lehigh ran high. At the time, the company's Oneida and Sheppton mines managed to continue operations, albeit with a reduced workforce. On the morning of October 9, a crowd of "Slavonians," men and women, gathered at the gates of the Oneida mine determined to shut it down. Men on their way to work were assaulted and later in the day, when an arriving locomotive attempted to enter the mine, numerous women blocked the track. The general superintendent of the mines, Edgar Kudlick, himself an immigrant, attempted to persuade the women to go home but was met with a barrage of stones. Eventually the escalating tensions led the crowd to begin attacking the works at the mine, and as one account reported, "A large woman [waving] a club over her head" began the charge. Inevitably shots rang out, however, this time the strikers themselves were well armed. When the violence subsided, two deputized officers and a Polish striker lay slain. Days later, eleven "Slavonians" were arrested for the killings.[18]

The outbreak of violence in Shenandoah, Lehigh, and elsewhere attracted significant press coverage. Such incidents, however, were not representative of the majority of Polish strikers. Despite the accounts emphasizing the tendency of Poles to "riot," most engaged in largely peaceful protests during the strike. Nowhere was the desire to avoid bloodshed more on display than in Lattimer, the scene of the 1897 massacre, when in early October Poles and other strikers marched through the town to enforce the shutdown of nearby collieries. During their march, the strikers met the local sheriff and a hundred of his deputies as well as a contingent of Pennsylvania Coal and Iron Police. The strikers were read the riot act and ordered to disband. Yet Poles and others refused to heed the order. Instead, one of the leaders cried out, "We demand the right of the highway." The crowd of striking men then raised their hands in the air to show they were unarmed and then pushed through the line of officers to continue their march into town.[19]

Polish militancy during the strike sparked surprise and outrage within middle-class circles. Even the UMW was forced to publicly disavow the more violent acts that occurred at Shenandoah or Lehigh. Unofficially, the UMW welcomed the willingness of Poles and other immigrant workers to enforce strike solidarity through acts of intimidation since the threats made against strikebreakers were proving effective. George Harris, a UMW organizer, noted that in the wake of the Shenandoah bloodshed, the "men responded to the request to quit work more rapidly and in larger numbers than expected."[20] Strike momentum increased throughout the Lehigh and Schuylkill fields. The number of those refusing to work grew rapidly, even with the presence of the military in the region. On September 22, the Philadelphia & Reading Railroad (P&R) ordered its coal agents not to accept any more coal orders at any price due to the outbreak of disturbances at its mines. Twenty of the thirty-nine P&R mines in the region were closed by September 23; two days later this figure increased to twenty-seven. At the end of the month, all three fields were largely at a standstill. On October 3, it was reported that of the 142,000 mine workers, only 5,000 remained at work.[21]

With the strike entering its third week, the solidarity exhibited by mine workers gave employers pause for caution; political pressure was also placed on the anthracite trust by prominent Republican leaders including Ohio Senator Mark Hanna, who worried about the effect the strike might have on President McKinley's reelection bid as well as general fears that the strike would starve the public of its main source of heating fuel just as winter was approaching.[22] The pressures wore on employers. By the end of September, operators offered workers a 10 percent increase in wages, mainly through the reduction in the price of a keg of blasting powder to $1.50. On October 1, the P&R posted notices offering these terms to workers who would return to work. Many other operators followed suit.[23]

Elated that the employers' united facade appeared to be cracking, miners rejected the initial offer.[24] Appreciating the fact that, in the short term, time was on the unions' side due to the coming elections in November, the UMW held a convention in Scranton on October 12 where they demanded the 10 percent increase, the abolishment of the sliding scale in the Lehigh and Schuylkill anthracite fields, and a guarantee that a strike settlement last until April 1, 1901.[25] On October 17, the P&R and the Lehigh Valley Coal Company agreed to these concessions, breaking ranks with the other operators.[26] Coal companies in the northern Wyoming field, where the sliding scale was never in effect, were appalled. William Truesdale, of the Delaware, Lackawanna & Western Railroad (DL&W), believed that the strike could still be broken if operators showed more solidarity with each other. Instead, employers were giving the UMW precisely what it needed to gain the confidence of the workers, a victory, however partial. In any event, such regret came too late. On October 24, operators in the northern field also officially posted notices granting a 10 percent raise. On the same day, the UMW declared an end to the strike and ordered workers to return to work on October 29.[27] The end of the strike marked an important turning point for workers in general and Poles in particular. For the first time since the early 1870s, workers of diverse ethnic backgrounds were able to maintain strike unity and gain wage concessions from employers. The UMW successfully withstood the test of a general strike and finally was able to gain a permanent foothold in the anthracite region. Equally important, the 1900 strike was a turning point in the process of Polish adaptation. During the strike, Poles played leading roles on the public stage, sending a powerful signal to employers, the middle classes, the union, and other workers, as well as themselves, that Polish interests could no longer be taken for granted or ignored.

Polish determination to see the strike through to a successful conclusion, to the point of risking life and limb, was driven by the desire to attain greater rights and recognition as citizens within their communities. This aspiration was put forcefully on display in the aftermath of the Shenandoah "riot," when the Polish community gathered to bury the Polish striker killed during the violence. As one contemporary observed,

> The Slavs made an impressive turn-out . . . when the man killed in the riot was buried. From far and near came hundreds of men to follow his body to the grave. A brass band led them, the United States flag was carried, and about 2,000 men followed the hearse, six abreast, marching with the precision of trained soldiers. They were all decently clothed, some of them in very good apparel, but all were serious to sullenness. Passing the head of the Eighth Regiment on the way, the marching men saluted the colors of the regiment, and the flag carried by the Slavs was saluted in response. The line of these men seemed interminable. They were not all miners, for it was a march of a race and not of a cause.[28]

This account demonstrates that Poles were making themselves visible within the public sphere, demanding that their voices be heard and interests respected. They also sought to allay nativist fears by conforming to accepted standards of respectability for their time, as evidenced by their dress, formation, and disposition. The reverence accorded to American symbols and military figures indicates that Polish strike militancy was not directed against the representatives of state power, instead it arose in response to the perceived illegitimate appropriation of American institutions and authority by employers. Finally, although the observer claims that this demonstration was a "march of a race and not of a cause," it was in fact both. Poles marched in Shenandoah not only to display their strength as an ethnicity but also to demand greater rights as full members of the working-class communities in which they lived.

In the wake of the 1900 strike, the UMW and its president John Mitchell grew in stature in the eyes of miners throughout the anthracite region. Miners even voted October 29, the official day the 1900 strike ended, to be "John Mitchell Day."[29] In April 1901, Mitchell agreed to a one-year extension of the existing agreement with employers in the belief that by doing so the UMW would gain recognition from the major coal companies.[30] The 1900 strike nevertheless left many issues unresolved, and by 1902 miners' dissatisfaction with their condition ran high.[31] Miners complained that no reform had been undertaken on issues such as the size of mine cars, the employment of independent check weighmen or check docking bosses, dead work, and the miner's ton. Growing inflation also significantly offset the hard-earned 10 percent wage increase. The price of basic foodstuffs, for example, rose 9.8 percent in the period between 1900 and 1902.[32] Consequently, in anticipation of the soon to expire 1901 settlement, the UMW approached anthracite operators in February 1902 to discuss wages and other workplace grievances. Employers ignored these entreaties and subsequently posted notices to their workers that they planned to maintain the current wage schedule for the coming year. In mid-March, a UMW convention in Shamokin discussed what to do given the refusal of employers to negotiate with them. Faced with an increasingly angry and militant base, the convention passed resolutions demanding an increase in wages of 20 percent for contract miners, an eight-hour day for company men, the payment of coal by weight, instead of car, to a legal ton of 2,240 pounds, a minimum price of 60 cents per ton, and the recognition of the UMW. A proposal was also made to stop work on April 1, though this was later tabled at the insistence of Mitchell, who wanted to attempt to negotiate with the mineowners through the mediation of the National Civic Federation (NCF), an organization chaired by Senator Hanna that sought to reconcile the interests of capital and labor through progressive reform.[33]

From the end of March through April, the NCF brokered various meetings between the heads of the major railroad companies and the UMW in New York. However, employers refused to accede to any of the union's demands, even after Mitchell reduced his wishes, calling for only a 10 percent wage increase, determination of pay by weight of coal mined as opposed to carload, and a nine-hour day.[34] The intransigence of the railroad heads eventually forced Mitchell to call an emergency meeting of anthracite district heads on May 8 in Scranton, where it was agreed to provisionally suspend work starting on May 12. Another UMW convention was organized for May 14 in Hazleton to decide whether to continue the strike. At that convention, opinion among the 811 delegates was split. Most of the leadership, most notably Mitchell, was reluctant to go on strike, believing that the time was inopportune for what would most likely be a protracted work stoppage. The UMW was still establishing itself in the region, union finances were not ideal, and there was a real danger that the organization would be destroyed. Most of the rank and file, however, were adamant in their desire to strike and argued that the union would lose all credibility in the eyes of ordinary workers if it backed down. In the end, the majority voted to strike.[35] With the decision made, workers in northeastern Pennsylvania embarked on one of the largest and longest strikes in American history. For six months, from May until the suspension of the strike on October 23, 1902, over 95 percent of the 147,000 mine workers laid down their picks and shovels, bringing the anthracite industry to a standstill.[36]

During the first two months of the strike, a general holiday atmosphere prevailed in much of the region. Mine workers were able to get by thanks to savings, UMW strike support, and the willingness of most storekeepers to extend credit. Moreover, anthracite workers were already accustomed to extended periods of unemployment given the nature of the industry. For their part, employers had anticipated the likelihood of a strike and began utilizing stockpiled coal reserves and securing their collieries with the aid of private armed guards and the Pennsylvania Coal and Iron Police.[37] The few collieries that provided company housing, such as Coxe Brothers, ordered striking workers to vacate their homes, though eviction notices were often ignored and went unenforced.[38] By and large, most coal companies did not initially attempt to work the mines with strikebreakers since overall demand for coal in the summer months was low. The reaction of the general public to the beginning of the strike was largely one of indifference. The somewhat surreal atmosphere of the situation was conveyed in the pages of the *UMWJ*, which at the end of May noted that despite "the most extraordinary strike that has ever taken place . . . there seems to be no external indication that a contest is going on. . . . Many of the mine workers are fishing . . . and the breaker boys are . . . having a little time for play in the fresh air and sunshine."[39] Tensions rose in the summer heat of July and August. At the beginning of July, an Italian striker was shot dead, and there were reports of sheriff's deputies beating striking "Hungarians" in their homes near Wilkes-Barre. In mid-August another miner was killed in the Lehigh region, while approximately twenty-five deputies in Duryea fired on a group of five hundred strikers, wounding several. Reports in local newspapers of strikers assaulting scabs were widespread.[40]

The most significant outburst of violence occurred in Shenandoah on July 30, when a crowd of Polish and Lithuanian workers attacked three strikebreakers and Thomas Beddal, their sheriff's deputy escort. The deputy fired a shot into the crowd and retreated with the strikebreakers to the local train depot. Highly agitated, the mob surrounded the building and began throwing stones. The deputy then telephoned his brother Joseph, the owner of a nearby hardware store, for help. As he ran to his brother's aid, the crowd surrounded Joseph Beddal and viciously beat him. He later died of his injuries. Meanwhile, local police also hurried to the depot, managing to extract the strikebreakers but not before several officers, including the police chief, were injured. A number of strikers also sustained injuries. By evening, the sheriff of Schuylkill County arrived with a large posse to restore order. Later that night, Governor Stone, for the second time in less than two years, ordered 1,500 state militiamen to take up positions in and around Shenandoah, where they would remain for the rest of the strike. Troops would also later occupy the Panther Creek Valley near Lehigh.[41]

With the presence of the state militia in the region, reports of violence declined. Eastern European workers, and especially Poles, nevertheless remained under suspicion by authorities as a great danger to public security. After Shenandoah, rumors ran wild that Poles and others with military training in the Prussian, Russian, and Austrian armies were arming and in the final stages of preparing an uprising. In reality, the story was false, though as with all good urban legends, based on a kernel of truth. Specifically, the rumors began after local residents observed a local Polish *Sokół* (Falcon) gymnastic association in Shenandoah drilling using blunted swords and wearing club uniforms, practices that were, in fact, part of their regular activities.[42] Altogether, what is remarkable about the 1902 strike was that it was conducted largely in a peaceful manner. There were fewer major incidents of violence than in either the 1897 or 1900 strikes and despite local worries that "Slavic hordes" were running wild in the region, Polish workers showed great restraint and discipline in their strike activities. Considering themselves by 1902 to be the backbone of the union, Poles adhered to the directives of their UMW leaders who feared that violence would turn public opinion against the strikers. To ease these fears, Polish union men held a mass rally in Shenandoah the first week of August where they denounced the violence of the previous week. They then swore to stand by the UMW until the strike was won.[43]

Poles subsequently maintained this solidarity for another two and a half months. By the end of August, the atmosphere between the UMW and employers was growing more acrimonious. During the late summer Mitchell tried to informally reach a solution to the work stoppage through back channel contacts with the NCF and representatives of J. P. Morgan.[44] Publicly, Mitchell made appeals for arbitration, hoping to win the public relations battle by demonstrating the miners' respectability and reasonableness. The railroad heads nevertheless held firm. The fight was no longer simply about wages, but about destroying the UMW and returning to the pre-1900 strike status quo. The DL&W president, William Truesdale, best highlighted the attitude of employers when he noted that "the vital question in this strike, from the operators' standpoint, is whether they shall resume the control and operation of their properties which they, as owners are entitled to and which they in a manner lost, as a result of the strike in the fall of 1900."[45]

To break the union, operators made aggressive efforts to recruit miners willing to work. In the effort to sow division, employers targeted Poles by playing off the animosities with the Irish. Circulars began appearing in the minefields asking, "Who is going to take care of you? Who gives your friends and relatives good chambers? Are they your countrymen? No, all Irish. Do John Mitchell, Fahy, Duffy, and Nicholls work for you? No, for themselves and their own class, the Irish. They use you and your countrymen to win their battle. . . . A pocket full of money is better than [a] strike benefit that is half stolen before you see it. The men who own the mines and pay you are better friends to you than those who lied to you and are still lying."[46] In early October, the *Straż* newspaper reported that an agent of one of the mine operators in the northern field offered the president of one local $2,500 and each member $100 to $200 if they returned to work.[47] Despite such attempts to bribe or cajole them to quit the strike, Poles held firm in their commitment to the work stoppage and to the UMW.

By September, the continuing stalemate between industry and labor, now in its fifth month, began to worry a public that was feeling the first chills of autumn. Newspaper headlines warned of a "coal famine," and the price of anthracite coal for domestic heating began to soar, going from $6 to more than $20 a ton. Anthracite coal grew so valuable that one unlucky bride in Brooklyn even received a ton of it as a wedding present.[48] In assessing blame for this state of affairs, public opinion was divided. *Harper's Weekly*, taking the side of employers, argued that it should "be plain to all clear-headed men, that there is no cause for arbitration." Taking the UMW to task for abrogating the right to work, *Harper's* asked whether "an American citizen [should be] deprived of the opportunity of doing work for which he is specially qualified by experience and skill, unless he will obey the order and submit to the pecuniary exactions of a particular association."[49] Meanwhile, the *American Monthly Review of Reviews* extolled the bravery of John Mitchell for being willing to arbitrate the strike and castigated the monopolistic coal barons for being "indifferent equally to the demands of miners and to the clamoring of the public."[50] Editorial cartoonists lampooned miners and employers for their mutual recalcitrance to settle.[51] Almost everybody agreed that the state needed to intervene and bring the strike to an end. As the usually staid *Wall Street Journal* proclaimed, "The public wants coal and must have it. If it does not get it, the consequences may be startling to everybody."[52]

With public pressure mounting and a midyear congressional election in the offing, Roosevelt intervened at the urging of Hanna. On October 1, the president personally invited Mitchell and the representatives of the major coal companies to meet with him in Washington. At the October 3 conference, Mitchell offered that striking miners would accept arbitration under the authority of the president, a proposal that the coal operators categorically refused. Employers then proceeded to criticize both the federal and state governments for their responses to the strike, claiming that instead of negotiating with instigators of disorder, the state should uphold the law and protect with force the right of men to work.[53] While accomplishing little, the meeting was a major public relations victory for the strikers and the UMW. Roosevelt and the general public were impressed by the moderate tone of Mitchell while outraged at the unyielding stance of the coal barons.[54]

Due to public anger with the operators, J. P. Morgan made an offer two weeks later to agree to an arbitration commission, provided that the panel be composed of a military engineer, a federal court judge from the United States Third District covering northeastern Pennsylvania, an independent mining engineer, a man with experience in the anthracite coal business, and a "man of prominence, eminent as a sociologist." Mitchell agreed to the panel, but also requested that it include a Catholic clergyman and a labor representative. The operators balked at the idea of a labor representative and threatened to scuttle the proposal altogether. Frustrated, Roosevelt agreed not to technically appoint a labor representative, though to the chagrin of the operators decided that Edgar Clark, the Grand Chief of the Order of Railway Conductors, would be appointed as the eminent sociologist.[55] With the general outlines of what became the Anthracite Coal Strike Commission (hereafter, the Anthracite Commission) established, focus turned to the miners and whether they would accept arbitration. Mitchell called for a UMW convention to meet in Wilkes-Barre on October 20–21. At the convention, miners' representatives unanimously agreed to accept arbitration. The *UMWJ* later reported that after this decision of "free men" was made, "a score of races mingled in the hall, Saxon and Celt, Teuton and Slav, Latin and the native-born . . . [all sang "My Country 'Tis of Thee"], one third of them not knowing the words or melody, but they knew that the hymn was of America and their hearts sang."[56] On October 23 workers returned to work to await the Anthracite Commission's final judgment.

After five months of work, the Anthracite Commission issued its report on March 21, 1903. The findings were mixed, offering both workers and employers the ability to claim victory. The Anthracite Commission found in favor of the strikers with regard to the issues of wages and hours. Contract miners were awarded a 10 percent increase in wages, and the working day of company men was reduced to nine hours, effectively increasing their wages likewise by a further 10 percent. Employers were placated with the rejection of the demand that coal be weighed by a ton of 2,240 pounds with a 60-cent minimum price. The Anthracite Commission ordered mine companies not to interfere with union organizing, but it did not require them to recognize the UMW as the miners' representatives. Other rulings included endorsing the use of independent check weighmen or docking men, requiring employers to pay miners' assistants wages directly by deducting them in advance from the miners' pay, thus circumventing the tradition of paying laborers in the saloon or elsewhere, and instituting a new sliding scale in which wages would increase, but never decrease, 1 percent for every five-cent rise in the wholesale price of coal.[57] The most important decision made was the imposition on employers and workers of a collective bargaining system in all but name only. The initial Anthracite Commission award was to last for a period of three years, after which it would be renegotiated in three-year periods. During the period an award was in effect, strikes and lockouts were prohibited. To aid in resolving any disagreements between management and labor, a Board of Conciliation was established made up of three employer representatives and three labor representatives. If the board could not settle disagreements, they were to be referred to an independent arbitrator. Over time, this arrangement would prove remarkably resilient.[58] The labor representatives on the board were the three UMW district presidents in the anthracite region, and in later years, these board members directly negotiated with employers over the renewal of labor contracts.

Historians have debated which side won the 1902 strike. Union leaders and a majority of workers generally hailed the outcome of 1902 strike as victory, though there were dissenters, particularly among the rank and file, who felt that the provisions of the award did not go far enough.[59] Given the state of trade unionism in the country at the time, the 1902 strike and the subsequent award represented a significant success for workers. Important in this regard was the imposition of binding arbitration and the creation of the Board of Conciliation, which forced the de facto recognition by employers of the UMW as the representative of the anthracite workers. The 1902 strike was also a triumph for Poles. Polish actions by and large cemented their integration into the region's working class. Although Poles would continue to face native discrimination and struggle to rise into the ranks of the middle class, they gained greater respectability and responsibility within union structures. They were more accepted as citizens within their working-class communities, especially within the male miner subculture. This can be seen in the transformation in the miners' minstrel songs about Poles. Whereas previously Poles were the targets of derision by the Irish, now they were held up as fellow brothers and citizens. One of the most popular Irish minstrel ballads in the region became "Me Johnny Mitchell Man." Telling the story of Joe Sokolsky, the song highlights a brave Pole willing to strike because he was both a union man and a citizen:

> Me no 'fraid fer nottink,
> Me dey nevair shcare,

Sure me shtrike tomorra night,
Dats de biziness, I dunt care.
Righta here me tellin' you–
Me no shcabby fella,
Good union citizen–
Johnny Mitchell man.[60]

Though the language of the Irish ballad, by contemporary standards, betrays a degree of prejudice against eastern Europeans, it also highlights how the 1902 strike, as historian Harold Aurand has noted, transformed Joe "from a Pole who happened to be miner . . . into a mine worker who happened to be Polish."[61] Further, it shows that the Irish increasingly accepted Poles as citizens, thereby promoting Polish mine workers' sense of belonging within the working-class community. Polish strike solidarity, as proven by action and represented in song, significantly contributed to the social integration of Poles within larger society.

The actions of Poles participating in the strike also sent a clear signal to established society that Polish needs could no longer be ignored. As the Reverend Charles Jefferson, speaking before an American Missionary Association gathering immediately after the end of the strike, proclaimed: "The other day that man quit working, but we paid no attention to his action, he was only a Slav. . . . But to our surprise he persisted in his refusal to work, and little by little the pillars of the Republic began to tremble. . . . That unnoticed foreigner . . . had by his labor made life comfortable and pleasant to millions who had never seen him. He has called for help repeatedly for many years, but no one went to his assistance. By refusing to work, he compelled the world to look at him."[62] Although the gaze lessened after the strike, the world was a different place for Poles in northeastern Pennsylvania. Polish miners, proving their willingness to stand as men, became active members of their working-class mining communities, a process that can also be observed in the Ruhr.

Poles, the ZZP, and the Ruhr Strike of 1905

In the wake of the 1899 Herne strike, working conditions in the Ruhr worsened. The boom of the late 1890s ended, and a recession that lasted from late 1900 to the middle of 1902 provided employers an opportunity to lower wages, cut back on hours, and dismiss troublesome employees.[63] For Polish workers, times were particularly difficult. In a tightening labor market, native unions and workers increasingly repeated the old refrain, so common in the 1890s, that Poles were stealing jobs. Employers, remembering the Herne strike, often targeted Poles when reducing their workforce. The difficulties Polish workers faced can be seen in their complaints to the Central State Mining Office in Dortmund. In February 1902, the Polish worker Ignatz Tskowiak protested against his physical mistreatment by his supervisor Wetterkamp, who became outraged and struck Tskowiak with a large stick, yelling "You dumb Pole, I'll finish you off!" after he tried to speak up for a fellow Polish worker who did not understand German. In his complaint, Tskowiak demanded justice: "Even if I am a Pole, I am also a Prussian and even the supervisor does not have the right to insult and threaten me." Other Poles objected to being unjustly fired, and younger Poles who worked as haulers complained that they were not being promoted to positions as mine laborers as previously promised.[64] Increasingly frustrated with their circumstances and finding little support from native workers or their unions, Poles looked toward organizing a trade union of their own.

Founded at the end of 1902 in opposition to the Christian Gewerkverein and the socialist Alter Verband, the ZZP initially emerged through the efforts of Polish middle-class figures such as Jan and Anton Brejski as well as leaders of the various Polish Catholic worker associations. The goals of the ZZP were to support "the moral and material advancement of its members [and] secure sufficient and steady earnings as well as the necessary esteem and respect of the community." To accomplish these aims, ZZP sought to defend Polish workers' rights by "all means allowed by Christian teaching and not forbidden by law." Though influenced by religion, the union was independent of the Catholic Church and officially barred members from discussing religious matters as well as "all agitation in the social-democratic spirit." Having national ambitions, the ZZP organized not only Poles in the Ruhr, but also other industrial workers throughout Germany. Owing to their large numbers, Polish miners from the Ruhr nonetheless constituted the majority of the union's total membership until the end of World War I.[65]

Within a few short years, the ZZP achieved significant organizational success. By 1905, the ZZP was the third largest miners union in Germany with approximately 28,000 members. In 1912, total membership in the ZZP's "miners' section" increased to approximately 50,000, compared with 78,000 in the Gewerkverein and 114,000 in the Alter Verband; total membership in the ZZP across Germany reached a peak of more than 77,000.

Although membership in the ZZP, as in German unions, fluctuated from year to year depending on economic conditions, the ZZP's achievement in organizing workers was impressive. By 1910, approximately 54 percent of Polish mine workers were union members, an organizational rate exceeding that of German workers, which stood at 37 percent.[66] Overall, drawing on the strength of their union, Polish workers would stand at the forefront of the struggle to achieve better working conditions and greater social equality, as can be better seen in the actions of Poles during the strike of 1905.

Many factors led to the 1905 strike. After the turn of the century, demand for Ruhr coal increased and employment rose while working conditions remained poor. Wages lagged below their 1900 levels; miners were required to work extended shifts; prices for food and rent soared. Although ethnic tensions eased somewhat, with native unions making greater efforts to attract Poles in an attempt to limit the growth of the ZZP, suspicions of Polish labor remained. Before German audiences, Alter Verband and Gewerkverein leaders railed against allowing more Poles to work in the Ruhr, blaming them for reducing wages and increasing the likelihood of accidents. The growth in levels of hookworm between 1902 and 1904, a disease attacking the intestines, brought new condemnations because Poles were blamed for bringing the illness with them from the East despite the fact that government studies concluded that the disease was due to poor working conditions in the mines. As a whole, the atmosphere among workers was dire. As government reports indicate, regardless of whether one was a German or Pole, increasing numbers of workers were quitting as a protest against the conditions under which they labored.[67]

The breaking point for Ruhr miners came at the end of 1904, when the Stinnes-owned Bruchstrasse mine in Bochum-Langendreer announced it was extending workers' shifts in order to accommodate changes in the transport of workers underground. Indignant German workers who constituted the majority of Bruchstrasse workers soon formed a workers' commission to meet with mine representatives and resolved to go on strike if their demands were not met. Under the auspices of the ZZP, Poles held mass meetings in early January that brought together thousands of Poles in support of a strike if the shift change directive was not rescinded. Great stress was placed on maintaining interethnic unity. As one Polish speaker declared at a January 1 meeting, "We will show that we are united with German workers and like them strive to improve our lot."[68] Soon mine workers throughout the Ruhr began closing ranks, believing that any precedent set in increasing hours at the Bruchstrasse mine would eventually affect them. Miners' determination would soon be tested. With no signs that management would change its position, Bruchtstrasse miners laid down their picks and shovels on Saturday, January 7. This wildcat strike soon spread to other nearby mines, with 12,000 mine workers idle by the following Monday. By January 12, the number of strikers rose to 64,000, or nearly a quarter of the entire Ruhr mining workforce. The rapid growth in the strike caught the various miners' unions off guard. Despite widespread worker discontent, leaders of both the Alter Verband and Gewerkverein nevertheless initially warned workers that a large strike at this time would have no chance of succeeding. Instead they urged miners to concentrate on organizing themselves into unions.[69] The rank and file, however, would not be that easily mollified. In order to gain control over the burgeoning strike movement, the four main unions in the Ruhr held a conference in Essen on January 12 to coordinate their responses and gain a hold over the chaotic strike.

At the Essen conference, 151 delegates including seven Poles met to discuss workers' demands and debate the merits of having a general strike. Representatives of the Gewerkverein were the most cautious, generally arguing against a strike given past failures in 1872 and 1889. A majority of those in the Alter Verband were in favor, believing that conditions were now different given the mass support workers had already shown for a strike. The ZZP delegates adopted a middle-of-the-road position, declaring that although the union did not necessarily favor a strike at the time, it would support whatever decision the majority decided. The Essen conference revealed ethnic prejudices that could endanger the success of any strike. At one point in the deliberations, a delegate declared, "It is a gratifying sign that the unorganized are with us [and] that now even the dumbest son of a Pole says it can't go on like this." The remark brought a sharp rebuke by Jan Brzeskot, the ZZP's legal affairs secretary, who remarked, "Despite [the comment] made by one of our German colleagues, we are ready to struggle with them."[70] The assembly of delegates ultimately approved a list of fifteen demands, the most significant of which were the shortening of the workday to eight hours within the next two years, the abolition of overtime, the ending of the *Wagennullen,* in which no credit was given to cars insufficiently loaded with coal, the appointment of independent check bosses, a minimum wage of 5 marks ($1.25) for contract miners and their assistants, 4.50 marks ($1.13) for company miners, and 3.80 marks ($0.95) for haulers, humane treatment, and the establishment of workers' committees within individual mines. It was further agreed to give the Bergbau Verein until January 16 to reply. If the mineowners rejected the demands, a general strike would commence on January 17. The conference also appointed a strike steering committee, known as the Siebenerkommission (Committee of Seven), which comprised two representatives each from the Alter Verband, the Gewerkverein, and the ZZP, and one from the liberal Hirsch-Dunker union. The establishment of this commission was particularly significant for Poles, enabling them to achieve an equal voice in trade union affairs for the first time.[71]

On January 16, the Bergbau Verein rejected miners' demands and refused to recognize the authority of the Siebenerkommission. With this response, all four miners' unions ordered a general strike. Ending three weeks later on February 9, the strike proved to be the largest seen in Europe to that time. By January 19, a total of 217,539 mine workers, approximately 78 percent of the workforce, were idle. Among underground workers, the percentage on strike reached a high on this day of 87.4 percent. Strike solidarity was especially strong in those regions with large Polish populations. Analyzing strike participation patterns in the seven "Polish" mining districts within the Ruhr, that is, those districts where migrants from eastern Prussia constituted over 40 percent of the workforce, the historian John Kulczycki found that in five out of the seven districts the numbers of strikers was greater than average each day between January 19 and February 9. Government officials in their daily reports also emphasized how Poles, along with the socialists, were "the first, who gladly greeted the outbreak of the general strike."[72] Polish militancy was quite evident at a miner assembly in Bochum on January 20, when Brzeskot told Poles that with solidarity comes victory, and soon "Herr Stinnes will have to kneel before us and acknowledge that we are people." He then urged Poles to set aside any past ethnic differences they had with Germans, exclaiming that "it does not matter if your fellow worker is a Pole or a German. Although much may keep us apart, we today feel like we are one people."[73] Poles were especially adamant that their countrymen take part in the strike. Polish strikebreakers were ostracized within the community, with Polish associations banning those members who refused to strike. Physical intimidation was also common, especially in the close-knit environment of the mine colonies. Through their ethnic networks, Poles even warned countrymen in the homeland not to let themselves be recruited by mine companies seeking to recruit scab labor from the East.[74]

The strike thoroughly surprised employers, who had expected that the work stoppage would quickly collapse because the majority of workers were unorganized, unions were unprepared, and relief funds limited. Yet the unorganized workers largely followed the directives of the Siebenerkommission, which itself proved a highly effective vehicle for rallying workers' support. Daily mass meetings were held throughout cities and towns in the Ruhr where representatives of the various trade unions shared the stage to urge the unorganized to join a union. Although there was some competition between the miners' unions for members, with ZZP officials often telling Poles to join only the Polish union, there were enough new recruits to limit significant intra-union conflict over the issue.[75] This growth in unionization rates can be seen particularly well on the local level. In the city of Gelsenkirchen, after the first week of the general strike, the Alter Verband added 400 new members to its rolls, the Gewerkverein 250, and the ZZP 1,200. By the end of the strike, the ZZP organized close to 8,000 new members in the city of Gelsenkirchen and the surrounding *Land* district, or 80 percent of its entire 1904 membership, and the Alter Verband increased its membership by 5,800. Only the Gewerkverein lagged, signing up only 400 new recruits, which indicates the extent to which this union's more conservative platform was not widely embraced.[76] Union recruitment efforts were also aided by the fact that the strike found widespread sympathy with the German public. Donations flowed in to the various union coffers, which in turn enabled them to offer limited strike support to previously unorganized workers.[77]

To counter union mobilization efforts, employers adopted tactics designed to break the strike. Individual mine companies organized their own private, armed security forces to protect those willing to work. Scab labor was imported from other parts of Germany, France, Holland, Italy, and Austria, though these workers were generally restricted to working above ground given their lack of mining experience. Certain mineowners threatened their workers with eviction from company housing if they continued to strike after January 31.[78] The Dorstfeld Mine Company was particularly malicious in dealing with striking workers when mine executives decided to mail miners' wage books detailing shifts worked and income earned to the homes of strikers. Typically, miners left these books at the mine. By sending them to miners' residences, miners' wives discovered how much their men actually made, causing, as later gleefully reported to the Bergbau Verein, "many unhappy scenes" as a consequence.[79] Employers also demanded that the Prussian government intervene militarily. In daily reports to the state mining offices in Herne and Dortmund, individual mine companies regularly complained about acts of violence and intimidation toward strikebreakers. Especially singled out were actions committed by Polish women.[80]

Employer appeals to law and order fell on deaf ears within Prussian officialdom, unlike in previous strikes. Widespread public support for the strikers made it difficult for the government to openly side with the employers. State officials were also exasperated by the conduct of employers. After ordering investigations, the Regierungspräsident in Münster reached the determination that most claims of violence "were either invented out of thin air or highly exaggerated." By and large, workers displayed significantly more discipline and restraint than in previous strikes, negating the need for the military to intervene. Such restraint was particularly evident among Poles, who followed the directions of ZZP leaders to avoid open confrontations. Attempts by employers to force workers back to work by threatening to evict them from company housing also came across as unfairly heavy-handed. When Thyssen executives in the Ruhrort district were planning such a move, the local Landrat warned that he "would not allow local police to assist such a purpose." Officials were further angered by the unconditional refusal of the Bergbau Verein to enter into any type of negotiations. Instead of considering the desire of the state to end the strike quickly, employers appeared much more intent on using the walkout to destroy the unions.[81]

The intransigence of employers eventually led the Prussian government for the first time to forcefully intervene. On January 30, the Prussian Trade Minister announced that a commission would be established to investigate mine workers' complaints and recommend to the Prussian state parliament any necessary amendments to the state mining law, a move that brought swift condemnation from employers, who labeled the action an undue infringement on the rights of capital. This intervention was not an altruistic act committed on behalf of the striking workers, but instead driven by political self-interest. At the time, there was an effort by socialists in the federal Reichstag, where the SPD was the largest party, to introduce an alternative, worker-friendly, Imperial Mining Law. By intervening, the Prussian government headed off this threat, an action that went far in placating public opinion, while undermining the solidarity of the miners' unions. After the announcement, the Gewerkverein urged an end to the strike, believing that this was the best outcome to be expected. Although the Alter Verband and the ZZP, given their backgrounds and largely negative experience in dealing with the Prussian administration, were more wary of government intentions, both were not prepared to weather the public furor an outright rejection of the state's overtures would bring. As a consequence, there was a general acknowledgment among the unions by the end of the first week of February that the strike should be called off, a belief reinforced by the fact that the various unions' strike funds were rapidly drying up.[82]

On February 9, a new workers' conference was held in Essen, where most of the delegates voted to end the strike, arguing that the Bergbau Verein was not going to change its position in the near future and that workers had suffered enough. Looking toward the promise of government to revise the state mining law, the conference passed a resolution demanding at minimum a maximum shift of 8 hours by January, 1, 1907; a ban on overtime and Sunday work, except in emergencies and on the practice of Wagennullen; the establishment of workers' committees, elected by secret ballot, at mines employing more than twenty workers; the reduction in fines, with a maximum of 50 pfennige per incident and 4 marks per month; and the equal contribution by employers to the Knappschaft pension fund. In addition, the delegates also agreed that the Siebenerkommission would remain in place to coordinate future union activity in the Ruhr.[83]

The decision by the four unions to abandon the strike was controversial. Many in the rank and file were adamantly opposed, and a number of union locals refused to recognize the order to abandon the strike, but the majority followed the Essen conference decision. Isolated strikes continued at certain mines for another week; however, 96 percent of the mine workforce was back to work by February 15 awaiting the outcome of government investigations into employment conditions.[84] The state inquiry would last until the end of March, and a Mine Reform Bill was passed by the Prussian parliament in May that fulfilled some worker demands. The workday was fixed at eight and one half hours, inclusive of transport time to and from the coal face, the Wagennullen was abolished, replaced by a system of deductions that were not to exceed 5 marks ($1.25) in any given month, and provisions were made for workers' committees, composed of employer and miner representatives, to be established at individual mines employing more than one hundred workers. Because the reform bill went through the caste-based Prussian parliament, the National Liberal Party was able to protect industrial interests. Much was left to be desired in the final legislation.

No changes were made to the regulation of overtime, nor were any limitations placed on the amount of various other fines that employers could charge workers. No effort was made to determine whether workers' wages were sufficient to meet the cost of living. Most important, strict limits were placed on the activities of the workers' committees and their composition. These committees were to serve only in an advisory capacity on secondary matters dealing with everyday work conditions and complaints. They could not serve as forums for collective bargaining. Discussion of larger issues such as wages and hours was strictly forbidden, and employers retained the right to ignore any proposed committee recommendations. Committee elections were not conducted by secret ballot, and the franchise was extended only to those workers who were over twenty-one years of age, worked at a given mine for more than a year, and held legal residency in the locality where they worked. Such qualifications effectively meant that more than half of the workforce was ineligible to vote. The requirements to become an actual representative were stricter still. Potential committee members needed to be at least thirty years of age, resident in their locality for several years, and fluent in German. There was also a proviso in the legislation that made workers who participated in past strikes ineligible to serve as representatives, though enforcement of this rule was left to the individual mine company's discretion. The various restrictions dealt a severe blow to the ability of workers' committees to act as effectual bodies representing mine workers' needs and desires. This was particularly true for Polish workers because the age and language provisions disproportionately affected them.[85]

Although on balance more of a defeat than victory for workers, given the meager concessions they ultimately obtained, the strike was not a complete failure. For the first time unions were able to put aside their ideological differences and establish the Siebenerkommission to closely coordinate their activities. Within the Siebenerkommision, the ZZP maintained its status as an equal to the other major unions. Among ordinary Polish workers, there was new willingness to join unions. The ZZP tripled its membership in the Ruhr, rising from 9,916 at the end of 1904 to 28,250 one year later.[86] The strike also provided the means through which Poles were able to begin building stronger class solidarities across ethnic lines. Although Poles continued to face discrimination, their sizable participation in the strike disproved beliefs popular in the native mind-set that they were undisciplined, unorganizable, or employers' lackeys. Polish actions also revealed their collective strength. As a whole, the 1905 strike represented a key turning point in Polish adaptation in the Ruhr, enabling greater political engagement within larger society.

The Stabilization and Integration of Poles into the Working-Class Milieu

Polish participation in strike actions between 1900 and 1905 led to the greater acceptance by native workers of Poles as fellow workingmen. In northeastern Pennsylvania, Poles increased their representational strength within the UMW in the wake of the 1902 strike, and the vice presidency of the three UMW districts in the region essentially became a "Polish" seat.[87] Native discourses regarding Poles also changed. A 1906 a *New York Times* report noted how Polish miners "have proved that they make good citizens. . . . [T]hey bring thoroughness and determination into every effort of their life and strong common sense is an attribute that has won them the respect of the people with whom they toil and with whom they reside."[88] A popular Irish minstrel ballad titled "A Greenhorn Makes Good" describes how the Slavic protagonist who initially worked for Paddy Burke eventually obtained his mining certificate, became a successful miner, and later hired Paddy's brother as his own laborer.[89]

The transformation in attitudes toward Polish and other eastern European labor is also evidenced by heated discussions that took place in 1914 and 1915 among foremen and other mid-level mine employees over "foreigners" within the pages of *Coal Age,* the primary trade journal of the industry. The debate started off innocuously enough with a letter to the editor in August 1914 about the need to better educate the "foreign element" in mining. By September, I. C. Parfitt, a mining official in western Pennsylvania, wrote a blistering letter to the editor, claiming that newly arriving immigrant miners were a deadly threat to both the moral health of the country and the mine industry itself.[90] The general response was swift and damning. For the next seven months, letters flooded in defending the "foreign" worker and his contribution to American society. Among the typical responses was the following from a "Pennsylvania engineer," who claimed that "it is my observation that these people learn very fast. . . . [T]he man who labors under the belief that they are not progressive is much mistaken, as when given half a chance they inevitably make good citizens."[91] Further evidence of a shift in native workplace attitudes toward Polish miners and the reconceptualizing of Poles as potential fellow citizens can be seen in a 1918 *Coal Age* editorial cartoon where an American miner reaches out to shake hands with a Slavic miner. As the caption of the cartoon notes, "Give the Foreigner your hand—and see Americanism break out all over him like a rash."[92] The door was opening for Poles. Within the white, working-class mining milieu of northeastern Pennsylvania they were increasingly accepted as workers first, Poles second.

Poles took advantage of this opportunity to raise their status and increasingly self-identified themselves as part of the native working class. One unidentified Polish miner expressed this sentiment as early as 1901 when he noted, "Me work at the breaker. I belong to a union and won't go back [to Poland] yet. In no hurry for you see me got plenty to do here just now."[93] This is not to say that ethnic identity receded in importance, only that other identities of class and gender were equally significant in the mind-set of the Polish miner. The pages of the *Straż* newspaper put this succinctly when it declared that a good Pole must also be a good union man.[94] Poles also remained militant in their defense of workers' rights, as evidenced by the month-and-a-half long strike that began in March 1912 where Polish participation was vital to the UMW's ability to eventually negotiate a wage increase of 10 percent.[95] Perhaps more tellingly, if somewhat off-putting, is the fact that some Poles began making themselves "whiter" by discriminating against other migrant minorities. In 1901, Polish UMW locals in the region, at the behest of UMW vice president Paul Pulaski, overwhelmingly supported a union resolution asking Congress for the continuation of the Chinese Exclusion Act, despite the fact that there was never a serious danger of Chinese workers ever coming to the northeastern Pennsylvania coalfields and that the majority of Poles were themselves recent immigrants, by and large not American citizens, and considered by many within the general public to be a danger to American values and ways of life.[96] In the early 1920s, Polish district leaders aligned themselves with the conservative "American" faction in the UMW and promoted efforts to halt the rise of "radical" Italian leaders within the union.[97]

In the Ruhr, developments similar to those in northeastern Pennsylvania occurred. The 1905 strike galvanized a sense of common cause between Polish and German workers. As ZZP leader Adalbert Sosinski declared in 1906, "We are all workers, regardless of whether we belong to this nation or another."[98] The growing integration of Poles in the workplace can be seen in the ZZP's closer collaboration with the Alter Verband. In 1908, the Siebenerkommission disbanded as a result of ideological clashes between the more conservative Gewerkverein and the three other miners' unions. The Christian union singled out Poles, in particular, for abandoning their religious heritage and drifting so far to the left that a majority of members now "stand very close, in their hearts, to Social Democracy."[99] In response, the Alter Verband, the ZZP, and the smaller Hirsch-Dunker union formed a new coordinating group known as the Dreibund (Triple Alliance) to discuss and debate trade union policy, a development that largely placed the Gewerkverein on the margins, while solidifying ZZP's credentials within the trade union mainstream.

Even more telling was the success of the ZZP in local elections to various representative bodies within the mine industry. From 1904 to 1910, the ZZP increased its representation on pension fund boards from five to twenty-nine seats. Similarly, in 1912 there were forty-four Poles serving as workers' committee members and ninety-one acting as safetymen. All told, approximately 8 to 9 percent of these various elected positions were held by Poles before the outbreak of World War I.[100] While such representation was not proportional to their overall percentage in the workforce, the election gains were notable given the obstacles Poles faced, such as needing to prove to the employer's satisfaction that a candidate was sufficiently fluent in German to serve in office. Poles also possessed greater clout than their elected numbers suggest. At mines where the ZZP did not have the strength to elect their own candidates outright, it formed electoral alliances with the Gewerkverein or, more commonly, the Alter Verband.[101] Altogether, the ZZP's participation in local elections for mine worker representatives enabled Poles to gain greater experience in navigating the political process, and it promoted interethnic cooperation.

In early 1912, that cooperative spirit would be tested again when the four miners' unions held meetings in February 1912 to determine whether to strike unless employers increased wages and made other improvements to working conditions. Opinion was split. Union leaders in the Triple Alliance felt that since the coal industry was entering a new boom period, the time was ripe to make new demands on employers, especially given that wages remained below their 1907 highs, inflation was making it difficult to make ends meet, the work process had intensified, and employers, through the hated Arbeitsnachweis, possessed greater control over labor mobility. Opinion within the Triple Alliance was more divided about whether to actually strike should their demands not be met, with the leaders of Alter Verband strongly in favor of a walkout, whereas those in the ZZP expressed a more cautious attitude.[102] By contrast, Gewerkverein representatives argued vehemently against confronting employers, believing that continuing economic growth would soon cause wages to increase and that a potential strike would end in disaster. By the second week of February, the

Gewerkverein withdrew from further talks with the other unions, declaring that it would not support any strike action.[103] Despite Gewerkverein opposition, the Triple Alliance forged ahead. On February 19, a list of demands was formally presented to the Zechen-Verband. The demands were a 15 percent wage increase and the bi-monthly payment of wages, the introduction of the eight-hour day, reduced hours when temperatures in the mines exceeded 22 degrees Celsius, the abolishment of overtime, limits on the imposition of fines, and reform of the Arbeitsnachweis. Employers were given until March 5 to respond. Aware of the division among the unions, the Zechen-Verband categorically refused to negotiate.[104]

That the employers refused to enter in to talks led representatives of the Triple Alliance to declare overwhelmingly, by a vote of 507 to 74, in favor of a general strike to begin on March 11. Meanwhile, confident that most mine workers would remain at work, the Gewerkverein continued to withhold its support. Arguing that the strike push was part of a socialist plot to destroy the other unions, the Christian union, in particular, believed that at least half of the Polish Catholic workforce would not follow the "radical direction" of the ZZP's leadership. The Gewerkverein was soon disappointed. On March 11, workers throughout the Ruhr heeded the call of the Triple Alliance and refused to enter the mines. Among the most willing to lay down their tools were Poles, who, as one mine director in Hamborn noted, were "striking to the last man." By March 13, the strike reached a high point when 70 percent of the underground and 61 percent of the aboveground workforce was idle.[105] The strike, however, was unable to sustain itself over the long term. The willingness of the Gewerkverein members to remain on the job enabled the mineowners to maintain operations at a reduced level. The strike garnered little public support, and the Prussian authorities used the police and 5,000 military troops to protect employers, hoping that a failed strike would destroy the socialist movement in the region. Meanwhile, operators declared that striking workers were in violation of their labor contracts, subjecting them to a week's loss of wages and a potential three-month ban on reemployment in the mines. On March 19, the Triple Alliance held a conference to determine whether to continue the strike. Although a majority of delegates voted in favor, the requisite two-thirds majority required for a continuation was not achieved. Consequently, a call to resume work the next day was issued.[106]

The repercussions of the unsuccessful strike were immense. Strike leaders soon found themselves blacklisted and barred from employment.

The state vigorously prosecuted strikers, who were accused of intimidation and violence during the strike; the number of court cases reached into the thousands.[107] Unions within the Triple Alliance, while blaming the Gewerkverein for the strike's defeat, nevertheless feuded among themselves; the acrimony caused the alliance to fall apart and soured the relationship between the Alter Verband and ZZP. Among many ordinary workers, the failed strike brought disillusionment. Both the Alter Verband and Gewerkverein suffered severe membership declines, while membership in employer-sponsored "yellow" unions rose. Only the ZZP was able to maintain its numerical strength, a testament to continued rank-and-file commitment to the union.[108]

Although the 1912 strike was a setback for the workers' movement, Poles once again demonstrated to their German counterparts a readiness to stand as good union men to defend workers' rights. When the strike failed, comfort was taken in the fact, as the ZZP noted in its 1912 annual report, that Poles "saved their honor, [and showed] that they are not, nor ever will be, strikebreakers and weaklings."[109] The strike also demonstrated that Poles believed they were integral members of the native Ruhr working class, a sentiment that would persist after the strike, as can be seen in a 1914 letter to the editor published in the *Narodowiec*, where a Pole from Bruch complained about seasonal Polish migrants employed as coke workers. Blaming these migrants for working "night and day" to the detriment of local workers, the letter writer goes on to note that "those people should, when they return here, adapt themselves to local conditions. They should join a union and endeavor to earn their money in an honorable way. . . . [A] great number of these people have no appreciation for the workers' movement. As a result of their reactionary outlooks, there exists for them neither a sense of amity nor community. . . . They do not concern themselves with either the Church or [Polish] cultural life, their main goal is to earn money."[110] The rhetoric in the letter is remarkably similar to that of earlier characterizations of uncultured, avaricious, and largely unassimilable Poles made by German workers, highlighting how long-resident Poles were adopting native attitudes and outlooks. As with their counterparts in northeastern Pennsylvania, Poles in the Ruhr developed their own biases toward more recent migrants and sought to raise their status in society through discriminatory rhetoric and actions that placed a premium on Polish honor, class consciousness, and respectability.

Assessing the Polish Workplace Experience

George Baer, head of the coal division of Philadelphia and Reading Railroad, was once asked during the 1900 strike in northeastern Pennsylvania to comment on the conditions under which his Polish workers labored. Baer replied, "They don't suffer. Why they can't even speak English."[111] The callousness of this remark exemplified the attitudes of many not only in America but also in Germany. In both countries, Poles were considered something less than human, an unseen labor force whose sole purpose was to serve. The structural position of Poles as producers contributing to the American and German national wealth, yet also as a group that was largely neglected and disenfranchised, made the Polish desire for economic and social justice urgent. To gain greater equality and respect in the workplace and in society, Polish mine workers turned to unions such as the UMW or ZZP and engaged in democratic protest to secure their rights and gain recognition as civilized beings, fellow workers, and good union men. With the 1902 and 1905 strikes, the position of Poles improved considerably in northeastern Pennsylvania and the Ruhr as Polish miners grew less "foreign" and more "respectable" in the eyes of native workingmen. Poles were able to rise within the ranks and exercise influence within the UMW, and the ZZP gained an equal voice in trade union affairs and greater representational clout on Ruhr pension fund boards and local mine workers' committees. The massive growth in Polish trade union membership, the behavior and disposition of Poles during strikes, and the embrace of native gender and racial discourses—all highlight Polish self-identification as part of the native working class. Becoming "mining men," Poles from the turn of the century onward enjoyed the privileges this status bestowed with regard to claiming rights as citizens as well as engaging in political activities in the public sphere.

There remained important differences between the Polish workplace experiences in each region. Poles in the Ruhr, driven by the existing political and social climate, formed the ZZP instead of joining a native union. Through this independent union, Poles eventually gained greater respect as equals. Nevertheless, trade union factionalism in the Ruhr, to which the ZZP contributed, did make overcoming ingrained confessional and ethnic differences more difficult than in northeastern Pennsylvania, where one big multiethnic union successfully established itself. Even more significant were the differing lengths and outcomes of strike actions after the turn of the century. In northeastern Pennsylvania, the 1900 and 1902 strikes were watershed events. For nearly eight months within a two-year period, work-ers were engaged in protracted struggles with mineowners to secure greater workplace rights. The length and intensity of the two strikes brought work-ers from diverse backgrounds closer together and forged lasting solidarities across ethnic lines. The strikes also eventually forced the government to decisively intervene and regulate labor relations. In the end, workers won significant concessions including wages increases, de facto union recogni-tion, and the institutionalization of a quasi collective bargaining regime; this was no small feat given the era. By contrast, although the 1905 strike in the Ruhr was also intense and united workers of diverse ethnic, confes-sional, and political backgrounds, the strikes limited duration meant that the bonds of solidarity were less mature. In addition, the 1905 strike ended in a less than favorable outcome, failing to reform underlying structural deficiencies in the workplace. Labor issues would continue to be a bone of contention that, depending on circumstances, could divide workers and reinforce parochial outlooks. This can aptly be seen during the 1912 strike. Although prior to 1914 Poles, by their actions, were able to elevate their status within working-class society in the Ruhr, the continued fractiousness of organized labor made the Polish position as fully integrated members of their communities more tenuous, as would become apparent when political and economic turmoil engulfed the Ruhr after World War I.

5 ⑪ Divided Hearts, Divided Faith

Poles and the Catholic Church

CATHOLICISM HAS TRADITIONALLY BOUND Poles together as a community. This was particularly the case for Polish migrants to the Ruhr and northeastern Pennsylvania. In both regions, the local Catholic parish was a visible, if highly contested, symbol that provided continuity with the past, while offering a key resource that Poles could use to build and strengthen their ethnic communities. The Catholic faith served as a wellspring for Polish working-class activism, demands for social justice, and claims to cultural rights within their adopted societies. This chapter investigates the profound influence religion had on Polish life and long-term integration patterns.

The Challenge of Polish Catholicism

The relationship between the native Catholic Church and Poles in the 1870s and 1880s was reasonably close, especially when compared to later years. In Germany, the *Kulturkampf* (struggle over culture) of the 1870s and its aftermath encouraged German and Polish Catholics to close confessional ranks. During the Kulturkampf, the Prussian government passed a variety of anti-Catholic laws in an effort to subordinate the church to the power of the state, attacks that occurred simultaneously with growing efforts by Prussia to suppress the supposed threat of Polish nationalism.[1] Within the rapidly industrializing Ruhr, the church also viewed the devout Polish population as a bulwark against the spread of socialism. In general, Catholic officials in the 1870s and 1880s propagated a vision, at least publicly, of interethnic unity not predicated on the outright cultural assimilation of Poles. As one Center Party official noted in an 1885 speech in Dortmund, before a joint audience of Germans and Poles, "You [Poles] are united with us in the same

Faith, in the same hopes and in the same love. . . . [Y]ou are and remain our Catholic brothers."[2] This idea of unity in difference manifested itself in two ways. The church permitted the formation at the parish level of Polish Catholic worker associations, rosary societies, and, later in the 1890s, various choral, women's, and youth organizations. It also recognized the need to recruit a spiritual caretaker to serve Poles in their native language. In 1885, the bishop of Paderborn, the primary diocese covering the Ruhr region, appointed the Polish priest Józef Szotowski for this task. During his tenure from 1885 to 1889, Szotowski expanded the number of Polish-language services and Polish Catholic worker associations, actions designed to ensure "proper" Polish spiritual development and limit the corrupting influences that might prey on largely young, overwhelmingly male, migrants. By allowing the formation of ethnically distinct organizations and Polish religious services, the church contributed to promoting a greater national consciousness, often for the first time, among Poles from disparate regions of Poland.[3]

In the United States, the Irish-dominated Catholic Church was also confronted with a significant, external threat in the form of nativist, Protestant groups that loudly campaigned against the danger "papists" posed to the democratic republic. Intolerance toward Catholics has a long political history, and during the 1880s and early 1890s, a wave of anti-Catholicism swept the nation, represented by the rise of organizations such as the Patriotic Order of the Sons of America (POSA) and the American Protective Association (APA).[4] Northeastern Pennsylvania was not immune to this wave of nativism. At the time, the Irish bore the brunt of nativist resentment since they were the largest and most dominant Catholic ethnic group; Poles were nevertheless also attacked. In 1887, the *Scranton Republican* endorsed the immigration platform of the APA, describing it as "practical and effective reform" because it would "exclude from our shores foreigners who do not possess the prerequisites of good citizenship," defined in terms of Anglo-Saxon Protestantism.[5] In the light of this anti-Catholicism, the Irish made concerted outreach efforts toward Poles in the name of a united Catholic front. In August 1888, the *Diocesan Record*, the Irish-owned, semiofficial weekly of the Scranton diocese, vigorously criticized Terence Powderly, Knights of Labor leader and former Scranton mayor, for his restrictionist views of the immigration of Poles and other eastern European immigrants. Even more significant was Irish participation at the Polish celebration of the hundredth anniversary of the May Third Constitution in

1891. At the gathering, Thomas Hoban, the brother of the future bishop of Scranton, spoke and called Poles "lovers of liberty and respectable people."[6] Beyond the rhetoric of interethnic confessionalism, the local Irish-dominated church took more concrete steps to aid Polish spiritual needs. The church permitted the emergence of Polish Catholic parish organizations similar to those in Germany and attempted to recruit Polish priests to serve their ethnic compatriots. Most important, the local Irish bishop William O'Hara allowed the formation of some ethnic Polish parishes. By 1890, there were nine such parishes in the Scranton diocese.[7]

Although Poles were permitted a degree of ethnic autonomy during the 1880s, the relationship between Poles and the Catholic hierarchies in each region was not built on a solid foundation. For native Catholic authorities, Poles were pious, yet unsophisticated confessional brethren who required constant guidance in the process of their assimilation into German or American society. This paternalistic, presumptuous attitude caused resentment and discontent, especially as the number of Polish Catholics in each region rapidly grew. During the 1890s nearly 100,000 Poles arrived in the Ruhr, only 10 percent of whom spoke German, raising the total population to well over 130,000. In northeastern Pennsylvania, the population increase was also sizable. By 1900, census reports indicate that there were 37,564 Poles in the region, while Polish sources place this figure at over 100,000.[8] The growth in population led to the increasing politicization of Polish Catholicism, particularly as the type of migrants arriving in the Ruhr and northeastern Pennsylvania changed. The earliest migrants to both regions came from Upper Silesia, where they had some exposure to industrial life and were more likely to be able to speak some German. This latter aspect is particularly significant because throughout the Ruhr and in many parts of northeastern Pennsylvania, Poles worshipped in ethnically German parishes. This sharing of facilities in the 1880s caused tensions, as Poles felt that their traditions were often not respected. Nevertheless, the divide separating ethnic religious practices was less than it was by the 1890s, when overwhelmingly monolingual Poles arrived in both regions from largely agrarian areas of partitioned Poland.[9]

The religious practices of newer Polish migrants were populist and grounded in rural traditions of the Polish countryside. This differed from the existing rationalist traditions of the German and American Catholic Church. For Poles, the local parish was a symbol of a moral community. The physical parish buildings were a form of moral property owned by the community and only managed by the local priest. Further, in the Polish peasant belief system, there were clear preferences for anthropocentric icons that were "of the people" as opposed to those that transmitted institutional power and authority. The most notable example of this is the widespread adoration of the figure of Mary, the mother and intercessor between God and the individual. By contrast, the worship of God himself was respectful though more detached, as he was a strict father figure. On a practical level, peasant beliefs encouraged expectations that their religious figures, both iconic and real, would serve them in material ways. Going to mass was not only about worship, but also viewed as a way to attain actual favors from saints and, more specifically, the priest.[10]

Within such a belief system, the influence of the local priest was considerable; there were nevertheless limits to his power. A priest was expected not only to provide moral guidance but also to serve and represent his flock. He needed to be careful not to appear to overstep his power.[11] As Thomas and Znaniecki highlight in their ethnographic analysis,

> The priest [is] a father of the parish, a representative of God (Jesus) by maintaining the social order, a representative of the parish by leading the acts of common worship. From his representation of Jesus results his superior morality, implicitly assumed wherever he acts, not as a private individual, but in his official religious character. Therefore his teaching, his advice, his praise or blame, whenever expressed in the church, from the chancel, or in the confessional, are listened to as the words of Jesus, seldom if ever doubted and obeyed more readily than orders from any secular power. This influence is extended beyond the church and manifests itself in the whole social activity of the priest, though there it loses some of its power, since it is not quite certainly established by the peasants whether the priest outside the Church is in the same sense a representative of Jesus.[12]

In essence, although the priest could act as a moral force, he had to be careful not to appear to impose his will, especially in nonreligious matters. Otherwise, he risked losing his authority within the ethnic community. Attempting a balance between providing leadership and not appearing authoritarian was difficult, particularly as the peasantry grew more politically conscious in the late nineteenth century.[13]

As Poles migrated into the Ruhr and northeastern Pennsylvania, they found fertile ground on which populist attitudes regarding religion could further evolve. The working-class milieu of both regions and the industrial workplace experience reinforced Polish communalistic beliefs and exposed

Poles to larger questions of social justice. At the same time, the discrimination Poles faced encouraged greater national awareness and recognition that the moral community needed to be reestablished in order to protect ethnic interests. The desire to seek redress for both class and ethnic inequalities caused Poles to become more politically sophisticated and active in the public sphere. Important early examples of such activism in the 1880s include the creation of various Polish Catholic worker associations, and, as Poles became more politically aware, religion took on added importance in Polish life. The local parish and church-affiliated institutions provided Poles an essential means to increase ethnic awareness, mobilize the community, and challenge their subordinate status.

Of particular concern for most Poles was the limited availability of Polish-language spiritual care. In both regions, the hierarchy was being pushed by Poles to increase the number of Polish or Polish-speaking priests, yet the church was not prepared to meet these demands. In the Ruhr, the hierarchy wanted, for political reasons, to avoid bringing in large numbers Polish priests from Prussian Poland, choosing instead to use German priests who either spoke or were willing to learn Polish. Yet the overall number of such Polish-speaking German priests remained small. By 1903, an estimate by a local Center Party politician placed the ratio of Polish Catholics to priests at 10,000:1. Meanwhile, in northeastern Pennsylvania, recruitment and training of Polish priests was also slow. In the early 1890s, only a few Polish priests were active in the region, and some held dubious clerical qualifications. At the turn of the century, there was still on average only one priest for every 2,800 Poles.[14] The unwillingness of the church to improve spiritual care led to bitterness among Poles. To the German and American church hierarchies such discontent seemed unfair. The growing demands for ethnically distinct spiritual care were unreasonable given the financial resources of the church; more important, such demands also undermined the principle of a universal church, could be politically dangerous, and were a direct challenge to the hierarchy's authority.

The growing outspokenness of Poles soon led hierarchies in both countries to attempt to assert greater control over Polish pastoral care within the church. In Germany, the change in the attitudes of the church hierarchy was primarily driven by the fear of state interference in ecclesiastical matters. Among Prussian authorities, there was great concern that the ongoing nationality conflict between Poles and Germans in eastern Germany would be carried west. To prevent this, the government actively sought the aid of the Catholic Church to help stifle the threat of Polish nationalism. In accordance with the government's policy of Germanization, the hierarchy and local clergy were expected to maintain a watchful eye on Polish activity and suppress any manifestations of nationalist sentiment. If the clergy failed in this duty, the relative autonomy enjoyed by the church since the ending of the Kulturkampf might be reversed.[15] Consequently, the church endeavored to demonstrate its loyalty to the state by keeping Poles in line through increased restrictions on Polish activities. As the church hierarchy and state bureaucracy began to work in partnership to discourage Polish nationalism, relations with Poles became increasingly fractious.[16]

The hierarchy's desire to rein in Polish activities was made explicit in 1894, when the bishop of Paderborn, at the behest of Heinrich Konrad von Studt, the minister-president of Westphalia, removed the Reverend Franciszek Liss from his position as Polish spiritual caretaker. When Liss first arrived in the Ruhr in 1890 as a replacement for Szotowski, German opinion viewed him favorably as someone who would protect Poles from the influence of Polish nationalism and socialism, something Szotowski was unfairly blamed for failing to do properly. The *Westfälische Anzeiger* newspaper proclaimed that Liss would reinforce morality and prevent Poles from being raised in an improper "religious and national manner."[17] With the tacit approval of his bishop, this energetic priest from West Prussia increased the number of Polish-language services held in the Ruhr, rapidly expanded the number of Polish Catholic associations and founded the *Wiarus Polski* (Old Polish Soldier), the most influential Polish newspaper in the Ruhr region. These activities quickly attracted scrutiny from German authorities concerned with the growing strength of Polish ethnic associations and the supposed nationalist threat these associations posed. By 1892, von Studt branded Liss a nationalist agitator and campaigned for his removal. German concerns regarding rising nationalist sentiment among Poles at this time were often overstated, and the characterization of Liss as an unabashed nationalist was pure hyperbole. Although Liss clearly desired to protect Polish ethnicity in the Ruhr, his confessional loyalty came first. At the prompting of church authorities in 1893, Liss removed himself from direct control of the *Wiarus Polski* and agreed to focus solely on the spiritual needs of Poles.[18] Moreover, he also agreed to champion the integration of the Polish Catholic worker associations into the German Catholic worker association movement, a position that quickly brought him under attack by elements within the Polish community who openly accused the priest of seeking to "de-nationalize"

Poles in the name of confessional unity.[19] Despite Liss's efforts to save his mandate, the pressure of the government caused the bishop of Paderborn to transfer Liss back to West Prussia in 1894, a removal that sparked outrage and bolstered the belief within the Polish community that the church was an agent of the government's Germanization campaign.[20]

In the United States, tensions between Poles and the hierarchy were also rapidly on the rise. Over the course of the late nineteenth century, Irish ethnics came to dominate the American Catholic Church and Irish bishops were reluctant to allow the religious traditions of other ethnic Catholics to permeate the church.[21] Poles, who bound national identity and Catholicism as closely together as the Irish, were seen as a particular danger. During the early 1890s, conflict between the Irish-American hierarchy and Poles especially grew over whether ethnic groups had the right to form and administer distinct national parishes. Within the hierarchy, a "modernist" view came into ascendance that viewed ethnic parishes, in contrast to territorial ones, as an impediment to their broader goal of using the church to Americanize immigrants. Eminent bishops such as John Ireland, James Gibbons, and John Spalding argued that the use of Polish for church services and in parochial school instruction was un-American and un-Catholic. Drawing on the Irish immigration experience, Catholic leaders envisioned a church that would actively promote immigrant assimilation; in assuming this task, the church would also finally end the loyalty question posed by Protestant nativists by proving itself a modern, loyal American institution.[22] In an 1899 speech at the Polish Seminary in Orchard Lake, Michigan, Bishop Ireland highlighted this sentiment when he declared that "from the numerous elements inhabiting our country, from the numerous nationalities, a homogeneous nation will someday emerge. The task of the clerical leaders of the Polish people is to choose the wisest road to this homogeneity."[23] Most Poles aligned against such a proposition, believing that the church's Americanization plans were a disguised form of "Anglo-Saxon racism," betraying what America stood for, namely the right to maintain and practice cultural traditions that were attacked in the homeland.[24]

In northeastern Pennsylvania, Polish desires for distinct ethnic parishes were present from the earliest days of their migration to the region because Poles viewed them as the surest way to preserve their culture and unite the ethnic community. With the rapid rise in population beginning in the 1890s, Polish entreaties for distinct national parishes grew, along with the pressure placed by Poles on the Diocese of Scranton to accede to them. Yet Bishop

O'Hara was frustrated by the growing independence of Poles on the matter of ethnic parishes. Particularly irksome was the fact that Poles often failed to obtain formal permission before building an ethnic church and that once built, the laity grew more assertive, not less, in resisting church regulations requiring the assignation of property titles to their bishop and complaining about the lack of lay oversight of parish finances. Many Poles believed they should have a say in controlling the management of their parishes, especially since the funds for erecting and maintaining ethnic churches came from the hard-won earnings of the parishioners. The mounting friction over ethnic parishes is aptly displayed by an 1894 dispute that broke out in Nanticoke between lay Poles and their pastor, Benevenuto Gramlewicz, over the control of finances at St. Stanislaus Church and the independence of eight Polish Catholic associations. Claiming that the priest was a dictator, about half the parish decided to leave and build their own church almost directly across the street at a cost of $25,000. O'Hara opposed the construction and told Poles he would refuse to consecrate the new building. Dissenting Poles then made appeals and sent a delegation to meet with the Vatican's apostolic delegate, Francesco Cardinal Satolli, in Washington, D.C. Although dispute exists over whether Cardinal Satolli applied pressure on the bishop, by the following year O'Hara reluctantly defused the situation by allowing the now completed Holy Trinity Church to be consecrated and appointing a newly arrived Polish priest named Franciszek Hodur as the parish's first pastor. The Nanticoke experience, however, solidified O'Hara's opposition to further enlarging the number of ethnic Polish parishes in the region; before his death in 1899, only one other was created in the diocese.[25]

A Covenant Broken and Renewed

The turbulent years of the early to mid-1890s left the relationship between Polish Catholics and the church in the Ruhr and northeastern Pennsylvania severely damaged. Polish desires to solidify the national community through the instrument of religion conflicted with the German and American hierarchy's interest in consolidating and protecting their authority. The divergence in goals left the hierarchy mistrustful of their Polish co-religionists and Poles struggling for ways to maintain loyalty both to their faith and their ethnicity. The anti-Polish attitudes displayed by the Catholic church hierarchies in the Ruhr and in northeastern Pennsylvania generated common reactions. In both regions, the Polish press condemned the oppression caused by a foreign church determined to Germanize or Americanize Poles. Newspapers in the Ruhr declared that priests were "wolves in sheep's clothing" and "costumed Germanizers" and called for the increased use of Polish clerics from eastern Germany because only they could understand the Polish character. In 1911, the Polish newspaper *Narodowiec* (Nationalist) went so far as to declare that "the entire Church organization within the hierarchy is working on attaining the Germanization of the Polish nation and the full domination over the Polish Catholic associations."[26] Similarly, in northeastern Pennsylvania, the *Straż* (Guard) regularly ran editorial cartoons depicting the Irish bishops with whips and chains stealing money from the *"lud polski,"* or ordinary Polish people.[27]

On the local level, tensions with the hierarchy weakened the bonds between Poles and ordinary clergy. For many priests, following church guidelines to rein in Polish activism while maintaining the support of their Polish congregations proved nearly impossible. Priests who attempted to assert their authority in nonreligious matters were seen as being self-interested, snobbish, and overbearing. They lost much of their moral authority. The image of priests was not aided by certain scandals involving conflicts between authoritarian priests and Poles that received significant attention in the ethnic press. In northeastern Pennsylvania, reports circulated in the early 1890s that the Irish priest Michael Hoban, later bishop of Scranton, withheld sacraments and threatened to excommunicate Poles who failed to meet assigned contributions. In the Ruhr, a priest in Hamborn engaged in a two-year legal battle with the Polish Catholic associations in his parish, at one point using the German police to retrieve property that the priest claimed was stolen from him.[28] Many priests questioned the loyalties of Poles to their Catholic faith.[29] Animosity between Poles and local clergy ran particularly high over continued priestly interference in the affairs of the Polish Catholic associations, and this conflict quickly accelerated the growth of secular associations. Anecdotal evidence suggests that dissatisfaction with priests also caused a decline in attendance at mass in both regions.[30] The agitation in the Polish press and conflict on the local level contributed to a belief among Poles on both sides of the Atlantic that they needed to reclaim their faith.

After the removal of Liss, overall authority for Polish spiritual care in the Ruhr was transferred to the conservative Redemptorist order, and the number of ethnically Polish priests was sharply curtailed. In their place, the hierarchy focused on utilizing Polish-speaking German priests; however, their numbers remained very limited in the period up until World War I.

By 1912, only seventy-five permanent priests were assigned to the spiritual care of a Polish Catholic community of approximately 300,000. Of these only three were ethnically Polish.[31] The lack of sufficient Polish-language spiritual care naturally caused discontent. As Tomasz Michalak of Duisburg observed, "Everywhere Polish-speaking clergy have been denied us. . . . [I]t is a shame that a Polish priest appears in a given community only two to three times a year to hold a service."[32] In 1898, Poles threatened to walk out of their electoral alliance with the Center Party if Polish concerns regarding their spiritual care were not addressed. Dismayed by the lack of progress by 1903, Poles abandoned their electoral support for the Center Party, an action that led the bishops of Münster, Paderborn, and Cologne to restrict Polish spiritual care even further.[33] In 1904, a set of declarations specifying the rights of Poles in the Catholic Church was announced. Poles were granted the right to have their confessions heard and have occasional services in Polish; however, all expressions "of Polish nationalist sentiment," such as the use of Polish songs in church, were banned, as was the speaking of Polish at baptismal, marriage, and funeral services. Perhaps most inflammatory, it was also ordered that "Polish children shall only be prepared for the holy sacrament [of communion] in German."[34]

The new restrictive measures of the hierarchy aroused Polish indignation. Yet it also brought forth a determination to maintain the faith and work toward improving the church from within. A member of a Polish Catholic association meeting in Castrop in 1905 best captured this sentiment when he declared that "we Poles and Catholics assembled in this meeting . . . resolve, as true sons of the Catholic Church, never to vacillate in our Faith in the fundamental tenets of the Catholic Church, even though we are increasingly oppressed in political and religious respects by the government and German clergy; just the same we will never depart from the demand for equality in the Church."[35] To obtain greater equality, Poles focused on recruiting more Polish priests, improving Polish-language spiritual care, and obtaining representation within the elective bodies of local parishes. Immediately after the 1904 bishops' decrees were announced, Poles issued a set of counterinitiatives at a regional "Polish Catholics in Rhineland-Westphalia" conference. At this meeting, Polish representatives demanded a repeal of the restrictions on the use of Polish in religious ceremonies such as first communion and funerals, a sizable increase in the number of Polish services, greater numbers of ethnic clergy from the East, and the reassignment of Polish-speaking German priests to predominantly Polish parishes in the

Ruhr. Believing the conference was the work of Polish national agitators, the hierarchy refused to entertain any of these demands.[36] In November 1906, another meeting of Polish Catholics in Rhineland-Westphalia was held in Essen. This assembly went further, resolving to embark on a strategy of continuing appeals to the German episcopate through the local clergy and preparing a deputation of Ruhr Poles to go to the Vatican to inform Pius X personally of the pastoral care problems facing the community.[37]

The idea of appealing to the pope had been circulating among Poles since the turn of the century, because many believed that he "did not know anything about how Poles were being treated by the government and the Church," and would be sympathetic to their plight.[38] The pope also appeared to encourage Poles in the Ruhr, albeit unintentionally, to undertake proactive steps to defend their faith. In 1905, the pope issued a declaration calling on Poles "to prove their faith not only through words, but also through actions," as well as encouraging them not to be "influenced by the enemies of God's laws."[39] Though the pope directed this exhortation to Poles in Russia, where the tsarist state and the Vatican were in conflict over restrictions on Catholic religious freedom, the proclamation struck a chord among Poles in the Ruhr who felt their faith was threatened.

As part of the decision to authorize a delegation to meet the pope, the Essen conference resolved that local Polish Catholic associations should sponsor forums for voicing the complaints and concerns of Poles, which could then be included in any future report provided to the Vatican.[40] In Essen, records of the meetings of one local Polish Catholic association from 1906 to 1907 provide valuable insight into the varied beliefs of ordinary Poles on the best method for achieving improved spiritual care, as well as their views of the German church. During the meetings of this association, the voices of a conservative base and more radical leadership emerge. For conservatives, the struggle to increase the number of Polish services and priests was dangerous since it might cause the clergy to further repress religious life. Some also felt that Poles in the organization were too willing to place the blame for their present lack of priests on the German church or the state. Franciszek Karlikowski noted that "the clergy does not deserve any blame; so far they have been inclined to leave us in peace."[41] At another gathering, Stefan Frackowiak argued that Poles should blame themselves for the poor state of spiritual care and observed that change would never be achieved "as long as indifference among Poles continues to exist." After these discussions, conservative support for sending a delegation to complain to the pope about spiritual care was limited. In the opinion of the conservatives, only after all other options were exhausted, including sending further representatives to meet with the German bishops, should this bold step be undertaken.[42]

The leadership and other members of the association were eager to make their concerns heard at a papal audience. Association chairman Wincenty Sosnowski felt that the German clergy discriminated against Poles to a far greater extent than any of the other ethnic minorities in the Ruhr. Moreover, it was believed that the German church was unwilling to alter its practices because it worked for the government.[43] Association secretary Stanisław Zaliss noted that Poles in the Ruhr wanted the same treatment afforded to Poles in the United States, namely the right to freely use their language.[44] In response to conservative opposition, Andrzej Przybyla and Jan Fabisch claimed that sending deputations to the German bishops was pointless since the bishops always promised improvement but never delivered. Moreover, Poles were not responsible for their present condition. Instead, blame must be assigned to the government and the clergy who "would love to see the Poles die out."[45] The acrimonious tone of the association's leadership vis-à-vis the German church stemmed from the fear that inadequate spiritual care was eroding Polish identity in the Ruhr. As Jan Wazny explained in one meeting, "Religion and nation are tightly bound together like the body and soul. . . . [I]f Poles lose their religion, then they lose their national identity as well."[46]

In the short term, the movement to send a delegation to the Vatican failed for lack of necessary funds as well as discontent over the pope's unwillingness to intervene on the side of Poles in Poznań during the 1906–7 Polish school strike.[47] Polish discontent with the church was briefly pacified in 1907 when the archbishop of Cologne ordered an increase in the number of Polish services held in the Essen/Düsseldorf region.[48] Although the beliefs and concerns of working-class Poles such as those in Essen never reached the Vatican, the drive and passion exhibited was important because it led to greater activism to secure equality and rights within the church. In early 1907, Andrzej Przybyla declared in a bold, though farsighted, statement, "We will . . . fight until we achieve victory. We will pound [on the door] until someone opens it for us. . . . [S]oon the time will come when our proposals will be granted."[49] In subsequent years, demands for Polish services and ethnically Polish priests continued and intensified, culminating in the 1913 Congress of Poles held in Winterswijk, the Netherlands. At this conference, a permanent central coordinating committee for all Polish organizations in the Ruhr was created to advocate for the installation of priests that were tied to the Polish nation through "the bonds of blood, language, and national traditions."[50]

The activism engendered by spiritual care issues also led Poles to make concerted efforts to change the church at the local level, especially by competing to gain elected seats on local church executive committees and councils. At the turn of the century, Polish representation on church councils and executive committees, which provided a means to influence parish administration, was insignificant. As tabulated in table 2 (see appendix), the 1904 statistics for Gelsenkirchen and Dortmund Stadt (city) and Land (rural) administrative units in the District of Arnsberg reveal that Poles were severely underrepresented relative to the percentage of the total Catholic population. In Gelsenkirchen-Stadt, for example, Poles controlled only 4.6 percent and 2.8 percent of the seats on parish executive committees and councils, respectively, despite constituting over 30 percent of the 1904 population. The figures for Dortmund-Stadt and Dortmund-Land show similar disparities. Only in Gelsenkirchen-Land did Poles achieve modest success at gaining representation in proportion to their numbers, with Poles in 12.5 percent and 19.6 percent of the seats on the executive committees and councils.[51]

By 1910 and 1912, this picture shifted dramatically. Although Polish Catholics were generally still unable to obtain representation comparable to their overall percentage in the Catholic population, as tables 3 and 4 (see appendix) highlight, sizable gains were made. From 1904 to 1912, Poles in both Gelsenkirchen and Dortmund city and rural administrative units, with two exceptions, increased their representation in local church offices. Changes in levels of Polish representation were particularly dramatic in Dortmund-Stadt. Whereas Poles in 1904 had no executive committee or council representation, by 1910 they had a combined fifteen seats. By 1912, Poles controlled 12.5 percent of the executive committee seats and 15.8 percent of the council seats, which paralleled closely the actual percentage of Polish Catholic inhabitants. Further, Poles were able to obtain majorities in certain parishes within the areas encompassed by Dortmund and Gelsenkirchen Stadt and Land boundaries. In 1913 and 1914, Poles held the majority of seats on the executive committees and councils in the parishes of Eving (Dortmund-Land), Gelsenkirchen-Hüllen (Gelsenkirchen-Stadt), and Wanne (Gelsenkirchen-Land), as well as a majority of seats on the council in Habinghorst (Dortmund-Land).[52]

Poles successfully attained greater representation in parish offices for various reasons. Local disputes with priests and German co-religionists as

well as the limited progress toward changing the church's anti-Polish policies were key motivators. After failing to secure the deputation to the pope
in 1907, Poles in Ruhrort were urged "man for man" to take part in the next
election for the church council.[53] In 1909, Poles in Holsterhausen, despite
the fact that they composed only one-third of the electorate, mobilized to
capture all of the executive committee and council seats after a conflict arose
with the priest and German members of the parish.[54] Polish achievements in
elections also resulted from cooperation with German Catholics. In some
parishes, Poles and Germans agreed on the percentage of seats each ethnicity
would be allotted in a given year; such agreements occurred in Wattenschied,
Derne, and Hordel in 1912. The existence of such negotiated pre-election
agreements are significant because they show the desire of Poles to protect
their autonomy while remaining within the fold of a larger inclusive Catholic Church, and they indicate that ethnic relations in the Ruhr were stabilizing, despite rising ethnic tensions at the national level. Although a degree
of suspicion and mistrust remained, the pragmatic preelection agreements
point to a growing recognition of Polish rights and demands for respect.[55]
Overall, the drive for representation went far in making Poles stakeholders
in Ruhr society and promoted integration prospects over the long term.
This can be seen most notably in the postwar period, where evidence from
local cities and towns suggests that those Poles who were active on parish
councils and in parish associations were more likely to remain than their
compatriots in the general population.[56]

In northeastern Pennsylvania, conflict over the contentious issues of
ethnic parishes and the independence of lay groups exploded in the latter
part of the 1890s, ultimately leading a segment of the Polish population to
quit the Catholic Church altogether and establish an independent, schismatic Polish National Catholic Church (PNCC).[57] The impetus for the
PNCC movement came from working-class Poles living in the heart of the
Scranton diocese. In 1896, a conflict between Polish activists and Richard
Aust, their German-Silesian parish priest, erupted over the control of parish finances at the Sacred Hearts of Jesus and Mary Church in Scranton.
Specifically, some parishioners, feeling that Aust was overstepping his au-
thority with regard to funds raised by parishioners for church renovations,
sought his removal. The ongoing conflicts between the priest and parish
members broke into open violence by early September, when Poles blocked
Aust from entering the church. When local police attempted to disband the
Polish protest, a melee ensued. In the aftermath of the "South-side mob

violence," as local papers dubbed it, Aust was reassigned to a parish in Hazleton and replaced by the Reverend Bronisław Dembinski, who quickly proved even less popular than Aust. His unpopularity led a segment of the congregation to raise more than $10,000 to build a new parish, without diocesan permission, in the immediate vicinity of Sacred Hearts. Outraged at the insolence of dissenting parishioners to his authority, Bishop O'Hara refused to consecrate the newly built church, now called St. Stanislaus.[58]

Firm in their desire for a new church, rebellious parishioners persuaded Francis Hodur, a former assistant at Sacred Hearts and since 1894 pastor of Holy Trinity Church in Nanticoke, to become their permanent priest in March 1897. For the working-class parishioners of St. Stanislaus, Hodur was an ideal choice. His background, together with the time he spent among Poles in both Scranton and Nanticoke, made him sympathetic to the plight of Polish workers, who in Hodur's view suffered under the burden of class and ethnic discrimination. With the support of his new congregation, Hodur used the newly established *Straż* newspaper to attack the policies of O'Hara and his eventual successor Michael Hoban, particularly their unwillingness to accept lay control over ethnic parishes.[59]

Between 1897 and 1900, attempts were made to reconcile the breakaway parish with the Catholic Church. In early 1898, Hodur undertook a trip to Rome to plead the cause of his parishioners, believing that the pope would prove sympathetic to Poles in Scranton if he only knew the conditions they faced. Hodur was never granted a meeting and returned to Scranton disillusioned with his Vatican experience.[60] Later that year, the split between the Catholic Church and the "independent" church widened as Bishop O'Hara excommunicated Hodur along with his parishioners. In response, Hodur burned the letter of excommunication in a public ceremony. Renewed attempts at a resolution of the conflict were made; however, by the end of 1900 members of St. Stanislaus voted for breaking altogether with the Catholic Church and its doctrine.[61] Over the next twenty years, the PNCC solidified its status as an independent church. In 1907, the PNCC entered into formal affiliation with the Church of the Union of Utrecht (Old Catholic Church), and Hodur was consecrated an apostolic bishop by the Old Catholics in a ceremony held in the Netherlands. Between 1904 and 1921, four PNCC synods were held to fashion the fundamental tenets of the new institution. Although retaining much of the outward pomp and ceremony associated with the Catholic Church, the PNCC rejected the concepts of hell, eternal damnation, and papal infallibility, abolished the celibacy requirement for priests and the requirement for auricular confession, held services in Polish, lowered parish dues, and ensured that parish property remained in the hands of parishioners.[62]

The rise of the independent movement initially posed a significant threat to the Catholic Church in northeastern Pennsylvania. Although the majority of Poles remained Roman Catholic, the independent movement gained in popularity. In Scranton, approximately one-third of the Polish community joined the PNCC by the turn of the century. Between 1898 and 1900, Hodur capitalized on Polish dissatisfaction elsewhere in the northeastern Pennsylvania region and organized four other independent parishes. The Scranton-based movement also spread to communities outside the anthracite fields, with "Hodurite" parishes appearing by 1900 in other parts of Pennsylvania, New Jersey, and Massachusetts. By 1906, the PNCC boasted twenty-four parishes in ten states with a total membership of 15,473.[63]

The quick success of the PNCC in establishing itself in the period 1896–1906 can be attributed to the following: First, many of the early PNCC organizers came from the most politically active strata within Polish working-class society and were involved in trade unions or political movements such as the Polish National Alliance (PNA) and the Polish Socialist Alliance.[64] This organizational experience helped the PNCC expand quickly. Second, when Poles compared the responses of the Catholic Church with those of the PNCC to various crises facing the Polish community, the Catholic Church cut a poor figure. The hierarchy's lack of sympathy for the plights of Poles was made obvious in the wake of the 1897 Lattimer Massacre that claimed the lives of nineteen striking mine workers, the majority of whom were Polish. Instead of expressing regrets over the loss of Polish life, the hierarchy appeared to endorse the local authorities' willingness to use deadly force. The church hierarchy was also ambivalent in its support of strikers during the 1900 and 1902 strikes. By contrast, the PNCC actively sided with the causes of Polish workers both at Lattimer and in later strikes.[65] Third, under the leadership of Hodur, the PNCC created an ideology deeply influenced by peasant populist and socialist thought that could inspire followers. Similar in many ways to contemporary "liberation theology," at the core of the PNCC's outlook was the belief that the organized Polish working class would serve as the vehicle through which the Polish nation could be spiritually and literally reborn. Hodur best encompassed this belief when he wrote that "our heroes arose from the huts of farmers and the artisans, or as children of landless tenants; they will sweat and shed blood not for kings, not in the name of the Pope, nor for privileges and rights for special individuals and classes . . . but will go into battle for their own freedom and the rights of man . . . for the assembly of workers, the factory bench, the stand of grain, giving bread to the people, the schools developing minds and warming the heart, the fine arts and literature and the Church."[66] The proletarian character of the PNCC movement is further seen in the independent church's symbol of an open bible lying on a cross and its motto—Prawdą, Pracą, Walką, Zwyciężymy (with Truth, Work, and Struggle, Victory).

In response to the challenge of the independent movement, the Catholic Church hierarchy concentrated on isolating and delegitimizing the PNCC in the eyes of Poles while stressing to Poles the immutable "thousand-year bond" uniting Poland and the church. Roman Catholic priests proclaimed thunderous sermons denouncing Hodur as the devil incarnate and suggested to parishioners that he was a Russian spy. Those who appeared sympathetic to the PNCC were threatened with excommunication. In place of *Straż*, rival Polish publications such as the *Przegląd* (Review) and *Górnik* (Miner) appeared that warned Poles of the danger that the new Polish "Protestant sect" posed. By labeling the PNCC Protestant, the hierarchy clearly hoped to capitalize on a common Polish association linking Protestantism to German nationalism.[67] The church also focused on promoting greater interethnic Catholic unity. In the English-language Catholic press, articles started to appear that complimented the contributions hard-working Poles made to America, as well as the historical suffering Poles were forced to endure for their faith in Poland. These articles helped begin the process of mainstreaming Polish Catholicism within American Catholic life.[68] Finally, the hierarchy strove to improve the quality of Polish spiritual care, the main source of Polish discontent. On the national level, a twenty-year-long campaign for the appointment of a Polish bishop in the American Catholic Church finally succeeded when Paul Rhode became an auxiliary bishop of Chicago in 1908.[69] Locally, Bishop Hoban proved amenable to allowing the number of ethnic parishes to increase and improved the quality of Polish priests. Between 1899 and 1916, the number of Polish parishes in the Diocese of Scranton increased from thirteen to forty-one.[70]

The actions undertaken by the church to improve spiritual care were successful in slowing the appeal of the PNCC. Between 1906 and 1916, census records show that the number of PNCC parishes increased from twenty-four to thirty-four, with only one new parish established in northeastern Pennsylvania.[71] During the interwar period, the PNCC was able to more effectively expand. More than seventy parishes in Poland were established and another seventy-four across the United States and Canada. By 1938, total membership within the United States approached 200,000.[72] Nevertheless, the PNCC movement was unable to attract enough congregants to challenge most Poles' loyalty to the Roman Catholic Church; even within the anthracite fields that gave birth to the PNCC, the majority remained firmly Roman Catholic. The long-term appeal of the PNCC was limited by a number of factors. When the PNCC first appeared in northeastern Pennsylvania, the region was embroiled in significant labor struggles. Poles were actively involved in the major strikes of 1897, 1900, and 1902, which in turn increased their radicalism. After 1902, the labor situation stabilized and the labor activism that helped sustain some of the PNCC growth declined. The PNCC also lost crucial support within the PNA as that organization grew more moderate and pro–Roman Catholic, a drift that led the PNCC to organize its own fraternal organization, the Polish National Union, in 1908.[73] Most important, the divisiveness of the PNCC constrained its popularity. The decision for a Pole to formally break with the Catholic Church was a monumental one. Although almost all Poles were dissatisfied with their treatment at the hands of the Irish-dominated church, discontent that would last for many decades, most were unwilling to sever ties to an institution that played such an elemental role in constructing their identities. As the chasm separating the Catholic Church from the PNCC widened after the turn of the century, being a PNCC member meant enduring the ostracism of the majority of Poles who remained loyal to the church. PNCC members were blamed for selfishly ripping apart families, and even today older Poles in the region derogatorily call those who joined the PNCC "kickers." Although PNCC members quickly formulated their own epithets, calling Polish Roman Catholics "suckers," the fact that joining the PNCC meant becoming, in essence, a "minority within a minority" ultimately limited the appeal of the movement. Finally, the PNCC was a victim of its own success. The gains Polish Catholics made in the church, particularly with regard to ethnic parishes, were due in no small part to the willingness of a minority of Poles to embrace schism. However, such gains also helped negate the need for an independent, breakaway church.[74]

Polish Religious Activism and Its Consequences

In the Ruhr and northeastern Pennsylvania, pre-migration populist religious beliefs emphasizing the protective role of religion in the lives of the *lud polski* combined with post-migration experiences of class and ethnic discrimination to transform Polish Catholicism into a powerful instrument of community empowerment. As the overall Polish population increased, Poles began to demand greater rights within the Catholic Church, including the right to Polish-speaking priests, associational autonomy, and, in northeastern Pennsylvania, ownership and control of ethnic parishes. The native Catholic hierarchies feared Polish Catholicism because it challenged their authority and endangered the political goals of the church in gaining acceptance as integral and loyal institutions within German and American society. As a consequence, by the 1890s the church in the Ruhr and northeastern Pennsylvania began adopting policies, such as limiting Polish-language spiritual care or restricting the formation of ethnic parishes, which were supposed to assimilate and make Poles complacent. Such a direct assault on Polishness within the church was bound to fail. For Poles, ethnic and confessional identities were inseparable. Limits placed on ethnic expression were perceived as an attack on faith and naturally resisted. In mobilizing to defend their interests against the actions of the hierarchy, Poles in both regions exhibited similarities, such as appealing their treatment first to representatives within the local hierarchy and, when rebuffed, to the pope himself. Nonetheless, more interesting and significant were the differences.

In the Ruhr, Poles focused on reforming the church from within, especially by concentrating on gaining representation on local parish representative bodies. By contrast, in northeastern Pennsylvania an independent movement emerged offering a unique, alternative vision of Catholicism embodying working-class immigrant Polish values. Although only a minority of Poles joined the PNCC, the existence of this independent church benefited all Poles because it pushed the Catholic Church hierarchy to improve Polish spiritual care, particularly with regard to ethnic parishes, the establishment of which represented a sizable material investment as well as a clear declaration of Polish intent to stay in their adopted communities. There were reasons for the disparity that occurred in Polish responses. Unlike in northeastern Pennsylvania, where the right to religious self-determination was enshrined in the constitution and religious denominationalism widespread, Poles in the Ruhr could not have realistically built their own ethnic parishes, let alone an independent national church, due to the policies of the Prussian state. Consequently, Ruhr Poles could attempt only to reform the church exclusively from within. Also significant was the fact that the PNCC emerged in northeastern Pennsylvania during a period marked by high levels of Polish worker radicalism, driven by the character of the capitalist production and labor relations in the region. By contrast, the periods of Polish radicalism in the Ruhr were comparatively less intense. Though pursuing different strategies to ensure their ethnic autonomy, the efforts to defend culture and faith nevertheless increased levels of integration by making Poles more visible stakeholders in their adopted communities.

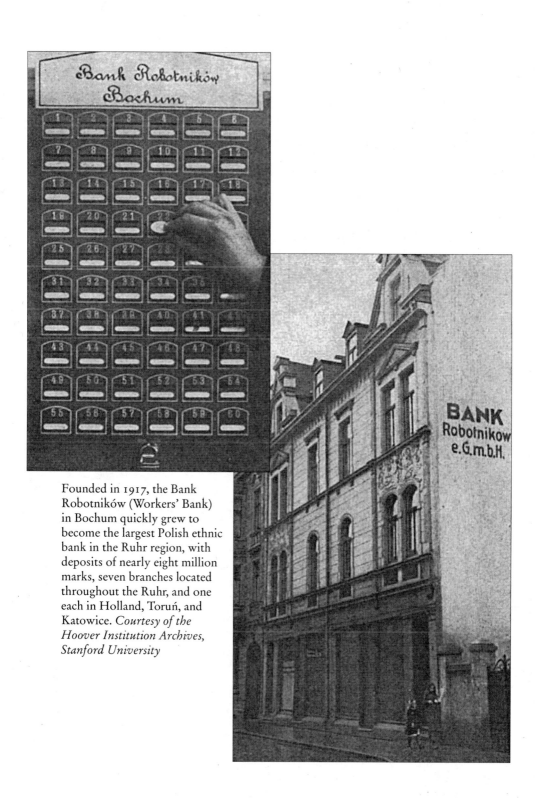

Founded in 1917, the Bank Robotników (Workers' Bank) in Bochum quickly grew to become the largest Polish ethnic bank in the Ruhr region, with deposits of nearly eight million marks, seven branches located throughout the Ruhr, and one each in Holland, Toruń, and Katowice. *Courtesy of the Hoover Institution Archives, Stanford University*

A Philadelphia & Reading–owned mining complex in northeastern Pennsylvania at the turn of the twentieth century. Because of the terrain, many mines in the region were slope shaft mines, where underground coal lay closer to the surface. In the Ruhr, most mines were deep shaft mines. *Reprinted from Roberts,* Anthracite Coal Communities

Pennsylvania miners working underground in Pittston, Pennsylvania. *Lewis Hine photograph courtesy of the National Archives, College Park, Maryland*

Breaker boys working under strict supervision at the Ewen Breaker of the Pennsylvania Coal Company in South Pittston, Pennsylvania. In the Ruhr, such child labor was forbidden. *Lewis Hine photograph courtesy of the National Archives, College Park, Maryland*

A Polish miner and his young son picking coal on a culm heap. *Reprinted from Roberts,* Anthracite Coal Communities

A typical mining settlement in northeastern Pennsylvania. *Reprinted from Roberts,* Anthracite Coal Communities

The Polish Miners' Association in Duryea, Pennsylvania, affiliated with the Polish National Catholic Church. *Reprinted courtesy of the Polish National Catholic Church*

Fryderyk Chopin girls' choir in Shenandoah, Pennsylvania, in the 1920s. *Reprinted courtesy of the Polish National Catholic Church*

A Sokoł (Falcon) association in Annen (Witten) in the Ruhr, c. 1917. *Courtesy of Valentina Maria Stefanski*

The Kościuszko Guards of Scranton, Pennsylvania, 1909. This association was named after the famous American Revolutionary War hero and Polish patriot Thaddeus Kościuszko. The Polish-style uniforms combined with the carrying of an American flag (see far right) display an emerging Polish-American identity. *Reprinted courtesy of the Polish National Catholic Church*

Notable Polish community organizers in the Ruhr included Jan Brejski (*left*) and ZZP Miners' section leader Francziszek Mańkowski (*below*). *Courtesy of Valentina Maria Stefanski*

Francziszek (Francis) Hodur, first bishop of the Polish National Catholic Church, founded in Scranton, Pennsylvania, in 1897. *Reprinted courtesy of the Polish National Catholic Church*

The symbol of the Polish National Catholic Church (PNCC) with the dictum "Truth, Work, Struggle." *Reprinted courtesy of the Polish National Catholic Church*

A 1918 opinion cartoon appearing in *Coal Age* magazine, emphasizing America's ability to assimilate "Slavic" miners. Though paternalistic in tone, the cartoon is notable for going against the rising wave of xenophobia in the United States that soon led to the immigration restriction measures of 1921 and 1924. *Courtesy of the Anthracite Mining Museum, Scranton, Pennsylvania*

In the interwar period, trying to ensure that second- and third-generation Poles living in Germany maintained their ethnic identity was important. To this end, the ZPwN attempted to promote "Polishness" by creating a variety of publications aimed at the young such as *Młody Polak w Niemczech* (Young Pole in Germany), a magazine for teenagers. Organizations such as the Związek Młodzieży Polskiej (Union of Polish Youth) were also established. Pictured is a blessing ceremony led by ZPwN president Father Bolesław Domański. *Courtesy of the Hoover Institution Archives, Stanford University*

The leadership of the ZPwN in 1937. Seated center is the ZPwN president Father Bolesław Domański. Standing directly behind on the right is Dr. Jan Kaczmarek, born in Bochum in 1895, general secretary of the ZPwN; and on the left, regional ZPwN leader for the Rhineland and Westphalia Józef Kalus. *Courtesy of the Hoover Institution Archives, Stanford University*

(*right*) A 1923 steamship advertisement asks "Czy jedziecie do domu w odwiedziny?" (Are you going home for a visit?). Return migration to Poland was frequent for Poles living in both the Ruhr and northeastern Pennsylvania. After World War I, however, Poles in both communities were confronted with the question of whether to permanently return. *From the 9 September 1923 issue of the* Republika Górnik Pensylvanski (*Scranton*)

(*below*) "Jesteśmy Polakami" (We are Poles), the dominating theme of the 1936 ZPwN meeting held in Bochum, Germany. The main symbol of the ZPwN was the *Rodło*, a graphic representation of the course of the Vistula River, along with the historic city of Kraków, that emphasized the ethnic roots of Poles in Germany. *Courtesy of the Hoover Institution Archives, Stanford University*

6 ııı Challenging State and Society

The "Polish Question" and the Rise of
Polish Ethnic Associations

WHEN POLES BEGAN ARRIVING in the Ruhr and northeastern Pennsylvania during the 1870s and 1880s, state authorities took little notice of
their presence, and anti-Polish sentiment within native society was limited.[1]
As Polish migration increased from the 1890s onward, attitudes quickly
changed; many within government and the general public grew concerned
about the danger this "foreign" element posed to the demographic and
moral health of society. The view that Poles were a threatening and undesirable element undermining social cohesion and the national interest became
widespread, raising the question: What should be done about the Poles?

Fears surrounding Polish migration emerged in large part as a legacy
of the imperfect nation-state building process in Germany and the United
States. The expansion of industry from the 1850s onward together with the
wars of (re)unification of the 1860s brought about a growing state centralization, albeit to different degrees, and the rise for the first time of tangible
"German" and "American" identities. Yet deep social and cultural divisions
remained, divides exacerbated by late nineteenth- and early twentieth-
century migration. Defining what is meant to be German or American—
and who could become a German or an American—grew critical. Debates
and investigations abounded regarding the costs and benefits of migration,
analyses that often led to different migrant population groups being accorded an "insider" or "outsider" status. As one of the largest immigrant
groups in both Germany and the United States, Poles were subject to particular scrutiny and, given their irreconcilably "foreign" ways, became the
target of measures intended to exclude them from the imagined national
community. This chapter explores the ways in which Poles were cast as an

internal "other" by examining government policies and public discourses on the Polish question as well as how Poles utilized ethnic associations to defend their interests and promote their greater inclusion within German and American society.

Government Policies Toward Poles in the Ruhr and Northeastern Pennsylvania

Government animosity toward the Polish presence in the Ruhr was stimulated, first and foremost, by the appointment of Heinrich Konrad von Studt as Oberpräsident (minister-president) of the Province of Westphalia in 1889. When von Studt became Oberpräsident, he already had extensive experience with the ongoing nationality conflict in the Prussian East, serving previously as a Landrat (county manager) in the Province of Posen, a Regierungspräsident (district president) in Königsberg, and in Interior Ministry posts in Berlin. Based on his experience, von Studt argued that it was unacceptable to allow a sizable Polish community to settle in the Ruhr without enacting stronger measures to prevent the rise of an irredentist Polish nationalism. In an 1896 report to the Prussian Interior Ministry he claimed that "it is in the fundamental interest of the state that the [Polish] element be Germanized and melted into native population as quickly as possible." In explaining why Poles had yet to become German, von Studt blamed the growth of ethnic Polish associations and the sorrowful indifference to national concerns exhibited by both Ruhr employers and the Center Party, who in their narrow economic and political self-interest were undermining state minority policies.[2]

In order to more effectively combat the danger posed by Poles and promote their Germanization, von Studt implemented a series of directives, based on policies already in place in eastern Prussia, though tailored to local conditions. These measures included requiring police to closely watch Polish associations; preventing ethnic Polish priests from entering the Ruhr; limiting the use of the Polish language in public meetings; and requiring that all school instruction, including religious education, be conducted in German. Poles were additionally prohibited from openly displaying certain symbols, club flags, pictures, and clothing. Specific Polish songs, books, and foreign newspapers deemed national in character were also banned. Finally, von Studt placed pressure on the Catholic Church hierarchy to rein in the activities of church-sponsored Polish ethnic associations and limit the availability of Polish-language spiritual care.[3]

After von Studt was appointed Prussian Minister of Culture in 1899, his successors and their subordinates held firm to this hard line. In subsequent years, almost all Polish associations were declared by authorities to be political organizations. This was an important designation because it required Poles to obtain police permission to hold their associational meetings and gave police the right to be physically present at such meetings. Attending policemen also had the option of disbanding meetings if they touched on nationality issues. The attitude of local officials to Polish associations is best encapsulated by a statement by the police chief in Borbeck. Justifying a decision to classify a local Polish lottery club as a political association, the official argued that "since the purpose of all Polish associations is to dissociate [Poles] from Germans and promote national-Polish sentiment, it must therefore follow that also the Polish lottery association should be seen as a political organization, even when there has been no evidence that the association has actually engaged in political activities."[4] By 1909, Polish associations in the Ruhr became such a perceived threat that the Prussian government organized a central office under the police president in Bochum to coordinate the surveillance of them. The reporting activities of this office lasted well into the late 1920s.[5] Perhaps the best example of the government's attempts to limit the growth of Polish organizations was the 1908 *Reichsvereinsgesetz* (law of association). This law forced the use of the German language in all Polish meetings open to the general public except for those related to political elections.[6]

To complement the measures implemented to constrain the development of Polish political and cultural life in the Ruhr, government officials also promoted divide-and-conquer strategies designed to limit the appeal of Polish nationalism among newly arriving migrants. Emphasis was placed in administrative circles on encouraging regionalism among the diverse groups of Polish-speakers in the Ruhr, such as Upper Silesians, Kashubes, and Masurians, with the hope of creating a successful, "model" migrant minority, an archetype that could then be used to justify further restrictions on those portions of the migrant population that continued to prove resistant to assimilation. In this regard, Protestant Masurians were particularly singled out as a group that could be "won" to the German cause. The transformation in administrative attitudes toward the Masurians can be seen in the way this group was officially defined over time. In the 1880s and into 1890s, Masurians were largely viewed within government circles as Poles because they spoke a Polish dialect. In census statistics, the Masurians were counted as Poles, and official reports referred to them simply as "evangelical Poles." By the late 1890s and especially after turn of the century, however, official Prussian definitions of the Masurian population changed. Although Poles from Posen, West Prussia, and Upper Silesia continued to be classified by their mother tongue as Poles, Masurians were now geographically defined for statistical and reporting purposes as "the native population of the same-named region" of East Prussia, thereby linking Masurians to the historically German lands of the Duchy of Prussia.[7]

The Prussian administration also undertook more concrete steps to win over the Masurians. Special treatment and economic support were accorded to institutions that furthered the development of an independent Masurian identity. From the 1890s onward, the state provided financial assistance to Polish-speaking evangelical pastors in the Ruhr who cared for the Masurians, and their number during this decade was higher than the number of Polish-speaking priests allowed to serve the much larger Polish Catholic population. Additionally, the government aided the development of a distinct Masurian press, local libraries, and East Prussian mutual-aid societies, organizations designed to provide limited financial and social support to "loyal" Masurian workers while offering protection from the dangers of Social Democratic or Polish agitation.[8] These efforts to encourage a Masurian identity were successful; in fact, they proved too successful. Instead of assimilating, Masurians began to develop a distinct subculture that proved resistant to assimilation. Although government reports and the German press constantly asserted beginning in the 1890s that the Masurians would easily be "melted" into German society, a report of the Bochum police president shows that by 1914 only 12.5 percent of Masurian men were active in German mutual-aid associations. This figure is not impressive when one considers that in Gelsenkirchen-Buer, a center of Masurian settlement, approximately 12 percent of the Masurian men in 1912 were members of the Polish ZZP trade union.[9] The apparent tendency of Masurians to remain *unter sich*, or to themselves, aroused significant consternation among those Germans that had lent support to the Masurian community in the years immediately prior to the war. In 1914, the primary spiritual caretaker of the Masurians, the Reverend William Mueckely, reported to the Bochum police president that the attempt to instill a German character in the Masurian workers through the Masurian mutual-aid societies was a complete failure. Such organizations actually posed the danger of fueling separatist sentiment. In contrast to an earlier stand, Mueckely proposed that the process of integration would be speeded if the number of Polish-language services for the Masurian community was reduced, which did occur later, after World War I.[10]

The limited level of social integration into German society evidenced by Masurians belies claims regarding the national orientation of this minority group. Although Masurians did not consider themselves to be Polish (nor could they, given the general Catholic orientation of Polish politics at the time), they were also not embracing a German national identity. Instead, the Masurian population gave every indication of taking advantage of its privileged position within Prussian minority politics to maintain their group independence and strengthen a burgeoning Masurian consciousness. The eagerness of the Prussian government to assimilate Slavic, Polish-speaking Masurians also highlights that policies toward Poles were driven primarily by politics, not ethnicity or race.[11]

Not all Prussian state institutions supported the policies of bureaucratic officials. Courts in the Ruhr especially proved invaluable in overturning the most onerous anti-Polish measures and protecting Polish civil rights. Germany has always prided itself on being a Rechtsstaat (a state ruled by the law) and in the pre–World War I period the courts were instrumental in upholding the right of Poles to hold meetings, march in processions, or otherwise engage in ethnic activity that the police and government officials wanted to restrict. As Prussian citizens, Poles readily turned to the courts to seek legal redress because they recognized that the judiciary was independent of the German executive and legislative branches. Although not all court cases were decided in the Poles' favor, many were, and the ability to sue in court was a highly valued right.[12]

This can be seen in the case brought by the police in Borbeck against Adalbert Kaczmarek, a leader of a local Sokół (Falcon) association. The police fined Kaczmarek for transgressing against the 1908 Reichsvereinsgesetz, specifically for not reporting in advance the meeting of an association deemed by authorities to be political, as well as for conducting a meeting in Polish open to the public. For his part, Kaczmarek claimed that the meeting was actually a closed meeting restricted to local members of the association. Consequently, he felt fully within his rights to speak in Polish since the 1908 Reichsvereinsgesetz did not prohibit the use of Polish in closed meetings. After hearing the case, the local *Schöffengericht*, or court of lay assessor, decided in Kaczmarek's favor, finding that the police could not provide sufficient evidence, outside of the personal testimony of an officer who attended the meeting, that the club was either open to the public or political.

The state appealed this decision to the *Königlicher Landgericht,* or district court, in Essen. However, the Essen court upheld the lower court decision finding that "the state's arguments not only have inconsistencies, but are also legally invalid. Just because the Sokół association has political tendencies, gave public notice of its meeting in the *Wiarus Polski,* and conducted its business in Polish does not mean that the meeting in question should be necessarily be seen as a political meeting requiring registration." The court then required the state to pay for all costs associated with the legal suit.[13]

Intriguing about this case is that while there was a question about whether the meeting was open to the public or closed to members-only, neither the petitioner nor the defendant disputed the fact that the meeting was indeed political. Given the wording of the 1908 Reichsvereinsgesetz, the meeting should have been registered in advance and the police were partially justified in their complaint. Yet both the local and appeals courts clearly demanded a higher burden of proof. The anecdotal impression of the police regarding what types of Polish clubs were political was not enough. Altogether, this case indicates that there was clear disagreement between the executive and judicial branches of government over the interpretation of the Reichsvereinsgesetz as well as the treatment of Poles. Despite various discriminatory measures, Poles could utilize the courts to fight against state discrimination and defend their legal rights.

In northeastern Pennsylvania, Poles did not face constant surveillance and were largely able to conduct their ethnic affairs without formal interference by state authorities. The lack of direct oversight, however, did not mean that the state took a hands-off approach to the growing Polish presence in the region. From the 1890s onward, there was increasing apprehension at all levels of government regarding the effects of new immigration on the moral and racial health of native society, anxiety that was also reflected in public opinion, where the push for immigration restriction was rapidly growing. In 1895 and 1897, Pennsylvania state legislators took up the cause of immigration reform by passing resolutions designed to restrict the influx of Slavic workers. Although no formal ban on entry and settlement was adopted, the legislature did approve a law requiring that eastern European miners demonstrate proficiency in English and required that coal operators pay a head tax of three cents a day for every eastern European worker they employed.[14]

The following year, courts in Lackawanna, Luzerne, and Schuylkill counties implemented a new set of provisions for naturalization that made it more expensive and difficult for immigrants to become citizens. Before

1897, when an immigrant worker wanted to obtain citizenship, he submitted "first" papers declaring his intent to naturalize. After a period of five years of continuous residence in the country and barring any criminal offenses, the immigrant could then obtain citizenship by paying a two-dollar fee. Under the new ordinances the five-year residence rule remained intact, however, applicants were also now required to engage a lawyer who would represent the immigrant before the court; bring two character witnesses to court who were citizens; publish a legal notice three times declaring an intent to become a citizen and hope that no objections were raised; and appear before a judge who would conduct, to his own satisfaction, an examination in English on the Constitution of both the United States and the Commonwealth of Pennsylvania as well as on the, never actually defined, duties of citizens. Altogether the costs to apply for citizenship (including legal fees, advertisement expenses, and the need to take time off from work and travel) amounted to between ten and fifty dollars. For a Pole, this represented at least one week's worth of wages, if not more. Although the sum may appear small by present-day standards, the same amount of money could buy passage back to the homeland or pay for a relative to come to America. Moreover, the fact that the granting of citizenship was at the judge's discretion meant that despite the increased expense, obtaining citizenship was no longer more or less automatic.[15]

Another restriction was adopted in 1906 that placed a new barrier to naturalization. Instead of courts deciding citizenship cases once a month, they now only convened hearings five times a year. Not surprisingly, applications for naturalization fell off sharply. In Schuylkill County, there were 1,307 petitions for citizenship for 1904 and 1905. After the new law went into effect, there were in the two-year period from October 1906 to 1908 only 73 applications.[16] All told, the various regulations on citizenship had a pronounced effect on the ability for Poles to become naturalized. By 1910, the overall percentage of Poles who were fully naturalized in northeastern Pennsylvania was 34 percent, with only an additional 8 percent having drawn the first papers necessary to later become full citizens. In Shenandoah, these figures were even lower. Of the 2,290 Poles living in the city, only 600, or 26 percent, were naturalized, while only an additional 79 Poles, or 5 percent, had their first papers.[17]

The desire to restrict immigration and access to citizenship has a long pedigree in U.S. history, and by the early twentieth century pressure at the federal level to limit the influx of eastern and southern Europeans was sizable, especially in the aftermath of the assassination of President McKinley by the Polish-American anarchist Leon Czolgosz.[18] In 1903, the commissioner general of immigration in New York decried the inadequacy of existing immigration law, noting that while "a strict execution of our present laws makes it possible to keep out what may be termed the worst element of Europe (paupers, diseased persons, and those likely to become public charges) . . . these laws do not reach large bodies of immigrants who, while not of this class, are yet generally undesirable . . . and unfitted mentally or morally for good citizenship." The commissioner then claimed that the arrival of increasing numbers of new immigrants benefited only one group, namely the steamship companies that made enormous profits in the transatlantic passenger trade.[19] Officials' concern about the danger of new immigrants led to extensive government studies being conducted to determine which immigrant "races," a term that by the turn of the century emphasized not just national, but increasingly biological distinctiveness, could be assimilated. Immigrant groups were "scientifically" categorized, ranked according to their perceived ability to assimilate and the cost/benefit various groups brought to American society. Inevitably such reports found that given their racial characteristics, eastern and southern Europeans were generally undesirable and unwelcome interlopers.

By far the most important study to emerge on the issues of immigration and immigration restriction was the 1907–10 investigation by the United States Senate Immigration Commission, chaired by Senator William Dillingham. Charged by President Roosevelt to determine the overall effects of immigration on American society, the immigration commission prepared an exhaustive forty-two volume report on field studies of immigrants working in all major American industries as well as their influence on the surrounding social environment.[20] Published in 1911, the *Reports of the Immigration Commission* found in specific reference to Poles and other new immigrants living in northeastern Pennsylvania that the arrival of eastern and southern Europeans brought an "infusion of a large element of foreign blood" and a "social and moral deterioration of the community." In distinguishing new immigrants from natives and earlier immigrants of Western European stock, the immigration commission highlighted differences in language, religious practice, and literacy. Much attention was given to the disparities in living customs, with emphasis placed on the general uncleanliness and immodesty of recent immigrants as well as their penchant for imbibing great quantities of alcohol. Attention was also given to the uniqueness of new immigrants' physical bodies. The immigration commission stressed in its *Reports* the physical strength of the new immigrants and their willingness to accept work requiring nothing but brawn. It further noted that despite living in unsanitary conditions, new immigrants appeared much more resistant to disease.

Altogether, the immigration commission concluded that the arrival of new immigrants and their interaction with the "native element" caused the following "evil effects . . . of a social and moral character" on the communities of northeastern Pennsylvania:

1. A lowering of the average intelligence, restraint, sensitivity, orderliness, and efficiency of the community through the greater deficiency of the immigrants in all of these respects;

2. An increase of intemperance and crime resulting from inebriety due to the drink habits of immigrants;

3. An increase of sexual immorality due to the excess of males over females;

4. A high infant mortality, due to the neglect and ignorance of hygiene and sanitary surroundings on the part of immigrant mothers;

5. A general loosening of the forces of social cohesion. The inability, owing to the lingual and educational barriers, of understanding the other's viewpoint prevents the development of sympathy and engenders a disintegrating hostility. Differences in modes of living hinder social intercourse;

6. A civic demoralization of the ruling class. The venality of the immigrants overcomes the scruples of the politically ambitious, and they succumb to the temptations of bribery. This reacts on the efficiency of the local government;

7. An enfeeblement of the power of public opinion through the weakness of the public press;

8. A general stimulation of the cupidity and avarice of the local business and professional men by the tempting prey of the ignorant foreigner;

9. A growth in the number of saloons (one for every 26 families) to satisfy the immigrant appetite, and as a consequent extension of the temptation to the native born, and increase in crime among all classes due to inebriety;

10. A coarsening of the fiber of the native-born through contact with the immodesties of the immigrant.[21]

The findings clearly declared that Poles were fundamentally different from natives and earlier immigrants both culturally and, in many ways, biologically. The *Reports* emphasize that Poles were a growing horde that posed a great danger to the moral and physical health of the American community. Poles were brutish, uncultured, less intelligent, and lawless. They spread disease and weakened the vitality of American institutions. In perhaps one of the best examples of blaming the victim, Poles were also held responsible, due to their intrinsic nature, for enticing and tempting natives, naturally against their will, to also become coarse, corrupt, and greedy; when sung by Polish sirens, the song of exploitation was apparently simply too strong for the native "ruling class" to resist.

The *Reports of the Immigration Commission,* together with the previous legal efforts taken to limit immigration and naturalization, heavily influenced both the public perception of immigration and subsequent government policy. The question of who could and should be included in the national community was answered by the government's confirmation, reflecting the biases within American society, that old immigrants were valuable members of the national community while new immigrants were a dangerous burden. By not addressing the fundamental social inequalities that limited new immigrant advancement, the various legislative actions and governmental reports helped delay by at least a generation the mainstream acceptance of Poles within American society, as well as Polish desires to become fully naturalized. The increasing belief in government circles that Poles and others new immigrants contributed little to the common good also spurred efforts that led to the passage of the 1921 Quota Act and 1924 National Origins Act, laws that effectively ended further immigration from eastern and southern Europe.

The Polish Immigrant in Popular Literature and Academic Thought

Finding an answer to the Polish question was not only the prerogative of governments. The Polish presence in German and American society became the subject of popular fiction as well as scholarly discussion. Within the realm of fiction, the success in Germany of Clara Viebig's 1903 novel *Das schlafende Heer* (The Dormant Army) is illuminating. The novel was written in the wake of the infamous 1901 Polish school strike in Września and chronicled the struggle between ethnic Germans and Poles in eastern Prussia, focusing on the Bräuer family and their attempt to establish themselves as German colonists in a predominantly Polish community in West Prussia.[22] The Bräuers are a symbol of German hope that this region can be civilized and brought within the orbit of German culture. However, the task proves to be overwhelming. Poles are uncultured, disloyal, and easily led astray by

Polish nationalists such as the local Catholic priest Górka, who at one point in the novel exclaims to his Polish flock that "you are the army that will arise to free Poland! Stand up and save yourselves! . . . Hold your Faith high! Your faith is your weapon, the strongest sword of Poland's freedom!" By the end of the novel, the growth in Polish nationalism, fostered under the shelter of the Catholic Church, thwarts the Bräuers' colonizing mission. The lessons to be drawn were clear. Left unchecked, Poles would arise from their current "dormancy" to overwhelm the German nation. To avert this, Poles needed to be strictly controlled, assimilated if possible, repressed when necessary.[23]

In the United States, popular fiction at the turn of the century also focused on the danger of the Polish presence. In 1904, Alice Ward Bailey penned a short story in *The Outlook* magazine titled "A Bright Green Pole," which chronicled the efforts of a benevolent male employer to instruct, in a *Pygmalion*-esque fashion, his naive Polish domestic Boronoca; he taught her English and instructed her in the proper ways of American household life. After several months, the employer achieved a degree of success. Boronoca learned rudimentary English and kept the home in an "American" fashion. Yet, she later betrays the employer's trust by working without permission outside of hours as an agricultural field laborer during the annual harvest; this was considered a primal reversion to type that highlighted her fundamentally flawed, backward nature. As Bailey describes it, "Outwardly she was intensely American . . . inwardly she was Polish," and the arrival of autumn "found the joints in the armor civilization had put on," touching "the wild nature beneath."[24] In a similar vein, E. S. Johnson penned a short story in 1906 for *American Magazine* titled "The Younger Generation," which portrayed the troubled domestic life of a young Polish-Lithuanian couple living in a coal-mining region. The main protagonist is Casimir Naktis, or Cass Knight, a conflicted soul who struggles to mask an instinctually violent nature and accept "the rigid limits of the American code of manners." After a fight with Gracie, his vain and jealous wife, the Casimir "of the old style" reawakes. Intoxicated, Casimir heads to work where he endangers the lives of his fellow workers. In a later scene, a drunken Casimir beats his wife in order to teach her "who's boss," after which Gracie admits her wrongdoing and need to be punished. Altogether, both characterizations underscore a common theme found in the fictionalized representation of Poles. Namely, while outwardly displaying American characteristics, they were at core an unreliable, wild, and potentially violent people.[25]

Such literary portrayals highlight middle-class fears of Poles. So too did many ethnographic investigations that focused on the Polish presence. In the Ruhr, Poles became the object of intense study after the 1899 Herne strike. In 1901, the Ruhr-Lippe district of the nationalist Alldeutscher Verband (Pan-German League) produced the first examination of the Ruhr Poles. Not surprisingly, given the group's ideology, the study concluded that Poles were an inferior, undesirable element that posed a great political and cultural threat to the German nation. Particularly dangerous was the growth in Polish ethnic associations in which "one can see . . . the highest form of insolence to the Prussian state that the Poles dare to offer." To alleviate the Polish menace, the Alldeutscher Verband recommended barring the use of Polish in ethnic association meetings and prohibiting Poles from purchasing land to prevent their permanent settlement in the Ruhr.[26] The fears that Poles threatened the integrity of the nation state can be further seen in Victor Bredt's 1909 study *Die Polenfrage im Ruhrkohlengebiet* (The Polish Question in the Ruhr Coal Region), which warned readers that "attention must be paid to those, who in ancient German lands . . . are attempting to build a particular 'state within a state' and reject all things German."[27] Franz Schulze seconded this sentiment in his own 1909 treatise, *Polnische Zuwanderung im Ruhrrevier und ihre Wirkung* (Polish Migration to the Ruhr and its Effect), which claimed that the Polish presence had an altogether negative effect on family life, the moral upbringing of children, and public safety.[28] The one significant exception in attitudes toward Polish-speaking migrants came in analyses of the Masurians, who were held up as a model minority due to their Lutheran faith, loyalty to the kaiser and Prussian rule, and perceived willingness to lift themselves up and embrace German language and culture.[29]

In northeastern Pennsylvania, the belief was widely held that "Anglo-Saxon" America was committing race suicide by allowing the continued immigration of undesirable peoples from eastern Europe. In 1904, Frank Warne claimed in *The Slav Invasion and the Mine Worker* that eastern Europeans were causing a "social revolution" by "retarding communal advancement" and "sending influences for evil deep down into the foundations of the social structure." In particular, Warne criticized Poles for stealing jobs and overturning the Protestant character of the region, as well as causing increased levels of crime, alcoholism, and political corruption.[30] The Immigration Restriction League also railed against the moral, economic, and especially eugenic danger of the Slavic influx. In 1910, it demanded the passage of laws that would enable the government to deport undesirable aliens "without time limit." As the league argued, such laws were necessary because "recent investigations in biology show that . . . there are certain parts of Europe from which all medical men and all biologists would agree that it would be better for the American race if no aliens at all were admitted. . . . We should see to it that we are protected, not merely from the burden of supporting alien dependents, delinquents, and defectives, but from . . . 'that watering of the nation's lifeblood,' which results from their breeding after admission." The viewpoint represented by the league had many supporters, especially in various institutions of higher learning. Presidents of twenty colleges and universities and 126 other educators endorsed the league's 1910 platform. The league's eugenicist arguments would subsequently prove influential in the passage of immigration restriction legislation in the early 1920s.[31]

There were opponents of the view that Poles threatened race and nation. Ludwig Bernhard's 1907 treatise on the Polish question in the Ruhr forcefully declared that it was Prussia's prejudicial Polenpolitik that was chiefly responsibly for the nationality conflict and concluded that Polish organizations "cannot simply be seen as *staatsfeindlich* (hostile to the state), since, contrary to their own will, they support the Prussian government on certain points by assuming and making easier tasks normally taken on by that state." In essence, the welfare and socialization activities of Polish associations' promoted Polish integration, taught Poles respect for the existing social order, and turned them into upstanding citizens.[32] Stanisław Wachowiak, a son of working-class Polish parents in the Ruhr, believed similarly. In *Die Polen in Rheinland-Westfalen* (The Poles in Rhineland-Westphalia) Wachowiak maintained that the willingness of Poles to ally with German workers belied assumptions that Poles were a closed national community. He further stressed that Polish political engagement through unions and ethnic associations demonstrated a clear embrace of democratic practices and German values.[33]

Comparatively, the voices advocating for greater toleration and understanding of Poles were louder in northeastern Pennsylvania. Peter Roberts argued in his 1904 work *Anthracite Coal Communities* that perceived declines in community standards resulted not from Polish immigration but the region's working-class radicalism, the greed of employers, and widespread political corruption. Once an environment that actually favored "social progress" was created, Poles could be raised to American standards since they naturally possessed positive "American" traits such as hard work and thrift. Roberts stressed that the "way to health" in integrating Polish immigrants into American society was for "the conservative and intellectual class" of American community leaders to become active on issues of immigration. As immigration secretary for the Young Men's Christian Association (YMCA), Roberts set about building programs through which the Pole could be "improved" and saved from the "deadly influence of social parasites now feeding upon" him. In particular, he advocated for greater government involvement in promoting immigrant "Americanization" by providing states with financing to establish English-language schools, making naturalization easier, and creating an employment bureau, in public/private partnership with leading ethnic fraternal associations and labor agencies, that could direct immigration to areas of the country where labor shortages existed.[34] Concrete aid to immigrants also came in the form of YMCA night schools, which, using the "Roberts' method of teaching," offered immigrants classes in the English language, citizenship, and industrial arts.[35]

Roberts's belief that Poles could be assimilated into American life was seconded by the prominent University of Chicago sociologists William Thomas and Florian Znaniecki, whose monumental *Polish Peasant in Europe and America* argued vigorously against the eugenicist perspective at the core of immigration restriction rhetoric. Published shortly before the 1921 Quota Act was passed, Thomas and Znaniecki claimed that the delinquency and moral corruption exhibited by some Polish migrants and cited by those wanting to restrict further Polish immigration was "due chiefly to the widely varying lines of their past cultural evolution rather than to divergent biological tendencies and unequal natural abilities." Essentially, it was the backward social environment of the homeland that left some Poles initially unprepared for life in the United States, not their innate nature. Once settled in America, Poles could become an asset to American society. They possessed a cooperative "social spirit" and with the aid of their ethnic organizations were overcoming a previous "wildness" and becoming respectable. Though "the cultural level of a 'Polonia Americana'" would always remain lower than that of American society, as Poles acclimated to their adopted country, they would shed their ethnicity and embrace "the wider and richer field of American civilization."[36]

Roberts, Thomas, and Znaniecki challenged arguments that Poles could not assimilate, though they believed that the maintenance of ethnic culture impeded Polish adaptation to "American" ways of life. The sooner Poles abandoned their ethnic identity and culture, the better. Not all proponents of Polish integration shared this view. Though in the clear minority, Emily Balch embraced a multicultural, pluralistic notion of citizenship. In her important 1910 work, *Our Slavic Fellow Citizens,* she posited that Polish isolation within their adopted society would end once America no longer represented "a rival nationality eager to make [Poles] forget their past and . . . abandon their ideals." The best way to promote integration was to respect Polish culture and its contribution to strengthening a common American identity. Concluding her study, Balch passionately argued that

> we must learn to connect our ideals and theirs . . . to work together with them for justice, for humane conditions of living . . . not merely formal, liberty. . . . [M]ovements in which different classes of citizens join to bring about specific improvements . . . are of infinite value as they conduce [a] higher unity, in which we may preserve every difference to which men cling with affection, without feeling ourselves any less fellow citizens and comrades.[37]

Conceiving citizenship in terms of equal membership in a shared cultural community and not just the formal legal relationship of an individual to the state, Balch emphasizes that Poles should embrace certain fundamental American values of justice, liberty, and obligations owed to the collective good, yet must also be allowed to maintain and practice their ethnic culture since it contributes to the advancement of a pluralistic, open society. Ultimately, successful integration of Poles as truly equal citizens necessitated interethnic rapprochement and a blending of American and Polish cultures, not the outright abandonment of the latter in favor of the former.

Polish Responses: Empowerment through Ethnic Associations

Polish communities in the Ruhr and northeastern Pennsylvania were able to thrive despite the hostility encountered in their adopted societies. In overcoming state discrimination and the public's moral panic over their presence, Poles utilized ethnic associations to defend their rights and become active citizens within the public sphere of their host societies. Between the 1880s and World War I, the Polish associational movement grew rapidly. By 1912, there were more than one thousand Polish ethnic associations across the Ruhr, or one for every three hundred Poles. The ratio of associations per inhabitant was similar in many urban centers of northeastern Pennsylvania.[38] The activities and types of Polish associations varied. In the early years of Polish migration, most associations developed under the auspices of the Catholic Church, though the need for more effective organizational responses to German and American anti-Polish policies soon spurred the growth of independent secular and politically active associations.[39] Although conservative, apolitical Polish Catholic Associations continued to maintain a significant presence in both the Ruhr and northeastern Pennsylvania, secular and partisan associations increasingly played a dominant role in ethnic life.

In the Ruhr, the first secular associations arose in the mid-1890s, and their growth accelerated after the turn of the century. The most notable secular association was the ZZP, discussed in earlier chapters, which focused on redressing economic injustice in the workplace. The earliest political organization was the Związek Polaków w Niemczech (Union of Poles in Germany—ZPwN), established in Bochum in 1894 under the leadership of Jan Brejski. In 1897, the Union of Poles established the Main Voting Committee for Westphalia, Rhineland, and the Neighboring Western Provinces, which played a prominent role in exposing Poles to modern democratic politics and forging a sizable Polish voting bloc for elections. By 1903, the effectiveness of this organization could be seen when the Main Voting Committee decided not to endorse any Center Party candidates for the Reichstag elections. Instead, Poles ran their own candidates despite the fact that this went against the political wishes of leading Polish politicians in Poznań. This action ultimately denied the Center Party victories in three voting districts. In later elections, the Main Voting Committee continued a policy of running Polish candidates in the first round of Reichstag elections. There were no illusions about actually winning, but by demonstrating electoral strength in the first round, Poles set themselves up as potential kingmakers who could extract concessions from German political parties in the inevitable second round of elections. On the local level, the Main Voting Committee also agitated for Polish candidates, though the electoral influence of Poles was less given the Prussian three-tiered voting system. Despite this disadvantage, thirty-two Poles were elected to local city and town council seats prior to World War I.[40]

The ability of the Main Voting Committee to direct Polish voting patterns was never absolute, especially as many working-class Poles grew dissatisfied with the orientation and domineering tendencies of the organization's middle-class leaders. In the second round of the 1912 Reichstag elections, the majority of Poles ignored the Main Voting Committee's support for the Center Party and instead cast their ballots for the SPD, thereby enabling the Socialists to pick up three seats in the Ruhr. Despite declining influence in later years, the Main Voting Committee gave Ruhr Poles a crucial political voice that was independent of the nobility, clergy, and middle-class nationalists in the homeland. As *Wiarus Polski* noted in the wake of the 1903 election, "The Poles *na obczyznie* [living in a foreign land], among which no nobles, lawyers, or doctors are found, are often assumed to be meek and obedient . . . but it was forgotten that the Polish people *na obczyznie* are not a herd of sheep that obey the whistle."[41]

Other political associations that arose around the turn of the century included the politically nationalist Oświata (Education), Straż (Guard), and Sokół (Falcon) groups. Of these, the most significant were the Sokoły, which were designed to prepare young Polish men for the cause of national liberation by building healthy minds through healthy bodies. Modeled after both German Turn (Gymnastic) and Czech Sokół associations, the Polish Sokół movement arose in the homeland during the late 1860s. The first Sokół in the Ruhr was founded in Oberhausen in 1899, and the organization quickly spread under the leadership of Stanisław Kunca. In 1911, there were 128 local Sokoły comprising a membership of 4,631 Poles, and the movement in the Ruhr was larger than the one in Posen; membership rose to approximately 7,000 by the end of 1912.[42] The growth of the Sokoły, their oftentimes right-wing, nationalist rhetoric and their use of blunted swords and lances in training exercises drew the ire of German authorities; officially they were viewed as paramilitary organizations that threatened public security. Closely watched, Sokół leaders were fined for any infraction against the Reichsvereinsgesetz, and public, military-style demonstrations were generally banned.[43] The efforts to fully suppress the Sokół movement were hampered by the German courts. In 1913, a court ruled that the activities of the Sokoły, including the carrying of blunted lances, essentially mirrored those of German nationalist student fencing societies and thus were to be permitted.[44] On the whole, the fears of authorities regarding the Sokoły were exaggerated. Although the leadership of the Sokół movement was strongly nationalist, most Poles joined because of the variety of sport and leisure activities offered, not to resurrect the homeland. Their success in recruitment was due primarily to the fact that the Sokoły provided a needed outlet where young Polish males could escape the drudgery of the mines and the boredom of mine colony life.

At the other end of the political spectrum, Polish socialists also undertook strenuous efforts to organize associations in the Ruhr. In 1898, the first Polish SPD-affiliated organization formed in Herne, and by 1910, Polish socialists organized ten local affiliates with a membership of approximately 300. As the membership figures highlight, the appeal of socialist associations was limited. The atheism underpinning socialist ideology made recruitment of Poles difficult. Poles who joined socialist groups faced ostracism within the community and excommunication from the Catholic Church. Although organizationally weak, socialists did find informal support within the Polish working-class community, much to the consternation of Polish middle-class leaders who constantly warned against the socialist menace.[45] The embrace of certain aspects of socialism can be seen in the ZZP, which after 1905 tended to align its agenda with that of the socialist Alter Verband on economic matters. Further backing for the socialists is evidenced by election returns, particularly the support Poles gave to the SPD in the 1912 elections.

In addition to the politically active organizations of the right and left, there were many nonpolitical cultural associations in the Ruhr. These included reading and choral societies, agricultural clubs, and abstinence societies. There were also a small number of ethnically mixed organizations that had both German and Polish members; these groups included the loyalist Kriegervereine (veterans' associations), choral groups, football and hunting clubs, and the ubiquitous Taubenvereine (pigeon-keeping associations). All told, by 1912, the rapid growth of Polish associations led German officials to observe that Polish organizational activity was more intense in the Ruhr than in Poznań.[46] The diversity and high growth rate of the Polish associations in the Ruhr is particularly impressive given the attempts by the government to stifle their growth, though ironically it was precisely this government pressure that catalyzed further associational development, as can be seen in the city of Gelsenkirchen, where the number of associations more than doubled in the years after the passage of the 1908 Reichsvereinsgesetz.[47] To circumvent the restrictions included in the Reichsvereinsgesetz on the use of the Polish language in public, Poles conducted "silent assemblies" where orators distributed copies of their speeches in Polish instead of actually speaking. After a 1909 court ruled this practice illegal, Poles opted to hold some of their larger meetings and celebrations across the border in the nearby Netherlands.[48]

Perhaps the most noteworthy example highlighting the ability of Polish organizations to thrive, even in an era of increasing government intervention, can be seen in the growth of Polish women's associations. Prior to the turn of the century, Polish women in the Ruhr participated relatively rarely in associational life. When they did, women usually joined apolitical rosary societies or choral groups. The causes for this lack of participation vary. There was immense social pressure on women to restrict their activities to the private, domestic sphere of the home. Further, the 1850 "Prussian Law of Association and Assembly" legally barred women in Prussia from participating in any association deemed by authorities to be political, which in the case of Poles presented a particular problem since authorities eagerly labeled every Polish association a political one. As more women settled permanently and became acclimated to the social environment of the Ruhr, their participation rates in associations rose. In early 1907, more than three hundred women came together in Herne to establish Wanda, the first sizable political women's association. The goals of the group included maintaining the Catholic faith, defending Polish language and culture, and ensuring the moral upbringing of children. As one leader of the association proclaimed, "As a bird defends her nest, [so too] should we . . . defend Poland and the Polish language." Emphasis was placed on women's leadership in the Polish community, especially their role in guaranteeing that their husbands maintain a proper "Polish consciousness." Such nationalist rhetoric, when espoused by women, soon proved too much for German officials, who quickly and successfully sued in court to have the club disbanded on the grounds that women could not form political associations.[49]

To the dismay of local authorities, the passage of the Reichsvereinsgesetz the following year made the court's decision moot. The new law now permitted Polish women for the first time to legally organize associations in which politics could be debated and discussed. After the Reichsvereinsgesetz, the number of politically oriented women's associations increased rapidly. In Gelsenkirchen, five political associations for women were created between 1908 and 1914. Others were established between 1908 and 1913 in Duisburg, Hamborn, Benrath, Düsseldorf, Oberhausen, Hamm, Schwerin, Castrop, Meiderich, and Eickel. Women also began, where possible, to join men's political associations such the Sokoły.[50]

A central coordinating office was created to oversee the further development of women's associations at the end of 1913. This office soon established eighty new women's locals throughout the Ruhr. A particular goal of activists in this central office was to promote a maternalist view of women as the chief protectors of the home and progenitors of the Polish nation. Directly challenging the state, women began organizing Polish-language courses for children, which at the time was illegal. In response, the government began to crack down. Surveillance of women's associations increased, and growing numbers of women were brought before the courts. Officials increasingly considered these organizations a greater threat than Polish men's associations, and the reactions they elicited from the state highlight how Polish women were becoming visibly active in the public sphere.[51]

In the United States, the late nineteenth and early part of the twentieth century bore witness to intense intraethnic factionalism over the direction of the associational movement. Polish communities in northeastern Pennsylvania were intimately caught up in these disputes. As in the Ruhr, various Polish associations competed to gain the allegiance of Polish immigrants, referred to as Polonia, and awaken in them a sense of national consciousness. The two most important Polish fraternal organizations operating in the United States were the Chicago-based Zjednoczenie Polskie-Rzymsko-Katolickie (Polish Roman Catholic Union—PRCU) and the larger Związek Narodowy Polski w Stanach Zjednoczonych Północnej Ameryki (Polish National Alliance in the United States of North America—PNA), founded in 1873 and 1880, respectively. During the 1880s, the PRCU and PNA subsumed many of the local Polish Catholic associations that existed in the Pennsylvania mining regions. By 1900, there were ninety-nine PNA and thirty-six PRCU locals located in the state, representing over 20 percent of the national number of affiliate members of each respective organization.[52]

Both the PRCU and the PNA played important economic and cultural roles in the lives of newly arriving Polish immigrants. As mutual-aid (insurance) societies, each provided sickness, disability, and death benefits to Polish workers and their families, especially important in a period of American history when state and employer welfare programs were virtually nonexistent. Through their locals, the two associations also provided Poles a social meeting space where cultures and traditions could be strengthened and ties to the homeland maintained. The PRCU and PNA were also active politically, promoting the socialization of Poles into American society. Various locals offered English classes and aided their members in applying for American citizenship. To redress the lack of higher learning institutions accessible to Poles in the United States, both organizations established liberal arts colleges designed to encourage greater social mobility.[53]

Most important, each organization was committed to representing Polish political interests on the local and national level. By turning out the ethnic vote, they became sizable ethnic lobby groups that raised the image and stature of American Polonia. In northeastern Pennsylvania, the PRCU and PNA were fervent election organizers. Although overall Polish participation in elections was low because many Poles were not legal citizens, the agitation of these associations was instrumental in helping Poles gain elected office. In Dickson City, near Scranton, a Polish mayor was elected in 1906, and Poles captured four local elected government seats in Shenandoah in 1909. One of the best election triumphs occurred in the city of Nanticoke, where Poles gained five city council seats, one school committee seat, and the office of city constable in 1902.[54]

On the national level, both the PRCU and PNA organizations campaigned for the appointment of an ethnic Polish bishop to the church hierarchy, efforts that led to Paul Rhode's becoming auxiliary bishop of Chicago in 1908. To counter the immigration restrictionists who sought to exclude Poles from the American body politic on moral and racial grounds, the PRCU and PNA campaigned against anti-immigration measures. Outreach efforts were organized to inform the American public of Polish contributions to the cause of democracy and Poland's historic links to the United States. In this regard, special emphasis was placed on the historical roles of Casimir Pułaski and Thaddeus Kościuszko, Polish officers who fought under George Washington in the American War of Independence and against the partitioning powers in the homeland. By 1910, the PNA successfully lobbied for congressional funding for the erection of public monuments in Washington, D.C., to these two figures.[55]

Despite sharing certain goals and functions, there were ideological differences between the PRCU and the PNA. The PRCU, established by exile priests from Prussian Poland who clashed with the Irish-led church hierarchy in the United States over issues of spiritual care, sought to blend Catholic traditionalism with elements of modern nationalist movements. Membership in the organization was limited to ethnic Poles who were Catholics and followed the teachings of the church.[56] Programmatically, the PRCU focused on "organic" work designed to develop and strengthen Polish Catholic religious life and culture in the United States, not on the struggle for Polish independence. Although the PRCU supported a free Poland and actively organized relief efforts to their countrymen in times of crisis, the tradition of religious conservatism within the organization made it more reluctant to actively engage in the partisan atmosphere of Polish homeland politics. When it did, the PRCU generally sympathized with the anti-German, right-wing National Democratic (Endek) Party.[57]

By contrast, although the majority of PNA members were Catholics, the association also included other ethnicities and faiths that came from within the historic boundaries of pre-partitioned Poland. Lithuanians and Ukrainians as well as Protestants and Jews could become members. In its first two decades of existence, the PNA was an anticlerical, socially liberal, and fervently nationalistic association. Many PNA founders were veterans of the 1863 January Uprising against Russian domination, and a key goal of the association, written into its constitution, was to promote among immigrants the cause of Polish independence within the historic boundaries of Poland "by all legitimate means." Though its leadership was largely liberal and middle-class, the PNA did have a fair number of socialists and their sympathizers within its ranks. This was particularly true in northeastern Pennsylvania, where at the turn of the century numerous local associations as well as PNA leaders associated themselves with the Polish National Catholic Church (PNCC) and its quasi-socialist, firebrand leader Francis Hodur. Such figures included John Kucki (vice-censor of the national PNA), John Sliwinski (regional organizer and from 1907 editor of the PNCC's *Straż* newspaper), W. G. Sawa (head of the PNA education commission), and Stanisław Dangel (member of the PNA press board, editor of *Straż* until 1907, and from 1913 to 1915 editor of *Zgoda*, the PNA's weekly newspaper).[58]

In the decade before and especially after World War I, the orientation of the PNA began to shift. Socialist influence declined, anticlericalism ebbed, and the political direction of the organization shifted to the right. This development was driven, first and foremost, by the triumph of midwestern conservatives over eastern liberals in internal PNA power struggles on issues regarding the role of Roman Catholicism in the association and homeland politics. Specifically, midwestern activists sought to abandon the association's traditional neutrality on religious matters, take the PNA in a publicly pro–Roman Catholic direction, and purge members with ties to socialist or independent religious movements. Related to this development was also a push to abandon the past support the PNA had shown to the Polish Socialist Party (PPS) in the homeland in favor of the National Democrats.[59]

In addition to the PRCU and the PNA, there were other sizable fraternal societies in northeastern Pennsylvania, including the left-wing, PNCC-affiliated Polsko-Narodowa Spójnia (Polish National Union—PNU) and the staunchly conservative Unia Polska w Stanach Zjednoczonych Ameryce Polnocnej Ameryki (Polish Union in the United States of North America—PU USA), both of which were founded in the region, but had a nation-wide reach.[60] In some of the larger communities where Poles lived, such as Scranton, Wilkes-Barre, and Shamokin, the New York–based Związek

Socjalistów Polskich (Alliance of Polish Socialists) and Polska Sekcja Socjalstycznej Partii (Polish Section of the [American] Socialist Party) also had a presence. In Coaldale, Polish socialists even managed to control the city council from 1902 to 1907, though the overall influence of socialist associations on Polish electoral politics was generally limited.[61]

For Polish youth, the primary political associations were local Sokoły affiliated with the Pittsburgh-based Związek Sokołów Polskich (Polish Falcons Alliance—PFA). American Sokoły were fully independent of their forebears in the homeland and in the Ruhr, though their political orientation and goals were similar. Namely, they targeted their efforts at preparing the minds and bodies of Polish youth for the independence struggle in the homeland. As the revised 1914 PFA charter declared, "The object of the Polish Falcons Alliance of America is to regenerate the Polish race in body and spirit and create of the immigrant a National asset, for the purpose of exerting every possible influence towards attaining political independence of the fatherland." In northeastern Pennsylvania, at least fifty Sokoły were organized by 1914; like their counterparts in the Ruhr, these organizations organized drills with blunted swords and public processions to display their readiness to defend their nationality.[62] At the same time, the Sokół movement recognized that it also had an obligation to aid the adaptation of Polish youth to American society and believed that the best means to accomplish this was through a strengthening of Polish identity. Felix Pietrowicz, who organized the American Sokoły in the late 1880s, best summarized this idea when he noted, "A 'Falcon' is the modern transformation of an ancient man into a modern man and . . . into a 'new' and different, better Pole and therefore better United States citizen."[63]

As in the Ruhr, there also developed a variety of nonpolitical cultural associations, such as choral societies and sports clubs, as well as independent women's associations.[64] The most influential women's association was the Związek Polek (Polish Women's Alliance—PWA), which aided women in obtaining a greater independent voice both within the ethnic community and the larger American society. Founded in 1898 in Chicago, the PWA grew to become the largest independent Polish women's association in the United States by World War I. Initially organized to aid women economically by providing needed insurance that the PNA refused to provide, the PWA subsequently developed a far-reaching cultural and political program designed to show, as organizer Emily Napieralski claimed, that women "could perform their home duties as well as before and notwithstanding that fact could also think broader, take deeper interest in social and national work."[65] To support its outreach effort, the PWA established in 1902 the *Głos Polek*, which had the largest circulation of any Polish-American women's daily. National and internationally, the PWA embraced a first-wave feminist agenda, lobbying hard for the passage of laws restricting child labor and women's labor, supporting the growing suffrage movement, and promoting the cause of an independent Poland. On the local level, PWA locals in northeastern Pennsylvania engaged in various cultural and educational activities including organizing Polish-language classes for women and children and other courses celebrating ethnic culture and history. The PWA also arranged summer camps for Polish youth and, in order to promote ethnic social advancement, offered financial support for those youths seeking a secondary education.[66] Altogether, the PWA encouraged the proposition that women could be active in political affairs and still fulfill traditional maternal roles, especially with regard to raising children, the future of the Polish nation. Although this political position increased Polish women's respectability and conformed to the gender norms of their host societies, it also placed limits on the degree to which the PWA could promote the emancipation and full equality of its members.

Polish Organizational Responses and Their Influence on Integration

Poles in the Ruhr and northeastern Pennsylvania confronted enormous challenges in gaining acceptance. The belief was widespread that this ethnic minority posed a threat to the security and health of the nation. Prussian officials sought a solution to its Polish question in the Ruhr by impinging on the civil rights of Poles, despite the fact that they were legal citizens, in the misguided belief that enough use of the proverbial stick would force Poles to eventually eat the carrot of Verschmelzung, or outright assimilation. Local, state, and federal governments in the United States interfered little in the day-to-day affairs of Poles, though starting in the 1890s a growing consensus emerged that Poles, on moral and racial grounds, were unfit to become Americans. Attempts were subsequently made to limit their presence and ability to become citizens. Such anti-immigrant attitudes reflected the panic over Polish immigration within the German and American public imagination. Though there were dissenters who argued that Poles could become good citizens and assets to the nation, this view increasingly was in the minority, especially in Germany.

In response to the efforts to exclude and discriminate against them, Poles focused on network building through ethnic associations to defend their rights. The types of ethnic associations varied widely, reflecting the diversity of immigrants. Some were religious, others secular. Some were right-wing and ethnically exclusive, others more inclusive and left-leaning. All were nationalist and committed to preserving Polish culture and identity. Regardless of orientation, Polish ethnic associations went far in helping Poles build their communities and promote their structural integration in their adopted societies. This can be seen in Germany, where despite attempts to impose restrictions on their activity, associations actively mobilized their members to participate in and achieve success in elections, use the courts to defend their rights, and become visible in the public sphere. In the United States, associations provided many Poles with an important degree of economic security not otherwise available to them. They aided Polish political mobilization at the local and national level. Exposing Polish immigrants to American political practices, associations also helped Poles challenge public perceptions that they were "un-American" through activities such as organizing civic education efforts linking Polish and American ideals and values. Perhaps the best illustration of the role of associations in promoting integration occurred in the development of women's associations, where women could build their own networks within patriarchal societies, promote their ethnic and gender interests, and begin practicing democracy at a time when they did not possess the vote.

Polish associations in northeastern Pennsylvania diverged from those in the Ruhr in three key respects. First, many in northeastern Pennsylvania were also mutual-aid (insurance) societies, which served important economic as well as political and cultural functions in the life of migrants. In the Ruhr, associations generally did not play as large an economic role because of the existence of state and employer-sponsored welfare programs. Second, Polish associations in northeastern Pennsylvania were more varied across the political spectrum, whereas in the Ruhr, right-leaning associations tended to predominate. Finally, associations in northeastern Pennsylvania were better vertically integrated into larger, national Polish federations possessing significant financial resources. This enabled Poles to effectively act as an ethnic lobby and make their voices heard on a national stage. The economic resources of Polish organizations in the Ruhr, and Germany as a whole, were paltry by comparison. Over the long term such differences made the Polish associational position in northeastern Pennsylvania stronger than in the Ruhr, a development that had important repercussions on community development and integration when tested by the burdens of World War I and its aftermath.

BY THE EVE OF World War I, stable and vibrant Polish communities were firmly established in the Ruhr and northeastern Pennsylvania. Although Poles continued to suffer discrimination at the hands of the state and the middle class, they were increasingly accepted as an integral part of working-class society in both regions, and Polish organizational activities promoted a strong degree of structural integration. World War I and its aftermath challenged this state of affairs, most notably in Germany, where defeat in the war fundamentally altered state and society, but also in the United States, where victory abroad gave new stimulus to defining who belonged to the American nation. This chapter examines how Polish attitudes, ethnic community cohesion, and the stability of prewar adaptation patterns were transformed during wartime and in the postwar period.

Polish Communities during World War I

Poles in both the Ruhr and northeastern Pennsylvania were loyal to the war efforts of their adopted societies. In the Ruhr, Polish organizations such as the ZZP declared their support for the *Burgfrieden,* the declared wartime civil truce between capital, labor, and the state, while thousands of Ruhr Poles joined the Prussian army. The first two years of the war were marked by a general decline in Polish activity. Many Poles previously active in Polish ethnic associations were called to serve and the Burgfrieden severely restricted the extent to which organizations such as the ZZP could be politically engaged. A telling example of the severe wartime political climate occurred in the matter of Russian-Polish forced labor in the mines. The ZZP, along with the Alter Verband, protested the use of wartime prisoners beginning in 1915, but were forced to retreat on the matter by early

1916 after the government threatened those who continued to raise the issue with fines, imprisonment, and charges of treason.[1] At the end of 1916, the Polish political position vis-à-vis the state improved after the German government declared that a nominally independent Poland would be established under the auspices of the Central Powers on successful conclusion of the war. The support the government gave for a postwar Polish state, made partly in reaction to Russian promises to Poles, led to the easing of most of the Prussian government's anti-Polish measures. Prohibitions that had been in place for decades, such as bans on the celebration of national holidays, the wearing of national symbols, and various language ordinances were rescinded by early 1917. Official police surveillance and harassment of Polish activities stopped.[2]

The increased freedom of action brought little relief to Poles suffering under the material, physical, and emotional hardships of war. Food shortages, a scarcity in consumer goods, and a decline in real wages made life in the Ruhr during the final two years of the war difficult, and by 1917 sporadic wildcat strikes by German and Polish miners occurred.[3] The fed-up, militant attitude of many Poles in the coalfields driven by economic deprivation led to the founding of the Narodowe Stronnictwo Robotników (National Party of Workers—NSR) at the end of the year. The NSR had its roots in the ZZP and was organized to channel dissatisfaction in a Christian-socialist direction and thus avert the danger that Polish workers would be attracted to radical socialist and communist organizations. The NSR officially disavowed class struggle, yet simultaneously called for far-reaching social reforms in German society.[4] Because the end of World War I radically altered the geopolitical landscape, the NSR had little chance to implement its political program in the Ruhr. Nevertheless, in postwar Poland, the NSR would achieve electoral success. After merging with other, smaller, working-class parties in Poland, the NSR renamed itself the Narodowa Partia Robotnicza (National Workers' Party—NPR) and captured twenty-eight seats in the first Polish parliament.[5]

In northeastern Pennsylvania, the late entry of the United States into the war meant that Poles there were never exposed to the same level of social dislocation and deprivation experienced by their ethnic brethren in the Ruhr. During the first three years of the war, rising demand for coal brought significant wage increases to Polish miners, and by the end of 1917, wages were 25 to 50 percent above their prewar levels. For the first time, the industry also managed to guarantee nearly full-time, year-round employment.

After the United States entered the war in April 1917, turmoil in the workplace did increase as production intensified and inflation began to eat into earlier wage gains, causing miners to complain bitterly that they were unable to make a living. As a consequence, rank-and-file militancy grew, culminating most visibly in a wildcat strike of more than 25,000 workers in September 1918. However, Poles in northeastern Pennsylvania remained in a far better economic position than their counterparts in the Ruhr.[6]

The same held true in terms of ethnic community development. During the war, Polish ethnic cultural activities expanded rapidly. Especially important were relief efforts to aid Poles in war-torn Poland. Tensions within the community did emerge between 1914 and early 1917 over which side to support in the war, with immigrant Poles from Prussia and Austria initially gravitating to the cause of the Central Powers, while those from Russian Poland tending to favor the Entente. This debate, however, became moot once the United States entered the conflict and, with the onset of war, Poles rallied around the flag in large numbers. More than 215,000 Poles enlisted in the United States Army, and another 20,000 joined the French-sponsored Polish legions under General Józef Haller. A grim, if telling, statistic of Polish dedication to the American cause is highlighted by the fact that although Poles comprised less than 4 percent of the American population, they accounted for approximately 12 percent of American losses on the battlefield. On the home front, Polish leaders and ethnic newspapers encouraged Poles to prove that they were "100% American" through actions such as buying war bonds. In one Pennsylvania mine district, it was claimed that Poles invested $11,000,000 in the Third Liberty Loan bond issue. Enthusiasm for the American war effort was especially strong after President Wilson's January 1918 "Fourteen Points" speech to Congress in which he called for an independent Poland, thus linking the destiny of Poland with that of the United States as never before.[7] Overall, the war was an important event in the history of American Polonia since it offered Poles new opportunities to become political actors on the public stage. Moreover, World War I provided a means through which Polish migrants could prove their loyalty in a period when anti-immigrant and anti-foreigner sentiment was running high.

The Polish Community in the Ruhr, 1919–1924

The end of the war and defeat of Imperial Germany in November 1918 brought forth many heartening changes for Poles. After 123 years, an independent, democratic Polish state was reestablished, fulfilling a dream that only a few years earlier seemed impossible. Under the republican Weimar government, trade unions such as the ZZP were officially recognized and given a genuine voice on labor matters vis-à-vis employers, raising hope that a more equitable society would emerge out of the destruction of war. In addition, the Versailles Treaty provided Poles living in Germany with wide-ranging minority protections, including the right to Polish-language education for children and an official end to formal police interference in organizational activities. The potential existed for Polish society in the Ruhr to develop free of past restrictions.[8] However, Poles also faced significant problems in the postwar environment. Many Germans could not understand how Germany lost the war and felt that the nation had been betrayed. The building of the Polish state through German territorial concessions, as mandated by the Versailles Treaty, produced widespread anti-Polish resentment among all German social classes. This antipathy grew as tensions between the German and Polish governments over final borders and the status of ethnic minorities in each country increased. Further, the fact that Poland was closely allied with France caused many in German society to view Poles as a potentially traitorous fifth column.[9]

The weakness of the early Weimar social order also adversely affected Poles. Economically, although employment in the immediate postwar period was plentiful due to the need of German industry to service war reparations, the growing rate of inflation, which exploded with the French occupation of the Ruhr in 1923, caused a decline in real wages; food shortages were also common.[10] Even more troublesome was the growing radicalization of politics on the left and the right. In 1919–20, strikes by revolutionary procommunist groups and the failed right-wing Kapp Putsch destabilized the entire region. Although Poles generally remained aloof from these events since they considered them "German matters," they caused widespread insecurity within the community. Further, Prussian administrative officials, many of whom remained from the old regime, suspected that Poles were behind some of the turmoil and surreptitiously again began to monitor their activities.[11] Most ominous was the growing hostility of working-class Germans toward Poles. Although all of the German trade unions in the Ruhr spoke out against interethnic animosity, many in the rank and file ignored these appeals. Communists blamed Poles for thwarting the success of the revolutionary movement in the Ruhr, particularly after the Soviet defeat in the Polish-Soviet War (1919–21). Newly arrived German refugees from Poland demanded that employers fire Poles in retribution for their own dislocation.[12] Anti-Polish resentment within the German working class was especially strong as a consequence of the 1921 plebiscite in Upper Silesia and the French occupation of the Ruhr in 1923.

To determine the final border between Germany and Poland, the Versailles Treaty mandated a plebiscite for March 1921 in the ethnically mixed counties of Upper Silesia. Many inhabitants of the Ruhr, both German and Polish, were eligible to participate in this referendum.[13] From the middle of 1920 onward, the campaign for the hearts and minds of Upper Silesians was waged with intensity. The Polish government sent activists into the Ruhr who worked with Polish political organizations such as the NPR to conduct mass meetings on behalf of the Polish cause. The German government tried to thwart these activities, arresting and even charging certain politically active Poles with treason.[14] The government also turned a blind eye to, and at times clandestinely aided, the actions of German working-class nationalist groups such as the Verband heimattreuer Oberschlesier (Association of Loyal Upper Silesians), which waged an intense and violent intimidation campaign against Poles planning to vote in the referendum.[15] In August 1920, Heimattreuer members held assemblies throughout the Ruhr demanding that the government undertake measures to deal with the Polish menace; their demands included the deportation of all Poles from the Ruhr, the confiscation of Polish property to make up for the losses suffered by Germans in the province of Posen, and the closing of Polish newspapers. At these meetings, the Entente powers were also accused of secretly planning to Polonize the Ruhr.[16] Throughout late 1920 and 1921, armed Heimattreuer members regularly broke up Polish meetings, threatening men, women, and children with clubs, knives, and guns. The extent of the violence led Stanislaus Kunca, editor of *Wiarus Polski,* to decry in April 1921 that the postwar security situation was intolerable, noting that "the Germans, with the exceptions of the courts which treat us fairly, are sowing ever more hate."[17]

Anti-Polish sentiment within the German working class further intensified after the French, with their Belgian allies, occupied the Ruhr industrial region in January 1923 in order to force Germany to fulfill reparation obligations mandated by the Versailles Treaty. Responding to the occupation, Ruhr workers refused to work the mines or man the factories and, with subsidies provided by the government in Berlin, organized a homegrown passive resistance campaign. Polish workers readily joined with their

German colleagues in this resistance effort. As an article in the *Wiarus Polski* declared in early January, "Polish workers, as the German workers, know quite well . . . how they should act. . . . [Fellow Poles] be ready to fulfill the duties to the state of which you are citizens." The ZZP likewise condemned "French and Belgian imperialism." Throughout the passive resistance campaign, German government reports confirmed that Poles, by and large, refused to cooperate with the occupation, severely disappointing French officials who hoped to persuade Poles to work as strikebreakers. Despite these facts, a widespread belief among German workers spread, especially from mid-1923 onward, that Poles were aiding the occupation authorities by operating the mines and factories, a misperception that further deteriorated the Polish position in the Ruhr.[18]

Altogether, postwar developments in the Ruhr promoted the attitude among many Germans that Poles could never be fellow citizens; they were instead *Fremdkörper*, or foreign bodies alien to the national community, a sentiment that strengthened the hand of Polish nationalists who likewise believed that German and Polish interests were irreconcilable and advised Poles to return to Poland. As a downward spiral of mutual recrimination and distrust developed, thousands of Poles decided it was indeed time to leave. Many Germans were glad to see them go.[19]

Leaders of the Polish community had been preparing for an eventual return to Poland as early as 1916, when the intention to create a Polish state under Central Power auspices was announced. After Poland reestablished its independence in 1918, a sizable number of Poles immediately emigrated. Polish organizations such as the ZZP, which was already firmly ensconced in the former Prussian eastern provinces, focused on building an independent trade union movement throughout the newly reunified country. Estimates are that by August 1919 approximately 40,000 Ruhr Poles returned to Poznań; figures for the other eastern provinces do not exist.[20]

The decision to either stay in the Ruhr or return to Poland was not easy. Poles had put down roots and achieved a degree of economic success. The choice of leaving for an uncertain future in Poland divided family and friends within the community, an insecurity that was not eased by the extremely chaotic nature of return migration in the immediate postwar period. The exact borders of the new state, visa requirements, and procedures for regulating settlement were not well defined. On returning to the homeland, many Ruhr Poles, given their experience in the west, expected to be greeted warmly and be able to obtain positions of influence within the new Polish society. Most were sorely disappointed by the dismal economic conditions and job prospects. In fact, many of the initial migrants later returned to the Ruhr, spreading news of the unstable conditions in Poland. By 1920 most Poles adopted a "wait and see" attitude to the idea of returning to the homeland, particularly after the outbreak of war with Soviet Russia.[21] Rising ethnic tensions in the Ruhr and Polish victory in war soon accelerated the migration of Poles back to Poland from the end of 1920 onward. Return migration was also stimulated by provisions in the Versailles Treaty requiring Poles in the Ruhr who wished to acquire Polish citizenship to declare their intent to do so by January 1922; otherwise, they would remain and henceforth be treated as German citizens. Eventually, the status of many Poles would be resolved only by final bilateral agreements signed by the Polish and German governments in August 1924.[22]

Exact statistics for 1919 to 1924 are unavailable, but rough estimates are that 100,000 to 130,000 Poles returned to Poland in that period. To aid those Poles who wished to return, the Polish government established a vice-consulate in Essen in 1920. A key duty of the vice-consulate was to screen applicants for Polish citizenship. Those wishing to gain a Polish passport first needed to prove to the satisfaction of officials that they were not only ethnically Polish but nationally minded as well, usually by producing a statement from an approved Polish organization testifying to the applicant's good character. This procedure was specifically adopted in order to prevent those Poles with socialist sympathies or other radicals from returning. In this capacity, the vice-consulate directly assisted 50,000–60,000 Poles in the Ruhr between 1920 and early 1922 in obtaining citizenship, though it should be noted that this figure was well below the total number of Poles who were eligible.[23]

One key reason that more Poles did not apply for citizenship was that, even as conflicts between Poles and Germans were rising, so too were tensions between Poles in the Ruhr and the Polish government. To limit the social problems that would ensue in Poland by a mass exodus from the Ruhr, the Polish government urged only those Poles to apply for citizenship who could financially support themselves in the homeland. However, this position left many feeling that the Polish government was abandoning them. Further, among some working-class Poles, there was also disillusionment with the state of Polish society. At a ZZP meeting of more than 350 Poles in Bochum-Wattenschied, a Polish speaker named Roschak highlighted this sentiment when he proclaimed that the "rule of the capitalists and the churchmen [in Poland] takes on increasingly worse forms. The entire press is in their hands. The princes and priests work in the same manner today as they did under the Prussian government. . . . Here people always blame the German capitalists; however, we must at the same time not forget, that the Polish capitalists are not any better."[24]

As an alternative to Poland, increasing numbers of Poles looked to migrate to northern France; the Polish government supported this development because it eliminated the threat returnees might pose to an already strained postwar economic situation, aided a key interwar ally, and deprived Germany of essential labor power for its recovery. For some Poles, France was an acceptable substitute destination. French mine companies were desperate for workers and keen to import skilled Polish miners from the Ruhr. In addition to offering stable social conditions, France was also not an altogether unfamiliar foreign environment. A community of twelve thousand Poles, originally from the Ruhr, had already settled in the mining regions of northern France before World War I. Beginning in 1920, French mine agents surreptitiously began recruiting Poles with the support of the Polish government and Essen vice-consulate; by year's end nearly three thousand miners had migrated. Recruitment slowed to a halt in 1921 after Poles who had worked in France returned to the Ruhr and circulated reports of the poor conditions in French mines. In 1922, migration increased again, with close to ten thousand workers leaving for France. After the occupation of the Ruhr by France in 1923 and labor unrest in the Ruhr in 1924, migration intensified. By the end of 1925, the vice-consul in Essen estimated that approximately twenty-five thousand Polish mine workers (and one hundred thousand dependents) moved to France.[25]

The Polish community in the Ruhr was a shadow of its former self after 1924. Although more than a hundred thousand Poles continued to live in the Ruhr, the vitality of the ethnic community declined. This can be seen in the dramatic drop in membership experienced by various Polish organizations. In 1920 there were 45,000 Poles organized in the ZZP's miners' union in 1920; only 3,000 members remained by 1925. There were 117 Sokół clubs with a total membership of 6,900 in 1912, yet in 1925 a mere 24 clubs with a total membership of 623 still existed.[26] More important, the ability of the ethnic community to survive and reproduce itself into the second and third generation was in jeopardy. Enrollment in Polish-language classes, which Poles organized with much fanfare beginning in 1919, fell dramatically. German sources note that whereas there were approximately

10,700 students enrolled in Polish-language classes in 1921, this number declined to fewer than 3,000 students by 1922. Polish sources suggest that there were still nearly 8,000 taking Polish-language classes in 1922, though this figure fell to fewer than 2,400 in 1928 and approximately 1,500 by the eve of World War II.[27] All told, the sizable decline in ethnic activity led the Polish consulate in Essen to report at the end of 1925 that the Polish community in the Ruhr could no longer be considered part of the *emigracja* (Polish emigration), but instead was now a "naturalized Polish colony" in the process of slowly dissolving itself into German society. Recognizing that Polish political loyalties were increasingly to the German state and society, the consulate concluded that the Polish government should concentrate on helping Poles preserve their ethnic traditions and culture in order to maintain a degree of influence.[28]

For those Poles who remained, the survival of the ethnic community in the face of massive emigration was of great concern. To aid in preserving ethnic consciousness, Polish leaders from the Ruhr, together with representatives of Polish minorities in Berlin and eastern Germany, established in 1922 a new Związek Polaków w Niemczech (Union of Poles in Germany, or ZPwN) with headquarters in Berlin. The goals of the newly constituted ZPwN were, in the light of changed postwar circumstances, to ensure the protection of Polish minority rights in Germany and preserve ties to the Polish nation, while maintaining a loyal relationship to the German state. The founding of the ZPwN was well received by Poles across Germany and sixteen thousand Ruhr Poles were members by 1930.[29]

The protection that the ZPwN offered was important. Despite minority rights guarantees provided by the Versailles Treaty, Ruhr Poles continued to face discrimination and derision in the 1920s and 1930s. Some teachers tormented the children of Polish leaders or those who took Polish courses. A town in the Herne region even prohibited Polish inscriptions on gravestones in the city cemetery. During the Nazi era, everyday discrimination intensified, despite an official accord on minority rights signed by the Nazi and Polish governments in 1934. Poles active in ethnic affairs were watched by the Gestapo, and those suspected of not being sufficiently loyal to the "German nation" singled out for sanction. In the workplace, those who did not join the Deutsche Arbeitsfront (German Work Front) faced difficulty in their jobs and younger Poles often failed to find apprenticeships unless they belonged to the Hitler Youth.[30] Against this inequity, the ZPwN made frequent appeals directly to the highest levels of government. Although unable to end all abuses, the ZPwN was successful in ensuring that the most egregious examples of discrimination were corrected. The outspokenness of the ZPwN, however, came with a tragic price. With the outbreak of World War II, the ZPwN leadership throughout Germany was arrested and placed in concentration camps. In the Ruhr, 249 representatives were detained. Of the 136 leaders of this organization that were eventually murdered by the regime, 41 came from the Ruhr region.[31] In spite of this brutality, the ZPwN persevered. After World War II, the organization was reestablished, with headquarters in Bochum, where it remains active to this day.

The formation and continued existence of the ZPwN highlights the determination of Poles in the Ruhr to preserve ethnic identity across generations and in difficult times. Nevertheless, Poles were unable to regain the high level of cohesion that marked the community before World War I. The lack of significant numbers of new migrants to the Ruhr after the early 1920s limited the extent to which the ethnic community could replenish its losses and remain dynamic. More important, the Poles of the first generation who remained in the Ruhr were the ones most comfortable within a German cultural milieu. For them, bonds to their local communities outweighed increasingly distant ties to the homeland. This was particularly true for their children, the majority of whom were born and raised in the Ruhr, spoke fluent German and did not need or want the protection that a strong ethnic community afforded, especially given the assimilationist pressure from within German society during the late 1920s and 1930s. Although this second generation would for the most part continue to value and venerate certain elements of its ethnic heritage, ethnicity became more of a sensibility than a primary means of self-identification. With this transformation, the history of the Polish community in the Ruhr gradually drew to a close.

The Polish Community in Northeastern Pennsylvania, 1919–1924

In northeastern Pennsylvania, the challenges faced by Poles after World War I were much less severe, but they still threatened ethnic community cohesion and survival. Economically, the position of miners reached an apogee after the war, when average annual earnings rose to nearly $1,500, an increase of approximately 40 percent over 1901 levels after adjusting for inflation. However, the postwar anthracite industry rapidly went into decline; jobs were lost and livelihoods became threatened. In 1920–21, a nationwide recession caused coal production to fall precipitously. Meanwhile, newer and cheaper fuels such as oil and natural gas were making steep inroads, breaking the monopoly on the domestic heating market that coal producers had enjoyed for years. The dismal performance of the industry led to the outbreak of significant labor strife, bringing to an end the twenty-year period of relative labor peace that had prevailed since the strike of 1902. In early 1922, employers demanded a 21.5 percent wage cut across the board because of declining profits. The UMW, claiming that employers were purposely underreporting income, refused and instead demanded a 20 percent increase in wages. The ensuing strike brought the industry to a standstill from April to September. In the end, both sides agreed to return to the old wage rates. In September 1925, another massive strike occurred, again over wages, which ended in February 1926 when both sides extended the existing wage structure for five years.[32]

Thanks to the support of Poles and other eastern and southern European laborers, the UMW was able to maintain it strength in the anthracite fields during the early to mid-1920s, a real accomplishment given the pitiful state of organized labor during the decade. The strikes, however, only added to the woes of the anthracite industry, as frustrated consumers permanently switched to alternative fuels. By 1930, coal production stood at 69 million tons, down from a prewar peak of 113 million tons in 1913. Employment correspondingly declined, and the onset of the Great Depression soon devastated what remained of the industry. By 1937, fewer than one hundred thousand laborers worked in mining.[33] Despite a brief resurgence during World War II, the decline of the anthracite industry led thousands of workers, including many Poles, to leave for better employment opportunities elsewhere in the country, a depopulation trend that continues to the present day among third and fourth generation Polish-American ethnics living in this economically depressed region.[34]

Politically and culturally, the postwar period was turbulent. With victory against the external enemy secured, the nation looked inward to fight perceived threats at home. In the immediate aftermath of the war and the Soviet revolution in Russia, campaigns against labor radicals and Bolsheviks, begun during the war, were waged with a new ferocity, culminating with the Red Scare period of 1919–20. In northeastern Pennsylvania, anticommunist hysteria ran particularly high given the large, and in the native mind-set oftentimes indistinguishable, eastern European industrial working class as well as the recent labor militancy that engulfed Pennsylvania and much of the nation during and after World War I. Falling victim to growing xenophobia,

Poles were viewed by many natives as disloyal and "un-American." In local newspapers, frequent warnings were issued from 1919 onward to be on the lookout for "reds" and foreign agitators, especially after eleven men with supposed ties to the IWW (Industrial Workers of the World) were arrested on April 1, 1919, for their activities in and around the predominantly Polish city of Nanticoke.[35] In early May 1919, the *Scranton Times* commented on the "Red Terror." Contrasting the "native born" with recent immigrants, the newspaper claimed that "the appeal of radicalism . . . is made to people primarily of foreign birth. This country has so many of them that there is always certainty of an audience or following. So many of them are people . . . unable to understand the false logic of the doctrines of the blatherskiites who preach to them from soap boxes. . . . America's Reds . . . are importations in 999 cases out of every 1000."[36]

To refute the perception that Poles were Bolsheviki, leading Polish citizens in Luzerne County organized a committee to combat the spread of Bolshevism. In late April 1919, this committee adopted a resolution declaring that:

> Whereas—Certain individuals interested in spreading Bolshevism throughout the world have been at work in the Wyoming Valley endeavoring to break down the good name and reputation of all loyal Polish citizens, and
> Whereas—The Polish citizens of this great valley have always been loyal to the laws of this country,
> Therefore, be it resolved—That it is the sense of this meeting that we protest against the false testimony as to the Polish citizens of this community being Bolsheviks and that we pledge ourselves to destroy any movement having for its object the spread of Bolshevism in our community.[37]

To further emphasize their allegiance, Polish leaders organized a "Polish loyalty" parade in May 1919 to visibly showcase the contributions made to the cause of American freedom as well as Polish sacrifice during World War I. Carrying banners declaring "America, Never to be Forgotten" and "America, We Thank Thee," more than ten thousand Poles marched in a parade through downtown Scranton with floats displaying the themes of Poland in distress and the German kaiser in chains as well as a funeral casket representing Polish and American losses in the war, attended by mourning women "symbolic of the womanhood of America and Poland." The local press commented very favorably on the latter float. Prominent politicians, including the lieutenant governor of the state, also spoke before those assembled to commend Poles on their service during World War I, and Poles passed resolutions praising President Wilson.[38]

Despite such public displays of loyalty, suspicions of "the foreigner" endured. At a Rotary Club meeting in Scranton in early May 1920, Homer Bobitt warned leading members of the community that "Scranton is surrounded by radicals." A former member of the American Expeditionary Force in northern Russia, Bobitt based his assessment on threats he received while visiting nearby Pittston, a working-class community with a large population of Poles and other eastern Europeans.[39] In 1923, the *Wall Street Journal* commented that the Pennsylvania anthracite region was a hotbed of communist radicalism, as witnessed by the 1922 strike, and warned of the dire consequences for the UMW if it did not exert control over its rank and file.[40]

The perception within "native" society that Poles, along with other eastern Europeans, were dangerous from a political standpoint was complemented by an equally strong belief that "the Slav" was racially inferior and posed a threat to the survival of "Anglo-Saxon" American society. From the late nineteenth century onward, laws and ordinances were passed to make it more difficult for new immigrants to naturalize, government studies were conducted to document "the immigrant problem," and increasing calls were made to restrict the influx of "undesirable races" from eastern and southern Europe. World War I gave new impetus to these efforts, as predictions that a flood of unwanted immigrants would swamp the country after the war became widely accepted. As *Coal Age* magazine reported in 1916, "Some authorities hold that the end of the war will bring a massive in-migration of people fleeing the desolation of Europe, a mass of despondent, destitute, needy, their sense of morality warped by memories of the past and the hopelessness of the future, their intellectual faculties deadened and brutalized by the scenes they were compelled to witness and the deeds they performed and their bodies weakened and diseased by exposure and an unsanitary environment." The magazine then concluded that such a development posed a "deadly peril for both American industry and American labor."[41]

Madison Grant's infamous *The Passing of the Great Race* was published that same year; it achieved enormous popular success. A member of the Immigration Restriction League, Grant galvanized support for the immigration restriction camp as never before. Claiming that morality and intellect derived from race, biologically defined, he warning that the superior "Anglo-Saxon" American race type was threatened with ruin by intermixture with the "human flotsam" of eastern and southern Europe.[42] By early 1917, fears of the immigrant threat led the United States Congress to ratify, over President Wilson's veto, legislation requiring immigrants to pass a literacy test before being granted admission into the United States. This literacy requirement became the first in a series of laws explicitly designed to reduce immigration from eastern and southern Europe. In late 1920, Congress passed a restriction bill limiting the number of immigrants from outside the Western Hemisphere to 3 percent of a given national group's representation within the general United States population, based on the 1910 census. Though vetoed by Wilson, Congress revisited the measure the following session at the urging of newly elected President Warren Harding, a fervent restrictionist. As passed and signed into legislation in May 1921, the Quota Act reduced the number of immigrants that could enter in a given year (July through June) to 357,803. Under the 3 percent rule, Poles received a maximum quota of 25,827, 31,146, and 30,977 for the 1921–22, 1922–23, and 1923–24 periods, respectively.[43]

The 1921 Quota Act was designed to discriminate against eastern and southern Europeans. Based on the 1910 census, such migrants received a significantly smaller immigrant quota than that assigned to Western European countries, whose quotas were larger and exceeded actual demand. Germany, for example, received a quota of 67,607 in 1922–23, yet only 49,250 Germans immigrated that year.[44] As passed, the Quota Act was a temporary measure. Yet the legislation's success in reducing unwanted immigration from eastern and southern Europe brought forth calls for a permanent quota system to be enacted. In 1924, Congress passed the National Origins Act, which applied an even more stringent quota system with regard to eastern and southern Europeans. As adopted, the yearly total number of immigrants from outside the Western Hemisphere allowed to enter the United States was limited to 164,667. The quota percentage assigned to each national group affected by the legislation was reduced to 2 percent and based on the older 1890 census. This change effectively brought to an end to all further migration of eastern and southern Europeans into the United States since most of these new immigrants settled in the country after 1890. Poland saw its annual quota reduced to 5,982 after 1924, whereas older immigrant nations such as Germany still enjoyed a generous quota of 51,227.[45]

Despite the rise in native animosity and the traditionally high rates of prewar return migration, the idea of going home after World War I was not appealing to the vast majority of Poles. Polish independence in 1918 did ignite a great euphoria among Poles in America who through their ethnic associations, including many throughout northeastern Pennsylvania, raised large sums of money for postwar relief work. Volunteers who had joined the Haller army left France and went to Poland to fight for the newfound state against the Red Army in 1920. Grey Samaritans, a Red Cross unit composed of Polish women, went to Poland to alleviate malnutrition and disease. The Scranton-based PNCC began transferring its populist, egalitarian ideological message back to the homeland. Nevertheless, the relationship between American Polonia and Poland in the postwar period was strained, and only approximately one hundred thousand Poles from across the United States decided to permanently return between 1919 and 1923.[46]

There were many reasons for this limited return rate. The immigration restrictions in the United States clearly played a role since Poles who were not citizens ran the risk, unlike in the prewar era, of not being permitted to reenter the United States should they go to Poland. More important, Poles were disillusioned by the stories they heard from those who did return. Economic conditions were dismal, and some of those who went back home lost all of their money on failed business ventures. Similar to their counterparts in the Ruhr, returning Polish migrants expected to be welcomed and play a prominent role in rebuilding Polish society; instead they were met with distrust. Members of the Polish government and leaders within the Catholic Church viewed returnees with suspicion, anxious that they would disrupt traditional power relationships. The foreign ministry conducted extensive background checks on American Poles wishing to return in the hopes of preventing those infected with the "socialist bug" from entering the country. The PNCC was never legally recognized and found its efforts to establish a sizable independent church movement largely frustrated. On the local level, priests in villages would complain to their bishops about the immorality of returnees who continually challenged their authority. Perhaps the most telling example of native Polish misgivings about returning migrants from the United States occurred in the case of the Haller Army, which after its transfer from France to Poland in 1919 was poorly supplied and largely abandoned by the Polish government during the Polish-Soviet War. The situation of the volunteers aroused sizable indignation among Poles in the United States, who looked to and later persuaded the United States government to send ships to retrieve some nineteen thousand members of that force.[47]

The advent of the Red Scare and the passage of various restrictive measures combined with the aversion to returning to Poland placed pressure on

Polish inhabitants in northeastern Pennsylvania to conform and "Americanize" as quickly as possible. Such pressure led Poles to stage displays of their loyalty through parades and proclamations, as occurred in Scranton in 1919. Americanization was also driven through citizenship campaigns as well as the rise of popular culture, where American identity was propagated in films, music, and other media.[48] The lack of new ethnic lifeblood entering the community after 1924 and the disgust with the treatment of Poles who did return to Poland forced migrants to ask themselves: Are we Polish or American?[49]

During the 1920s and through to the end of World War II most Poles attempted to split the difference, choosing to embrace a new Polish-American identity and culture. As the historian Hieronim Kubiak describes, "News of the fate of the returning immigrants disavowed in America the old conception of the task of the Polish immigration toward their independent fatherland and at the same time forced a transformation of the emigrant cultural and national institutions from their function from 'immigration for the old country' to 'immigration for the immigration.'" This new Polish-American culture would reach its zenith in the 1920s and 1930s, as highlighted by membership figures for Polish fraternal associations, which nearly doubled from 350,000 to 650,000 between 1924 and 1935.[50] Over the long term, sustaining the ethnic community would become difficult. Although Polonia organizations remain quite active in both the United States as a whole and in northeastern Pennsylvania in particular, overall membership has steadily declined due to socioeconomic transformations that occurred after World War II. These include changes in occupational mobility, suburbanization, as well as the rise of a third and fourth generation that speaks little Polish and often possesses only a vaguely defined sense of Polish identity.[51]

Polish Communities at the Crossroads

The First World War and, especially, its aftermath altered the relationship between Poles and their host societies considerably, forcing Poles to make hard choices about who they were and the direction of their communities. The position of Poles in the Ruhr after World War I was far more tenuous than that in northeastern Pennsylvania. Defeat in war and the tremendous economic hardship that followed gave rise to an unstable, at times violent social climate in which anti-Polish sentiment ran high. Despite officially gaining new minority protections under the Weimar government, these advances mattered little in an environment where the state often turned a blind eye to infringements on Polish civil rights. For minority groups, life in "illiberal" Wilhelmine Germany was in many ways a paradise compared to what came later under the Weimar regime.

The growing ethnic animosity and the deteriorating security situation led the majority of Poles in the Ruhr to leave the region and migrate back to Poland or on to France by 1924. However, a large minority of approximately 100,000 Poles, or one-third of the pre–World War I community, chose to stay, testifying to the roots that many Poles planted in the region during the Wilhelmine era. For those remaining after 1924, maintaining ethnic group cohesion was difficult. Polish ethnic institutions never recovered from the loss of two-thirds of the prewar Polish population, and assimilation pressures were intense. This was especially true in the case of second generation Poles. As a consequence, although Ruhr Poles would not become fully accepted as Germans until after World War II, the process of their assimilation, albeit in many respects forced by both German and Polish government policies, was well under way in the interwar period.

Poles in northeastern Pennsylvania never experienced the same degree of economic privation and social adversity between 1914 and 1924, though they too faced enormous challenges as levels of nativism, xenophobia, and nationalism within American society reached new heights. Fears ran rampant that foreigners and Bolsheviks were threatening the social order, prompting many to cast aspersions on Poles and others of Slavic origin. To this were added dire warnings claiming that the "Anglo-Saxon" nation was committing race suicide, leading the federal government to pass a series of discriminatory immigration restrictions, culminating in the racist National Origins Act of 1924. Within such a political atmosphere, Poles in northeastern Pennsylvania needed to decide whether to remain in the United States or return to Poland. The vast majority ultimately chose to stay. The reasons for this decision vary. Poles already had progressed far in becoming stakeholders within local society, while poor economic conditions in Poland and the difficulties returning Poles encountered in readapting to a society that in many ways was now "foreign" limited the appeal of returning. The passage of the immigration restrictions also played a major role since, unlike before the war, Poles who left might not be able to return. Most important, Poles in northeastern Pennsylvania could still maintain a sufficiently independent social space in which they could pass their ethnic culture on to the second generation, as long as they couched that culture in the rhetoric of loyal

Americanism. This was something Poles in the Ruhr attempted through organizations such the ZPwN but could not achieve in the 1920s and 1930s. Moreover, although the existence of a strong and vital Polish-American culture in northeastern Pennsylvania in the 1920s and 1930s did delay the full integration of Poles, it was also thanks to that culture that Poles were able later to successfully integrate on their own terms as "un-hyphenated" Americans after World War II.

CONCLUSION ılı

Determining the Borders of Integration

DURING THE LATE NINETEENTH and early twentieth centuries, hundreds of thousands of Poles, driven by diverse economic, cultural, and political factors, left their homeland and migrated to the coal regions of the Ruhr and northeastern Pennsylvania. Arriving in each region, Poles faced severe challenges. The majority entered industrial environments that differed vastly from the largely agricultural settings to which they were accustomed. Cast as an internal "other" against which German and American national identities became defined, Poles experienced significant levels of discrimination; their presence both in the workplace and larger society was increasingly deemed undesirable, even dangerous, by large segments of the general public and the state. Despite such hostility, Poles persevered and ultimately thrived during the pre–World War I period within their adopted societies. In order to overcome discrimination and isolation, to challenge their subordinate position in the social hierarchy, and to make themselves subjects of their own history, Poles initially turned inward. Poles established vibrant cultural communities, sustained by familial and extended kinship networks, Catholicism and the local parish, and a diverse array of informal and formal Polish institutions. Participation in ethnic life went far in forging a common ethnonational identity among diverse groups of Poles who, prior to migrating, possessed local or at best regional identities. At the same time, the Polish communities in the Ruhr and northeastern Pennsylvania were never closed subcultures, and ethnicization aided the adaptation of Polish migrants in the long run by providing needed stability and, more important, the means to become active participants in the public life of their host societies, especially from the 1890s onward.

In the workplace, Poles responded to intolerable conditions and native animosity by organizing themselves into formal unions such as the UMW and ZZP after the turn of the century. These institutions enabled Poles to begin to redress the economic and cultural disparities under which they labored and, more important in terms of integration, to acquire a strong and influential voice in working-class affairs. Within the confessional sphere, Poles rallied their ethnic communities to protest assaults on their religious practices and traditions. Through such mobilization, Poles in the Ruhr were able to obtain equal representation on many church councils and executive boards between 1904 and 1912. In northeastern Pennsylvania, Polish activism led to an increase in Polish ethnic parishes, though such growth was also dependent on the willingness of a minority of Poles to break away from the Catholic Church altogether and establish the PNCC, an independent, nationalist, working-class religious institution supporting working-class struggle as a means to liberation both in the Pennsylvania coalfields and in Poland. Perhaps the best example of ethnicization as a means to greater integration occurred with the growth of Polish ethnic associations. Although such associations were ethnically exclusive, they provided Poles with invaluable lessons in democratic organizational practices. As the associational movement matured, it grew increasingly secular, diverse, and politically active on a wide range of issues. Preserving ethnic culture and national awareness was a constant goal of these associations, regardless of political orientation, but many simultaneously advanced interests based on class, confession, and gender.

Taken as a whole, the experience of migration, living in the culturally diverse milieus of the Ruhr and northeastern Pennsylvania, and organizing large numbers of their community broadened Polish outlook. By the eve of World War I, Poles in both regions possessed identities that were highly pluralistic and transnational in character, influenced by homeland and host societies, yet also distinct from both. This can be seen in the way Poles viewed themselves. Many embraced a concept of "Polishness" that incorporated class and gender perspectives derived from the host cultures in which they lived. In the case of male miners, a "true" Pole was someone who fulfilled not only certain ethnolinguistic/religious criteria, agitated for the cause of Polish independence, and defended his ethnicity against the forces of Germanization or Americanization, but was also a class-conscious, respectable worker and producer, a male breadwinner who acted as protector of the family and upholder of the social order. Meanwhile, a "proper" Polish woman was politically aware and active in the public sphere, though within limits; her first duty was to ensure a respectable home life and imbue the children with a national awareness.

The emergence of transnational identities can also be discerned in the changing relationship Polish migrants had to the homeland society they left behind. Having absorbed Western ways and practices, Poles in both regions came to consider themselves more culturally and politically advanced than their "backward" countrymen who remained under the influence of morally bankrupt and ineffectual elites in partitioned Poland. This self-assertiveness later served as a driving force behind attempts to transplant the political culture as well as democratic institutions formed in the emigration, such as the ZZP and PNCC, back to Poland so that they could then be put into the service of building an independent state and more egalitarian society. However, as those Poles who returned to Poland before and especially after World War I quickly learned, time spent abroad fundamentally changed outlooks, and many returnees were seen as and felt themselves to be "foreigners" in their native land.

The formation of multifaceted, transnational identities in the emigration was important for aiding the process of Polish integration in the pre–World War I period since such identities could enable Poles in both regions to establish significant points of contact with natives, while preserving and enhancing ethnic awareness. Nevertheless, transnational identities could advance the process of integration only so long as they did not conflict with the demands of citizenship within their host societies. Before 1914, this was not an issue. Despite the many flaws of German and American political culture in this period, Polish migrants in both the Ruhr and northeastern Pennsylvania were able to carve out independent, transnational social spaces within which they could maintain links to the homeland and assert their national identity, while participating in the public life of their host societies.

After World War I, political conditions in both countries changed. Between 1918 and 1924, Poles were confronted with a significantly more intense, integral German and American nationalism, transcending social class, which was driven by the war, its aftermath, and the growing hysteria over potential internal enemies. In this atmosphere, anything less than conformity and the embrace of a clear national identity was suspect. Maintaining a transnational identity was no longer feasible. Poles had to choose whether they were German, American, or Polish. Confronted with this choice, a majority of Poles in the Ruhr decided to leave by 1924, returning to Poland or migrating to France. The ethnic Polish community of approximately one hundred thousand that remained was, in subsequent years, unable to maintain ethnic cohesion and steadily dissolved into German society. In northeastern Pennsylvania, the vast majority of Poles decided not to return to Poland during the interwar period. Instead, they remained in Pennsylvania, where they gave birth to a distinctly Polish-American culture. Meanwhile, those Poles who returned to Poland found that Polish society had little tolerance for those who failed to embrace an identity other than a purely national one.

On the whole, the patterns of adaptation that emerged after World War I revealed the limits of transnationalism and highlighted how integration levels were dependent on Poles becoming full, or at least fuller, citizens within their host societies over the long term. Modern citizenship must encompass not only political and civic rights but also genuine social and cultural rights necessary to live as civilized and equal human beings; Polish struggles for inclusion and recognition a century ago highlight this fact. Comparatively, Poles in the Ruhr, as Prussian citizens, possessed more political, civil, and social rights than their counterparts in northeastern Pennsylvania, who slowly naturalized and did not have access to the same range of legal and economic protections. When it came to cultural rights, however, the reverse was true. Whereas Ruhr Poles could exercise their ethnic culture, they did not enjoy the same degree of security derived from inclusion within a larger cultural community as Poles in northeastern Pennsylvania. This was because of underlying, interconnected structural differences between the two regions in the organization of industry and markets, the role of the state in economic and cultural affairs, and the relative strength of civil society in the pre–World War I period, disparities that would manifest themselves under the burden of war and postwar dislocation.

To elaborate, I find that in order to build a shared cultural community, one in which Polish migrants could maintain ethnic culture while embracing a larger sense of membership in the immigrant-receiving society, Poles needed to become visible and active participants in the public sphere. Oftentimes, this meant having the ability to engage in social conflicts within the bounds of civil society as Poles, workers, Catholics, men, and women. Through such conflicts, Poles came into direct contact with native members of local society, producing an exchange with the "other" that served to break down and reshape mental borders. They became less "foreign" in their ways and practices in the eyes of natives. Poles also began adopting native habits and viewpoints, enabling them to become better accepted as fellow social citizens. In both regions, specific conflicts emerged, such as labor strikes, battles for ethnic rights within the Catholic Church, and struggles over ethnic associations, which supported the ongoing process of Polish integration in the workplace and society. Nevertheless, Poles in northeastern Pennsylvania had greater opportunities to be active in civil society, both as a group and as individuals, than Poles in the Ruhr. This led to more extensive integration patterns evolving in northeastern Pennsylvania.

The structural variations between the two regions and their effect on integration can be seen in the workplace. Differences in industrial organization as well as the actions of the state in the Ruhr placed greater limits than in Pennsylvania on the intensity of social conflict and integration levels. In the Ruhr long-standing corporatist traditions grounded in German culture, which emphasized the mutual obligations between employers and employees, constrained the level of labor conflict. The Knappschaft pension fund, the rise of the more conciliatory Christian Gewerkverein trade union as a counterbalance to the socialist Alter Verband, and the status that the occupation of miner traditionally held in the Ruhr—all bear witness to this corporatist heritage. Reinforcing these traditions was the marketplace. The high cost of labor, as a percentage of profits, and the year-round demand for workers driven by a diversified coal market, encouraged employers to provide mine workers with high levels of employer-sponsored welfare, such as company housing, improved work facilities, and other benefits, in lieu of better wages. The lower wages together with the various welfare measures had the added benefit of giving employers greater control over their workforce, thereby serving to inhibit the outbreak of labor conflicts. By contrast, in northeastern Pennsylvania, there were no long-standing corporatist traditions influencing the organization of the work environment. Anthracite coal production was geared to satisfying the demands of a captive, highly seasonal market, resulting in high wages, though there were noticeably fewer employer-sponsored welfare benefits and less job security. Within such an environment, it is not surprising that labor relations were volatile, workers more militant, and strikes violent and lengthy.

When strikes did occur, workers in the Ruhr were at an immediate disadvantage compared with their American counterparts. Aside from the fact that they could lose their homes or pension benefits, low wages made it difficult to endure long work stoppages. The economic weakness and fractiousness of German trade union organizations, which often held opposing viewpoints on labor goals, also made unity difficult to maintain. In northeastern Pennsylvania, the UMW was better positioned. Demands centered primarily on wages, making it easier to unite diverse groups of workers around a single issue; the "one big union" of the UMW had greater financial resources; and workers were used to long periods of unemployment due to the seasonality of the coal industry.

Added to this were the disparities in levels of government intervention. Prussian authorities, in the name of preserving social order, more readily intervened in labor conflicts. During the 1899 and 1912 strikes, state officials mobilized the military within a few days to ensure a speedy end to the work stoppages. In the 1889 and 1905 strikes, the government, while not using the military, nevertheless pressured both employers and workers to end the strikes within a month. In northeastern Pennsylvania, state and federal officials were less likely to directly interfere in workplace relationships, thus ensuring that labor disputes were protracted. The strikes of 1887–88, 1897, and 1912 brought forth no significant state intervention by military authorities. In the two major strikes when the government did step in, namely the one-and-a-half month 1900 strike and the six-month 1902 strike, such intrusion occurred only after a significant period of intense, direct conflict between mine operators and workers. When American officials did finally interfere, they proved much more effective in promoting a durable solution to labor problems than their Prussian counterparts, whose reforms after the 1905 Ruhr strike were minor by comparison. Altogether, for Polish workers in northeastern Pennsylvania, the experience of engaging in multimonth struggles with workers of other backgrounds and ethnicities went far in forging a common class identity that could promote integration. Although interethnic solidarities were also achieved due to strikes in the Ruhr, their limited intensity and duration resulted in bonds that were less substantial.

Within larger society, differences in the role assumed by the state in directing minority policy also influenced the extent to which Poles could become full actors in their local communities. Responding to public pressure emanating from within middle-class society, state officials in the Ruhr took a leading role in dealing with "the Polish question." However, the heavy-handedness of the Germanization policies, while obstinately designed to accelerate the melding of the Polish minority into the majority, produced an ethnic backlash as Poles engaged in an intense conflict with the government. The struggle did compel Poles to become more active citizens, as testified to by the numerous appeals Poles made to the German courts to protect their rights; yet it also inhibited Polish identification with the Prussian state and made it difficult for Poles to challenge anti-Polish sentiment in larger society. Moreover, though the German courts provided Poles an important means to prevent the implementation of the most onerous of anti-Polish policies, the Polish community was left in a precarious position of being dependent on the goodwill of the courts to safeguard Polish rights.

In contrast, in northeastern Pennsylvania, the government rarely interfered in the daily activities of Poles. Despite growing restrictionist sentiment, the state administrative apparatus remained in the background while issues of Americanization and immigration were publicly debated. This enabled Poles to be able to better identify themselves with government institutions and imagine that they could be both loyal Poles and Americans. Further, Poles responded to the efforts designed to either Americanize or exclude them from society by directly challenging public conceptions of the "Pole." In the first decade of the twentieth century, Polish ethnic associations undertook a lively campaign designed to educate society about Polish contributions to American democracy. Such direct Polish participation in the debate about immigration helped promote splits in native opinion. A vocal faction developed within the middle-class progressive movement that advocated greater efforts to reach common ground with the immigrant Polish population. Although this outreach, organized through institutions such as the YMCA, could oftentimes be contemptuous of ethnic culture, it was nevertheless an important first step along the path to better understanding between Poles and natives in northeastern Pennsylvania, a step that was never undertaken in the Ruhr.

There were also clear economic disparities that influenced integration outcomes. Poles in northeastern Pennsylvania developed, over time, a much greater economic stake in their host society than their counterparts in the Ruhr. This was in part because of disparities in levels of social welfare entitlements. Unlike the Poles in Germany, Poles in northeastern Pennsylvania did not have access to state-sponsored health and insurance benefits. Employer-funded pension plans, when they existed, offered negligible benefits. As a result, Poles relied on ethnic associations such as the PNA and PRCU to create and administer mutual-aid insurance programs in order to provide a degree of economic security. For the most part, this situation was different from that in the Ruhr, where ethnic associations did not play nearly as great an economic role in the lives of Poles. In the end, the fact that ethnic associations in northeastern Pennsylvania were important political, cultural, *and* economic institutions is noteworthy because the need for sophisticated insurance programs led to an early amalgamation and centralization of the associational movement into several large, nationwide organizations. The sizable amount of capital that associations such as the PNA and PRCU eventually accumulated, thanks to their ability to vertically integrate resources, made them formidable political players on the national stage. The greater fiduciary responsibility of associations, both at the national and local level, also made them stable institutions over the long term. Through their investments, Polish economic interests became closely tied to those of their host society.

Another essential economic difference between the Ruhr and northeastern Pennsylvania came in the form of property ownership. By the eve of World War I, at least 13 percent of Poles owned their own homes in northeastern Pennsylvania, while in the Ruhr less than 2 percent did. The reasons for this vary. In the Ruhr, Poles often had the benefit of company housing. Meanwhile, in northeastern Pennsylvania, the lack of company housing, the inexpensive land values, and the lower tax rates combined to spur Poles to acquire property. Similarly, the number of Poles who owned small businesses, most often saloons, was generally higher in northeastern Pennsylvania than in the Ruhr. Furthermore, all Poles in northeastern Pennsylvania held in common, if not in actual legal deed then in spirit, another type of property, namely the local parish. Unlike in the Ruhr, where Polish Catholics joined existing territorial parishes, Poles in northeastern Pennsylvania were able to form their own distinct ethnic parishes, oftentimes with ethnic elementary schools attached. The richly endowed, majestic churches that arose in the region, whether Roman Catholic or Polish National Catholic, represented a large investment by Poles in their local communities and a declaration of intent to stay. By acquiring property and building public monuments such as churches, Poles in northeastern Pennsylvania were conforming to a typically American pattern of settlement that contributed to making Poles appear less foreign in the eyes of natives.

Exploring Polish integration patterns in the early twentieth century can provide insight into contemporary issues of immigration and integration. Although exact comparisons between the past and present can never be drawn, the varied Polish experiences in the Ruhr and northeastern Pennsylvania highlight how integration must be seen as a drawn-out process involving a complex series of social and cultural negotiations between migrants and their host societies. In this process, migrants must become similar in some, though not necessarily all, respects to a reference community that itself changes under the influence of immigration. In attempting to promote integration, the state must recognize that its powers are limited; it cannot achieve integration by decree. Policies adopted to encourage integration by either restricting ethnic rights or, alternatively, granting immigrants complete autonomy, often do not accomplish their objectives and generate hierarchies of privileged and disadvantaged minorities as well as resentment within the native population. This argues for a cautious, judicious approach to integration policy. The state must be willing to tolerate a degree of social conflict within the bounds of civil society, since this exchange ultimately helps break down mental barriers separating ethnic and social classes. Yet the state must not abrogate its responsibilities in the matter of immigrant integration. Obviously, expectations that immigrants adhere to certain fundamental values such as respect for democratic practices and, in our present age, the rights of women are important. Moreover, the state must foster a sufficiently secure environment within which integration can happen. The post–World War I situation in the Ruhr provides an excellent example of what occurs when a government refuses to fulfill its obligations to protect minority rights against the tyranny of the majority. Generally, the best way for governments to promote integration is to ensure that immigrants have sufficient opportunity to become economic stakeholders in their adopted society through such things as home ownership, small business development, and other types of financial investment. Although a secure economic base will never ensure integration, it makes it more likely.

Finally, in order for fuller integration to occur, it is necessary for migrants to be politically active participants within the public sphere of their host societies. The experiences of Poles in northeastern Pennsylvania, and to a lesser extent the Ruhr, show that the ability of migrants to cross ethnic divides and make contacts with natives on their own terms was vital for broadening Polish identities and promoting social and cultural integration; yet this activism could occur only in an environment where immigrants had the freedom to redress grievances. Regrettably, present-day levels of communication between migrants and natives in many Western countries are weak. The difficulties in overcoming barriers are seemingly insurmountable, especially in the light of legal measures that emphasize fundamental differences between "us" and "them." Ultimately, in order to begin to bridge the chasm separating present-day immigrants from their host societies, there must be an increase in volunteeristic, grassroots activities within the bounds of civil society on both sides of the ethnic divide. Only by building a shared cultural community can immigrants feel themselves to be full citizens of the host societies in which they live and the borders of integration redrawn.

Appendix

Table 1. Comparison of production, employment, productivity, wages, and labor costs in the Ruhr and northeastern Pennsylvania, 1901–14

Year	Yearly Coal Production (in tons, 1=2,000 pounds) Ruhr	NEPA**	Total Employees (includes managers) Ruhr	NEPA	Yearly Production per Man (in tons) Ruhr	NEPA	Average Days Worked* Ruhr	NEPA	Average Daily Production per Man (in tons) Ruhr	NEPA	Average Daily Shift Wage of all Workers ($) Ruhr***	NEPA	Average Yearly Earnings ($) Ruhr***	NEPA	Labor Cost (per ton) of Coal Mined ($) Ruhr***	NEPA	Price (per ton) at Market ($) Ruhr***	NEPA	Percent of Market Price due to Labor Cost Ruhr	NEPA
1901	58,447,657	67,094,635	243,926	147,651	240	454	300	195	0.80	2.33	$1.02	N/A	$305	N/A	$1.27	N/A	$2.19	$3.86	58%	N/A
1902	58,038,594	41,340,995	243,963	148,139	238	279	296	116	0.80	2.41	$0.96	N/A	$283	N/A	$1.19	N/A	$2.10	$3.98	57%	N/A
1903	64,689,594	75,232,535	255,992	151,827	253	496	311	211	0.81	2.35	$0.97	$2.07	$301	$437	$1.19	$0.88	$2.07	$4.30	58%	20%
1904	67,533,681	73,594,439	270,259	161,330	250	456	304	213	0.82	2.14	$1.00	$2.48	$302	$528	$1.21	$1.16	$2.06	$4.30	59%	27%
1905	65,373,531	78,647,020	267,798	168,254	244	467	295	208	0.83	2.25	$1.01	$2.24	$297	$466	$1.22	$1.00	$2.10	$4.30	58%	23%
1906	76,811,054	72,139,510	278,719	166,175	276	434	321	206	0.86	2.11	$1.09	$2.39	$351	$492	$1.27	$1.13	$2.19	$4.30	58%	26%
1907	80,182,647	86,056,412	303,089	168,774	265	510	321	227	0.82	2.25	$1.22	$2.36	$391	$536	$1.48	$1.05	$2.31	$4.30	64%	24%
1908	82,664,647	83,543,243	334,733	174,503	247	479	310	193	0.80	2.27	$1.21	$2.23	$374*	$47*	$1.51	$0.98	$2.52	$4.30	60%	23%
1909	82,803,676	80,223,833	340,567	171,195	243	469	301	205	0.81	2.29	$1.12	$2.34	$333	$480	$1.39	$1.02	$2.49	$4.30	56%	24%
1910	86,864,504	83,683,994	345,136	168,175	252	498	304	212	0.83	2.35	$1.14	$2.41	$345	$511	$1.37	$1.03	$2.45	$4.30	56%	24%
1911	91,329,140	90,917,176	352,555	173,338	259	525	308	234	0.84	2.24	$1.17	$2.46	$362	$576	$1.39	$1.10	$2.45	$4.30	57%	26%
1912	100,264,830	84,426,059	363,879	175,098	276	482	324	220	0.85	2.19	$1.26	$2.72	$407	$598	$1.48	$1.24	$2.59	$4.49	57%	28%
1913	110,765,495	91,626,954	397,339	175,310	279	523	327	242	0.85	2.16	$1.34	$2.65	$439	$641	$1.57	$1.23	$2.75	$4.52	57%	27%
1914	94,851,288	91,189,641	372,886	180,899	254	504	314	229	0.81	2.20	$1.29	N/A	$405	N/A	$1.59	N/A	N/A	N/A	N/A	N/A
AVG.					255	470	310	209	0.82	2.25	$1.13	$2.40	$350	$521	$1.37	$1.07	$2.33	$4.27	58%	25%

Sources: Franz-Josef Brüggemeier, Leben vor Ort: Ruhrbergleute und Ruhrbergbau (Munich: C. H. Beck, 1983), 278; Christoph Klessmann, Polnische Bergarbeiter im Ruhrgebiet, 1870–1945: Soziale Integration und nationale Subkultur einer Minderheit in der deutschen Industriegesellschaft (Göttingen: Vandenhoeck und Ruprecht, 1978), 263–65; M. J. Koch, Die Bergarbeiterbewegung im Ruhrgebiet zur Zeit Wilhelm II (Düsseldorf: Droste Verlag, 1954), 148–50; Carl Ludwig Holtfrerich, Quantitative Wirtschaftsgeschichte des Ruhrkohlenbergbaus im 19. Jahrhundert (Dortmund: Gesell. f. West. Wirtschaftsgeschichte, 1973), 22–24, 51–56; W. Jett Lauck, Comparison of Earnings and Wage Rates in the Anthracite and Bituminous Mines of Pennsylvania (Washington, D.C., 1920), 13, 15; Irregularity of Employment in the Anthracite Industry (Washington, D.C., 1920), 8, 23; Wholesale and Retail Prices of Anthracite Coal 1913 to 1920 (Washington, D.C., 1920), 3; Report of the Department of Mines of Pennsylvania, Part 1 Anthracite—1919–1920 (Harrisburg, Penn., 1921), 25, table 6, and 59, table 20: Report of the Department of Mines of Pennsylvania, Part 1 Anthracite—1914 (Harrisburg, Penn., 1915), 72, table 13, and 89, table L; Report of the Anthracite Coal Strike Commission, 25; Eliot Jones, The Anthracite Coal Combination in the United States (Cambridge: Harvard University Press, 1914), 156–57.

* Based on a 312-day work year fifty-two weeks times six days a week). Excesses in average number of days worked was due to overtime.

**NEPA = Northeastern Pennsylvania.

*** Figures calculated on the basis of the 4:1 exchange ratio of Reichmarks to U.S. dollars, based on gold, in effect until 1914.

Table 2. Statistics on Polish church representation in the Arnsberg (Ruhr) district for 1904

				Church Executive Committee (Vorstande)			Church Council (Gemeindevertretung)		
Region	No. of Catholics	No. of Polish Catholics	Polish Catholics as % of Total Catholic Population	Total No. of Seats	No. of Seats Held by Poles	%	Total No. of Seats	No. of Seats Held by Poles	%
Gelsenkirchen									
Stadt	70,330	21,501	30.6%	65	3	4.6%	213	6	2.8%
Land	61,079	15,740	25.8%	56	7	12.5%	112	22	19.6%
Dortmund									
Stadt	75,691	4,866	6.4%	34	0	0%	75	0	0%
Land	85,426	18,959	22.2%	116	7	6%	345	24	7%

Source: STAM RA 6037—1904 Statistics of the Regierungs-Präsident Arnsberg

Table 3. Statistics on Polish church representation in the Arnsberg (Ruhr) district for 1910

				Church Executive Committee (Vorstande)			Church Council (Gemeindevertretung)		
Region	No. of Catholics	No. of Polish Catholics	Polish Catholics as % of Total Catholic Population	Total No. of Seats	No. of Seats Held by Poles	%	Total No. of Seats	No. of Seats Held by Poles	%
Gelsenkirchen*									
Stadt	84,445	10,136	12%	79	2	2.5%	229	13	5.7%
Land	77,481	24,013	31%	88	17	19.3%	242	49	20.3%
Dortmund									
Stadt	100,837	14,7392	14.6%	47	4	8.5%	118	11	9.3%
Land	107,707	6,814	24.9%	153	22	14.4%	457	77	16.9%

Source: STAM RA 6351—1910 Statistics of the Regierungs-Präsident Arnsberg

*The boundaries between Gelsenkirchen-Stadt and -Land shifted between 1904 and 1910, which may partly account for the significant drop in the number of Poles living in Gelsenkirchen-Stadt (see 1904 census). For the purposes of this study, such a drop does not affect the determination of % representation vs. % of overall Catholic population.

Table 4. Statistics on Polish church representation in the Arnsberg (Ruhr) district for 1912

				Church Executive Committee (Vorstande)			Church Council (Gemeindevertretung)		
Region	No. of Catholics	No. of Polish Catholics	Polish Catholics as % of Total Catholic Population	Total No. of Seats	No. of Seats Held by Poles	%	Total No. of Seats	No. of Seats Held by Poles	%
Gelsenkirchen									
Stadt	87,965	11,680	13.3%	79	8	10.1%	231	27	11.7%
Land	81,734	26,047	31.9%	85	21	24.7%	256	59	23.1%
Dortmund									
Stadt	108,443	14,297	13.2%	40	5	12.5%	120	19	15.8%
Land	120,557	33,526	27.8%	164	29	17.7%	545	84	15.4%

Source: STAM RA 5758—1912 Statistics of the Regierungs-Präsident Arnsberg

Notes

Guide to Abbreviations in Notes

AMM—Anthracite Mining Museum, Scranton
APP—Archivum Panstowe Miasta Poznania i Wojewodztwa Poznanskiego
BA—Bergamt
BAD—Bergamt Dortmund
BAH—Bergamt Herne
BBA—Bochum Bergbau Museum Archive
BR—Bergrat
BRD—Bergrat Dortmund
BRH—Bergrat Herne
Coxe—Coxe Family Papers
CPNCC—Collections of the Polish National Catholic Church
CUA—Catholic University of America Archives
DHP—Daniel Hastings Papers
ESC—Ethnic Studies Collections
HSP—Historical Society of Pennsylvania
HSTAD—Hauptstaatsarchiv Düsseldorf
JMP—John Mitchell Papers
LA—Landesamt
LAM—Landesamt Moers
LR—Landrat
LRB—Landrat Bochum
LRD—Landrat Dortmund
LRG—Landrat Gelsenkirchen
LRH—Landrat Hattingen
LRR—Landrat Recklinghausen
MdI—Minister des Innern
MG—Manuscript Group
OBD—Oberbergamt Dortmund
OPRP—Oberpräsident der Rhein Provinz, Koblenz
OPW—Oberpräsident der Provinz Westfalen, Münster
PDB—Polizeidirektor Bochum
PHMC—Pennsylvania Historical and Museum Commission
PP—Polizeipräsident
PPB—Polizeipräsident Bochum

PPE—Polizeipräsident Essen
PV—Polizeiverwaltung
RA—Regierung Arnsberg
RD—Regierung Düsseldorf
Rep.—Report
RG—Record Group
RM—Regierung Münster
RPA—Regierung Präsident Arnsberg
RPD—Regierung Präsident Düsseldorf
RPM—Regierung Präsident Münster
SOHP—Scranton Oral History Project
SPP—Samuel Pennypacker Papers
STAM—Staatsarchiv Münster
StB—Stadtarchiv Bochum
StG—Stadtarchiv Gelsenkirchen
StO—Stadtarchiv Oberhausen
WSP—William Stone Papers

Introduction: Migration and Citizenship in a Globalizing World

1. Stephen Castles and Mark J. Miller, *The Age of Migration: International Population Movements in the Modern World* (London: Macmillan, 1996).

2. "The United Nations on Levels and Trends of International Migration and Related Policies," *Population and Development Review* 29, no. 2 (2003): 335–40; United Nations Department of Economic and Social Affairs, *World Economic and Social Survey: International Migration* (New York: United Nations Publishing Section, 2004); "In a World on the Move, A Tiny Land Strains to Cope," *New York Times*, June 24, 2007. United Nations Development Programme, *Human Development Report 2009: Overcoming Barriers: Human Mobility and Development* (Basingstoke, UK: Palgrave Macmillan, 2009), 1–2. Globally, the number of internal migrants, i.e., those who move inside their own country, is conservatively estimated to be 740 million as of 2009. This means that worldwide, approximately one in seven persons have had some experience of migration in their lifetime.

3. Peter Schuck and Rainer Münz, eds., *Paths to Inclusion: The Integration of Migrants in the United States and Germany* (New York: Berghahn Books, 1998); "Where the Minorities Rule," *New York Times*, Feb. 10, 2002. Although the total number of legal immigrants in the United States has surpassed previous all-time highs, as a percentage of the population, immigration today remains below the historic high of 14 percent for the early 1900s.

4. For a broader discussion of this point see Larry Jones, ed., *Crossing Boundaries: German and American Experiences with the Exclusion and Inclusion of Minorities* (Oxford: Oxford University Press, 2001). In particular, see Klaus Bade's article, "Immigration, Naturalization, and Ethno-National Traditions in Germany from the Citizenship Law of 1913 to the Law of 1999," in the same volume.

5. For assimilationist approaches see Robert Park, *Race and Culture* (Glencoe, Ill.: Free Press, 1950); Oscar Handlin, *The Uprooted: The Epic Story of the Great Migrations That Made the American People* (Boston: Little, Brown, 1951); Milton Gordon, *Assimilation in American Life* (Oxford and New York: Oxford University Press, 1964). Charles Hirschman, "America's Melting Pot Reconsidered," *Annual Review of Sociology* 9 (1983): 397–423. The classic "reactive ethnicity" work remains Nathan Glazer and Daniel Patrick Moynihan, *Beyond the Melting Pot: The Negroes, Puerto Ricans, Jews, Italians, and Irish of New York City* (Cambridge, Mass.: MIT Press, 1963). In this vein, see also William L. Yancey, Eugene P. Eriksen, and Richard N. Juliani, "Emergent Ethnicity: A Review and Reformulation," *American Sociological Review* 41, no. 3 (1976): 391–403; Susan Olzak, "Contemporary Ethnic Mobilization," *American Review of Sociology* 9, no. 1 (1983): 367–68.

6. For a broader discussion of debates and changes in thinking about integration and assimilation during the 1990s and beyond see Herbert Gans, "Second Generation Decline: Scenarios for the Economic and Ethnic Futures of Post-1965 Immigrants," *Ethnic and Racial Studies* 15, no. 2 (1992): 173–92; Alejandro Portes and Min Zhou, "The Second Generation: Segmented Assimilation and Its Variants," *Annals of the American Academy of Political and Social Science* 530 (November 1993): 74–96; Richard Alba and Victor Nee, "Rethinking Assimilation Theory for a New Era of Immigration," *International Migration Review* 31, no. 4 (1997): 826–74; Ewa Morawska, "In Defense of the Assimilation Model," *Journal of American Ethnic History* 13, no. 2 (1994): 76–87; Kathleen Conzen, "Thomas and Znaniecki and the Historiography of American Integration," *Journal of American Ethnic History* 16. no. 1 (1996): 16–26; Rogers Brubaker, "The Return of Assimilation? Changing Perspectives on Immigration and Its Sequels in France, Germany, and the United States," *Ethnic and Racial Studies* 24, no. 4 (2001): 531–48; Christian Joppke and Ewa Morawska, "Integrating Immigrants in Liberal Nation-States: Policies and Practices," in *Towards Assimilation and Citizenship: Immigrants in Liberal Nation-States*, ed. Christian Joppke and Ewa Morawska (Basingstoke, UK: Palgrave Macmillan, 2003), 1–36.

7. Klaus Bade, *Legal and Illegal Immigration into Europe: Experiences and Challenges* (Antwerp: Netherlands Institute for Advanced Study, 2003).

8. Ulrich Herbert, *Arbeit, Volkstum, Weltanschauung: Über Fremde und Deutsche im 20. Jahrhundert* (Frankfurt: Fischer, 1995), 218, cited in Diethelm Blecking, "Polish Community before the First World War and Present-Day Turkish Community Formation—Some Thoughts of a Diachronistic Comparison," in *Irish and Polish Migration in Comparative Perspective,* ed. John Belchem and Klaus Tenfelde (Essen: Klartext, 2003), 183.

9. Klaus Bade and Michael Bommes, "Migration und politische Kultur im 'Nicht-Einwanderungsland,'" in *Migrationsreport 2000,* ed. Klaus Bade and Rainer Münz (Bonn: Bundeszentrale für politische Bildung, 2000), 168. Bade and Bommes note that the size of the number of "foreign-born" places Germany on par with the United States, the "classic" country of immigration. Included in this 14 percent are guestworkers, though not their children, asylum seekers, and ethnic Germans from Eastern Europe.

10. Gérard Noiriel, "Immigration: Amnesia and Memory," *French Historical Studies* 19, no. 2 (1995): 368.

11. Gérard Noiriel, *Le creuset français: Historie de l'immigration XIXe–XXe siècles* (Paris: Du Seuil, 1988); Dirk Hoerder, ed., *Labor Migration in the Atlantic Economies: The European and North American Working Classes during the Period of Industrialization* (Westport, Conn.: Greenwood Press, 1985); Klaus Bade, *Auswanderer, Wanderarbeiter, Gastarbeiter: Bevolkerung, Arbeitsmarkt und Wanderung in Deutschland seit der Mitte des 19. Jahrhunderts*, 2 vols. (Ostfildern: Scripta Mercaturae, 1984); Colin Holmes, *John Bull's Island: Immigration and British Society, 1871–1971* (Basingstoke, UK: Macmillan, 1988).

12. Since the 1930s, the Warsaw-based sociologists of the Instytut Gospodarstwa Społecznego (Institute of Contemporary Society) began extensive examinations of Polish immigration, compiling numerous memoirs of Polish immigrants abroad and return migrants. See, for example, *Pamiętniki chłopów*, vols. 1–2 (Warsaw: Instytut Gospodarstwa Społecznego, 1935–36); *Pamiętniki emigrantów: Stany Zjednoczone*, vols. 1–2 (Warsaw: Książka i Wiedza, 1977). Prominent migration scholars include the late Andrzej Brożek and Adam Walaszek. See Andrzej Brożek, *Polish Americans, 1854–1939* (1977; repr., Warsaw: Interpress, 1985); Adam Walaszek, *Reemigracja ze Stanów Zjednoczonych do Polski po I. wojnie światowej, 1919–1924* (Cracow: Nakl. Uniwersytetu Jagiellonskiego, 1983); Walaszek, ed., *Polska diaspora* (Cracow: Wydawnictwo Literackie, 2001).

13. Klaus Bade, "German Emigration to the United States and Continental Immigration to Germany in the Late Nineteenth and Early Twentieth Centuries," *Central European History* 13, no. 4 (1980): 348.

14. For an overview of these debates, see Richard Alba, "Assimilation, Exclusion, or Neither?" in *Paths to Inclusion: The Integration of Migrants in the United States and in Germany*, ed. Peter H. Schuck and Rainer Münz (New York: Berghahn Books, 1998), 1–31; Leslie Page Moch, *Moving Europeans: Migration in Western Europe since 1650* (Bloomington: Indiana University Press, 2003); Leo Lucassen, David Feldman, and Jochen Oltmer, eds., *Paths of Integration: Migrants in Western Europe, 1880–2004* (Amsterdam: Amsterdam University Press, 2006); Leo Lucassen, "Old and New Migration in the Twentieth Century: A European Perspective," *Journal of American Ethnic History* 21, no. 4 (2002): 85–101; Leo Lucassen, *The Immigrant Threat: The Integration of Old and New Migrants in Western Europe since 1850* (Urbana: University of Illinois Press, 2005); Richard Alba and Victor Nee, *Remaking the American Mainstream: Assimilation and Contemporary Immigration* (Cambridge, Mass.: Harvard University Press, 2003).

15. Portes and Zhou, "The Second Generation"; Gans, "Second Generation Decline"; Nina Glick Shiller, Linda Basch, and Cristina Szanton Blanc, "Transnationalism: A New Analytic Framework for Understanding Migration," in *Towards a Transnational Perspective on Migration: Race, Class, Ethnicity, and Nationalism Reconsidered*, ed. Nina Glick Schiller, Linda Basch, and Cristina Szanton Blanc (New York: New York Academy of Sciences, 1992); Douglas Massey, "The New Immigration and Ethnicity in the United States," *Population and Development Re-*

view 21 no. 3 (1995): 631–52; Min Zhou, "Segmented Assimilation: Issues, Controversies, and Recent Research on the New Second Generation," *International Migration Review* 31, no. 4 (1997): 975–1008; Christian Joppke, *Immigration and the Nation-State: The United States, Germany, and Great Britain* (Oxford: Oxford University Press, 1999).

16. Alejandro Portes and Rubén G. Rumbaut, *Immigrant America: A Portrait* (1990; Berkeley: University of California Press, 1996), 7–8.

17. Lawrence Fuchs, *The American Kaleidoscope: Race, Ethnicity, and the Civic Culture* (Hanover, N.H.: University Press of New England, 1990); Nancy Foner, *From Ellis Island to JFK: New York's Two Great Waves of Immigration* (New Haven, Conn.: Yale University Press, 2000); Lucassen, Feldman, and Oltmer, eds., *Paths of Integration;* Lucassen, "Old and New Migration in the Twentieth Century"; Lucassen, *The Immigrant Threat.*

18. David Roediger, *The Wages of Whiteness: Race and the Making of the American Working Class* (New York: Verso, 1991); Noel Ignatiev, *How the Irish Became White* (New York: Routledge, 1995).

19. John Bodnar, *The Transplanted: A History of Immigrants in Urban America* (Bloomington: Indiana University Press, 1985); John Bodnar, *Lives of Their Own: Blacks, Italians, and Poles in Pittsburgh, 1900–1960* (Urbana: University of Illinois Press, 1982)

20. For overviews of this rich history, see Moch, *Moving Europeans;* Mark Wyman, *Round Trip to America: The Immigrants Return to Europe, 1880–1930* (Ithaca, N.Y.: Cornell University Press, 1993); Michael Piore, *Birds of Passage: Migrant Labor and Industrial Societies* (Cambridge, UK: Cambridge University Press, 1979); Roger Daniels, *Coming to America: A History of Immigration and Ethnicity in American Life* (New York: Harper Collins, 1990). For examples from the Polish experience see Ewa Morawska, *For Bread with Butter: The Life-Worlds of East Central Europeans in Johnstown, Pennsylvania, 1890–1940* (Cambridge, UK: Cambridge University Press, 1985). For Italians and Slovaks, see Dino Cinel, *The National Integration of Italian Return Migration, 1870–1929* (Cambridge, UK: Cambridge University Press, 1991); M. Mark Stolarik, *Immigration and Urbanization: The Slovak Experience, 1870–1918* (New York: AMS Press, 1989).

21. Nina Glick Schiller, Linda Basch, and Cristina Szanton Blanc, eds., *Towards a Transnational Perspective on Migration: Race, Class, Ethnicity, and Nationalism Reconsidered* (New York: New York Academy of Sciences, 1992); Alejandro Portes, Luis E. Guarnizo, and Patricia Landolt, "The Study of Transnationalism and the Promise of an Emergent Research Field," *Ethnic and Racial Studies* 22, no. 2 (1999): 217–37; Michael Smith and Luis Guarnizo, eds., *Transnationalism from Below* (New Brunswick, N.J.: Transaction Publishers, 1998); Peter Kivisto, "Theorizing Transnational Immigration: A Critical Review of Current Efforts," *Ethnic and Racial Studies* 24, no. 4 (2001): 549–77; Thomas Faist, *The Volume and Dynamics of International Migration* (Oxford: Oxford University Press, 2000); Faist, "Transnationalization in International Migration: Implications for the Study of Citizenship and Culture," *Ethnic and Racial Studies* 23, no. 3 (2000): 189–222.

22. Faist, "Transnationalization in International Migration," 191–98.

23. Ibid., 191; Portes, Guarnizo, and Landolt, "The Study of Transnationalism," 223; Ewa Morawska, "Immigrants, Transnationalism, and Ethnicization: A Comparison of This Great Wave and the Last," in *E Pluribus Unum? Contemporary and Historical Perspectives on Immigrant Political Incorporation,* ed. Gary Gerstle and John Mollenkopf (New York: Russell Sage, 2001), 198.

24. The 2003 *International Migration Review* special issue dealing with transnational migration is a useful starting point for understanding the approaches taken by differing disciplines to transnationalism. See especially Ewa Morawska, "Disciplinary Agendas and Analytic Strategies of Research on Immigrant Transnationalism: Challenges of Interdisciplinary Knowledge," *International Migration Review* 37, no. 3 (2003): 611–40. Also see Robert Smith, "Diasporic Memberships in Historical Perspective: Comparative Insights from the Mexican, Italian, and Polish Cases," *International Migration Review* 37, no. 3 (2003): 724–59; Morawska, "Immigrants, Transnationalism, and Ethnicization," 175–212; Luis Eduardo Guarnizo, "On the Political Participation of Transnational Migrants: Old Practices and New Trends," in *E Pluribus Unum? Contemporary and Historical Perspectives on Immigrant Political Incorporation,* ed. Gary Gerstle and John Mollenkopf (New York: Russell Sage, 2001), 212–63. For a critique of tendencies in many transnational studies to overlook the role of states in delimitating transnational spaces, see Roger Waldinger and David Fitzgerald, "Transnationalism in Question," *American Journal of Sociology* 109, no. 5 (2004): 1177–95.

25. This position contrasts with that of Portes, who argues that the levels of transnationalism correspond to the levels of education and professional skills that an immigrant or immigrant community possesses, i.e., higher educational levels lead to greater transnationalism. See Portes, Guarnizo, and Landolt, "The Study of Transnationalism," 224–27.

26. Archiwum Państwowe Miasta Poznania i Województwa Poznańskiego (APP)—Polizeipräsidium 2714—*Zgoda* (*Harmony*, Chicago, Ill.), Dec. 17, 1903; *New York Times,* June 15, 1904; Aug. 17, 1907; Aug. 8, 1908; Jan. 24, 1913. The inflation-adjusted figures are based on the change in the Consumer Price Index from 1904 as calculated by Samuel H. Williamson, "Six Ways to Compute the Relative Value of a U.S. Dollar Amount, 1774 to Present," MeasuringWorth, http://www.measuringworth.com/uscompare/ (accessed July 31, 2009).

27. Peter Kivisto argues a similar point in his analysis of transnationalism. See Kivisto, "Theorizing Transnational Immigration," 571.

28. Christian Joppke, "How Immigration Is Changing Citizenship: A Comparative View," *Ethnic and Racial Studies* 22, no. 4 (1999), 644–47; Kivisto, "Theorizing Transnational Immigration," 572; Faist, "Transnationalization in International Migration," 217.

29. Instytut Gospodarstwa Społecznego, *Pamiętniki chłopów,* vol. 2 (Warsaw, 1936), Memoir 2.

30. For a discussion of how citizenship influenced immigrant transnationalism in postwar Europe, see Ruud Koopmans and Paul Stratham, "How National Citizenship

Shapes Transnationalism: Migrant and Minority Claims-Making in Germany, Great Britain and the Netherlands," in *Toward Assimilation and Citizenship: Immigrants in Liberal Nation-States,* ed. Christian Joppke and Ewa Morawska (Basingstoke, UK: Palgrave Macmillan, 2003), 195–238.

31. T. H. Marshall, *Citizenship and Social Class* (Cambridge, UK: Cambridge University Press, 1950), 28–29.

32. Ibid., 11

33. Reinhard Bendix, *Nation-Building and Citizenship: Studies of Our Changing Social Order* (1964; Berkeley: University of California Press, 1977).

34. This is a point also advanced by gender scholars in considering issues of citizenship. See, for example, Nira Yuval-Davis, "Women, Citizenship and Difference," *Feminist Review* 57, no. 1 (1997): 5. Also in the same issue, Ruth Lister, "Citizenship: Towards a Feminist Synthesis," 28–43. For a larger discussion of recent trends in broadening the domains of citizenship, see Linda Bosniak, *The Citizen and the Alien: Dilemmas of Contemporary Membership* (Princeton, N.J.: Princeton University Press, 2006), 20–23.

35. Niklas Luhmann, "Inklusion und Exklusion," in *Nationales Bewusstsein und kollektive Indentität: Studien zur Entwickelung des kollektiven Bewusstseins in der Neuzeit,* ed. Helmut Berding (Frankfurt a.M.: Suhrkamp, 1994), 15–45; Rogers Brubaker, *Citizenship and Nationhood in France and Germany* (Cambridge, Mass.: Harvard University Press, 1992), 1–22; Lister, "Citizenship," 36.

36. Carole Pateman, "The Fraternal Social Contract," in *Civil Society and the State,* ed. John Keane (London: Verso, 1988), 101–28; Carole Pateman, *The Sexual Contract* (Stanford, Calif.: Stanford University Press, 1988); Joan Wallach Scott, "French Feminists and the Rights of 'Man': Olympe de Gouge's Declarations," *History Workshop Journal* 28, no. 1 (1989): 1–21; Lynn Hunt, *The Family Romance of the French Revolution* (Berkeley: University of California Press, 1992). A classic example of women's exclusion, even when coupled with newfound political rights, appears with the rise of the Western welfare state in the twentieth century. In many countries, the drive to extend greater social rights to "male breadwinners" complemented maternalist policies that forced women to become more economically dependent on men and relegated them to the nonpolitical, private familial sphere. See Susan Pederson, *Family Dependence and the Origins of the Welfare State: Britain and France, 1914–1945* (Cambridge, UK: Cambridge University Press, 1993); Carole Pateman, "The Patriarchal Welfare State," in *Democracy and the Welfare State,* ed. Amy Gutman (Princeton, N.J.: Princeton University Press, 1988), 231–60; Christian Eifert, "Coming to Terms with the State: Maternalist Politics and the Development of the Welfare State in Weimar Germany," *Central European History* 30, no. 1 (1997): 25–47; Theda Skocpol, *Protecting Soldiers and Mothers: The Political Origins of Social Policy in the United States* (Cambridge, Mass.: Harvard University Press, 1992).

37. Joppke, *Immigration and the Nation-State,* 6–7.

38. Lister, "Citizenship," 37; Eric Hobsbawm, "Identity Politics and the Left," *New Left Review* 1, no. 217 (1996): 38–47.

39. For a critical, philosophical treatment of the difficulty in balancing group versus individual rights see Will Kymlicka, *Multicultural Citizenship: A Liberal Theory of Minority Rights* (Oxford: Clarendon Press, 1995).

40. Jürgen Habermas, "Anerkennungskämpfe im demokratischen Rechtsstaat," in *Multikulturalismus und die Politik der Anerkennung*, ed. Charles Taylor, Amy Gutman, and Jürgen Habermas (Frankfurt: S. Fischer, 1993), 175–76. For a fuller elaboration of Habermas's ideas regarding the public sphere, see Jürgen Habermas, *Structural Transformation of the Public Sphere: An Inquiry into a Category of Bourgeois Society* (Cambridge, Mass.: MIT Press, 1989); Jürgen Habermas, *The Theory of Communicative Action*, 2 vols. (London: Heinemann, 1984/1987); and Jürgen Habermas, *The Inclusion of the Other*, ed. Ciaran Cronin and Pablo De Greiff (Cambridge, Mass.: MIT Press, 1998).

41. For the view that the American national project is ultimately inclusive see Philip Gleason, "American Identity and Americanization," in *Concepts of Ethnicity*, ed. William Petersen, Michael Novak, and Philip Gleason (Cambridge, Mass.: Belknap Press of Harvard University Press, 1982), 57–143; For important works examining the historically exclusive nature of American citizenship see Rogers M. Smith, *Civic Ideals: Conflicting Visions of Citizenship in U.S. History* (New Haven, Conn.: Yale University Press, 1997); Evelyn Nakono Glenn, *Unequal Freedom: How Race and Gender Shaped American Citizenship and Labor* (Cambridge, Mass.: Harvard University Press, 2003); Aristide Zolberg, *A Nation by Design: Immigration Policy in the Fashioning of America* (New York: Russell Sage, 2006).

42. For important examples of the *Sonderweg* argument, see Hans Ulrich Wehler, *Das Deutsche Kaiserreich* (Göttingen: Vandenhoeck and Ruprecht, 1973); Ralf Dahrendorf, *Society and Democracy in Germany* (London: Weidenfeld and Nicolson, 1968); Fritz Stern, *The Failure of Illiberalism: Essays on the Political Culture of Modern Germany* (1972; repr., New York: Columbia University Press, 1992); George L. Mosse, *The Crisis of German Ideology: Intellectual Origins of the Third Reich* (1964; New York: Schocken Books, 1981). Since those books came out, this essentializing view of German history brought about by the Sonderweg has declined. See David Blackbourn and Geoff Eley, *The Peculiarities of German History: Bourgeois Society and Politics in Nineteenth-Century Germany* (Oxford: Oxford University Press, 1984); Margaret Lavinia Anderson, *Practicing Democracy: Elections and Political Culture in Imperial Germany* (Princeton, N.J.: Princeton University Press, 2000); Geoff Eley and Jan Palmowski, eds., *Citizenship and National Identity in Twentieth-Century Germany* (Stanford, Calif.: Stanford University Press, 2008).

43. The 1913 Citizenship Law standardized naturalization procedures throughout Germany, granting the right to citizenship only to those who could prove German ancestry through male bloodline descent. From 1949 to 1999, the law, with certain modifications to allow for maternal descent and some administrative discretion, provided the primary basis for determining naturalization rights within West Germany and post-1990 unified Germany. Generally, when considering the nature of citizenship in Germany during the Wilhelmine period, state interests often trumped ethnocultural considerations. In the case of the 1913 Citizenship Law, the state in-

sisted for political and military reasons that "bloodline descent" would continue to be determined on the basis of gender, that is, hereditary descent from a male citizen within the multinational empire, not on the basis of ethnicity or race, much to the annoyance of German nationalists at the time. The law also made provisions for the naturalization of foreigners who served in the armed forces. For further information on the 1913 Citizenship Law, see Dieter Gosewinkel, *Einbürgern und Ausschliessen: Die Nationalisierung der Staatsangehörigkeit vom Deutschen Bund bis zur Bundesrepublik Deutschland* (Göttingen: Vandenhoeck and Ruprecht, 2001), 324–27.

44. Dieter Gosewinkel, "Citizenship and Naturalization Politics in the Nineteenth and Twentieth Centuries," in *Challenging Ethnic Citizenship: German and Israeli Perspectives on Immigration,* ed. Daniel Levy and Yfaat Weiss (New York: Berghahn Books, 2002), 71.

45. For an overview of legal changes in citizenship law in post–World War II Germany, see Simon Green, *The Politics of Exclusion: Institutions and Immigration Policy in Contemporary Germany* (Manchester: Manchester University Press, 2004).

46. In this regard it might also be noted that from 1790 until the passage of the McCarren-Walter Act in the early-1950s, the right of first generation immigrants to naturalize in the United States was restricted to "free white persons."

47. Since 1992, elements of *jus sanguis* within French citizenship codes have become more pronounced after passage of legislation that required second generation children of immigrants who were born in France to formally apply for French citizenship at adulthood, instead of being automatically accorded it from birth. Similarly, in the United Kingdom, the British Nationality Act of 1981 introduced *jus sanguis* by creating a distinct category of "British" citizen, defined as a person born within England, Wales, Scotland, Northern Ireland, or a dependent territory. This designation, which alone confers the right to residence in the United Kingdom, was designed to limit the ability of immigrants from the Commonwealth to enter Britain. In the United States, while *jus soli* remains the law of the land, there are renewed efforts, taken up against the backdrop of current debates over changing immigration law, to prevent the children of largely nonwhite illegal immigrants living in the United States from automatically gaining the right of citizenship at birth.

48. William Hagen, *Germans, Poles, and Jews: The Nationality Conflict in the Prussian East, 1772–1914* (Chicago: University of Chicago Press, 1980); Richard Blanke, *Prussian Poland in the German Empire, 1871–1900* (Boulder, Colo.: East European Monographs, 1981).

49. Unfortunately, Brubaker acknowledges the experience of Poles in the Ruhr with only a footnote. See Brubaker, *Citizenship and Nationhood,* 192n.

50. Yasemin Soysal, *The Limits of Citizenship* (Chicago: University of Chicago Press, 1994). Soysal argues that we are entering a new era of "postnational" citizenship in which present-day immigrants are able to attain membership within a community even when they do not possess legal citizenship. This is because in most western nations the rights of citizenship have expanded to incorporate post-1945 concepts of human rights that provide legal immigrants the same social and cultural protections enjoyed by actual citizens.

51. For a greater consideration of this argument within the context of German history see Eley and Palmowksi, *Citizenship and National Identity in Twentieth-Century Germany.*

52. For works emphasizing the limited integration prospects of Poles in the Ruhr and northeastern Pennsylvania, see Hans Ulrich Wehler, "Die Polen im Ruhrgebiet bis 1918," in *Moderne deutsche Sozialgeschichte,* ed. Hans Ulrich Wehler (Cologne: Kiepenheuer and Witsch, 1966); Krystyna Murzynowska, *Die polnische Erwerbsauswanderer im Ruhrgebiet während der Jahre 1880–1914* (1972; Dortmund: Forschungsstelle Ostmitteleuropa, 1979); Christoph Klessmann, *Polnische Bergarbeiter im Ruhrgebiet, 1870–1945: Soziale Integration und nationale Subkultur einer Minderheit in der deutschen Industriegesellschaft* (Göttingen: Vandenhoeck und Ruprecht, 1978); Jerzy Kozłowski, *Rozwój organizacji społeczno-narodowych wychodżstwa polskiego w Niemczech w latach 1870–1914* (Wrocław: Zakład Narodowy im. Ossolińskich, 1987); Michael A. Barendse, *Social Expectations and Perception: The Case of the Slavic Anthracite Workers* (University Park: Pennsylvania State University Press, 1981); Perry K. Blatz, *Democratic Miners: Work and Labor Relations in the Anthracite Coal Industry, 1875–1925* (Albany: State University of New York Press, 1994). Studies that stress greater integration include Richard Charles Murphy, *Guestworkers in the German Reich: A Polish Community in Wilhelmine Germany* (Boulder, Colo.: East European Monographs, 1983); Valentina-Maria Stefanski, *Zum Prozess der Emanzipation und Integration von Aussenseitern: Polnische Arbeitsmigranten im Ruhrgebiet* (Dortmund: Forschungsstelle Ostmitteleuropa, 1984); John J. Kulczycki, *The Foreign Worker and the German Labor Movement: Xenophobia and Solidarity in the Coal Fields of the Ruhr, 1871–1914* (Providence, R.I.: Berg, 1994); John J. Kulczycki, *The Polish Coal Miners Union and the German Labor Movement in the Ruhr, 1902–1934* (Oxford: Berg, 1997); Susanne Peters-Schildgen, *"Schmelztiegel" Ruhrgebiet: Die Geschichte der Zuwanderung am Beispiel Herne bis 1945* (Essen: Klartext, 1997); Victor Greene, *The Slavic Community on Strike: Immigrant Labor in Pennsylvania Anthracite* (Notre Dame, Ind.: University of Notre Dame Press, 1968); Harold W. Aurand, *From the Molly Maguires to the United Mine Workers* (Philadelphia: Temple University Press, 1971); Pien Versteegh, "Glück Auf: The Polish Labor Movement in the United States and Germany, 1890–1914," *Polish American Studies* 62, no. 1 (2005): 53–66. Quotation from Kulczycki, *Foreign Worker,* 262. For an excellent recent anthology that brings together various Polish and German historians and their perspectives regarding the Polish experience and integration in the Ruhr, see Dittmarra Dahlmanna, Alberta S. Kotowskiego, and Zbigniewa Karpusa, eds., *Schimanski, Kuzorra i inni: Polacy w Zagłębiu Ruhry 1870/71–1945* (Toruń: Wydawnictwo Adam Marszałek, 2006).

Chapter 1: Migration and Settlement

1. Florian Stasik, *Polska emigracja zarobkowa w Stanach Zjednoczonych Ameryki 1865–1914* (Warsaw: Państwowe Wydawnictwo Naukowe, 1985) 33–40, 46; William Thomas and Florian Znaniecki, *The Polish Peasant in Europe and*

America, 5 vols. (Boston: G. Badger, 1918), 5:1–28; Victor Greene, "Poles," in *Harvard Encyclopedia of American Ethnic Groups*, ed. Stephan Thernstrom (Cambridge, Mass.: Harvard University Press, 1980), 787, 792; Norman Davies, *God's Playground: A History of Poland* (Oxford: Clarendon Press, 1981), 2:180, 279. In 1914, the Polish lands had a population of approximately 24 million. Between 1870 and 1914, conservative estimates place Polish migration to the United States at over 2 million. Others suggest 3–4 million. At least 500,000 Poles moved from eastern Prussia to central and western Germany, with another 600,000–700,000 seasonal migrants to Germany from Austrian Galicia and Russian Poland. In addition, sizable Polish communities existed by 1914 in Brazil, Canada and France.

2. U.S. Bureau of the Census, "Native and Foreign Born Population, by Counties," *Tenth Census of United States, 1880—Population* (Washington, D.C.: Government Printing Office, 1883), 525–26; Christoph Klessmann, *Polnische Bergarbeiter im Ruhrgebiet, 1870–1945: Soziale Integration und nationale Subkultur einer Minderheit in der deutschen Industriegesellschaft* (Göttingen: Vandenhoeck und Ruprecht, 1978), 261. In the Ruhr, the figure given does not include those classified separately as Masurians, Kashubes, or other Polish-speaking foreigners, e.g., those from Russia or Austria. For northeastern Pennsylvania, the actual population figure was most likely several thousand higher due to the misclassification of Poles as Germans, Austrians, or Russians.

3. Staatsarchiv Münster (STAM) OP 5758—Rep. RPA to OPM, "Zahlenmässige Angaben über das Polentum im rheinisch-westfälischen Industriebezirke, 1912," March 27, 1913; Klessmann, *Polnische Bergarbeiter*, 262. In this study, the Masurian population, which spoke a dialect of Polish, is treated as an ethnic group distinct from Poles. Masurians came to the Ruhr from the southern districts of East Prussia (present-day northeast Poland) and were overwhelmingly Lutheran in their religious affiliation. For a general history of the Masurians in East Prussia, see Richard Blanke, *Polish-Speaking Germans? Language and National Identity among the Masurians since 1871* (Cologne: Bohlau, 2001).

4. In the 1910 U.S. census, Poles are not enumerated as a distinct national group. Instead, they are classified either as Germans, Austrians, or Russians based on where they were born in partitioned Poland. To determine the approximate number of Poles in the northeastern Pennsylvania region, I have relied on employment statistics from Pennsylvania, Department of Mines, *Report of the Department of Mines of Pennsylvania*, Part 1—Anthracite, 1914 (Harrisburg: Wm. Stanley Ray, State Printer, 1915), 55–56; statistical information on marital status, occupation, and family size provided by the 1907–1911, United States Senate, *Reports of the U.S. Senate Immigration Commission* (also known as the Dillingham Commission Reports), in particular volume 16, "Immigrants in Industries—Part 19: Anthracite Coal Mining" (Washington, D.C.: Government Printing Office, 1911), 598 (table 12), 662, and 726 (table 30); and Frank Warne's *The Slav Invasion and the Mine Workers* (Philadelphia: J. B. Lippincott, 1904), 60–64, which provides approximations of the ethnic composition of the region. From these sources the following calculations have been made. In 1914, there were 31,812 foreign-born, Polish mine workers, and practically

all foreign-born, Polish males of working age, were employed in mining. As estimated by the Dillingham Reports, 52 percent (16,542) of the foreign-born, Polish mine workers were married heads of household. The average Polish household size, including wife and children under sixteen years, likewise according to the Dillingham Reports, comprised 6.86 members. Using these figures, it can be extrapolated that there were 113,479 Poles in households consisting of foreign-born, married Polish men, their wives and children. Combining this figure with the 15,270 foreign-born, unmarried Polish miners yields 128,749 foreign-born Poles. In addition, there was a sizable number of second generation, native-born Polish men and women sixteen years of age and older. Figures for the number of second-generation Polish females are unavailable. For second-generation Polish men, Frank Warne, a contemporary observer in northeastern Pennsylvania, claimed that the majority of those listed as "native-born" in census reports by the turn of the century were of Slavic origin. Approximately half of those Slavic migrants from Eastern Europe in northeastern Pennsylvania (according to the 1900 census) were Polish. It can thus be extrapolated that of the 58,416 workers listed as "American" in the 1914 mine census statistics, one-quarter, or 14,604, were of Polish origin. Of these Polish mine workers, approximately 9 percent (1,315) were married, thus yielding 9,207 Poles in households consisting of native-born, married Polish men, their wives, and children. Approximately 13 percent, or 2,184, of second-generation Polish men over age sixteen did not work in the mines, mostly because they were either in school or employed in other occupations. Adding these second-generation figures ([14,604–1,315] + 9,207 + 2,184 = 24,680) to first-generation totals (128,749) yields 153,429 Polish persons. Due to the fact that the number of independent, unmarried Polish women over the age of sixteen is unknown as well as the likelihood that employment statistics also undercounted the number of foreign-born Poles, classifying some as Austrians, Russians, or Hungarians, I conservatively estimate that the actual number of Poles was higher, hence the 160,000 figure. The total population in the seven counties constituting the coal-producing regions of northeastern Pennsylvania was in 1910 approximately 1,160,000. See U.S. Bureau of the Census, "Composition and Characteristics of the Population for the State and for Counties," *Thirteenth Census of United States, 1910—Population* (Washington, D.C.: Government Printing Office, 1913), 3:572–85.

    5. Thomas and Znaniecki, *Polish Peasant*, vols. 1, 5; Klessmann, *Polnische Bergarbeiter*, 23–28, 32–37; Victor Greene, *The Slavic Community on Strike: Immigrant Labor in Pennsylvania Anthracite* (Notre Dame, Ind.: University of Notre Dame Press, 1968), 11–12; Richard Charles Murphy, *Guestworkers in the German Reich: A Polish Community in Wilhelmine Germany* (Boulder, Colo.: East European Monographs, 1983), 28–29. For individual accounts of attempts of mine operators to recruit workers in the United States, see *Harper's Magazine*, July 28, 1888; PHMC (Pennsylvania Historical and Museum Commission) MG-409, SOHP—Interview with Theodore Myknik (1973); Instytut Gospodarstwa Społecznego, *Pamiętniki emigrantów, 1878–1958* (Warsaw: Czytelnik, 1960), Memoir of Stanisław Kazimierowski, 721; Donald Miller and Richard Sharpless, *The Kingdom of Coal* (Easton, Penn.: Canal History and Technology Press, 1998), 173; M. Accursia, "Polish Min-

ers in Luzerne County, Pennsylvania," *Polish American Studies* 3, no. 1 (1946): 10. For the Ruhr, see HSTAD RD Präs 835, *Rheinisch-Westfälische Arbeiter Zeitung*, April 30, 1897; HSTAD RD 24720—*Der Bergknappe*, Dec. 1, 1898; STAM BAD 6052—Rep. Bergrevierbeamten Revier III to OBD, Sept. 3, 1906; STAM BAH 7405—Rep. Zeche Shamrock (Hibernia Gesellschaft) to Bergrevierbeamten Herne, Feb. 1906. In the United States, direct recruitment of foreign contract labor was outlawed in 1885, though recruitment at ports of entry continued. In the Ruhr, no ban on recruitment existed, despite repeated calls from both middle- and working-class representatives to halt the practice. By the 1890s, employer recruitment in the Ruhr was for the most part unnecessary as Poles increasingly arrived of their own accord.

6. For a comparative overview of state policies across partitioned Poland, see Benjamin Murdzek, *Emigration in Polish Social-Political Thought, 1870–1914* (Boulder, Colo.: East European Monographs, 1977). For Prussian Poland, see Martin Broszat, *Zweihundert Jahre deutsche Polenpolitik* (Munich: Ehrenwirth, 1963); William Hagen, *Germans, Poles, and Jews: The Nationality Conflict in the Prussian East, 1772–1914* (Chicago: University of Chicago Press, 1980); Richard Blanke, *Prussian Poland in the German Empire, 1871–1900* (Boulder, Colo.: East European Monographs, 1981). For Russian Poland, see Robert Blobaum, *Rewolucja: Russian Poland, 1904–1907* (Ithaca, N.Y.: Cornell University Press, 1995).

7. PHMC MG-409, SOHP—Interview with Stanley Adamovitch (1973). Adamovitch, a miner from northeastern Pennsylvania, recounted that his father "decided to come to America" only when he thought he would have to follow his brothers into the Russian army. In the Ruhr, the total number of Poles from Russia and Austrian Galicia in the Ruhr reached approximately 1,400 by 1912. See STAM OP 5758—Rep. RPM to OPW, "Zahlenmässige Angabe," March 27, 1913.

8. Murphy, *Guestworkers in the German Reich*, 28. All told, land prices increased 250 percent over their 1888 levels by 1906.

9. StO Amt Osterfeld 185—Rep. Polizeiverwaltung Osterfeld, Oct. 21, 1906. For many Poles, the dream of owning farmland would remain out of reach, especially after an amendment to the 1904 *Ansiedlungsgesetz* (Settlement Law) that prohibited Poles in the province of Posen/Poznań from building permanent structures on land acquired as part of the parcelization of former noble estates.

10. Literacy and education rates did vary between Prussian, Russian, and Austrian Poland. In 1911, there were 2,992 schools in the Province of Posen, serving a population of approximately two million. By contrast, there were only 4,000 schools serving a population of almost ten million in Russian Poland. See Davies, *God's Playground*, 124.

11. Thomas and Znaniecki, *Polish Peasant*, 5:16. Later scholars have highlighted the significant levels of regional and seasonal migration that occurred in preindustrial regions of Central and Eastern Europe. See, for example, Steve Hochstadt, *Mobility and Modernity: Migration in Germany, 1820–1989* (Ann Arbor: University of Michigan Press, 1999); Dorota Praszolowicz, "Jewish, Polish, and German Migration from the Prussian Province of Posen/Poznań during the 19th Century," in *Irish and Polish Migration in Comparative Perspective*, ed. John Belchen and

Klaus Tenfelde (Essen: Klartext, 2003); Annemarie Steidl, *Auf nach Wien! Die Mobilität des mitteleuropäischen Handwerks im 18. und 19. Jahrhundert am Beispiel der Haupt- und Residenzstadt Wien* (Munich: Oldenbourg, 2003).

12. Michał Lengowski, *Mój Życiorys* (Olsztyn: Pojezierze, 1974), 23.

13. *Pamiętniki emigrantów*, vol. 1, memoir 25, 559–70.

14. STAM RA 14044—"Rep. LRB to RPA," June 12, 1883. Thomas and Znaniecki, *Polish Peasant*, 5:30–32; Witold Kula, Nina Assorodobraj-Kula, and Marcin Kula, *Writing Home: Immigrants in Brazil and the United States, 1890–1891*, ed. and trans. Josephine Wtulich (New York: Columbia University Press, 1986), 256, 337–38, 420–22, 491–92; Krystyna Murzynowska, *Die polnische Erwerbsauswanderer im Ruhrgebiet während der Jahre 1880–1914* (1972; Dortmund: Forschungsstelle Ostmitteleuropa, 1979), 47–48. In the United States, the importance of family ties is highlighted by 1908 statistics that claim that of the 68,105 Poles admitted into the United States, only 1,010, or 1.4 percent, were not arriving to join a relative or friend. See "Annual Report for the Commissioner of Immigration for the Year Ended June 30, 1908," 15, cited in Emily Balch, *Our Slavic Fellow Citizens* (New York: Charities Publication Committee, 1910), 433.

15. Ewa Morawska, "Labor Migrations of Poles in the Atlantic World Economy, 1880–1914," *Comparative Studies in Society and History* 31, no. 2 (1989): 254; Greene, "Poles," 793; John Bukowczyk, *And My Children Did Not Know Me: A History of the Polish Americans* (Bloomington: Indiana University Press, 1987), 32. For personal accounts of reasons for migrating as well as returning to Poland, see Lengowski, *Mój Życiorys; Pamiętniki chłopów*, vols. 1–2; *Pamiętniki emigrantów*, vols. 1–2. The classic study on Polish return migration after World War I remains Adam Walaszek, *Reemigracja ze Stanów Zjednoczonych do Polski po I. wojnie światowej, 1919–1924* (Cracow: Nakl. Uniwersytetu Jagiellonskiego, 1983).

16. Accursia, "Polish Miners," 10–11; Greene, *Slavic Community on Strike*, 15; Klessmann, *Polnische Bergarbeiter*, 38–39; John J. Kulczycki, *The Foreign Worker and the German Labor Movement: Xenophobia and Solidarity in the Coal Fields of the Ruhr, 1871–1914* (Providence, R.I.: Berg, 1994), 28–29.

17. For more information of Polish agricultural laborers in the Prussian East see Hagen, *Germans, Poles, and Jews*, 132–33, 137, 210.

18. Klessmann, *Polnische Bergarbeiter*, 266. By 1914, of the 133,033 workers in the Ruhr with eastern origins, 7.4 percent came from Upper Silesia, 41.9 percent from Posen, 12.9 percent from West Prussia, and 37.8 percent from East Prussia.

19. U.S. Bureau of the Census, *Twelfth Census of the United States, 1900—Population* (Washington, D.C.: Government Printing Office, 1902), 779–80.

20. Thomas and Znaniecki, *Polish Peasant*, vol. 1; Karen Majewski, *Traitors and True Poles: Narrating a Polish-American Identity, 1880–1939* (Athens: Ohio University Press, 2003), 22–23. For the French peasant experience, see Eugen Weber, *Peasants into Frenchmen: The Modernization of Rural France, 1870–1914* (Stanford, Calif.: Stanford University Press, 1976).

21. Stanislaus Wachowiak, *Die Polen in Rheinland-Westfalen* (Leipzig: Robert Noske, 1916), 100.

22. For a further discussion of Polish immigrant involvement in immigrant affairs, see Brian McCook, "Becoming Transnational: Continental and Transatlantic Polish Migration and Return Migration, 1870–1924," in *Relations among Internal, Continental, and Transatlantic Migration,* ed. Annemarie Steidl, Josef Ehmer, Stan Nadel, and Hermann Zeitlhofer (Göttingen: Vandenhoeck and Ruprecht Unipress, 2009), 151–74.

23. STAM RA 14051—Rep. PDB to RPA, July 23, 1920; For a complete history of the ZZP, see John J. Kulczycki, *The Polish Coal Miners Union and the German Labor Movement in the Ruhr, 1902–1934* (Oxford: Berg, 1997).

24. M. B. Biskupski, "Bishop Hodur, the Pilsudskiites, and Polonia Politics on the Eve of World War I: Documents and Commentary," *Polish National Catholic Church Studies* 7, no. 1 (1986): 39–52; PHMC MG-215, ESC, "Fortieth Anniversary Book of the Good Shepherd Church in Plymouth, PA" (1938). For a complete history of the PNCC, see Hieronim Kubiak, *The Polish National Catholic Church in the United States of America from 1897 to 1980* (Cracow: Nakl. Uniwersytetu Jagiellonskiego, 1983); Stephen Włodarski, *The Origin and Growth of the Polish National Catholic Church* (Scranton, Penn.: PNCC Press, 1974).

25. Peter Roberts, *Anthracite Coal Communities* (New York: Macmillan, 1904), 2, 4–5; Miller and Sharpless, *Kingdom of Coal,* 3–5.

26. Franz-Josef Brüggemeier, *Leben vor Ort: Ruhrbergleute und Ruhrbergbau* (Munich: C. H. Beck, 1983), 271; Klessmann, *Polnische Bergarbeiter,* 262; U.S. Bureau of the Census, *Seventh Census of United States, 1850—Population* (Washington, D.C.: Government Printing Office, 1853), 158–59; *Thirteenth Census of the United States, 1910—Population,* 3:543, 546, 572–85.

27. By the first decade of the twentieth century, approximately 90 percent of the population in Ruhr belonged to the working class, whereas only 5–8 percent was "middle-class." For a broader discussion of class divisions in the Ruhr see Gerhard Ritter and Klaus Tenfelde, *Arbeiter im Deutschen Kaiserreich, 1871 bis 1914* (Bonn: Dietz, 1992), 113–54. For northeastern Pennsylvania see Miller and Sharpless, *Kingdom of Coal,* 77–82.

28. Among the earliest outsiders to arrive in the Ruhr were English, and especially Irish, mine engineers, whose experience in British mines was highly prized by the growing number of German firms engaged in mining operations. Mines with names such as Hibernia, Erin, and Shamrock bear witness to the often forgotten Anglo-Irish presence in the Ruhr coalfields. See Susanne Peters-Schildgen, *"Schmelztiegel" Ruhrgebiet: Die Geschichte der Zuwanderung am Beispiel Herne bis 1945* (Essen: Klartext, 1997), 16–23, and Klaus Tenfelde, *Sozialgeschichte der Bergarbeiterschaft an der Ruhr im 19. Jahrhundert* (Bonn: Verlag Neue Gesellschaft, 1977), 235.

29. STAM BAH 7396—Rep. OBD, Jan. 28, 1905; STAM BAD 6052—Rep. OBD, Sept. 3, 1906; HSTAD RD 15939—Rep. PPE to RPD, Oct. 11, 1912; HSTAD RD 15944—PV Hamborn to RPD March 28, 1912; S. H. F. Hickey, *Workers in Imperial Germany: The Miners of the Ruhr* (Oxford: Oxford University Press, 1985), 33.

30. William Jones, *Wales in America* (Scranton, Penn.: University of Scranton Press, 1997); Roberts, *Anthracite Coal Communities*, 18; *Report of the Department of Mines, 1914*, 55–56.

31. Tenfelde, *Sozialgeschichte der Bergarbeiterschaft an der Ruhr*, 51–53; Hickey, *Workers in Imperial Germany*, 81.

32. Roberts, *Anthracite Coal Communities*, 58, 209–211; AMM-*Diocesan Record*, April 9, 1898; April 18, 1898. In determining the number of Protestants, Roberts estimates that there were 62,580 communicants among the various Protestant churches, which represented 39 percent of the practicing Protestant population. Anti-Catholic sentiment in the northeastern Pennsylvania declined due to the efforts of the Catholic hierarchy to promote the church as an "American" institution, and, in relation to immigrants, an "Americanizing" one. See Chapter 5 for a fuller discussion.

33. Klessmann, *Polnische Bergarbeiter*, 40.

34. Joh. Victor Bredt, *Die Polenfrage im Ruhrkohlengebiet: Eine Wirtschaftspolitische Studie* (Leipzig: Duncker and Humblot, 1909), 17–18. According to Bredt, the mines (and percentage of the workforce who were Polish) were in Revier Gelsenkirchen: Pluto (74.7%), Unser Fritz (54.6%), Konsolidation (55.3%), Hibernia (50.1%), Wilhelmine Viktoria (52.2%); in Revier Recklinghausen: König Ludwig (61.9%), Ewald (85%), Graf Bismarck (71%); in Revier Herne: Viktor (51.2%), Friedrich der Grosse (62.5%), v.d. Heydt (57.5%), Julia (52.5%); in Revier Wattenscheid: Rheinelbe (51.3%); in Revier West Essen: Prosper I (63.6%), Prosper II (69.6%); in Revier Ost Essen: Zollverein (52.2%), Friedrich-Ernestine (50.6%); in Revier Süd Essen: Ludwig (63.8%); in Revier Süd-Bochum: Dannenbaum (71.9%). Not all of these workers were in fact "Polish." Many were either Germans or Masurians from the Prussian East. Further, John Kulczycki argues that there in fact only eleven collieries could be considered "Polish mines" and that the figures provided by Bredt were inflated in order to raise German nationalist alarms about the Polish presence in the Ruhr. See John J. Kulczycki, "Polscy górnicy w Zagłębiu Ruhry," *Przegląd Polonijny* 13, no. 3 (1987): 21–26; Kulczycki, *Foreign Worker*, 36.

35. HSTAD LA Essen 101—*Wiarus Polski*, Oct. 28, 1908; Franz Schulze, *Die polnische Zuwanderung im Ruhrrevier und ihre Wirkung* (Munich: Josefs Druckerei, Bigge, 1909), 23–43; Klessmann, *Polnische Bergarbeiter*, 38–40; Kulczycki, *Foreign Worker*, 35–40; Murphy, *Guestworkers in the German Reich*, 28; Peters-Schildgen, *"Schmelztiegel" Ruhrgebiet*, 34–47. Günter Mertins, *Die Kulturlandschaft des westlichen Ruhrgebiets (Mühlheim-Oberhausen-Dinslaken)* (Giessen: Wilhelm Schmitz Verlag, 1964), 139–42; Tenfelde, *Sozialgeschichte der Bergarbeiterschaft an der Ruhr*, 42.

36. STAM OP 5758—Rep. RPM to OPW, "Zahlenmässige Angabe," March 27, 1913.

37. Accursia, "Polish Miners," 5; Greene, *Slavic Community on Strike*, 35–39.

38. Warne, *Slav Invasion and the Mine Workers*, 47–51.

39. Klessmann, *Polnische Bergarbeiter*, 268; Roberts, *Anthracite Coal Communities*, 57.

40. For the Ruhr, see Klessmann, *Polnische Bergarbeiter*, 268. Divided by subgroup, gender ratios in the Ruhr were more equal within the Masurian community than in the Polish, though this is primarily attributable to the fact that the migration flow of Poles, particularly those from Posen, lagged about a decade behind that of the Masurians from East Prussia. For northeastern Pennsylvania, see *Reports of the U.S. Senate Immigration Commission*, vol. 16, "Immigrants in Industries—Part 19: Anthracite Coal Mining," 637, table 46. The ratio is based on a sample of 428 Polish males and 277 females.

41. Murphy, *Guestworkers in the German Reich*, 103, 108–10; Roberts, *Anthracite Coal Communities*, 64; *Reports of the U.S. Senate Immigration Commission*, vol. 16, "Immigrants in Industries—Part 19: Anthracite Coal Mining," 635, table 45. The Immigration Report notes that in northeastern Pennsylvania, 87.6 percent of Polish males between the ages of 30 and 44 years were married.

42. STAM OP 5758—Rep. RPM to OPW, "Zahlenmässige Angabe," March 27, 1913; Roberts, *Anthracite Coal Communities*, 58; PHMC MG-409, SOHP—Interview with Henry Klonowski, Aux. Bishop of Scranton (1973). In 1912, only 3.2 percent of Polish men and 2.2 percent of Polish women in the Ruhr were married to Germans. Even among the Protestant Masurians, this figure only reached approximately 5 percent for males and 3 percent for females. In northeastern Pennsylvania, interethnic marriage rates were similarly low. Although exact statistics are unavailable, observers of the period note that such marriages were rare. Peter Roberts, an ethnographer of the northeastern Pennsylvania coalfields at the turn of the century, noted that "the foreign born are generally endogamous as to race . . . out of 118 Sclav [*sic*] young men [sampled], only two of them married Sclav [*sic*] women of a different race from that of their own." Rates of interethnic marriage began to increase after World War I, as a second generation of Poles born and reared in the Ruhr and northeastern Pennsylvania began to marry; however, such marriages generally remained taboo until after World War II.

43. For the Ruhr, see Schulze, *Die polnische Zuwanderung im Ruhrrevier*, 40–43. The estimate is derived from 1906 statistics for Poles living in the Regierungsbezirk Arnsberg. In 1906, there were 41,562 married Polish women and 96,962 children under the age of fourteen, which yields an average of 2.33 children per married Polish woman. It should be noted that this calculation does not account for infant mortality or those over the age of fourteen, so the average number of children born to Polish mothers is most likely closer to three. This number also accords with later estimates made by Christoph Klessmann and Jan Molenda. See Klessmann, *Polnische Bergarbeiter*, 42; Jan Molenda, "The Role of Women in Polish Migration to the Rhine-Westphalia Industrial Region at the Beginning of the Twentieth Century," *Polish Review* 42, no. 3 (1997): 323. For northeastern Pennsylvania, see *Reports of the U.S. Senate Immigration Commission*, vol. 16, "Immigrants in Industries—Part 19: Anthracite Coal Mining," 662; Roberts, *Anthracite Coal Communities*, 73.

44. Outside of the cities of Scranton and Wilkes-Barre, less than 5.5 percent of wage earners were female in northeastern Pennsylvania at the turn of the century.

In Scranton itself, 22.7 percent of wage earners were female, while in Wilkes-Barre, this figure stood at 23.6 percent. See Roberts, *Anthracite Coal Communities,* 14, 137–38; *Reports of the U.S. Senate Immigration Commission,* vol. 16, "Immigrants in Industries—Part 19: Anthracite Coal Mining," 614. In the Ruhr, approximately 3 percent of Polish women worked as industrial wage earners in 1907. The total number engaged in industrial, commercial, and agricultural work in 1912 was 19,000, or approximately 30 percent of all Polish women. See Murzynowska, *Die polnische Erwerbsauswanderer im Ruhrgebiet,* 37–43; Molenda, "The Role of Women in Polish Migration to the Rhine-Westphalia Industrial Region," 322–24.

45. HSTAD RD Präs. 867—Rep. OPW (von Studt) Oct. 31, 1896. After World War I, Polish-language gymnasiums were erected in Marienwerder and Bytom. Approximately, 80 Polish students from the Ruhr region attended. See Helena Lehr and Edmund Osmańczyk, *Polacy spod znaku rodła* (Warsaw: Wydawnictwo Ministerstwa Obrony Narodowej, 1972), 84.

46. *Reports of the U.S. Senate Immigration Commission,* vol. 33, "The Children of Immigrants in Schools—Scranton and Shenandoah, Pennsylvania" (Washington, D.C.: Government Printing Office, 1911), 377–91, 471–81; Roberts, *Anthracite Coal Communities,* 154–57, 166–67. On average, boys attended school for four and a half years until the age of eleven, while girls attended for slightly over five years until the age of twelve. In Scranton and Shenandoah, approximately 50 and 40 percent attended Catholic parochial schools, respectively.

47. Ralf Karl Oenning, *Du da Mitti, polnische Farben: Sozialisationserfahrungen von Polen im Ruhrgebiet 1918 bis 1939* (Münster: Waxmann, 1991); PHMC MG-409, SOHP—Interview with Henry Dende (1973). When asked if there was difficulty going to school because of his Polish background, Dende replied: "No, but we always had an inferiority complex. Those that were Irish didn't have any difficulties, and the English and the Welsh. And the Germans didn't have it too bad but when the Polish people came it was too bad. And you had the feeling of a second class citizen and you were treated that way. And they would call you a Hunky, or a greenhorn."

48. *Reports of the U.S. Senate Immigration Commission,* vol. 33, "The Children of Immigrants in Schools—Scranton and Shenandoah, Pennsylvania," 386. Among elementary school age children, the Immigration Commission found that 34.4 percent of all Polish children were retarded versus an average of 18.2 percent for native-born children. The percentage of retardation increased as children grew older. Among ten-, eleven-, twelve-year-olds, the rate of what was thought of as Polish retardation stood at 65.1 percent versus 26.8 percent for native children.

49. In the Ruhr, the primary scholarship program was the St. Josephat Collection, created in 1891 to support the training of young Poles as priests. In 1907, the goals of this fund expanded to include support for general higher educational purposes, especially with the aim of supporting the development of a Polish middle class and intelligentsia in the Ruhr. Between 1892 and 1914 more than 200 students received a stipend. For more on the St. Josephat fund, see HSTAD RD Präs. 867—Rep. OPW (von Studt) Oct. 31, 1896; StB LA 1306 Bd. 2—Rep. RPA to MdI, Nov. 28, 1907;

Jerzy Kozłowski, *Rozwój organizacji społeczno-narodowych wychodżstwa polskiego w Niemczech w latach 1870–1914* (Wrocław: Zakład Narodowy im. Ossolińskich, 1987), 161–63. In northeastern Pennsylvania, a few young men were eligible for scholarships through Polish fraternal organizations such as the Polish National Alliance (PNA), the smaller Polish Roman Catholic Union (PRCU), and the Polish National Union, the latter affiliated with the Polish National Catholic Church.

50. HSTAD RD Präs. 835—*Bergknappe*, Feb. 26, 1897; RD 24720—*Deutsche Berg- und Hüttenarbeiterzeitung*, Oct. 15, 1898; PHMC MG-409, SOHP—Interview with Father Bocianski (1973); Klessmann, *Polnische Bergarbeiter*, 72; Hickey, *Workers in Imperial Germany*, 20; Roberts, *Anthracite Coal Communities*, 13–16; Thomas Dublin and Walter Licht, *The Face of Decline: The Pennsylvania Anthracite Region in the Twentieth Century* (Ithaca, N.Y.: Cornell University Press, 2005), 40–41. In the pre–World War I era, a few women in both the Ruhr and northeastern Pennsylvania were able to work as clericals within the mine complex. The demands of World War I and its aftermath significantly increased the employment of women in the mines. Although still restricted from working underground, women filled many above-ground ancillary positions. In the Ruhr, the ZZP miners' union organized a women's auxiliary in 1918. Women's experience in mining was not easy, as evidenced by complaints about favoritism and sexual harassment in the workplace. See HSTAD LA Moers 395 Bd.1—"Rep. to LR Moers," June 2, 1918; HSTAD RD 16020—"Rep. PPB to RPA" Aug. 11, 1918; STAM BAH 7553—"Complaint of Maria Andrasky (pseud.) to BR Herne," Oct. 20, 1919.

51. Brüggemeier, *Leben vor Ort*, 276.

52. Anthracite Coal Strike Commission, *Report to the President on the Anthracite Coal Strike of May–Oct. 1902* (Washington, D.C.: Government Printing Office, 1903), 43; Roberts, *Anthracite Coal Communities*, 120–22.

53. Brüggemeier, *Leben vor Ort*, 276.

54. Roberts, *Anthracite Coal Communities*, 125.

55. Ibid., 107; STAM BAD 6067—Rep. OBD May 14, 1914. In the Ruhr, for example, the number of animals raised in the Erin, Westhausen, and Hansa mining colonies were as follows: Erin mine: 3 cows, 62 pigs, 275 goats, 5 sheep, 497 chickens and 1,923 roosters, geese, and ducks; Westhausen mine: 704 pigs, 182 goats, 4 sheep, 565 chickens, 1,569 roosters, geese, and ducks; Hansa mine: 431 pigs, 220 goats, 11 sheep, 565 chickens, 1,450 roosters, geese, and ducks.

56. *Reports of the U.S. Senate Immigration Commission*, vol. 16, "Immigrants in Industries—Part 19: Anthracite Coal Mining," 669; PHMC MG-409, SOHP—Interview with Henry Klonowski, Aux. Bishop of Scranton (1973); interview with Sidney Grabowski (1973).

57. Many observers of the period and subsequent historians have argued that the Ruhr Poles tended to remain "unter sich" (to themselves), holding up the mine colonies as a prime example of the way Poles were segregated from larger society. Many colonies, however, were quite integrated. In Gelsenkirchen-Buer, a survey of names and addresses of those living on streets around the mines Bismarck, Wilhelm Victoria, Unser Fritz, and Hugo displays no pattern of segregation between Poles

and Germans. See Stadtarchiv Gelsenkirchen (StG), *Adressbuch der Stadt Buer,* *1910/1911.*

58. *Reports of the U.S. Senate Immigration Commission,* vol. 16, "Immigrants in Industries—Part 19: Anthracite Coal Mining," 639; Roberts, *Anthracite Coal Communities,* 135

59. STAM OP 5758—Rep. RPM to OPW, "Zahlenmässige Angabe," March 27, 1913. The total number of Polish-owned homes in the Ruhr in 1912 was 1,052, while the total number of male heads of household was 63,020.

60. STAM Kreis Recklinghausen, Nr. 14—see various police reports from 1902–1903; STAM OP 5758—Rep. RPM to OPW, "Zahlenmässige Angabe," March 27, 1913. In 1912, there were 35,486 Polish boarders. For a localized analysis of levels of boarders, see StG, Buer II/5/6—Police reports for December 1912. Employers in the Ruhr also encouraged the keeping of boarders, since the system contributed to stabilizing the workforce. In fact, some placed pressure on their employees to board laborers, causing some dissatisfaction as evidenced by the fact that one of the demands made by miners during the 1912 strike was that they no longer be forced to take in boarders. For more information see Bochum Bergbau Museum Archive (BBA), Bestand 20, File 563—Demands of the Verband der Bergarbeiter Deutschlands, Polnische Berufsvereinigung (Bergarbeiterabteilung), Gewerkverein der Bergarbeiter Hirsch-Dunker, Feb. 19, 1912.

61. Klessmann, *Polnische Bergarbeiter,* 262, 271. In 1902, government statistics report that there were 29,872 boarders within a Polish-speaking population of 162,578 in the province of Westphalia. In 1912, there were 35,486 boarders for a Polish-speaking population of 356,448.

62. *Reports of the U.S. Senate Immigration Commission,* vol. 16, "Immigrants in Industries—Part 19: Anthracite Coal Mining," tables 33 and 34, 626.

63. STAM Kreis Recklinghausen, Nr. 14. For examples of the intimate problems of the boarding house see various police reports for 1902–1903 including the case of Andreas Losinski vs. Ignatz Olejniczak (July–September 1902). The perception that the overcrowding brought about by the boarding system posed health hazards and weakened moral standards caused the Prussian government to forcibly intervene. In 1892, a law was adopted that required at least one bed and washbasin be provided for every two boarders who slept in the same bed on alternate shifts. To this were other regulations requiring each miner to obtain police permission prior to housing boarders and provisions established for the immediate revocation of this permission should improprieties in the boarding arrangement be discovered. See also in same file a copy of Regierungs-Polizei Verordnung, Jan. 12, 1892.

64. AMM-*Diocesan Record,* Aug. 25, 1888.

65. *Reports of the U.S. Senate Immigration Commission,* vol. 16, "Immigrants in Industries—Part 19: Anthracite Coal Mining," 669–76.

66. BBA Bestand 72, File 1029—Letter from Deutscher Verein für Gasthaus- reform to Oberbergrat Recklinghausen, July 18, 1913; Roberts, *Anthracite Coal Communities,* 232. In 1913, the Deutscher Verein für Gasthausreform (German Association for Public House Reform) in Recklinghausen noted that saloons were

responsible for "impoverishing workers" and likened them to "vampires who were sucking the working class dry." In his treatise on northeastern Pennsylvania, Peter Roberts asked the question, "If left to the unrestrained influence of the saloon, which today plays so prominent a part in [workers'] social and economic life, what type of worker will be evolved, upon whom will rest the obligation of faithful and efficient workmanship in this risky business of digging coal?"

67. E. P. Thompson was one of the first historians to aptly recognize the socializing role of the saloon or public house in working-class life. Practitioners of *Alltagsgeschichte* have also provided adept analyses of the importance of the saloon to ordinary workers. See, for example, Brüggemeier, *Leben vor Ort*. For other studies that address the role of the saloon, and drinking culture in general, see Susanna Barrows and Robin Room, eds., *Drinking: Behavior and Belief in Modern History* (Berkeley: University of California Press, 1991); Madelon Powers, *Faces Along the Bar: Lore and Order in the Workingman's Saloon, 1870–1920* (Chicago: University of Chicago Press, 1998).

68. Brüggemeier, *Leben vor Ort*, 144;

69. Roberts, *Anthracite Coal Communities*, 238.

70. An apt example of Polish women's use of the saloon as a means to participate more fully in public life is provided by a 1907 *Märkischer Sprecher* newspaper account of a meeting held by the Polish women's club *Wanda* in a local Herne saloon. The owner of the public house attempted to get the women to end their meeting early because he was frustrated that, due to all of their passionate speaking, they were not ordering any drinks or food. The meeting nevertheless continued well into the evening, and when the women asked the saloon owner to turn the gas lights on, he refused, saying he was not going to lose any more money on gas. In response, some women then went and fetched lanterns from their home and continued the meeting. See STAM RA 1417—*Märkischer Sprecher* (Bochum), Feb. 21, 1907. Peter Roberts noted in his study, "It is nothing unusual to see both women and men of the Sclav races taking their social glass in public houses. The Poles . . . are considered the heaviest drinkers in the coal fields." See Roberts, *Anthracite Coal Communities*, 242.

71. Roberts, *Anthracite Coal Communities*, 259; STAM OP 5758—Rep. RPM to OPW, "Zahlenmässige Angabe," March 27, 1913. Many Polish associations borrowed and adapted practices of native organizations. In the Ruhr, the bylaws of early Polish-Catholic associations were often copied directly from German-Catholic associations. Members of the "Unity" association in Langendreer discussed in 1905 adopting a formal ceremony for the burial of its members. The head of the club acknowledged that he had no experience in this regard, at which point members suggested they simply copy the ceremony that other German associations traditionally performed. For further information, see STAM RA 14044—Rep LR Bochum to RPA, Jan. 10, 1884; StB Amt Langendreer 350—Police Report, March 28. 1905.

72. HSTAD RD Präs. 867—Rep. OPW (von Studt) Oct. 31, 1896.

73. STAM OP 6396—"Stand der Polenbewegung," April 15, 1911. After World War I, the *Narodowiec* grew more conservative relative to the *Wiarus Polski*.

74. STAM OP 5758—Rep. RPM to OPW, "Zahlenmässige Angabe," March 27, 1913.

75. Joseph Wieczerzak, "Bishop Francis Hodur and the Socialists: Associations and Disassociations," in *Bishop Francis Hodur: Biographical Essays,* ed. Joseph Wieczerzak (Boulder, Colo.: East European Monographs, 1998), 118.

76. The influence of the *Górnik Pensylwanski* in its first years of existence is difficult to determine as no early issues of the paper were preserved. However, the vociferous condemnation by *Straż* of this rival indicates that the paper found support among Poles in northeastern Pennsylvania. See Collections of the Polish National Catholic Church (CPNCC)—*Straż* (Scranton), Aug. 30, 1902; Feb. 7, 1903. In the early 1920s, the *Górnik Pensylwanski* was taken over by the Dende Publishing Company, renamed the *Republika-Górnik Pensylwanski,* and embraced a stronger conservative-nationalist direction. See also PHMC MG-409, SOHP—Interview with Henry Dende (1973).

77. For a greater discussion of Polish newspapers in the United States, see James Pula, *Polish Americans: An Ethnic Community* (New York: Twayne, 1995). Definitive circulation figures for these various newspapers are unavailable. Attached to many of these various Polish newspapers were also publishing houses, which fostered the emergence of a robust Polish-American émigré literature in the late nineteenth and early twentieth centuries. For further information, see Majewski, *Traitors and True Poles,* 30–51.

78. The level of remittances to the homeland was high. In 1915, it was estimated that in northeastern Pennsylvania, approximately ten million dollars was transferred annually to Central and Eastern Europe. See AMM-*Coal Age,* July 3, 1915. In 1908, in Shenandoah, Pennsylvania, one company claimed that its workers alone sent two hundred thousand dollars to Eastern Europe. See *Reports of the U.S. Senate Immigration Commission,* vol. 16, "Immigrants in Industries—Part 19: Anthracite Coal Mining," 684. In the Ruhr, the exact levels of remittances are difficult to reconstruct due to the lack of sufficient data. However, the concern among German officials that monies earned by Poles in the Ruhr were not being reinvested in the local economy, but instead sent to Poland, was sizable. See HSTAD LA Moers 467—Rep. RPD to LA Moers, March 11, 1910; Rep. Bürgermeister Baerl to LA Moers, April 7, 1910; April 17, 1910.

79. HSTAD LA Moers 467—Rep. RPD to LA Moers, March 11, 1910; CPNCC-*Straż,* June 6, 1906; STAM RM VII, Nr. 33—Rep. PPB to RPA, Nov. 5, 1913; STAM RM VII, Nr. 35—"Stand der Polenbewegung," May 4, 1914; Aug. 31, 1920; *Reports of the U.S. Senate Immigration Commission,* vol. 16, "Immigrants in Industries—Part 19: Anthracite Coal Mining," 683.

80. *Reports of the U.S. Senate Immigration Commission,* vol. 16, "Immigrants in Industries—Part 19: Anthracite Coal Mining," 683; STAM RM VII Nr. 35—"Stand der Polenbewegung," May 4, 1914.

81. STAM RM VII, Nr. 33—Rep. PPB to RPA, Nov. 5, 1913; *Reports of the U.S. Senate Immigration Commission,* vol. 16, "Immigrants in Industries—Part 19: Anthracite Coal Mining," 683–84.

82. STAM OP 5758—Rep. RPM to OPW, "Zahlenmässige Angabe," March 27, 1913.

83. *Reports of the U.S. Senate Immigration Commission,* vol. 16, "Immigrants in Industries—Part 19: Anthracite Coal Mining," 690–92.

Chapter 2: The Face of Mining

1. Christoph Klessmann, *Polnische Bergarbeiter im Ruhrgebiet, 1870–1945: Soziale Integration und nationale Subkultur einer Minderheit in der deutschen Industriegesellschaft* (Göttingen: Vandenhoeck und Ruprecht, 1978), 264; State of Pennsylvania, *Report of the Department of Mines of Pennsylvania,* Part 1—Anthracite, 1914 (Harrisburg: Wm. Stanley Ray, 1915), 57, table 2; U.S. Bureau of the Census, *Fourteenth Census of the United States, 1920—Mines and Quarries,* vol. 11 (Washington, D.C.: Government Printing Office, 1923), 258, table 8.

2. S. H. F. Hickey, *Workers in Imperial Germany: The Miners of the Ruhr* (Oxford: Oxford University Press, 1985), 110–11; Franz-Josef Brüggemeier, *Leben vor Ort: Ruhrbergleute und Ruhrbergbau* (Munich: C. H. Beck, 1983), 75; Max J. Koch, *Die Arbeiterbewegung im Ruhrgebiet zur Zeit Wilhelms II* (Düsseldorf: Droste, 1954), 139; Peter Roberts, *The Anthracite Coal Industry* (New York: Macmillan, 1901), 107; *Thirteenth Census of the United States, 1910—Mines and Quarries 1909: General Report and Analysis,* vol. 11 (Washington, D.C.: Government Printing Office, 1913), 232; *Report of the Department of Mines of Pennsylvania,* Part 1—Anthracite, 1914, 56; Harold W. Aurand, *From the Molly Maguires to the United Mine Workers* (Philadelphia: Temple University Press, 1971), 37.

3. STAM OP 5758—Rep. RPM to OPW, "Zahlenmässige Angabe," March 27, 1913; Klessmann, *Polnische Bergarbeiter,* 43; John J. Kulczycki, *The Foreign Worker and the German Labor Movement: Xenophobia and Solidarity in the Coal Fields of the Ruhr, 1871–1914* (Providence, R.I.: Berg, 1994), 34; Frank Warne, *The Slav Invasion and the Mine Workers* (Philadelphia: J. B. Lippincott, 1904), 60–64; *Twelfth Census of the United States, 1900 Population,* 779–80; M. Accursia, "Polish Miners in Luzerne County, Pennsylvania," *Polish American Studies* 3, no. 1 (1946): 10; Donald Miller and Richard Sharpless, *The Kingdom of Coal* (Easton, Penn.: Canal History and Technology Press, 1998), 186. By 1912 approximately 60 percent of Poles in the Ruhr were employed in mining, while the other 40 percent were in other industries. In northeastern Pennsylvania over 80 percent of Poles were employed in mining prior to 1914 because of the lack of alternative industries.

4. Bernd Weisbrod, "Arbeitgeberpolitik und Arbeitsbeziehungen im Ruhrbergbau: Vom 'Herr-im-Haus' zur Mitbestimmung," in *Arbeiter, Unternehmer und Staat im Bergbau: Industriellen Beziehungen im Internationalen Vergleich,* ed. Klaus Tenfelde and Gerald Feldman (Munich: C. H. Beck Verlag, 1989), 113; Hickey, *Workers in Imperial Germany,* 14–17.

5. Brüggemeier, *Leben vor Ort,* 83; Weisbrod, "Arbeitgeberpolitik und Arbeitsbeziehungen im Ruhrbergbau," 114, 118–19; Hickey, *Workers in Imperial Germany,* 15–16; Kulczycki, *Foreign Worker,* 15–16; Carl Ludwig Holtfrerich, *Quantitative*

Wirtschaftsgeschichte des Ruhrkohlenbergbaus im 19. Jahrhundert (Dortmund: Gesellschaft für Westfälische Wirtschaftsgeschichte, 1973), 30–35.

6. William Walsh, *The United Mine Workers of America as an Economic and Social Force in the Anthracite Territory* (Washington, D.C.: Catholic University Press, 1931), 87–88; The Office of Inspector of Mines was created due to pressure regarding mine safety conditions, particularly in the wake of the 1869 Avondale Mine Disaster, where a mine fire in the vicinity of Plymouth, Pennsylvania, caused the deaths of 108 men and boys. To this day, the Avondale mine fire remains the worst disaster in the history of anthracite mining.

7. Aurand, *From the Molly Maguires to the United Mine Workers*, 15–18; Victor Greene, *The Slavic Community on Strike: Immigrant Labor in Pennsylvania Anthracite* (Notre Dame, Ind.: University of Notre Dame Press, 1968), 7–11; Miller and Sharpless, *Kingdom of Coal*, 82, 286; *Thirteenth Census of the United States, 1910—Mines and Quarries 1909*, 199; Talcott Williams, "A General View of the Coal Strike," *American Monthly Review of Reviews* 26, no. 1 (1902): 64–66; Rosamond Rhone, "Anthracite Coal Mines and Mining," *American Monthly Review of Reviews* 26, no. 1 (1902): 62; Thomas Dublin and Walter Licht, *The Face of Decline: The Pennsylvania Anthracite Region in the Twentieth Century* (Ithaca, N.Y.: Cornell University Press, 2005), 19–20. The railroad companies were the Reading Company (which controlled the Philadelphia & Reading Railroad, the Philadelphia & Reading Coal and Iron Company, and the Central New Jersey Railroad), the Delaware, Lackawanna & Western Railroad, the Lehigh Valley Railroad (which also controlled the Delaware, Susquehanna & Schuylkill Railroad), the Erie Railroad (which also controlled the New York, Susquehanna & Western Railroad and the Pennsylvania Coal Company), the New York, Ontario & Western Railroad, the Pennsylvania Railroad, and the Delaware and Hudson Coal and Navigation Company.

8. Prior to deregulation, the special status accorded mine workers included the right to be at least partially excluded from taxation, a dispensation from military service, various fishing and hunting rights as well as the right to wear distinct uniforms that conveyed miners' corporate status within the Prussian state. For further information on the development of mining and mine-worker organization see Klaus Tenfelde, *Sozialgeschichte der Bergarbeiterschaft an der Ruhr im 19. Jahrhundert* (Bonn: Verlag Neue Gesellschaft, 1977). Also for an examination of the early history of mining, see Otto Hue, *Die Bergarbeiter: Historische Darstellung der Bergarbeiter-Verhältnisse von der ältesten bis in die neue Zeit,* 2 vols. (Stuttgart: Dietz Verlag, 1910, 1913).

9. For further information on the Knappenvereine see Evelyn Kroker and Werner Kroker, *Solidarität aus Tradition: Die Knappen Verein im Ruhrgebiet* (Essen: C. H. Beck, 1988). The word *Knappschaft* has a dual meaning. In addition to the word's use as the designation for the pension fund, an older meaning was frequently used to refer to mine workers as a corporate body.

10. Klaus Tenfelde, "The Herne Riots of 1899," in *The Social History of Politics: Critical Perspectives in West German Historical Writing since 1945,* ed. Georg Iggers (Dover, N.H.: Berg, 1985), 292–93.

11. Hickey, *Workers in Imperial Germany*, 84–90, 94–105; Michael Schäfer, *Heinrich Imbusch: Christlicher Gewerkschaftsführer und Widerstandskämpfer* (Munich: C. H. Beck, 1990), 22–24. Brüggemeier, *Leben vor Ort*, 182–85; Karl Ditt and Dagmar Kift, "Der Bergarbeiterstreik von 1889: Ein Testfall für die sozialpolitische Reformfähigkeit des Kaisserreichs," in *1889 Bergarbeiterschaft und Wilhelminische Gesellschaft*, ed. Karl Ditt and Dagmar Kift (Hagen: Linnepe, 1989), 12–13. The Gewerkverein was Christian-social in orientation although a strong Catholic influence remained within the organization that limited the overall appeal of this union to Protestant workers. In addition, there was a liberal-capitalist Hirsch-Dunker union established in 1883, with total membership in the low thousands throughout the period under examination.

12. Walsh, *United Mine Workers*, 47–65. In 1849, the Bates union, the first formal worker organization, appeared in the region, however, it quickly collapsed when the leader of the union, a former chartist from England, absconded with the union purse in 1850.

13. The history of the Molly Maguires has been well documented by several excellent works including Aurand, *From the Molly Maguires to the United Mine Workers;* Kevin Kenny, *Making Sense of the Molly Maguires* (New York: Oxford University Press, 1998); Wayne Broehl Jr., *The Molly Maguires* (Cambridge, Mass.: Harvard University Press, 1964). After several violent murders during the mid-1870s, a coordinated effort by mineowners, the Pinkerton Detective Agency, the State of Pennsylvania, and the federal government was undertaken to destroy the group. By the end of the 1870s, the power of the "Mollies" was completely broken after several leaders were captured, tried, and later executed.

14. Walsh, *United Mine Workers*, 72–98; Greene, *Slavic Community on Strike*, 122–28.

15. Heinrich Herkner, *Die Arbeiterfrage: Eine Einführung* (1921; Berlin and Leipzig: de Gruyter, 1922), 1:440.

16. "Letter from G. Baer to W.F. Clark, July 17, 1902," reprinted in *United Mine Workers Journal (UMWJ)*, Aug. 28, 1902.

17. HSTAD LA Moers 788—"Rep. of Polizei Inspektor to Polizei Verwaltung Moers," Oct. 28, 1906. Excerpt from speech given by H. Löffler to an open meeting of 1,000 mine workers.

18. STAM BAD 6052—Various Reports of Mine Companies to Revier Dortmund III, July 21, 1903; Weisbrod, "Arbeitgeberpolitik und Arbeitsbeziehungen im Ruhrbergbau," 124; Hickey, *Workers in Imperial Germany*, 139; Roberts, *Anthracite Coal Communities*, 34–35; Aurand, *From the Molly Maguires to the United Mine Workers*, 37; Perry K. Blatz, *Democratic Miners: Work and Labor Relations in the Anthracite Coal Industry, 1875–1925* (Albany: State University of New York Press, 1994), 14; Greene, *Slavic Community on Strike*, 54.

19. STAM BAH 7405—"Rep. OBD," Feb. 23, 1910. The establishment of the *Arbeitsnachweis* was an employers' response to the official ban on keeping blacklists. In northeastern Pennsylvania, the geographic areas covered by the anthracite fields as well as the seasonality of work made the appearance of an *Arbeitsnachweis*

impractical, hence workers were more likely to be able to obtain new employment elsewhere if fired. For further information see Walsh, *United Mine Workers,* 44.

20. Brüggemeier, *Leben vor Ort,* 94–96; Kulczycki, *Foreign Worker,* 42; Blatz, *Democratic Miners,* 12; *Report of the Department of Mines of Pennsylvania,* Part 1—Anthracite, 1903 (Harrisburg, 1904), xiv–xviii; Walsh, *United Mine Workers,* 83–84. The presence of child labor in the anthracite fields elicited enormous condemnation in the American press, particularly after the turn of the century. The issue of *Harper's Weekly,* Aug. 11, 1906, quoting from John Spargo's *Bitter Cry of the Children,* noted the following "joys" of young workers in the Pennsylvania anthracite fields: "For ten or eleven hours a day, children of ten and eleven stoop over the chute and pick out the slate and other impurities from the coal as it moves past them. The air is black with coal dust, and the roar of the crushers, screens, and rushing mill-race of coal is deafening. Sometimes one of the children falls into the machinery and is terribly mangled, or slips into the chute and is smothered to death. Many children are killed in this way. Many others, after a time, contract coal-miners' asthma and consumption, which gradually undermine their health. Breathing continually, day after day, the clouds of coal dust, their lungs become black and choked with small particles of anthracite."

21. Blatz, *Democratic Miners,* 12–18; Kulczycki, *Foreign Worker,* 42–45, 90–93.

22. State of Pennsylvania, "Legislative Investigating Committee Report on Conditions Existing Among the Miners and those Employed in and about the Mines in the Anthracite Coal Regions." *Journal of the Senate of the Commonwealth of Pennsylvania for the Session begun at Harrisburg of the 5th day of January 1897,* II (Harrisburg: Wm. Stanley Ray, State Printer, 1897), 1830. Anthracite Coal Strike Commission, *Report to the President on the Anthracite Coal Strike of May–Oct. 1902* (Washington, D.C.: Government Printing Office, 1903), 68–69; HSTAD LA Moers 788—*Ruhrorter Zeitung,* Jan. 12, 1905; STAM BAH 7396—*Essener Volkszeitung,* Feb. 9, 1905.

23. For examples of such studies see David Roediger, *The Wages of Whiteness: Race and the Making of the American Working Class* (New York: Verso, 1991), and Noel Ignatiev, *How the Irish Became White* (New York: Routledge, 1995).

24. STAM Kreis Gelsenkirchen 53—*Arbeiter Zeitung,* Dec. 23, 1899; Catholic University Archives (CUA), John Mitchell Papers (JMP) Collection 3, Box 3—"Letter to William D. Ryan," Sept. 24, 1900; Stanislaus Wachowiak, *Die Polen in Rheinland-Westfalen* (Leipzig: Robert Noske, 1916), 42.

25. More specifically, anthracite coal has a carbon content between 86 and 98 percent and a heat value of approximately 15,000 BTUs-per-pound. Bituminous coal has a carbon content between 45 and 86 percent and a heat value of 10,500 to 15,500 BTUs-per-pound. In Germany, both anthracite and bituminous coal were classed together as "Steinkohl," or hard coal, and divided into seven graded levels of impurity. These coal grades (impurity levels by percentage) are: Anthrazit (<10%), Magerkohle (10–14%), Esskohle (14–19%), Fettkohle (19–28%), Gaskohle (28–35%), Gasflammkohle (35–40%) and Flammkohle (>40%). For further information, see American Coal Foundation, "Coal: Ancient Gift Serving Modern Man,"

http://www.ket.org/Trips/Coal/AGSMM/agsmmtoc.html (accessed July 15, 2009); Walter Bischoff, *Das kleine Bergbaulexikon* (Essen: Verlag Glückauf, 1985).

26. AMM-*Coal Age*, April 3, 1919.

27. See Appendix 1; *Thirteenth Census of the United States, 1910—Mines and Quarries 1909*, 199; AMM-*Coal Age*, Feb 12, 1916. For the anthracite region, this figure represented an improvement over the 1890s when the number of days worked in a given year was well below 200.

28. The sliding scale was first adopted in 1869. The scale tied base wages in the southern and middle anthracite fields to the selling price of coal at Port Carbon, Pennsylvania, or Elizabeth, New Jersey. Until 1903, companies in the northern anthracite field set their own individual rates, as in the Ruhr; however, employers in the northern field did keep their rates on par with those offered in the other anthracite regions. Workers in Pennsylvania initially welcomed the sliding scale, yet in 1875 the scale minimum was abolished, which soon led to overproduction, falling prices, and declining wages. By 1900, workers in the middle and southern fields pushed for the abolition of the sliding scale and eventually won this concession later that year during the 1900 Anthracite Strike. The sliding scale was resurrected in 1903 by the Anthracite Coal Strike Commission and adopted throughout all three regions. A new basis was adopted tied to the selling price of coal in New York City and a relatively generous minimum granted to workers. In 1912, the scale was once again abolished as part of the labor agreement between workers and employers.

29. See Appendix 1; Brüggemeier, *Leben vor Ort*, 33–36; Henry George Jr., "What the Single Tax Is Doing," in *Great Leaders and National Issues of 1912* (New York: L. T. Myers, 1913), 142–46; Aurand, *From the Molly Maguires to the United Mine Workers*, 23–24.

30. Kulczycki, *Foreign Worker*, 106; Klessmann, *Polnische Bergarbeiter*, 263; Hickey, *Workers in Imperial Germany*, 126–27. Employers and employees had equal representation on the boards that managed the Knappschaft fund at each coal company. Until 1908, employers were responsible for only 25 percent of the fund's contributions, versus 75 percent for workers. This meant that they had a greater voice on the management of the Knappschaft than their share of contributions would justify. After 1908, employers' contributions increased to 50 percent.

31. *Report of the Department of Mines of Pennsylvania*, Part 1—Anthracite, 1903, ix–xiii, xiv–xviii; Aurand, *From the Molly Maguires to the United Mine Workers*, 160–61; Herkner, *Die Arbeiterfrage*, 1:414. In particular, the mining subsidiaries of the seven large railroad companies in the region generally offered a limited pension scheme. For example, the Lehigh Valley Railroad created a relief fund in 1878 that was supported by a worker's contribution of one day's wages per year, an amount the company then matched. The Lehigh Coal and Navigation Company had a system in place starting in 1884 in which workers contributed 0.25–0.5 percent of their earnings per year. Nevertheless, union efforts to make the establishment of employer pension schemes mandatory as part of the negotiated settlement to the 1902 Anthracite Strike failed in 1903. Among independent operators, pension-style benefits were almost nonexistent. A key exception existed at

202 | *Notes to Pages 47–49*

the mines owned by the Coxe Brothers Coal Company, which provided a worker's insurance and pension fund financed exclusively from company contributions. During the 1890s, the fund provided infirm workers five dollars, widows of fallen miners three dollars, and orphans one dollar a week, respectively, sums that still accounted for less than half an average miner's regular salary. For further information on Coxe Brothers, see State of Pennsylvania, "Legislative Investigating Committee Report," 1826; Sharon Ann Holt, "Life and Labor of Coxe Miners," *Pennsylvania Legacies* 1, no. 1 (2001): 10.

32. Brüggemeier, *Leben vor Ort,* 177–78. Company housing in Germany was usually cheaper and more spacious than that available on the open market. For a discussion of housing conditions, see Chapter 1. Other forms of social welfare included company pension plans, family insurance schemes, company clubs, and company-sponsored amusements.

33. In the early 1890s, the issue of proper bathing facilities and changing rooms was a point of contention between workers, employers, and unions in the Ruhr. Unions advocated for improved facilities, while workers themselves remained divided over the issue, with some preferring to bathe at home because of concerns with cleanliness and disease in the bathhouses, catching cold with a wet head on the way home, and worries about theft. Soon the Prussian state became involved, conducting extensive surveys and encouraging employers to improve their facilities. For more detail see various documents in STAM BAD 6101, BAD 6073, including excerpts from the *Rheinisch-Westfälische Arbeiter Zeitung.* Immediately before the war the issue of bathhouses in coal regions of Pennsylvania came to the fore through the agitation of Progressive reformers who cited the excellent bathhouses in the Ruhr as an example that should be copied. See AMM-*Coal Age,* Oct. 14, 1911, Jan. 27, 1912; Roberts, *Anthracite Coal Communities,* 143–44. Both sources focus on the issue of showers and their need to be implemented in every mine in the belief that the miner could be "morally uplifted" and be spared the moral degradation and risk of disease that came from bathing at home. The issue of baths is also insightful for showing the growing concern of the German state with hygiene at the turn of the century as well as the transfer of later ideas regarding sanitary practices to the United States.

34. Anthracite Coal Strike Commission, *Report to the President,* 28; Hickey, *Workers in Imperial Germany,* 120. For the German coal industry as a whole the fatality rate was 2.45 per thousand.

35. Herkner, *Die Arbeiterfrage,* 1:422–23. For example, the housing contracts at the Hannover mine, owned by Krupp, required workers to leave their company homes on the same day they quit or were fired from work. Other mine companies generally required workers to leave their homes by the end of the calendar month of their discharge.

36. *Report of the Department of Mines of Pennsylvania,* Part 1—Anthracite, 1914, 13.

37. Pennsylvania, "Legislative Investigating Committee Report," 1827.

38. Walsh, *United Mine Workers,* 80. Often powder had to be purchased from the company at exorbitant rates. At some mines, companies charged workers $2.75

for a keg of powder that would retail for $1.10. For an overview of conditions in Ruhr Mines, see STAM BAH 7395—"Results of Survey of Workplace Conditions in the Westphalian Hardcoal Region," Aug. 30, 1889.

39. State of Pennsylvania, "Legislative Investigating Committee Report," 1839–41; Walsh, *United Mine Workers*, 94. In the Legislative Investigating Committee Report, the exploitative nature of the company store is more fully elaborated upon. In one instance a miner noted that if workers did not buy from the store, word would get back to their foreman who then would assign them a mine chamber that was more difficult to work. A manager of a company store even noted to the Committee that "the store was not run for the benefit of the miner."

40. Roberts, *Anthracite Coal Communities*, 114. Roberts bases his estimate on the work of the economist F. S. Nitti; Robert Hunter, *Poverty* (New York: Macmillan, 1904), 52, cited in Blatz, *Democratic Miners*, 25; B. Hetmann and K. Freudenberg, *Morbität und Mortalität der Bergleute im Ruhrgebiet* (Essen, 1925), cited in Brüggemeier, *Leben vor Ort*, 284. The figure cited for the Ruhr is based on the year 1909.

41. Hickey, *Workers in Imperial Germany*, 130; Brüggemeier, *Leben vor Ort*, 82–86. Some miners did vigorously criticize the Kohlensyndikat, rightly claiming that production limits accelerated the closing of older mines in the southern Ruhr regions.

42. Weisbrod, "Arbeitgeberpolitik und Arbeitsbeziehungen im Ruhrbergbau," 126; AMM-*Coal Age*, March 7, 1914. A good example of the relative weakness of state intervention occurred in 1904 when the government attempted to gain a majority stake in the mine company Hibernia A.G. In response, Kohlensyndikat members banded together to ensure that the government obtained only 46 percent of the company's shares and no influence over its management. There were four mines fully owned by the state in the Ruhr region north of Gelsenkirchen that supplied coal primarily to the growing German navy.

43. George, "What the Single Tax Is Doing," 146; *New York Times*, Nov. 30, 1906; Eliot Jones, *The Anthracite Coal Combination in the United States* (Cambridge, Mass.: Harvard University Press, 1914), 156–218; *Wall Street Journal*, April 1, 1916, 6.

44. Herkner, *Die Arbeiterfrage*, 1:437; Ditt and Kift, "Der Bergarbeitstreik von 1889," 12–13; Hickey, *Workers in Imperial Germany*, 208–9.

45. Aurand, *From the Molly Maguires to the United Mine Workers*, 20–26; Miller and Sharpless, *Kingdom of Coal*, 142–43.

46. Brüggemeier, *Leben vor Ort*, 186–90; 231–33.

47. For details of the 1902 Anthracite Strike settlement see Anthracite Coal Strike Commission, *Report to the President*, and chapter 4.

48. Anthracite Coal Strike Commission, *Report to the President*, 39–41; HSTAD LA Moers 788—*Ruhrorter Zeitung*, Jan. 13, 1905.

49. The 1905 Ruhr Strike lasted from early January to mid-February 1905, whereas the 1902 Anthracite Strike lasted from the beginning of May until mid-October. The approximate duration of the other major strikes in the Ruhr are as follows: 1889 Ruhr Strike (May 4–28, 1889), 1899 Herne Strike (June 23–July 4, 1899), 1912 Ruhr Strike (March 11–19, 1912). In northeastern Pennsylvania the duration of major strikes was

as follows: 1887–1888 Anthracite Strike (Sept. 1, 1887–March 1, 1888), 1897 Lattimer Strike (Aug. 14–Sept. 21, 1897), 1900 Anthracite Strike (Sept. 1–Oct. 24, 1900).

50. The Siebenerkommission emerged in during the 1905 Ruhr Strike to coordinate the actions of all four unions. The Alter Verband, the Gewerkverein, and the ZZP each had two representatives, while the Hirsch-Dunker Union had one representative on the commission. After the 1905 Ruhr Strike, a growing split between the Gewerkverein and the other three unions over tactics and goals led to the commission's effective demise by 1908. In its place a "Dreibund," or Pact of Three, was formed between the Alter Verband, Hirsch-Dunker union, and the ZZP in 1910. For further information on the activities of the Siebenerkommission in the post-1905 strike period see HSTAD LA Moers 788—"Reps. PV Moers" Oct.14, 1906; Nov. 11, 1906; Nov. 19, 1906.

Chapter 3: Breaking Barriers

1. "Letter from Joseph and Josephine Lipinski," Feb. 21, 1891, cited in *Writing Home: Immigrants in Brazil and the United States, 1890–1891*, by Witold Kula, Nina Assorodobraj-Kula, and Marcin Kula, ed. and trans. Josephine Wtulich (New York: Columbia University Press, 1986), 337–38.

2. PHMC MG-409, SOHP—Interview with Stanley Nycz (1973); interview with Theodor Myknyk (1973).

3. *Ninth Census of United States, 1880*—Population, 525–26; Christoph Klessmann, *Polnische Bergarbeiter im Ruhrgebiet, 1870–1945: Soziale Integration und nationale Subkultur einer Minderheit in der deutschen Industriegesellschaft* (Göttingen: Vandenhoeck und Ruprecht, 1978), 260; STAM RA 14044—LRB to RPA, June 12, 1883. Many of the first Polish migrants also spoke some German, which eased settlement not only in the Ruhr but also in northeastern Pennsylvania due to the sizable numbers of German immigrants to that region.

4. STAM RA 14044—LRB to RPA, June 12, 1883; Joh. Victor Bredt, *Die Polenfrage im Ruhrkohlengebiet: Eine Wirtschaftspolitische Studie* (Leipzig: Duncker and Humblot, 1909), 6; *Pottsville Republican*, Sept. 20, 1897, cited in George Turner, "The Lattimer Massacre," *Proceedings of the Second Annual Conference on the History of Northeastern Pennsylvania* 2, no. 1 (1990): 5; *Górnik*, Dec. 15, 1897, cited in Hans Jürgen Brandt, *Die Polen und die Kirche im Ruhrgebiet* (Münster: Aschendorff, 1987), 134–35; *Catholic Light*, Aug. 9, 1890; *Hazleton Sentinel*, Oct. 30, 1880; STAM RA 14044—LRB to RPA, June 12, 1883; M. Accursia, "Polish Miners in Luzerne County, Pennsylvania," *Polish American Studies* 3, no. 1 (1948): 7.

5. HSP-Coxe RG II, Series 2, Box 553, Folder 1—*Freeland Progress*, Oct. 6, 1887. For further information on Polish activities in the strike, see also Coxe RG II, Series 2, Box 564, Folder 15; Coxe RG II, Series 2, Box 553, Folder 3, 5.

6. John J. Kulczycki, *The Foreign Worker and the German Labor Movement: Xenophobia and Solidarity in the Coal Fields of the Ruhr, 1871–1914* (Providence, R.I.: Berg, 1994), 58–59, 61; STAM OP 2828 Bd. 1—LRR to OPW, May 9, 1889; STAM OP 2828 Bd. 2—LRH to OPW, May 10, 1889.

7. STAM BAD 6101—"Jahresberichte der Bergrevier Dortmund III," for 1894, 1896, 1898, and 1900; *Eleventh Census of the United States, 1890—Population,* 653–54; *Twelfth Census of the United States, 1900—Population,* 779–80. Harold W. Aurand, *From the Molly Maguires to the United Mine Workers* (Philadelphia: Temple University Press, 1971), 37; Kulczycki, *Foreign Worker,* 42; Klessmann, *Polnische Bergarbeiter,* 261, 265.

8. State of Pennsylvania, *Laws of the General Assembly of the Commonwealth of Pennsylvania, passed at the Session of 1895* (Harrisburg: Edwin Meyers, 1897), 643; *Laws of the General Assembly of the Commonwealth of Pennsylvania, passed at the Session of 1897* (Harrisburg: Clarence Busch, 1899), 546; State of Pennsylvania, "Legislative Investigating Committee Report," 1831–33; HSTAD RD 24720—*Der Bergknappe,* Dec. 1, 1898; HSTAD RD Präs. 835—*Rheinisch-Westfälische Arbeiter Zeitung,* Jan. 23, 1897; April 3, 1897. For their part, Poles often complained that the process of becoming a certified miner was too slow. Examples of the Polish perspective can be found in STAM BAH 7405; Peter Roberts, *The Anthracite Coal Industry* (New York: Macmillan, 1901), 18.

9. In northeastern Pennsylvania, a roof collapse at the Twin Shaft mine in Pittston claimed fifty-eight lives, including nine Poles. See State of Pennsylvania, *Reports of the Inspectors of Coal Mines of Pennsylvania, 1896* (Harrisburg: Edwin Meyers, 1897), 79–85, 96–97. Meanwhile in the Ruhr, a disaster claiming twenty-eight lives occurred in December 1896 at the General Blumenthal mine near Recklinghausen. STAM BAD 6101—*Rheinisch-Westfälische Arbeiter Zeitung,* Jan. 22, 1897; HSTAD RD 24720—"Rep. PV Oberhausen," Oct. 10, 1898.

10. *Reports of Inspectors of Coal Mines, 1896,* xxvii–xxx, cvii–cxi. See in particular changes to section 5. Fees were raised from 50 cents to a dollar. In addition, a worker lost a day's wages to take the test as well as usually having to pay the wages of the miner who vouched for him. For workers who lived in outlying, rural areas of the region, costs were higher due to greater travel expenses. After passage of the "head tax" on foreign labor, John Fahy argued that the tax should have been higher, exclaiming: "What a world of good this law would do to the American citizens who try to earn their living in the coal mines, if the tax were one dollar per day. I have an idea it would also do the foreign born . . . a power of good by keeping them out of the coal mines where all is cruel poverty and misery." See *UMWJ,* July 1, 1897, cited in Perry K. Blatz, *Democratic Miners: Work and Labor Relations in the Anthracite Coal Industry, 1875–1925* (Albany: State University of New York Press, 1994), 54.

11. HSTAD RD 24720—*Deutsche Berg- und Hütten Arbeiter Zeitung,* April 15, 1899; *Bergpolizeiverordnung,* Jan. 25, 1899, cited in Franz Schulze, *Die polnische Zuwanderung im Ruhrrevier und ihre Wirkung* (Munich: Josefs Druckerei, Bigge, 1909), 71; Kulczycki, *Foreign Worker,* 90; Klessmann, *Polnische Bergarbeiter,* 64.

12. HSTAD RD Präs. 835—*Rheinisch-Westfälische Arbeiter Zeitung,* April 3, 1897; PHMC MG-409, SOHP—Interview with Stanley Nycz (1973); Emily Balch, *Our Slavic Fellow Citizens* (New York: Charities Publication Committee, 1910), 288–89, 291. Balch further claimed that the general expansion of industry, the role of unions in setting wage rates, and the Slavic "temperament," from which flowed a

"capacity for cohesion and discipline" in the industrial struggle against employers, mitigated against wage exploitation.

13. Schulze, *Die polnische Zuwanderung im Ruhrrevier*, 72; *Report of the Department of Mines of Pennsylvania*, Part 1—Anthracite, 1905, iiv, table H; *UMWJ*, Jan. 9, 1901.

14. For a greater discussion of the stigmatizing of foreign workers in mining, see John J. Kulczycki, "Scapegoating the Foreign Worker," in *The Politics of Immigrant Workers: Labor Activism and Migration in the World Economy since 1830*, ed. Camille Guerin-Gonzales and Carl Strikwerda (New York: Holmes and Meier, 1993), 133–52.

15. *Laws of the General Assembly of the Commonwealth of Pennsylvania, passed at the Session of 1895*, 643, cited in Turner, "The Lattimer Massacre." There were 6,497 fatal accidents between 1892 and 1905. Of those killed, 1,698 were Poles.

16. HSTAD RD Präs. 835—Speech by Dr. Adolf Wagner, Jan. 31, 1897; *Rheinisch-Westfälische Zeitung* (no. 88), March 29, 1897; *Berg- und Hütten Arbeiter Zeitung*, Jan. 16, 1897; Jan. 21, 1897; *Rheinisch-Westfälische Arbeiter Zeitung*, April 3, 1897.

17. Since World War I, the term Hun has commonly been used to mean a German. In northeastern Pennsylvania, the term derived from the word Hungarian and the more derogatory "Hunkie," which was widely used to refer to anyone of East European descent.

18. George Korson, *Minstrels of the Mine Patch: Songs and Stories of the Anthracite Industry* (Hatboro, Penn.: Folklore Associates, 1938), 132–33.

19. HSTAD RD Präs. 835—*Essener Volkszeitung*, March 27, 1897.

20. Blatz, *Democratic Miners*, 51; Klessmann, *Polnische Bergarbeiter*, 116. The decline in UMW membership also reflected the lack of any significant organizing push after the early months of 1896. In the Ruhr, Polish membership in the Gewerkverein and the Alter Verband declined to approximately 3,000 and 1,000, respectively, by 1902.

21. PHMC MG-145, DHP, Box 18. Turner, "The Lattimer Massacre," 2–3; Victor Greene, *The Slavic Community on Strike: Immigrant Labor in Pennsylvania Anthracite* (Notre Dame, Ind.: University of Notre Dame Press, 1968), 129–31; Aurand, *From the Molly Maguires to the United Mine Workers*, 137–39.

22. *Hazleton Daily Standard*, Aug. 16, 1897; *Pottsville Republican*, Sept. 2, 1897, cited in Turner, "The Lattimer Massacre," 8–9; Aurand, *From the Molly Maguires to the United Mine Workers*, 138–39.

23. PHMC MG-145, DHP, Box 18—Report of Sheriff Martin; *New York Times*, Sept. 18, 1897; *Hazleton Daily Standard*, Sept. 4, 1897, in Turner, "The Lattimer Massacre," 9.

24. PHMC MG-145, DHP, Box 18—Report of Sheriff Martin; *New York Times*, Sept. 11, 1897; Sept. 12, 1897; Sept. 21, 1897; Greene, *Slavic Community on Strike*, 138–39; Aurand, *From the Molly Maguires to the United Mine Workers*, 139, Turner, "The Lattimer Massacre," 15–16.

25. For example, expressions of solidarity came from as far away as Kansas, where Anchor Federal Labor Union No. 6540 declared, "[We express] sympathy

with our murdered brethren," who shall be forever memorialized as "martyrs to the cause of downtrodden labor." Meanwhile, on the international stage, the Austro-Hungarian government issued formal protests to Washington over the violation of the rights of its citizens. See PHMC MG-145, DHP, Box 18; *New York Times,* Oct. 14, 1897; March 13, 1898; March 24, 1898.

26. AMM-*Diocesan Record,* Sept. 11, 1897; Sept. 25, 1897; CPNCC-*Straż,* Sept. 18, 1897; *Carbondale Herald,* reprinted in *Diocesan Record,* Sept. 18, 1897; *New York Times,* March 10, 1898.

27. CPNCC-*Straż,* Sept. 18, 1897; Sept. 25, 1897; Feb. 19, 1898.

28. As discussed in Chapter 5, Aust previously had a quite stormy relationship with Poles he pastored in Scranton. For further information on the relief committee, see George Turner, "Ethnic Responses to the Lattimer Massacre," in *Hard Coal, Hard Times,* ed. David Salay (Scranton: Anthracite Museum Press, 1984), 133–34.

29. Craig Phelan, *Divided Loyalties: The Public and Private Life of Labor Leader John Mitchell* (Albany: State University of New York Press, 1994), 106.

30. Blatz, *Democratic Miners,* 121–22; Turner, "Ethnic Responses to the Lattimer Massacre," 133–34. The growth in membership is particularly impressive given the fact that in the immediate aftermath of the strike, organized labor appeared to care little for the suffering of Poles and other Eastern Europeans, choosing to contribute only $391 to the relief committee aiding the families of the stricken men.

31. *UMWJ,* Sept. 15, 1898, cited in Blatz, *Democratic Miners,* 66. Some ethnic locals were formed that lasted well into the World War I era. See *UMWJ,* Dec. 20, 1906; April 7, 1910; April 10, 1913; Sept. 2, 1915; Jan. 6, 1916.

32. Blatz, *Democratic Miners,* 70–78; Phelan, *Divided Loyalties,* 98. Polish pride in joining the UMW, and being better union men than native workers, was highlighted by Frank Gwisedoskey, who reported to the *United Mine Workers Journal:* "The Polish, Litevish and Slavish elements are joining the union. The English speaking people are slow in coming in, especially the Americans . . . they seem to have doubts about the organization being successful." See *UMWJ,* March 31, 1898, cited in Blatz, *Democratic Miners,* 60.

33. HSTAD RD 24720—*Deutsche Berg- und Hütten Arbeiter Zeitung,* Oct. 1, 1898; Oct. 15, 1898; *Der Bergknappe,* Dec. 1, 1898; Rep. PV Oberhausen—Oct. 10, 1898; Dec. 19, 1898; RD Präs 835—Rep. RPD, Feb. 10, 1897; Rep. MdI to OPK, March 4, 1897. Both German trade unions believed that a wage of approximately 4.90 marks was necessary to meet the average needs of a worker with a family. Although younger, single workers could live on less, the article notes that unskilled laborers were marrying at an increasing rate.

34. HSTAD RD 24720—Rep. RPA, June 27, 1899; Rep. of Polizeikommissar Essen to RPD, June 27, 1899; STAM Kreis Gelsenkirchen 53—*Emscher Zeitung,* July 1, 1899; *Deutsche Berg- und Hütten Arbeiter Zeitung,* July 8, 1899; *Rheinisch-Westfälische Arbeiter Zeitung,* June 30, 1899. The fact that no changes were made to the requirement that workers reach 30 years of age before they became fully vested in the Knappschaft and were thus able to vote for the worker representatives to pension boards was a further source of discontent.

35. HSTAD RD 24720—*Rheinisch-Westfälische Arbeiter Zeitung*, June 27, 1899.

36. STAM RA 14321—Bezirkskommissar Bochum to RPA, June 25, 1899; HSTAD RD 24720—Rep. RPA, June 27, 1899; *Rheinisch-Westfälische Arbeiter Zeitung*, June 28, 1899; BBA Bestand 32, File 4258—Rep. Bergwerkgesellschaft Hibernia, Aug. 1, 1899; STAM Kreis Gelsenkirchen 53—*Rheinisch-Westfälische Zeitung*, June 29, 1899; *Rheinisch-Westfälische Arbeiter Zeitung*, June 29, 1899.

37. HSTAD RD 24720—Rep. LRE to RPD, June 28, 1899; STAM Kreis Gelsenkirchen 53—*Emscher Zeitung*, June 29, 1899; *Rheinisch-Westfälische Zeitung*, June 29, 1899; *Rheinisch-Westfälische Arbeiter Zeitung*, June 28, 1899. The figures cited are based on private communication between the Landrat and various mine companies. Publicly released figures were lower.

38. STAM Kreis Gelsenkirchen 53—*Rheinisch-Westfälische Arbeiter Zeitung*, June 30, 1899; *Emscher Zeitung*, June 29, 1899; *Wiarus Polski*, June 29, 1899; STAM BAH 7396—See strike statistics 26 June–4 July 1899.

39. STAM Kreis Gelsenkirchen 53—Rep. PV Eickel, Aug. 4, 1899; BBA Bestand 32, File 4358—Rep. Bergwerkgesellschaft Hibernia, Aug. 1, 1899; STAM Kreis Gelsenkirchen 53—*Rheinisch-Westfälische Arbeiter Zeitung*, Dec. 23, 1899; Kulczycki, *Foreign Worker*, 140, 145; Jerzy Kozłowski, *Rozwój organizacji społeczno-narodowych wychodżstwa polskiego w Niemczech w latach 1870–1914* (Wrocław: Zakład Narodowy im. Ossolińskich, 1987), 211. At the Shamrock mine alone, 44 Polish, 17 German, and 5 Masurian workers, most of whom were between 20 and 25 years of age, lost their jobs. Interestingly, not only strikers were victims of zealous prosecutors. Dr. Theodore Reismann-Grone, former head of the Bergbau-Verein and owner/editor of the national, liberal *Rheinisch-Westfälische Zeitung*, was fined three hundred marks for his supposedly inflammatory reporting of the Herne strike. While holding Poles in contempt for the actions during the strike, the paper also specifically faulted the Gendarmenwirtschaft of Herne, or regime of police and mayoral incompetence, for the violence that ended in the Bahnhofstrasse battle. For further information, see STAM Kreis Gelsenkirchen 53—*Rheinisch-Westfälische Zeitung*, June 29, 1899; BBA Bestand 32, File 4258—*Rheinisch-Westfälische Zeitung*, Nov. 24, 1899, *Märkischer Sprecher*, Dec. 2, 1899; StB LA 1271—Rep. of Polizeikommissar Essen, Oct. 10, 1899. Insult was added to injury for Herne victims in October 1899 when 19 of the 31 Herne police officers were awarded commendations, and along with the mayor received the Königlichen Kronen-Orden medal (third class) for their actions during the strike. At Christmas, mineowners gave police bonuses for their work. See BBA Bestand 32, File 4258—*Märkischer Sprecher*, Oct. 3, 1898; Reply of Bergwerkgesellschaft Hibernia, Dec. 22, 1899. The idea for a bonus actually came as a result of a direct request of the police. In replying to the mine with a note of thanks, the Amtmann of Recklinghausen declared that the bonus money of 100 marks brought "great Christmas joy" and that the mine "will be served with even greater attention to duty" should disturbances occur in the future.

40. STAM Kreis Gelsenkirchen 53—RPA to LRG, June 27, 1899. Even after the incident of Sunday, certain independent observers blamed the escalation of tensions not on the striking Polish workers but on the incompetence of officials in Herne.

The police commissioner of Essen, in a confidential report to the Regierungspräsident in Düsseldorf, noted that in his opinion the conflict intensified because of a "highly foolish, hurried, and tactless action of the Police Commissioner in Herne. . . . [I]t is hard to comprehend the nervousness that the local police there have unleashed." See HSTAD RD 24720—PKE to RPD, June 27, 1899.

41. HSTAD RD 24720—Rep. RPA, June 27, 1899; STAM OP 2847a—Rep. RPA to OPW—July 17, 1899; Kulczycki, *Foreign Worker*, 113. Local officials in fact took Szczotkowski and the other 14 members of the pitifully small Polish socialist association in Herne into protective custody, releasing them only on July 11. For further information on socialist development in Herne see STAM RA 14086—various reports 1903–1907.

42. STAM Kreis Gelsenkirchen 53—*Rheinisch-Westfälische Zeitung*, June 29, 1899, *Emscher Zeitung*, July 5, 1899; STAM OP 2847a—see various newspaper clippings. For papers affiliated with the National Liberal party, which acted as the traditional mouthpiece of industry, the opportunity to cast aspersions on socialist loyalty by linking the SPD with the Polish nationalism was particularly satisfying.

43. HSTAD RD 24720—PKE to RPD, June 27, 1899; *Herne Zeitung*, Aug. 1, 1899, cited in Peters-Schildgen, *Schmelztiegel Ruhrgebiet: Die Geschichte der Zuwanderung am Beispiel Herne bis 1945* (Essen: Klartext, 1997), 88; HSTAD RD 24720—*Rheinisch-Westfälische Arbeiter Zeitung*, June 28, 1899; STAM Kreis Gelsenkirchen 53, *Rheinisch-Westfälische Arbeiter Zeitung*, June 29, 1899, June 30, 1899. In the wake of the strike, the socialists' attitude toward Poles did soften, as Alter Verband and SPD leaders saw in the anti-Polish propaganda of middle-class press a larger attack on the working-class as a whole and believed that continued anti-Polish agitation on their part would only bind Poles closer to the Center Party. Consequently, while continuing to attack the Center for misleading the tractable Poles, the socialist press did paternalistically note that "we still see in the Poles the proletarian, the class comrade, who we have to enlighten and draw into the organization, so that they will learn to recognize that only by organizing can they improve their position over the long term." See STAM Kreis Gelsenkirchen 53—*Rheinisch-Westfälische Arbeiter Zeitung*, July 5, 1899 as well as the July 8, 1899 edition which analyzes the Herne strike at great length.

44. StB LA 1271—*Wiarus Polski*, July 4, 1899.

45. According to Brejski, the 1899 Herne strike served as the direct impetus for the creation of the ZZP. See Jan Brejski, "Dlaczego powstało Z.Z.P.," in *Ćwierć wieku pracy dla Narodu i Robotnika* (Poznań: Nakładem Zarządu Centralnego Zjedn. Zawod. Polskiego, 1927), 514, cited in Kulczycki, *Foreign Worker*, 151.

Chapter 4: Becoming Mining Men

1. Emily Balch, *Our Slavic Fellow Citizens* (New York: Charities Publication Committee, 1910), 291–92.

2. HSTAD RD Präs. 870—PV Caternberg to LRE, Dec. 15, 1902.

3. *UMWJ*, March 15, 1900; April 12, 1900; *Reports of the U.S. Senate Immigration Commission*, vol. 16, "Immigrants in Industries—Part 19: Anthracite Coal

Mining" (Washington, D.C.: Government Printing Office, 1911), 695; Perry K. Blatz, *Democratic Miners: Work and Labor Relations in the Anthracite Coal Industry, 1875–1925* (Albany: State University of New York Press, 1994), 66. The UMW's industrial unionizing program mirrored in many ways the later inclusive organizing drives of the CIO in the 1930s.

4. For a general history of American unionism in the late nineteenth and early twentieth century, see David Montgomery, *The Fall of the House of Labor: The Workplace, the State, and American Labor Activism, 1865–1925* (New York: Cambridge University Press, 1987); Melvyn Dubofsky and Foster Rhea Dulles, *Labor in America: A History*, 6th ed. (Wheeling, Ill.: Harlan Davidson, 1999); David Brody, *In Labor's Cause: Main Themes on the History of the American Worker* (New York: Oxford University Press, 1993).

5. Blatz, *Democratic Miners*, 121–22.

6. Victor Greene, *The Slavic Community on Strike: Immigrant Labor in Pennsylvania Anthracite* (Notre Dame, Ind.: University of Notre Dame Press, 1968), 154–55.

7. CPNCC-*Straż*, March 29, 1902.

8. *Report of the Department of Mines of Pennsylvania*, Part 1—Anthracite, 1904 (Harrisburg, 1905); Anthracite Coal Strike Commission, *Report to the President on the Anthracite Coal Strike of May–Oct. 1902* (Washington, D.C.: Government Printing Office, 1903), 23, 26.

9. CUA-JMP, Collection 3, Box 3—Letter of the United Mine Workers of America, Districts 1, 7, and 9 to the Operators of the Anthracite Coal Fields of Pennsylvania, Aug. 16, 1900. *New York Times*, Aug. 13, 1899; May 11, 1899; See also William Walsh, *The United Mine Workers of America as an Economic and Social Force in the Anthracite Territory* (Washington, D.C.: Catholic University Press, 1931), 77–82; Blatz, *Democratic Miners*, 90.

10. CUA-JMP, Collection 3, Box 3—Letter of James Crosbie to John Mitchell, Sept. 26, 1900; Blatz, *Democratic Miners*, 24.

11. Anthracite Coal Strike Commission, *Report to the President*, 79. In the wake of the 1902 strike, this practice was reformed, with miners reporting to the company the amount of money due to their laborers, which was then paid to the laborer directly by the company.

12. Talcott Williams, "A General View of the Coal Strike," *American Monthly Review of Reviews* 26, no. 1 (1902): 64–66.

13. CUA-JMP, Collection 3, Box 3—Letter of the United Mine Workers, Aug. 16, 1900; *UMWJ*, Sept. 13, 1900; Letter of James Crosbie, Sept. 26, 1900; Blatz, *Democratic Miners*, 83.

14. *New York Times*, Aug. 29, 1900; Sept. 6, 1900; CUA-JMP, Collection 3, Box 3, "Correspondence." Mitchell to W. C. Scott, Sept. 22, 1900; to Tom Davis, Sept. 22, 1900; Address by John Mitchell in Wilkes-Barre, Oct 2. 1900.

15. *UMWJ*, Sept. 13, 1900.

16. Associated Press (AP) Night Report, Shenandoah, Sept. 21, 1900, in *Los Angeles Times*, Sept. 22, 1900; *New York Times*, Sept. 22, 1900.

17. *Los Angeles Times*, Sept. 22, 1900; *New York Times*, Sept. 22, 1900; Sept. 23, 1900; Sept. 24, 1900; Sept. 27, 1900; Oct. 6 1900; Greene, *Slavic Community on Strike*, 168.

18. *New York Times,* Oct. 11, 1900; *Los Angeles Times,* Oct. 18, 1900; *Hazleton Daily Standard,* cited in Greene, *Slavic Community on Strike,* 172.

19. *UMWJ,* Oct. 4, 1900, 1.

20. Craig Phelan, *Divided Loyalties: The Public and Private Life of Labor Leader John Mitchell* (Albany: State University of New York Press, 1994), 109–10; CUA-JMP, Collection 3, Box 3—"Correspondence," John Mitchell to W. C. Scott, Sept. 23, 1900; *New York Times,* Sept. 23, 1900; Sept. 26, 1900.

21. *UMWJ,* Oct. 4, 1900; *New York Times,* Sept. 22, 1900; Sept. 23, 1900; Sept. 25, 1900; Sept. 27, 1900; Oct. 4, 1900.

22. *New York Times,* Sept. 15, 1900; AP Night Report, Scranton, Sept. 27, 1900, in *Los Angeles Times,* Sept. 28, 1900.

23. *UMWJ,* Oct. 4, 1900; *New York Times,* Oct. 1, 1900; Oct. 2, 1900. As the *New York Times* noted, the 10 percent offer was just as beneficial to the operators as to the strikers since the companies constituting the anthracite trust could make up the increase in labor costs by raising freight rates on their railroad lines, thereby squeezing smaller, independent coal companies out of the market.

24. CUA-JMP, Collection 3, Box 3, "Correspondence"—John Mitchell to Daniel Keefe, Oct. 4, 1900; *UMWJ,* Oct. 4, 1900.

25. *New York Times,* Oct. 13, 1900; *Los Angeles Times,* Oct. 14, 1900.

26. *New York Times,* Oct. 15, 1900; Oct. 18, 1900.

27. Blatz, *Democratic Miners,* 95–96.

28. *New York Times,* Sept. 25, 1900.

29. Phelan, *Divided Loyalties,* 119; *UMWJ,* Nov. 7, 1901; Nov. 14, 1901. In 1901, Mitchell Day celebrations brought out over 70,000 miners who marched in various parades. Poles took an active part in these celebrations, and Polish organizers for the UMW spoke at rallies in Hazleton, Pottsville, Ashland, Plymouth, and Wilkes-Barre.

30. Blatz, *Democratic Miners,* 103–4; Phelan, *Divided Loyalties,* 127–32; *UMWJ,* April 19, 1901.

31. CPNCC-*Straż,* Feb. 8, 1902.

32. Anthracite Coal Strike Commission, *Report to the President,* 46.

33. Ibid., 33; *UMWJ,* March 20, 1902. For a history of the NCF, see Christopher J. Cyphers, *The National Civic Federation and the Making of a New Liberalism, 1900–1915* (Westport, Conn.: Greenwood, 2002).

34. Blatz, *Democratic Miners,* 128.

35. Ibid., 128–31; Anthracite Coal Strike Commission, *Report to the President,* 33–37; *UMWJ,* May 8, 1902; May 15, 1902.

36. Greene, *Slavic Community on Strike,* 188. The total numbers of workers employed in mining operations during the months of the strike were as follows: June 16,353, July, 6,552, August, 7,706, September 8,236. These estimates were originally taken from U.S. Bureau of the Census, *Mines and Quarries, 1902* (Washington, D.C.: Government Printing Office, 1905), 667.

37. HSP-Coxe RG II, Series 2, Box 560, Folder 2; *UMWJ,* June 26, 1902. As during earlier strikes, many of these guards were college students home for the summer.

38. HSP-Coxe RG II, Series 2, Box 560, Folders 8 and 13.

39. *UMWJ*, May 29, 1902. See also *UMWJ*, June 12, 1902.

40. *UMWJ*, July 10, 1902; *UMWJ*, Aug. 21, 1902; Aug. 28, 1902; *UMWJ*, Sept. 25, 1902; HSP-Coxe RG II, Series 2, Box 560, Folders 10, 14, and 19.

41. *UMWJ*, Aug. 7, 1902; CPNCC-*Straż*, Aug. 2, 1902; PHMC, MG-181, WSP, Box 2, Folder 1; Greene, *Slavic Community on Strike*, 190–92; Blatz, *Democratic Miners*, 135.

42. *UMWJ*, Aug. 7, 1902. For a greater discussion of the Sokół movement, see Chapter 6.

43. *UMWJ*, Aug. 7, 1902. See speech given by UMW Vice-President Paul Pulaski and crowd responses.

44. "The Progress of the World," *American Monthly Review of Reviews* 26, no. 5 (1902): 516; Blatz, *Democratic Miners*, 135.

45. Blatz, *Democratic Miners*, 136. John Markle, head of GB Markle and Company, offered a similar view when discussing the strike in the pages of the *Philadelphia Sun*, noting, "It is wholly within the bounds of truth to say that from the time when the concessions of 1900 were granted there has existed in the anthracite coal regions a condition of anarchy in the management of the vast industries centered there. Mr. Mitchell has found the exact word which describes it—a condition that was intolerable." See HSP-Coxe RG II, Series 2, Box 560, Folder 1, *Philadelphia Sun*, Sept. 11, 1902.

46. *UMWJ*, Oct. 9, 1902.

47. CPNCC-*Straż*, Oct. 4 1902.

48. HSP-Coxe RG II, Series 2, Box 560, Folder 1, *Philadelphia Public Ledger*, Oct. 5, 1902; CPNCC-*Straż*, Sept. 27, 1902; *New York Times*, "Women Here & There," Nov. 2, 1902. Unfortunately, the bride received the coal toward the end of the strike, and with the settlement the value plummeted. As the report notes, "As she has seen her stock in coal drop lower and lower she is disgusted, and wishes that something had been given her that would have had a par value."

49. *Harper's Weekly*, Sept. 12, 1902, 1278.

50. "The Progress of the World," 515–16.

51. See *American Monthly Review of Reviews* 26, no. 5 (1902): passim.

52. *Wall Street Journal*, Sept. 30, 1902.

53. *New York Times*, Oct. 4, 1902; Blatz, *Democratic Miners*, 137–38.

54. *New York Times*, Oct. 5, 1902. See remarks of Senators George Vest, Henry Cabot Lodge, as well as Cardinal Gibbons.

55. *New York Times*, Oct. 15, 1902; Oct. 16, 1902; Oct. 17, 1902; Blatz, *Democratic Miners*, 137–38, 305. In addition to Clark, the other members of the Anthracite Commission were George Gray (chair), former U.S. Senator and judge on the Third Circuit Court; Brigadier General John Wilson, former head of the Army Corps of Engineers; Edward Parker, chief statistician of the Coal Division of the United States Geological Survey; Thomas Watkins, former partner in the Simpson and Watkins Coal Company; John Spalding, bishop of Peoria, Illinois; and Carroll Wright (recorder), Commissioner of Labor.

56. *UMWJ*, Oct. 30, 1902.

57. Anthracite Coal Strike Commission, *Report to the President*, 42–79.

58. Ibid., 81.

59. Blatz, *Democratic Miners*, 173–172. For a broader discussion of rank-and-file opinion, see Joseph Gowaskie, "John Mitchell and the Anthracite Mine Workers: Leadership Conservatism and Rank-and-File Militancy," *Labor History* 27 (Winter 1985–86): 54–83.

60. George Korson, *Minstrels of the Mine Patch: Songs and Stories of the Anthracite Industry* (Hatboro, Penn.: Folklore Associates, 1938), 234–36.

61. Harold W. Aurand, *From the Molly Maguires to the United Mine Workers* (Philadelphia: Temple University Press, 1971), 165–66.

62. *New York Times*, Oct. 22, 1902.

63. John J. Kulczycki, *The Foreign Worker and the German Labor Movement: Xenophobia and Solidarity in the Coal Fields of the Ruhr, 1871–1914* (Providence, R.I.: Berg, 1994), 155–56; STAM BAH 7396—Rep. Zeche v. d. Heydt to BAH, May 12, 1902; STAM BAD 6052—*Dortmunder Zeitung*, Oct. 16, 1901.

64. STAM BA Herne 7405—Complaint by Ignatz Tskowiak to OBD, Feb. 15, 1902. See also complaint of mistreatment by Franz Lesnik, filed on August 9, 1902, as well as other various complaints to the OBD in this file covering the period from 1901 to 1904.

65. HSTAD RD Präs 870 Rep. I'V Caternberg to LRE, Dec. 15, 1902; Stanislaus Wachowiak, *Die Polen in Rheinland-Westfalen* (Leipzig: Robert Noske, 1916), 72, 78; John J. Kulczycki, *The Polish Coal Miners Union and the German Labor Movement in the Ruhr, 1902–1934* (Oxford: Berg, 1997), 20, 31; Christoph Klessmann, *Polnische Bergarbeiter im Ruhrgebiet, 1870–1945: Soziale Integration und nationale Subkultur einer Minderheit in der deutschen Industriegesellschaft* (Göttingen: Vandenhoeck und Ruprecht, 1978), 112. Interestingly, one factor influencing the Brejski brothers in their efforts to form the ZZP was their view that Poles in the United States were far better organized than in Germany.

66. Franz-Josef Brüggemeier, *Leben vor Ort: Ruhrbergleute und Ruhrbergbau* (Munich: C. H. Beck, 1983), 283; Kulczycki, *Polish Coal Miners Union*, 77, 253. The high Polish organizational rate disproves beliefs of German trade unionists and many historians since that Poles were less willing to organize. For examples within the academic literature, see S. H. F. Hickey, *Workers in Imperial Germany: The Miners of the Ruhr* (Oxford: Oxford University Press, 1985), 206; Klaus Tenfelde, *Sozialgeschichte der Bergarbeiterschaft an der Ruhr im 19. Jahrhundert* (Bonn: Verlag Neue Gesellschaft, 1977), 511–14.

67. STAM BAD 6053—Mine Company Reports (various) to BAD Revier III, July 1903; STAM BAD 6101, Feb. 2, 1902; Kulczycki, *Foreign Worker*, 160–65; Hickey, *Workers in Imperial Germany*, 124–25; Brüggemeier, *Leben vor Ort*, 213. According to Brüggemeier, there were 30,000 cases of ringworm in 1902. In 1904, there were 14,000. Most likely one cause for the higher rates of worm disease among Poles was the fact that they often received less desirable, "wetter" chambers at the mine face.

68. Kulczycki, *Foreign Worker*, 168–69; Kulczycki, *Polish Coal Miners Union*, 48; HSTAD LA Moers 788—*Niederrheinische Volkszeitung*, no. 19, Jan. 9, 1905.

69. Brüggemeier, *Leben vor Ort*, 212. The Alter Verband placed special emphasis on the need for Poles to organize. According to Hermann Sachse and Otto Hue, many Poles currently "stood on the wrong path." See HSTAD LA Moers 788—*Ruhrorter Zeitung*, Jan. 4, 1905.

70. HSTAD LA Moers 788—*Niederrheinische Volkszeitung*, Jan. 14, 1905; Kulczycki, *Foreign Worker*, 171–72.

71. HSTAD LA Moers 788—*Ruhrorter Zeitung*, Jan. 13, 1905. The ZZP representatives on the commission were Jan Brzeskot and ZZP chairman Jósef Regulski.

72. STAM BAH 7396—Reply *Verein für die Bergbauliche Interesse*, Jan. 16, 1905; Brüggemeier, *Leben vor Ort*, 214; Klessmann, *Polnische Bergarbeiter*, 121; Kulczycki, *Foreign Worker*, 77–78.

73. STAM OP 2849 Bd. 3—*Stenographischer Bericht über die öffentliche Bergarbeiter Versammlung*, Jan. 20, 1905.

74. STAM BAD 6054—Reports Zeche Germania II to Bergrevierbeamte Dortmund III, Jan. 19, 1905; Jan 21, 1905; Jan. 23, 1905; STAM BAH 7396—Reports Zeche Victor, Feb. 11, 1905; STAM OP 2849 Bd. 3—*Stenographischer Bericht*, Jan. 20, 1905.

75. Kulczycki, *Polish Coal Miners Union*, 52–53.

76. StO Amt Osterfeld 184—Rep. RPM to LRR, Jan. 28, 1905; HSTAD RD 15925—Rep. RPM to MdI, Feb. 5, 1905; Kulczycki, *Polish Coal Miners Union*, 53–54, 255–54. At the end of 1904, there were 9,916 members in the ZZP.

77. Brüggemeier, *Leben vor Ort*, 214. After the strike ended, public support for those workers who lost their positions as a result of their activities remained high. In Mannheim, for example, a commission comprising union leaders, priests, workers, and officials was created in April 1905 to manage a relief fund of 5,000 marks to aid families made destitute by the strike. See StO Amt Osterfeld 184—Rep. Oberbürgermeister Mannheim to Amt Osterfeld, April 7, 1905.

78. STAM BAH 7396—Rep. BAD to Bergrevierbeamten, Jan. 28, 1905.

79. STAM BAD 6054—Rep. Gewerkschaft Dorstfeld to Bergbau Verein, Jan. 21, 1905.

80. STAM BAH 7396—Rep. Zeche Julia to Bergassessor Luethgen, Jan. 18, 1905, Rep. Gewerkschaft Victor to Bergrevierbeamte Herne, Jan. 21, 1905; Rep. Zeche Friedrich d. Grosse to Bergrevierbeamte Herne, Jan. 30, 1905; STAM BAD 6054—Reports Zeche Germania II to Bergrevierbeamte Dortmund III, Jan. 19, 1905.

81. STAM OP 2849 Bd. 3—*Stenographischer Bericht*, Jan. 20, 1905; Brüggemeier, *Leben vor Ort*, 215, 236, 341, 347; Wachowiak, *Die Polen in Rheinland-Westfalen*, 76.

82. Brüggemeier, *Leben vor Ort*, 215–16; Kulczycki, *Foreign Worker*, 190–92

83. STAM BAH 7396—*Essener Volkszeitung*, Feb. 9, 1905; HSTAD RD 15925—Rep. RPM to MdI, Feb. 9, 1905.

84. HSTAD RD 15925—Rep. RPA to MdI, Feb. 11, 1905; Kulczycki, *Foreign Worker*, 192–93.

85. HSTAD LA Moers 788—Rep. PV Homberg, Nov. 14, 1905; Brüggemeier, *Leben vor Ort*, 217–18; Kulczycki, *Foreign Worker*, 196–201.

86. Kulczycki, *Polish Coal Miners Union*, 253.

87. Blatz, *Democratic Miners*, 231, 235, 252.

88. *New York Times*, Feb. 16, 1906.

89. Korson, *Minstrels of the Mine Patch*, 134–35.

90. AMM-*Coal Age*, Sept. 12, 1914. For a full examination of this debate, see *Coal Age*, Aug. 22, 1914; Sept. 12, 1914; Oct. 3, 1914; Oct. 17, 1914; Nov. 7, 1914; Dec. 26, 1914; Jan. 2, 1915; Jan. 16, 1915; Jan. 30, 1915; April 3, 1915.

91. AMM-*Coal Age,* Nov. 7, 1914. For a complete examination of this debate, see *Coal Age,* Aug. 22, 1914; Sept. 12, 1914; Oct. 3, 1914; Oct. 17, 1914; Nov. 7, 1914; Dec. 26, 1914; Jan. 2, 1915; Jan. 16, 1915; Jan. 30, 1915; April 3, 1915.

92. AMM-*Coal Age,* Dec. 19, 1918.

93. "Strike Good Thing for Green Ridge," *Plain Speaker,* Sept. 14, 1902, 1, cited in Greene, *Slavic Community on Strike,* 187.

94. CPNCC-*Straż,* Aug. 4, 1906; Aug. 18, 1906; Aug. 25, 1906; Sept. 8, 1906; Sept. 22, 1906; Sept. 29, 1906.

95. AMM-*Coal Age,* April 6, 1912; April 27, 1912; May 25, 1912.

96. *UMWJ,* Nov. 21, 1901, Nov. 28, 1901. See Chapter 6 for a greater discussion of attempts to hinder Polish immigration and naturalization.

97. Blatz, *Democratic Miners,* 247–48

98. HSTAD RD 15933—Transcript of the Essen Conference, Feb. 11–12, 1906.

99. HSTAD RD 15921—"Geschäftsbericht des Gewerkverein Christlicher Bergarbeiter Deutschlands (1911)."

100. Klessmann, *Polnische Bergarbeiter,* 284; Wachowiak, *Die Polen in Rheinland-Westfalen,* 82.

101. The increasing tendency of the ZZP to ally with the Alter Verband brought rebuke from the Gewerkverein, which complained about ZZP election practices in which the Polish union "not only ran candidates where they had a chance to be elected" but also divided the Christian workforce by running them "in elections where they could not win, thereby aiding the comrades [i.e., socialists] to victory. At other times [the Poles], without any official voting pact, forewent running any candidate and voted directly for the Social Democratic candidates." For a further discussion, see StO Amt Osterfeld 186—*Bergknappe,* Sept. 24, 1910.

102. Appendix 1 provides an overview of yearly wage movement for the period between 1907 and 1912. For a greater discussion of Triple Alliance demands, see BBA Bestand 72, File 516—Report on wages and price conditions prepared by the Alter Verband, ZZP, Gewerkverein, Hirsch-Dunker to the Königliche Bergwerksdirektion Recklinghausen, Feb. 9, 1912; BBA Bestand 20, File 563—Demands of the Alter Verband, ZZP and Hirsch Dunker unions, Feb. 19, 1912; HSTAD RD 15939—Rep. PPE to RPD, Feb. 7, 1912.

103. HSTAD RD 15939—Rep. PPE to RPD, Feb. 7, 1912; Rep. PPE to RPD, Feb. 9, 1912.

104. HSTAD RD 15939—Rep. PPE to RPD, Feb. 21, 1912; BBA Bestand 20, File 563—Demands of the Alter Verband, ZZP and Hirsch Dunker unions, Feb. 19, 1912; BBA Bestand 20, File 563—Rep. Zechen-Verband, March 12, 1912.

105. HSTAD RD 15939—Rep. PPE to RPD, March 6, March 10, and March 13, 1912; STAM RM, Nr. VII 14, Bd. 3—Rep. RPA to RPM, March 12, 1912; BBA Bestand 20, File 563—"Aufstandsbewegung im Ruhrgebiet," Ermittelung des Bergbau Vereins, March 11–20, 1912; Kulczycki, *Foreign Worker,* 226, 229–30; Brüggemeier, *Leben vor Ort,* 230; BBA Bestand 20, File 563—"Aufstandsbewegung im Ruhrgebiet," Ermittelung des Bergbau Vereins, March 11–20, 1912.

106. Kulczycki, *Foreign Worker*, 232, 247; Brüggemeier, *Leben vor Ort*, 230–31; Wachowiak, *Die Polen in Rheinland-Westfalen*, 87; HSTAD RD 15939—Rep. PPE to RPD, March 20, 1912.

107. HSTAD RD 15939—Rep. PPE to RPD, May 29, 1912; BBA Bestand 72, File 516—Rep. Bergbau Verein to Verbandszechen, April 6, 1912; Brüggemeier, *Leben vor Ort*, 232; Wachowiak, *Die Polen in Rheinland-Westfalen*, 87.

108. Brüggemeier, *Leben vor Ort*, 232, 282–83; Kulczycki, *Foreign Worker*, 251–58; Kulczycki, *Polish Coal Miners Union*, 253. Between year end 1911 and 1913, total membership in the Alter Verband declined from 120,136 to 101,986. In the same period Gewerkverein membership fell from 84, 321 to 63,129. By 1914, there were 21,000 miners organized in employer-sponsored unions, also known as yellow unions because such employee associations were typically acquiescent to the wishes of employers. At the beginning of 1912, ZZP's Ruhr miner's section had 30,164 members organized in 171 locals. At year-end, the ZZP had 30,354 members organized in 182 locals. In 1913, ZZP membership did decline somewhat to 28,936, though this loss was not nearly as great as that experienced by German unions.

109. Wachowiak, *Die Polen in Rheinland-Westfalen*, 87.

110. STAM RM VII, Nr. 36c—*Narodowiec*, July 22, 1914.

111. Michael A. Barendse, *Social Expectations and Perception: The Case of the Slavic Anthracite Workers* (University Park: Pennsylvania State University Press, 1981), 34.

Chapter 5: Divided Hearts, Divided Faith

1. William Hagen, *Germans, Poles, and Jews: The Nationality Conflict in the Prussian East, 1772–1914* (Chicago: University of Chicago Press, 1980), 129–30; Lech Trzeciakowski, "The Prussian State and the Catholic Church in Prussian Poland, 1871–1914," *Slavic Review* 26, no. 4 (1967): 624–25; Lech Trzeciakowski, *Kulturkampf w zaborze pruskim* (Poznań: Wydawnictwo Poznańskie, 1970); Helmut Walser Smith, *German Nationalism and Religious Conflict: Culture, Ideology, and Politics, 1870–1914* (Princeton, N.J.: Princeton University Press, 1995), 45; Owen Chadwick, *A History of the Popes, 1830–1914* (Oxford: Clarendon Press, 1998), 433. Anti-Polish elements of the Kulturkampf included laws requiring the use of German in classroom instruction and in all affairs related to public administration in Polish-majority regions of Poznań. More audaciously, in 1874 the Prussian government arrested the Polish archbishop Mieczysław Ledochowski of Gniezno-Poznań for his refusal to comply with the anti-Catholic May Laws, sentencing him to two years in prison and eventually forcing him into exile in Rome.

2. STAM RA 14044—Rep. PV Dortmund to RPA, June 2, 1885; Christoph Klessmann, *Polnische Bergarbeiter im Ruhrgebiet, 1870–1945: Soziale Integration und nationale Subkultur einer Minderheit in der deutschen Industriegesellschaft* (Göttingen: Vandenhoeck und Ruprecht, 1978), 57–58. The speech was given by Center Party representative Bachem in Dortmund on May 31, 1885, and reported in *Tremonia* (Dortmund), June 1, 1885.

3. STAM OP 2748 Bd.1—Rep. RPA to OPM, Jan. 8, 1886; STAM RA 14044—Rep. LR Bochum to RPA on the St. Barbara Verein in Gelsenkirchen, June 12, 1883; STAM OP 2748 Bd. 1, Rep. RPA to OPM, Dec. 27, 1890. Prior to Szotowski's arrival, there had been intermittent visits to the region by Polish priests. For a history of Polish spiritual care and associational activity during the 1870s, 1880s and 1890s, see Witold Matwiejczyk, *Katolickie towarzystwa robotników polskich w Zagłębiu Ruhry, 1871–1894* (Lublin: Towarzystwo Naukowe Katolickiego Uniwersytetu Lubelskiego, 1999); Jerzy Kozłowski, *Rozwój organizacji społeczno-narodowych wychodżstwa polskiego w Niemczech w latach 1870–1914* (Wrocław: Zakład Narodowy im. Ossolińskich, 1987), 68–73, 83–85; John J. Kulczycki, "The First Polish Clergymen in the Ruhr: Religion in Service of National Identity," in *States, Societies, Cultures: East and West: Essays in Honor of Jaroslaw Pelenski,* ed. Janusz Duzinkiewicz, Myroslav Popovych, Vladyslav Verstiuk, and Natalia Yakovenko (New York: Ross Publishing, 2004), 513–21; Anastazy Nadolny, "Problemy duszpasterstwa Polaków w Zągłębiu Ruhry na przykładzie losów księży Józefa Szotowskiego i Franciszka Lissa," in *Schimanski, Kuzorra i inni: Polacy w Zagłębiu Ruhry 1870/71–1945,* edited by Dittmarra Dahlmanna, Alberta S. Kotowskiego, and Zbigniewa Karpusa (Toruń: Wydawnictwo Adam Marszałek, 2006), 106–32; Witold Matwiejczyk, "Mieędzy integracją kościelną a izolcją społeczną: Katolicy polscy w Zągłębiu Ruhry w latach 1871–1914," in *Schimanski, Kuzorra i inni,* 5–32. In the early years of associational activity, not all Polish associations identified themselves as Polish. In 1884, Upper Silesian Poles in Schalke (Gelsenkirchen) established a St. Barbara Association (St. Barbara was the patron saint of miners) and were insistent that the association be known as an Upper Silesian Catholic worker association. For more information, see STAM RA 14044—Rep. LR Bochum to RPA, March 4, 1884.

4. The APA movement spread rapidly throughout the country on a platform specifically created to counter the supposed Catholic influence in national life, including the threat posed by Catholic immigrants. In addition to the APA and POSA, other anti-Catholic groups gaining in popularity during the 1880s include the Templars of Liberty (1881), the Patriotic League of the Revolution (1882), the Order of American Freedom (1884), and the National Order of the Videttes (1886). Interestingly, much of the rhetoric of the APA and other movements borrowed heavily from the arguments put forth by Bismarck during the Kulturkampf. See Les Wallace, *The Rhetoric of Anti-Catholicism: The American Protective Association, 1887–1911* (New York: Garland, 1990), 1–2, 30–31.

5. AMM-*Diocesan Record* (Scranton), Aug. 18, 1888; *Scranton Republican,* July 9, 1887.

6. AMM-*Diocesan Record,* Aug. 25, 1888; May 16, 1891.

7. AMM-*Directory of the Diocese of Scranton* (1990).

8. Klessmann, *Polnische Bergarbeiter,* 261; Hans Ulrich Wehler, "Die Polen im Ruhrgebiet bis 1918," in *Moderne deutsche Sozialgeschichte,* ed. Hans Ulrich Wehler (Cologne: Kiepenheuer and Witsch, 1966), 439–44; *Eleventh Census of the United States, 1890—Population,* 653–54; *Twelfth Census of United States, 1900—Population,* 779–80. Wacław Kruszka, *A History of Poles in America to 1908,* edited

by James Pula, 3 vols. (Washington, D.C.: Catholic University Press, 1993), 1:65–66; 3:110, 117–18, 125. For northeastern Pennsylvania, the total number of Poles most likely stood between the census estimate, which did not include second-generation children and was known for undercounting Poles, and Kruszka's, which are based on the compilation of parish surveys Kruszka conducted through local priests in the region.

9. STAM OP 2748 Bd. 1, Rep. RPA to OPM, Aug. 8, 1889; M. Accursia, "Polish Miners in Luzerné County, Pennsylvania," *Polish American Studies* 3, no. 1 (1946): 8; John Gallagher, *A Century of History: The Diocese of Scranton, 1868–1968* (Scranton, Penn.: Diocese of Scranton, 1968), 152. For more specific details on the German case see Brian McCook, "Divided Hearts: The Struggle between National Identity and Confessional Loyalty among Polish Catholics in the Ruhr, 1904–1914," *Polish Review* 47, no. 1 (2002): 67–96.

10. William Thomas and Florian Znaniecki, *The Polish Peasant in Europe and America*, 5 vols. (Boston: G. Badger, 1918), 1:182, 250–52, 274–75; Barbara Les Strassberg, "The Origins of the Polish National Catholic Church: The 'Polish National' Factor Reconsidered," *Polish National Catholic Church Studies* 7, no. 1 (1986): 29–31; John Bukowczyk, *And My Children Did Not Know Me: A History of the Polish Americans* (Bloomington: Indiana University Press, 1987), 40–41. See also Barbara Les, *Kościół w procesie asymilacji Polonii amerykańskiej: Przemiany funkcji polonijnych instytucji i organizacji religijnych w środowisku Polonii chicagowskiej* (Wrocław: Zaklad Narodowy im. Ossolinskich, 1981).

11. Helena Znaniecka Lopata, *Polish Americans* (New Brunswick, N.J.: Prentice Hall, 1994), 59. For a fictionalized account of the intricate priest/peasant relations in a Polish village see Ladislas St. Reymont, *The Peasants*, 4 vols., trans. Michael Dziewicki (New York: Knopf, 1925).

12. Thomas and Znaniecki, *Polish Peasant*, 1:285.

13. Ibid., 4:154–74; Lopata, *Polish Americans*, 59.

14. Klessmann, *Polnische Bergarbeiter*, 139; Gallagher, *A Century of History*, 157; Kruszka, *History of Poles in America to 1908*, 110, 125, 331. Kruszka claims that there were six Polish priests in the Diocese of Harrisburg and twenty-eight in the Diocese of Scranton. In addition, there were three priests in the anthracite regions covered by the Diocese of Philadelphia. James Pula, the editor of Kruszka's *History of Poles in America to 1908*, has revised these figures noting that there were two Polish priests in the Diocese of Harrisburg and sixteen in the Diocese of Scranton serving four and twenty-five parishes, respectively. This indicates that one in thirty-six priests in the Diocese of Harrisburg and one in ten within the Diocese of Scranton were Polish.

15. HSTAD RD Präs. 902—Rep. RPD to LR Moers, May 3, 1907; HSTAD RD Präs. 902—Rep. Father Bresser to Bishop of Münster, March 30, 1906; HSTAD LA Moers 467—Letter of the Archbishop of Köln to the OPR, Jan. 30, 1911; Klessmann, *Polnische Bergarbeiter*, 140. The church's concern about state intervention was well founded. Throughout the period before World War I, the Prussian bureaucracy kept a watchful eye on church activities. In 1911, for example, the

Oberpräsident of the Rhine Province wrote the archbishop of Cologne concerned about reports of Polish-language services in the Düsseldorf region. The archbishop, annoyed by the Oberpräsident's interference, responded that services in the Polish language helped limit the appeal of socialism and that his handling of Polish spiritual care had the approval of the Kaiser. The Oberpräsident nevertheless subsequently ordered his subordinates to make full reports on the number of Polish services and their influence on Poles.

16. Trzeciakowski, "The Prussian State and the Catholic Church in Prussian Poland," 626. The willingness of the hierarchy to embrace the government's Germanization program was aided by the fact that due to the Kulturkampf, there was only one Polish bishop left in the German Catholic hierarchy by 1900.

17. STAM OP 2848—*Westfälische Anzeiger*, Nov. 29, 1890. During Szotowski's time in the Ruhr, he was viewed with suspicion by German authorities, who suspected that he hid his Polish nationalist sympathies beneath his clerical robe. For further information, see STAM OP 2748—Rep. RPA to Ministerium der geistlichen, Unterrichts- und Medicinal-Angelegenheiten, Jan. 8, 1886.

18. HSTAD RD Präs. 867—Rep. OPW, Oct. 31, 1896. Most Polish Catholic associations at this time remained deeply conservative in outlook, and nationalism within the associations was only starting to emerge in the 1890s in the wake of various government restrictions on Polish activities, such as an 1892 ordinance banning association symbols, such as uniforms and flags, deemed by authorities to be too Polish in character. S. See STAM RA 14044—Rep. LR Gelsenkirchen to RPA, May 22, 1891; STAM RA 14045—Rep. of Amtmann GE-Ueckendorf to LR Gelsenkirchen, Nov. 23, 1892; Rep. of OPW to RPA, Feb. 16, 1893.

19. STAM RA 14045—Rep. OBM TO RPA, May 9, 1893; Sept. 12, 1893; Rep. of OBD to RPA, Sept. 10, 1893; Oct. 27, 1893; *Orędownik*, Oct. 26, 1893; Nov. 22, 1893; Nov. 29, 1893; *Wiarus Polski*, Dec. 5, 1893.

20. HSTAD RD Präs. 867—Rep. OPW, Oct. 31, 1896; Klessmann, *Polnische Bergarbeiter*, 59.

21. Hieronim Kubiak, *The Polish National Catholic Church in the United States of America from 1897 to 1980* (Cracow: Nakl. Uniwersytetu Jagiellonskiego, 1983), 56, 62; Jay P. Dolan, *The American Catholic Experience: A History from Colonial Times to the Present* (New York: Doubleday, 1985), 302. Dolan notes that by 1900 two-thirds of the Catholic bishops in the United States were of Irish descent.

22. Dolan, *American Catholic Experience*, 294–320; Kubiak, *Polish National Catholic Church*, 56–66; Joseph A. Wytrwal, *The Poles in America* (Minneapolis: Lerner, 1971), 49; Theodore Maynard, *The Story of American Catholicism* (New York: Macmillan, 1942), 510–11.

23. Kruszka, *A History of Poles in America to 1908*, 1:100.

24. Dolan, *American Catholic Experience*, 180, 297, 300–302; Kubiak, *Polish National Catholic Church*, 58–59; Kruszka, *A History of Poles in America to 1908*, 1:100–101.

25. Gallagher, *A Century of History*, 156–57, 163–69; Kruszka, *A History of Poles in America to 1908*, 127–28; AMM-*Scranton Diocesan Directory* (1990). For a

detailed description of the battle over ethnic parishes in northeastern Pennsylvania and Bishop O'Hara's involvement in them, see Gallagher, *A Century of History,* 163–69; James Earley, *Envisioning Faith: The Pictorial History of the Diocese of Scranton* (Devon, Penn.: Cooke, 1994), 109–25.

26. STAM RM VII, no. 31—"Stand der Polenbewegung," April 22, 1912.

27. CPNCC-*Straż*. Class was also a very relevant theme in these cartoons. The depictions of the Irish bishops were meant to evoke images of the Polish gentry, and the term *lud polski* was very specifically understood to mean the Polish working class and peasantry in contrast to the gentry and capitalist bourgeoisie. In another article from *Straż*, dated March 29, 1902, specific parallels between the *szlachta* in the homeland to the Irish bishops in America are drawn.

28. CPNCC-*Straż*, June 12, 1897; HSTAD RD Präs. 897—Rep. OB Hamborn to RPD, Aug. 28, 1913; Aug. 28, 1914.

29. STAM RM VII 31—"Stand der Polenbewegung," May 4, 1914; CPNCC-*Straż*, July 16, 1898

30. STAM OP 6396—"Stand der Polenbewegung," April 22, 1912; HSTAD RD 42815—Rep. on Polish Meeting in Bruch, Feb. 10, 1898; Hans Jürgen Brandt, *Die Polen und die Kirche im Ruhrgebiet* (Münster: Aschendorff, 1987), 24; Gallagher, *A Century of History,* 163.

31. STAM RM VII 31—"Stand der Polenbewegung," May 3, 1913. The three ethnically Polish priests were Father Szczech in Eving, Father Makowski in Gelsenkirchen, and Father Mazurowski in Köln.

32. HSTAD RD Präs. 902—Rep. OB Duisburg, Oct. 24, 1905.

33. HSTAD RD 42815—*Wiarus Polski,* Feb. 5, 1898; HSTAD RD Präs. 883–884—*Wiarus Polski,* 1903 (various dates). On the local level, Polish refusal to support the Center Party led to recriminations by parish priests. In the town of Caternberg (Essen Land), a local priest banned the St. Stanisław Kostka association from taking part in parish processions and refused to allow the association to hang its banner in the church. The priest later lifted these restrictions in June 1904, but only after the Poles in the association renounced the *Wiarus Polski,* made a declaration that they wished to remain strictly a religious organization and agreed that the priest could exercise veto power over all future decisions of the association. For further information see HSTAD LA Essen 101—Rep. Bürgermeister zu Stoppenberg to LR Essen, Sept. 29, 1904.

34. HSTAD LA Essen 101—Rep. RPD to LR Essen, Aug. 25, 1904; HSTAD RD Präs. 902—Rep. Bezirkspolizeikommissar Essen to RPD, Nov. 28, 1906; Smith, *German Nationalism,* 189.

35. *Wiarus Polski* (Bochum), July 2, 1905.

36. HSTAD RD Präs. 902—Rep. Kgl. Bezirkspolizeikommissar Essen to RPD, Nov. 28, 1906; LA Essen 101—Rep. RPD to Landraethe, Feb. 23, 1907.

37. HSTAD RD Präs. 902—Rep. Kgl. Bezirkspolizeikommissar Essen to RPD, Nov. 28, 1906.

38. HSTAD RD Präs. 902—Rep. PV Essen, Dec. 4, 1906.

39. HSTAD RD Präs. 902—Press excerpt of Dec. 12, 1905, cited in Polish press reports compiled by the Königliche Regierung Düsseldorf.

40. HSTAD RD Präs. 902—Rep. Kgl. Bezirkspolizeikommissar Essen to RPD, Nov. 28, 1906.

41. HSTAD RD Präs. 902—Rep. PV Essen, May 14, 1906.

42. HSTAD RD Präs. 902—Rep. PV Essen, Feb. 25, 1907. See statements by Albert Grzekowiak.

43. HSTAD RD Präs. 902—Rep. PV Essen, March 18, 1907.

44. HSTAD RD Präs. 902—Rep. PV Essen, Dec. 4, 1906. See statements by Stanisław Zaliss.

45. HSTAD RD Präs. 902—Rep. PV Essen, Feb. 25, 1907.

46. HSTAD RD Präs. 902—Rep. PV Essen, March 18, 1907.

47. For a history of the school strikes in Poland, see John J. Kulczycki, *School Strikes in Prussian Poland, 1901–1907: The Struggle over Bilingual Education* (Boulder, Colo.: East European Monographs, 1981).

48. HSTAD RD Präs. 902—Rep. PV Oberhausen to RPD, June 24, 1907; *Wiarus Polski*, Jan. 24, 1907.

49. HSTAD RD Präs. 902—Rep. PV Essen, Feb. 25, 1907.

50. STAM RM VII 31—"Stand der Polenbewegung," May 4, 1914; Richard Charles Murphy, *Guestworkers in the German Reich: A Polish Community in Wilhelmine Germany* (Boulder, Colo.: East European Monographs, 1983), 148.

51. Within the Gelsenkirchen-Land region, Poles were most successful within the city of Wanne, where Poles enjoyed electoral success in 1903 and by 1908 even achieved parity with German Catholics in terms of parish council seats. For more information, see STAM RA II E No. 714—Report LR Gelsenkirchen to RPA, March 8, 1908; Report LR Gelsenkirchen to Kreisschulinspector, May 2, 1908.

52. STAM RM VII 31—"Stand der Polenbewegung," May 3, 1913; "Stand der Polenbewegung," May 4, 1914. In addition, Poles also had majorities in both executive committees and church councils in Bottrop. For a more detailed listing of elections at the parish level between 1900 and 1914 see STAM RA II E No. 714.

53. HSTAD RD Präs. 902—Rep. Königliche Landrat Ruhrort (Kreis) to RPD, June 14, 1907.

54. STAM OP 6396—"Stand der Polenbewegung," May 20, 1910.

55. STAM RM VII 31—"Stand der Polenbewegung," April 22, 1912.

56. It is difficult to determine the exact nature of the out-migration from the Ruhr in the early 1920s because accurate statistical data from both German and Polish government sources is unavailable. In individual towns, some information on the types of out-migrants can be ascertained by examining local city address books. For example, in the city of Gelsenkirchen, of the sixteen Poles who held seats on various church councils in 1910, ten, or 63 percent, were still living in Gelsenkirchen in 1924/25, well after the massive out-migration of the early 1920s. See Stadtarchiv Gelsenkirchen—*Adressbuch Gelsenkirchen*, 1910, 1920, and 1924/25. Similarly, twelve Polish associations, three of them connected to the church, existed in the district of Osterfeld (city of Oberhausen) prior to 1921. By 1927, only four associations remained, including the three same religious associations that existed in 1921. See Stadtarchiv Osterfeld—*Adressbuch Osterfeld*, 1921, 1927.

222 | *Notes to Pages 114–115*

57. Key works on the history of the PNCC include Polish National Catholic Church, *Księga Pamiątkowa "33"* (Scranton, Penn.: PNCC Press, 1930); Paul Fox, *The Polish National Catholic Church* (Scranton, Penn.: PNCC Press, 1957); Stephen Włodarski, *The Origin and Growth of the Polish National Catholic Church* (Scranton, Penn.: PNCC Press, 1974); Kubiak, *Polish National Catholic Church.*

58. *Scranton Republican*, Aug. 11, 1896; Sept. 7, 1896; Kubiak, *Polish National Catholic Church*, 102–7. Aust has often been described as a snobbish, overbearing German or (even worse) Prussian whose nationality made conflict inevitable. Such descriptions, however, fail to adequately understand his background or character. Aust was a Polish-speaking German-Silesian catering to a congregation composed of many Polish-Silesians, hence the nationality divide between the priest and his parishioners was not particularly large. Further, after his transfer to Hazleton, Aust became a leading figure within that Polish community, acting as a chief defender of Poles in the aftermath of the Lattimer Massacre in 1897. In the end, the conflict that erupted in Scranton under Aust was less about nationality and more about issues of power and control in the parish. The naming of this parish after a Polish patron saint was a deliberate challenge to O'Hara's authority, especially since St. Stanislaus was renowned for successfully challenging his king over a land dispute.

59. Of peasant birth, Hodur grew up in the Austrian Silesian mining community of Zarki. In the early 1890s, he entered the seminary at the Jagiellonian University in Kraków. During this time he became an admirer of the populist priest Stanisław Stojałowski, an activist who agitated for peasant rights and attempted to form a peasant populist party in Galicia. Under circumstances that are not entirely clear, he did not complete the seminary program and immigrated in 1893 to the United States, eventually arriving in the Diocese of Scranton. In Scranton, he was permitted to complete his preparation for the priesthood and was ordained by Bishop O'Hara in August 1893. Kubiak, *Polish National Catholic Church*, 118–19; Włodarski, *The Origin and Growth of the Polish National Catholic Church*, 40–41; CPNCC-*Straż*, April 16, 1898. In addition to attacks on the Irish hierarchy in America, Hodur vigorously railed against what he viewed as the corruption of the Polish Catholic Church in Poland. See, for example, CPNCC-*Straż*, Sept. 16, 1897.

60. For a fuller account of the trip, see CPNCC-*Straż*, March 19, 1898. Arriving in Rome without prior notice or evidence of permission from his bishop, Hodur was only able to meet with a few minor-level Vatican officials. His efforts to see the pope were ultimately rebuked by Cardinal Mieczysław Ledóchowski, the archbishop of Gniezno-Poznań and primate of Poland during the Kulturkampf, who, after his forced exile from Prussia in 1875, became head of the Sacred Congregation for the Propagation of the Faith, a position that made him Superior for Catholic Church affairs in the United States. After returning to Scranton, Hodur's bitterness about his Rome experience was evidenced by his attacks on Ledóchowski as a traitor in league with Prussian Germanizers. See, for example, CPNCC-*Straż*, Aug. 16, 1902.

61. Włodarski, *The Origin and Growth of the Polish National Catholic Church*, 65–66; Kubiak, *Polish National Catholic Church*, 107. A final attempt at reconcilia-

tion occurred in late 1900, when the new bishop of Scranton, Michael Hoban, presented Hodur terms for lifting the excommunication decree. These terms required Hodur to repudiate and do penance for his actions as well as the assignment of parish ownership to a committee consisting of the bishop and two lay members of the parish. The majority of St. Stanislaus members rejected this offer and at a meeting on December 16, 1900, voted to sever all ties with the Roman Catholic Church.

62. Much of the ideology and precepts of the church developed over the first three decades after the PNCC's founding. The basic tenants of the church are laid forth in the "11 Principles of the Polish National Catholic Church," first published on the 25th anniversary of the PNCC in 1923. See Polish National Catholic Church, *Po Drodze Życia* (Scranton, Penn.: PNCC Press, 1923).

63. Kruszka, *A History of Poles in America to 1908*, 1:66, 2:130; CPNCC—List of PNCC parishes with founding dates; Polish National Catholic Church, *Księga Pamiątkowa "33"*; U.S. Bureau of the Census, *Census of Religious Bodies, 1936—Bulletin No. 30* (Washington, D.C.: Government Printing Office, 1940), table 2, 2. In addition to Scranton, independence movements emerged in Chicago and Buffalo during the 1880s and 1890s. The PNCC integrated these other movements by World War I.

64. Kruszka, *A History of Poles in America to 1908*, 1:97; Kubiak, *Polish National Catholic Church*, 116–17. See also Chapter 6 for a fuller description of the PNA and Polish Socialist Alliance.

65. AMM-*Diocesan Record*, Sept. 11, 1897; CPNCC-*Straż*, Sept. 18, 1897; Sept. 25, 1897. For more information on the Lattimer Massacre, see Chapter 3. During the 1902 strike, the PNCC was, for example, even willing to mortgage its properties to aid striking workers.

66. *Prace i pisma księdza biskupa Franciszka Hodura* (Scranton, 1939), 69, cited in Kubiak, *Polish National Catholic Church*, 134.

67. CPNCC-*Straż*, April 2, 1898; July 16, 1898; Oct. 1, 1898; Kruszka, *A History of Poles in America to 1908*, 3:135; Włodarski, *The Origin and Growth of the Polish National Catholic Church*, 73–75.

68. AMM-*Diocesan Record*, June 4, 1898; *Catholic Light* (formerly *Diocesan Record*), June 3, 1909; Feb. 17, 1910; May 27, 1909.

69. For a discussion of the struggles over appointment of Polish bishops, see William Galush, "Both Polish and Catholic: Immigrant Clergy in the American Catholic Church," *Catholic Historical Review* 70, no. 3 (1984): 407–27; Daniel Buszek, "Equality of Right: Polish American Bishops in the American Hierarchy?" *Polish American Studies* 62, no. 1 (2005): 5–28.

70. AMM-*Scranton Diocesan Directory* (1990).

71. U.S. Bureau of the Census, *Census of Religious Bodies, 1936—Bulletin No. 30*, table 2, 2. PNCC membership stood at 28,245 in 1916. The most significant source of growth in the 1906–16 period occurred when the PNCC subsumed into its organization other Polish independent movements in Chicago and Buffalo. For further information on PNCC development in this decade see Kubiak, *Polish National Catholic Church*, 122–24. Robert Jankowski, in his documentary work on PNCC history,

claims that two PNCC parishes were created in northeastern Pennsylvania between 1910 and 1916 and twenty-one parishes overall across the country. The sources for his figures, however, are not provided. See Robert Jankowski, ed., *The Growth of a Church: A Historical Documentation* (Scranton, Penn.: Straż Printers, 1965), 47.

72. Kubiak, *Polish National Catholic Church*, 121; Polish National Catholic Church, *Księga Pamiątkowa "33,"* 565–86; PHMC, MG-215, ESC, 40th Anniversary Book of the Good Shepherd Church in Plymouth, Penn., 1938.

73. See Chapter 6 for more detail on this split as well as Donald Pienkos, *PNA: A Centennial History of the Polish National Alliance of the United States of North America* (Boulder, Colo.: East European Monographs, 1984); Joseph Wieczerzak, "Bishop Hodur and the Polish National Alliance (1896–1908): Re-viewing a Relationship," in *Bishop Francis Hodur: Biographical Essays*, ed. Joseph Wieczerzak (Boulder, Colo.: East European Monographs, 1998), 153–64.

74. PHMC MG-409, SOHP—Interview with Henry Klonowski, Aux. Bishop of Scranton (1973); Stanley Adamovitch, miner (1973); Stanley Nycz, second generation miner (1973).

Chapter 6: Challenging State and Society

1. The first discussion of Poles by government officials in the Ruhr occurred in 1883. See STAM RA 14044—various. In northeastern Pennsylvania, discussion of Poles was limited to reports on Polish workers given by the *Reports of the Inspectors of Mines of the Anthracite and Bituminous Coal Regions of Pennsylvania* for the 1880s.

2. HSTAD RD Präs. 867—Rep. OPW, Oct. 31, 1896.

3. STAM RA 14045—RPA to OPW, May 17, 1893; Amtmann GE-Ueckendorf to LRG, Nov. 22, 1892; LRG to RPA—Dec. 5, 1892; HSTAD RD Präs. 867—Rep. OPW, Oct. 31, 1896; HSTAD RD 42815—Rep. OPW to OPRP, Nov. 2, 1897. For a complete list of banned books as of 1911, see HSTAD RD Präs. 903.

4. HSTAD LA Essen 101—Rep. Polizeiverwaltung Borbeck to LR Essen, Jan. 13, 1909. Among the three Regierungsbezirke there were slight differences in the treatment of Poles. Specifically, in the Regierungsbezirk Düsseldorf, part of the Rhineland Province, regulations were sometimes not as rigorously enforced as they were in the Regierungsbezirke Münster and Arnsberg. The chief reasons for this were that within the Regierungsbezirk Düsseldorf, the majority of the population was Roman Catholic, officials tended to be slightly more liberal in their politics toward Poles, and there were fewer Poles who lived within the region. Thus they were not perceived to be as great a threat.

5. STAM RM VII Nr. 35—Rep. MdI to OPW, July 13, 1909; HSTAD LA Essen 97—Rep. RPD, Aug. 2, 1910. As part of its efforts to track the development of Polish activities in the Ruhr, the Bochum *Polenüberwachungsstelle* (Polish oversight office) issued annual *Stand der Polenbewegung* reports in the years from 1910 to 1914 and 1919 to 1928. Copies of the reports are located in the Staatsarchiv Münster. See STAM OP 5758; STAM RM VII Nr. 35.

6. HSTAD RD 16035—RPA to RPD, July 2, 1908; HSTAD LA Essen 97—RPA to LR Essen; HSTAD LA Essen 101—various 1908–1909, 86–175. Section 12 of the Reichsvereinsgesetz banned the use of Polish in public meetings, depending on the size of the Polish minority among the German population within a given district. It is important to note that this regulation referred only to "public" meetings, defined as assemblies that anyone could attend. Local associations that held "closed," members-only meetings could still use the Polish language. Public assemblies related to elections were also unaffected.

7. STAM RA 14044—Rep. LRG to Regierung Arnsberg, Innere Abteilung, Dec. 31, 1886; Rep. RPA, March 3, 1887; Rep. LRG to RPA, July 23, 1887; HSTAD LA Essen 101—Rep. PPB to LRE, Oct. 17, 1911. Poles from Upper Silesia were occasionally treated as a separate group; however, there was no general attempt by the Prussian government to foster an Upper Silesian identity.

8. STAM OP Münster Polizei 5426. Masurians were allowed a church service in Polish every fourteen days. By comparison, Poles, who were double the population, were generally granted a Polish service on an ad hoc basis, usually around Easter. After the turn of the century, support for Masurian parishes was permanently incorporated into the budget of the Ministry for Spiritual, Educational, and Medical Affairs. The development of Masurian newspapers is fascinating for highlighting the attempt to use them as a tool for Germanization. Whereas in the 1890s, the first Masurian paper was titled the *Polski Przyjaciel Familii* (Polish family friend), after the turn of the century Masurian papers bore titles such as *Altpreussische Zeitung* (Old Prussian newspaper) and *Heimatgrüsse* (Homeland greetings). These newspapers, which were printed partly in German and partly in Polish using a Gothic script with which Masurians were most familiar, spread historically questionable propaganda "proving" the Germanic origins of the Masurian community. As the first issue of *Heimatgrüsse* declared in 1911, "Our old and distant homeland was and remains German like other areas of our great and beautiful Fatherland; our forefathers were German, we are German and our children shall remain German!" Masurian mutual-aid societies also underwent an evolution from the 1890s to World War I. When the first such associations were founded, they bore names such as "polnische-evangelischer Arbeiterverein" (Polish-Evangelical worker association) and "evangelisch-polnischer Unterstützungverein" (Polish-Evangelical support association). Later these names changed, with the word "polnisch" (Polish) being replaced by "ostpreussisch" (East Prussian).

9. STAM OP Münster Polizei 5426—Rep. PPB, March 13, 1914; StG Buer II/5/6—Police Revier Reports for Buer for 1912. Overall, the majority of Masurians were significantly less active than Poles in local society and politics. For example, while in 1912 there was an ethnic organization for every 277 Poles, statistics show that there was only one such organization for every 2,316 Masurians. In number of seats held on church councils, the statistics are similar. Whereas in 1912, the Poles held 6.1 percent of seats on local Catholic administrative councils throughout the Ruhr region, the Masurians controlled only 0.35 percent of the seats on councils of the local evangelical parishes. While some Masurians belonged to Protestant religious communities not officially recognized by the state, the disparity remains noticeable.

For more information, see STAM OP 5758—Rep. RPM to OPW, "Zahlenmässige Angabe," March 27, 1913; STAM OP 5758—Rep. PPB to RPA, "Zahlenmässige Angaben," March 15, 1913.

10. STAM OP 5426—Report Rev. William Mueckely to PPB, April 24, 1914.

11. For its part, the Polish national movement was largely ineffective in counteracting German propaganda efforts. For many years, Polish circles made only crude, haphazard attempts to find support within the Masurian community. In the early 1890s, for example, the *Wiarus Polski* argued that Masurians needed to convert to Catholicism before they could aid the Polish cause. See STAM OP 2748 Bd. 2—RPA to OPW, March 19, 1891. For years afterward, many Polish leaders in the Ruhr, not to mention ordinary Poles, continued to believe that only a Catholic could be a true Pole, thus effectively alienating most Masurians from the Polish appeals for ethnic solidarity. For more information on Polish attempts to "win" Poles, see STAM OP Münster Polizei 5426—Rep. PPB, March 13, 1914.

12. For various examples of court cases that ended in decisions in favor of Poles, see HSTAD RD 16029; LA Essen 101.

13. HSTAD LA Essen 101—Decision of the Königlichen Landgerichts Essen, March 11, 1909. For further courts cases see STAM OP 2748 Bd. 11—Decision of the Kreisausschuss des Kreises Gelsenkirchen-Land, June 8, 1907, in Rep. RPA to OPW, June 20, 1910; HSTAD RD 16029—Decision of the Königlichen Landgerichts Essen, Aug. 29, 1905; HSTAD RD 16035—Reports on cases printed in *Wiarus Polski*, Feb. 19, 1914, May 15, 1914.

14. Perry K. Blatz, *Democratic Miners: Work and Labor Relations in the Anthracite Coal Industry, 1875–1925* (Albany: State University of New York Press, 1994), 54; "Legislative Investigating Committee Report," 1831–33. The courts later overturned the head tax.

15. Peter Roberts, *Anthracite Coal Communities* (New York: Macmillan, 1904), 44–45; U.S. Senate, "Statements and Recommendations Submitted by Societies and Organizations Interested in the Subject of Immigration," *Reports of the U.S. Senate Immigration Commission*, vol. 41 (Washington, D.C.: Government Printing Office, 1911), 85–86.

16. U.S. Senate, "Immigrants in Industries—Part 19: Anthracite Coal Mining," *Reports of the U.S. Senate Immigration Commission*, vol. 16 (Washington, D.C.: Government Printing Office, 1911), 695.

17. Ibid., 641, 695.

18. For a general account, see Aristide Zolberg, *A Nation by Design: Immigration Policy in the Fashioning of America* (New York: Russell Sage, 2006). In the late nineteenth century, the restrictionist impulses manifested themselves notably with the 1882 Chinese Exclusion Act, the 1885 law banning contract labor, the congressional 1889 Ford Committee Report, and the takeover of immigration control by the federal government in early 1890s.

19. PHMC MG-171, SPP, Box 28—"Extracts from the Report of the Commissioner-General of Immigration for the year ending June 30, 1903," *Publications of the Immigration Restriction League*, no. 38 (Boston, 1903), 70. Attached to Letter from Prescott Hall (Secy. Immigration Restriction League) to Samuel Pennypacker (Pennsylvania Governor), Nov. 27, 1903.

20. For an overview of the immigration commission's work, see Robert Zeidel, *Immigrants, Progressives, and Exclusion Politics: The Dillingham Commission, 1900–1927* (DeKalb: Northern Illinois Press, 2004).

21. U.S. Senate, "Immigrants in Industries—Part 19, Anthracite Coal Mining," *Reports of the U.S. Senate Immigration Commission*, 16:671–72, 675. Quoted here as printed in the original.

22. On the 1901 Września school strike see John J. Kulczycki, *School Strikes in Prussian Poland, 1901–1907: The Struggle over Bilingual Education* (Boulder, Colo.: East European Monographs, 1981), 49–81; Bolesław Święciochowski, ed., *Strajk szkolny we Wreśni w. 1901 r.* (Września: Wrzesińskie Tow. Kulturalne i Muzeum Regionalne we Wreśni, 2001). For a perspective on Polish immigrant reactions in America to the strike, see Stanislaus Blejwas, "American Polonia and the School Strike in Wrzesnia," *Polish American Studies* 58, no. 2 (2001): 9–59.

23. Clara Viebig, *Das schlafende Heer* (1903; repr., Berlin: Egon Fleischel, 1910), 241. Between 1903 and 1910, the book was reprinted twenty-six times.

24. Alice Ward Bailey, "A Bright Green Pole," *The Outlook* 76, no. 6 (1904): 368–77.

25. E. S. Johnson, "The Younger Generation," *American Magazine* 62, no. 5 (1906): 369–77.

26. *Die Polen im rheinisch-westfälischen Steinkohlen-Bezirk*, published by Gau "Ruhr and Lippe" des Alldeutschen Verbandes (Munich: I. F. Lehmans Verlag, 1901), 65; HSTAD RD Präs. 871—*Rheinisch-Westfälische Zeitung*, Feb. 24, 1903; Christoph Klessmann, *Polnische Bergarbeiter im Ruhrgebiet, 1870–1945: Soziale Integration und nationale Subkultur einer Minderheit in der deutschen Industriegesellschaft* (Göttingen: Vandenhoeck und Ruprecht, 1978), 88–89. For another example of Alldeutscher opinions regarding Poles see Otto Hössch, *Die dringendste Aufgabe der Polenpolitik* (Munich: I. F. Lehmanns Verlag, 1907). For a complete history of the Alldeutscher Verband, see Roger Chickering, *We Men Who Feel Most German: A Cultural Study of the Pan German League* (Boston: Allen and Unwin, 1984).

27. Joh. Victor Bredt, *Die Polenfrage im Ruhrkohlengebiet· Eine wirtschafts politische Studie* (Leipzig: Duncker and Humblot, 1909), 7, 33. For Bredt, the main culprit behind this state of affairs were the Polish leaders in the Ruhr, particularly Jan and Anton Brejski, the publishers of the *Wiarus Polski*, and the leadership of the ZZP, who were leading ordinary Poles astray. The inability of Germans and Poles to find common ground was directly attributable to "the program" of such leaders "who wish to hinder in any way the joining of western Poles with the German nation."

28. Franz Schulze, *Die polnische Zuwanderung im Ruhrrevier und ihre Wirkung* (Munich: Josefs Druckerei, Bigge, 1909), 90–91.

29. Bredt, *Die Polenfrage im Ruhrkohlengebiet*, 8. See also STAM Kreis Gelsenkirchen 53; STAM OP 5426—Rep. RPA to MdI, June 14, 1910. The transformation in the status of Masurians was most notably made evident through the efforts of German nationalists to reclaim this group for the German nation through intensified educational programs designed to teach Masurians about their "true" ethnic German roots. Interestingly, there were concerns among nationalists that Masurians were not integrating fast enough because of the government's minority policy toward

them. In 1910, the National Liberal *Rheinisch-Westfälische Zeitung* criticized this policy, noting that "when the 'true German character' of the 'Old Prussian' is so certain . . . then we do not understand why their actual amalgamation into German society is still artificially postponed [since] the deeper their solidarity with a great people, the less the danger exists that they will fall into the hands of the Poles." See STAM OP 5426—*Rheinisch-Westfälische Zeitung,* Nov. 1, 1910.

30. Frank Warne, *The Slav Invasion and the Mine Workers* (Philadelphia: J. B. Lippincott, 1904), 82, 99–100, 105–6, 108–12.

31. "Statement of the Immigration Restriction League," Oct. 24, 1910, in *Reports of the U.S. Senate Immigration Commission,* vol. 41, "Statements and Recommendations," 103, 106–7, 110–38.

32. Ludwig Bernhard, *Das polnische Gemeinwesen im preussischen Staat: Die Polenfrage* (Leipzig: Duncker and Humblot, 1907), 188–89, 671–75. Bernhard's book enjoyed a degree of popularity. In 1910, a second edition was published and the book was also translated into Russian.

33. Stanislaus Wachowiak, *Die Polen in Rheinland-Westfalen* (Leipzig: Robert Noske, 1916), 41, 68, 106–7. Wachowiak's life story itself is remarkable. Born in eastern Prussia, Wachowiak came to the Ruhr in 1898 with his working-class parents. Despite his class background, he was fortunate to receive financial support from the St. Joseph's Fund, a scholarship program established by Poles to promote higher education access for promising students, and as a consequence was able to enroll in a gymnasium (a college-preparatory high school) in Recklinghausen. In 1911, he became an editor for the Polish ZZP union newspaper *Głos Górnika* (Miner's Voice) and contributor to the *Wiarus Polski* (The Old Polish Soldier). Prior to and during World War I, Wachowiak attended Humboldt University in Berlin, University of Münster, University of Strassburg (at Münster and Strassburg he ran afoul of university and Prussian authorities), and finally Munich's Ludwig-Maximilian University where he studied under Lujo Bretano. After World War I, Wachowiak returned to Poland, became a representative in the Polish Sejm and an official in the Polish province of Pomorze (formerly West Prussia). After the 1926 Piłsudski coup, he became involved in Polish diaspora affairs and in the 1930s took a prominent position with the Bank Handlowy (Trade Bank). During the German occupation of World War II, he served as a representative for the Main Polish Occupation Committee in the district of Warsaw. After the war, he again organized the Bank Handlowy before fleeing Poland in 1946 and eventually settling in Brazil in 1952. He died in 1972. For more information see Stanisław Wachowiak, *Czasy, które przeżyłem, 1890–1939* (Warsaw: Czytelnik, 1983); STAM OP 2748 Bd. 12—Rep. PPB, April 10, 1913; Rep. Disziplinaramt der Universität Strassburg, June 25, 1913.

34. Roberts, *Anthracite Coal Communities,* 25–26; 343–78; "Statement of the International Committee of Young Men's Christian Associations," Oct. 14, 1910, in *Reports of the U.S. Senate Immigration Commission,* vol. 41, "Statements and Recommendations," 85–87; Peter Roberts, *The Problem of Americanization* (New York: Macmillan, 1920). The YMCA was particularly active in northeastern Pennsylvania, where the organization retained a special secretary to work among the

region's various immigrant groups. Another organization aiding immigrants in the region was the North American Civic League for Immigrants, with offices in Hazleton, Pottsville, and Reading.

35. Examples of the Roberts method of teaching can be found in Peter Roberts, *English for Coming Americans: A Rational System for Teaching English to Foreigners* (New York: Young Men's Christian Association Press, 1909); *Civics for Coming Americans* (New York: Young Men's Christian Association Press, 1912); *English for Coming Americans Advanced Course: History, Geography, Government, Language Lessons* (New York: Young Men's Christian Association Press, 1917); *English for Foreigners* (Urbana: University of Illinois, 1914); *Report of the Department of Mines of Pennsylvania*, Part 1—Anthracite, 1912, (Harrisburg: Wm. Stanley Ray, State Printer, 1913), 12–13. In northeastern Pennsylvania, such schools proved popular. Course content was often based on miners' own work experiences, making it accessible to non-English speakers. English comprehension exercises, for example, were taught within the context of a mine safety lesson showing proper and improper mining methods, with photos and simple captions stressing and repeating important words.

36. William Thomas and Florian Znaniecki, *The Polish Peasant in Europe and America*, 5 vols. (Boston: G. Badger, 1918), 5:341–45.

37. Emily Balch, *Our Slavic Fellow Citizens* (New York: Charities Publication Committee, 1910), 424–25.

38. STAM OP 5758–Rep. RPM to OPW, "Zahlenmässige Angabe," March 27, 1913; Roberts, *Anthracite Coal Communities*, 259.

39. STAM OP 6037—Statistical Report on Poles in Westphalia for 1902; Roberts, *Anthracite Coal Communities*, 198.

40. HSTAD RD 42815—*Wiarus Polski*, Dec. 16, 1897; Klessmann, *Polnische Bergarbeiter*, 126; Valentina-Maria Stefanski, *Zum Prozess der Emanzipation und Integration von Aussenseitern: Polnische Arbeitsmigranten im Ruhrgebiet* (Dortmund: Forschungsstelle Ostmitteleuropa, 1984), 161; STAM OP 5758—Rep. RPM to OPW, "Zahlenmässige Angabe," March 27, 1913. Due to the three-tiered voting system, the Main Voting Committee generally did organize Poles for Prussian Landtag elections. The exception occurred in the 1908 elections, when the Committee supported the Center Party.

41. Klessmann, *Polnische Bergarbeiter*, 126–27; STAM OP 6396—"Stand der Polenbewegung," April 15, 1911.

42. HSTAD RD 42815—Rep. RPD April 28, 1899; STAM RA 14049—Bericht des Verbandsturnwarts für das Jahr 1911 (trans.), March 15, 1912; STAM OP 5758—Rep. RPM to OPW, "Zahlenmässige Angabe," March 27, 1913. For a more expansive history, see Diethelm Blecking, *Die Geschichte der nationalpolnischen Turnverien Sokół im deutschen Reich, 1884–1939* (Dortmund: Forschungstelle Ostmitteleuropa, 1987).

43. STAM RA 14131—*Rheinisch-Westfälische Zeitung*, Feb. 12, 1903, May 14, 1903.

44. STAM RM VII, Nr. 340—Decision of the Oberverwaltungsgericht, May 15, 1913.

45. STAM OP 6396—"Stand der Polenbewegung," May 20, 1910; STAM RM VII Nr. 35—"Stand der Polenbewegung," May 4, 1914. For further information on Polish socialist activities in the Ruhr, see also STAM OP 2847—Rep. RPA to OPW, July 17, 1899; APP Polizeipräsidium 2692—*Wiarus Polski,* Sept. 21, 1904; *Gazeta Robotnicza* (Katowice), July 1, 1905; HSTAD LA Moers 467—Rep. RPD to PPE, March 21, 1910; Rep. PPE to RPD, April 11, 1910; John J. Kulczycki, *The Foreign Worker and the German Labor Movement: Xenophobia and Solidarity in the Coal Fields of the Ruhr, 1871–1914* (Providence, R.I.: Berg, 1994), 84, 163–64. For a history of Polish socialism in Germany, see Krzysztof Rzepa, *Socjaliści polscy w Niemczech do 1914 roku* (Warsaw: Książka i Wiedza, 1988).

46. HSTAD RD Präs. 867—Rep. RPM to RPD, Oct. 21, 1895; STAM OP 5758—Rep. RPM to OPW, "Zahlenmässige Angabe," March 27, 1913. It should be noted that politics were never completely absent from these various associations. The mere act of coming together as Poles was in many respects a political statement in itself and taken as such by authorities in the Ruhr.

47. STAM RA 14056—Reports on Polish associations in Gelsenkirchen, dates vary. Whereas prior to 1908, there were twenty associations, by 1914 there were fifty-five.

48. HSTAD LA Essen 101—*Wiarus Polski* (Bochum), Oct. 11, 1908, Oct. 14, 1908; STAM RM VII Nr. 35—"Stand der Polenbewegung," May, 3, 1913; May 4, 1914.

49. STAM RA 14174—Rep. PV Herne, Feb. 18, 1907; *Ludensch-Generalanzeiger,* Feb. 20, 1907; March 25, 1907; *Herner Zeitung,* Nov. 12, 1907. The name Wanda refers to a legendary Polish princess from the Middle Ages who chose to kill herself rather than marry a German prince.

50. HSTAD LA Essen 101—Rep. PV Borbeck, Sept. 29, 1908; STAM RA 14056—Reports on Polish associations in Gelsenkirchen, dates vary; STAM RM VII Nr. 35—"Stand der Polenbewegung," May 3, 1913; STAM RA 14049, Sokół (Posen) March 15, 1912; STAM RA 14169—Rep. RPA, July 15, 1914.

51. STAM RM VII Nr. 35—"Stand der Polenbewegung," May 4, 1914; Rep. PPB, May 23, 1914.

52. For a history of these two organizations see John Radzilowski, *The Eagle and the Cross: A History of the Polish Roman Catholic Union of America, 1873–2000* (Boulder, Colo.: East European Monographs, 2003), 104; Donald E. Pienkos, *PNA: A Centennial History of the Polish National Alliance of the United States of North America* (Boulder, Colo.: East European Monographs, 1984). The PNA drew more core support from Poles living in the eastern United States than the PRCU. Before moving to Chicago, the PNA was originally founded in Philadelphia, and through the years there were repeated attempts to have the organization's headquarters returned East. For further information, see Joseph Wieczerzak, "Bishop Hodur and the Polish National Alliance (1896–1908): Re-viewing a Relationship," in *Bishop Francis Hodur: Biographical Essays,* ed. Joseph Wieczerzak (Boulder, Colo.: East European Monographs, 1998), 157.

53. Pienkos, *PNA: A Centennial History of the Polish National Alliance,* 25, 57, 91–92; Radzilowski, *The Eagle and the Cross,* 66–70, 73–74, 91–92, 178. The

PRCU established the first Polish seminary in the United States in Orchard Lake, Michigan (Detroit area), in 1885. Although initially designed for preparing males for the priesthood, the seminary later expanded to provide both liberal arts and college preparatory curricula. Today the school continues in the form of Ave Maria University. The PNA subsequently founded Alliance College in Cambridge Springs, Pennsylvania, in 1912, which remained in existence until 1987.

54. CPNCC-*Straż*, Feb. 22, 1902, Oct. 6, 1906; U.S. Senate, "Immigrants in Industries—Part 19, Anthracite Coal Mining," *Reports of the U.S. Senate Immigration Commission,* 16:696.

55. Pienkos, *PNA: A Centennial History of the Polish National Alliance,* 28, 78, 90, 110–11; Radzilowski, *The Eagle and the Cross,* 124, 140–45.

56. In later years, the qualifications for membership in the PRCUA have expanded somewhat to include other Eastern European ethnic groups. The requirement that members be Roman Catholics in good standing remains. As recent promotional literature notes, "Insurance, Annuity and membership offers are available only to applicants who are of Polish nationality or descent, members of the Roman Catholic Church, or those related by marriage to an individual who is eligible for membership. We also admit Slavs, Ruthenians, and Lithuanians who are members in good standing in the Catholic Church, according to the Roman, Armenian or Greek rites." See Polish Roman Catholic Union of America, "About PRCUA," http://www.prcua.org/about.htm (accessed July 29, 2009).

57. Radzilowski, *The Eagle and the Cross,* 89–93; John Bukowczyk, *And My Children Did Not Know Me: A History of the Polish Americans* (Bloomington: Indiana University Press, 1987), 45–46.

58. Pienkos, *PNA: A Centennial History of the Polish National Alliance,* 59, 73–78, 95, 216; Bukowczyk, *And My Children Did Not Know Me,* 45–46; Stanislaus Blejwas, *The Polish Singers Alliance of America, 1888–1998* (Rochester: University of Rochester Press, 2005), 20–21, 36; Wieczerzak, "Bishop Hodur and the Polish National Alliance," 156–57; 163–64. According to Wieczerzak, by 1904 there were seventeen PNA locals affiliated with the PNCC.

59. Pienkos, *PNA: A Centennial History of the Polish National Alliance,* 97–98, 101–3, 127–49, 215–16; Bukowczyk, *And My Children Did Not Know Me,* 47–48; Stanislaus Blejwas, "Polonia and Politics," in *Polish Americans and their History: Community, Culture, and Politics,* ed. John Bukowczyk (Pittsburgh: University of Pittsburgh Press, 1996), 124–28.

60. Hieronim Kubiak, *The Polish National Catholic Church in the United States of America from 1897 to 1980* (Cracow: Nakl. Uniwersytetu Jagiellonskiego, 1983), 170–73; James Pula, *Polish Americans: An Ethnic Community* (New York: Twayne, 1995), 36; Radzilowski, *The Eagle and the Cross,* 102–3; CPNCC-*Straż,* Oct. 27, 1900.

61. CPNCC—*Straż,* Oct. 27, 1900; Joseph Wieczerzak, "Bishop Francis Hodur and the Socialists: Associations and Disassociations," in *Bishop Francis Hodur: Biographical Essays,* ed. Joseph Wieczerzak (Boulder, Colo.: East European Monographs, 1998), 117, 124–27; AMM-*Catholic Light,* Feb. 6, 1908; *Smull's Legislative*

Hand Book and Manual of the State of Pennsylvania (Harrisburg: Harrisburg Publishing, 1907–15).

62. Donald E. Pienkos, *One Hundred Years Young: A History of the Polish Falcons of America, 1887–1987* (Boulder, Colo.: East European Monographs, 1987), 83–89; 231–57; Polish Falcons of America, "About Us—History," http://www.polishfalcons.org/aboutus/index.html (accessed July 29, 2009); *UMWJ*, Aug. 7, 1902.

63. Arthur Waldo, *The Falcon Ideology of Felix L. Pietrowicz: Creator of the Polish Falcons of America in 1887* (Pittsburgh: Polish Falcons of America, 1975), 2–3, cited in Pien Versteegh, "'The Ties That Bind': The Role of Family and Ethnic Networks in the Settlement of Polish Migrants in Pennsylvania, 1890–1940," *History of the Family* 5, no. 1 (2000): 124.

64. For information on Polish singing associations, see Blejwas, *The Polish Singers Alliance;* Victor Greene, *A Singing Ambivalence: American Immigrants between Old World and New, 1830–1930* (Kent, Ohio: Kent State University Press, 2004), 94–113. An introduction to the role of sport in Polish-American life is provided by Thomas Tarapacki, *Chasing the American Dream: Polish Americans and Sports* (New York: Hippocrene, 1995).

65. Emily Napieralski, "The Polish Women's Alliance," *Głos Polek*, Aug. 22, 1918, cited in Versteegh, "The Ties That Bind," 131.

66. Versteegh, "The Ties That Bind," 132; Thaddeus Radzilowski, "Family, Women, and Gender: The Polish Experience" in *Polish Americans and Their History: Community, Culture, and Politics,* ed. John Bukowczyk (Pittsburgh: University of Pittsburgh Press, 1996), 72.

Chapter 7: War and Polish Communities Transformed, 1914–24

1. STAM RM VII, Nr. 35a—Rep. Constantine der Grosse to Bergbau Verein, Oct. 26, 1915; HSTAD RD 9082—Rep. MdI to RPD, May 6, 1915; Rep. MdI, May 11, 1915; Rep. PPE to RPD, July 21, 1915; HSTAD RD 9081—Rep. Stellvertr. Generalkommando VII. Armee to RPA, April 18, 1916.

2. STAM RM VII 35—Rep. MdI to RPM, Feb. 9, 1917; HSTAD LA Essen 97—Rep. MdI to RPD, Feb. 9, 1917; See also HSTAD LA Moers 467—Rep. MdI to RPD, March 8, 1918, for exceptions to the easement in restrictions.

3. BBA Bestand 20, File 563—Internal reports for Zeche Amalie and Helene; STAM BAD 6054—Reports between OBD, Bergrevierbeamten Dortmund III, and affected mines, Feb. 1917–Jan. 1918; HSTAD LA Moers 395 Bd.1—Rep. PV Friemersheim to LR Moers, June 14, 1918; HSTAD LA Moers 395 Bd.1—Rep. PV Hochemmerich to LR Moers, June–July 1918; HSTAD LA Moers 395 Bd.1—Rep. PV Camp to LA Moers, Sept. 9, 1918.

4. HSTAD RD 16020—Rep. PPE to RPD, 1918 (p. 322); HSTAD LA Moers 395, Bd. 1—Rep. PV Hochemmerich to LR Moers, June 12, 1918; PV Hamborn to LR Moers, May 27, 1918; John J. Kulczycki, *The Polish Coal Miners Union and the German Labor Movement in the Ruhr, 1902–1934* (Oxford: Berg, 1997), 151–54;

Christoph Klessmann, *Polnische Bergarbeiter im Ruhrgebiet, 1870–1945: Soziale Integration und nationale Subkultur einer Minderheit in der deutschen Industriegesellschaft* (Göttingen: Vandenhoeck und Ruprecht, 1978), 129.

5. STAM RA 14051—Rep. PDB to RPA, July 23, 1920; For a history of the relationship between the ZZP and NPR in Poland during the early 1920s see Tadeusz Kotłowski, *Zjednoczenie Zawadowe Polskie: Zasięg wpływów i działalność społeczno-polityczna w latach 1918–1939* (Poznań: Uniwersytet im. Adama Mickiewicza, 1977), 55–77.

6. Perry K. Blatz, *Democratic Miners: Work and Labor Relations in the Anthracite Coal Industry, 1875–1925* (Albany: State University of New York Press, 1994), 229–33; Thomas Dublin and Walter Licht, *The Face of Decline: The Pennsylvania Anthracite Region in the Twentieth Century* (Ithaca, N.Y.: Cornell University Press, 2005), 40, 50

7. Mieczysław Haiman, *Polacy w Ameryce* (Chicago: Nakładem Polskiej Katolickiej Spółki Wydawniczej, 1930), 74–80; James Pula, *Polish Americans: An Ethnic Community* (New York: Twayne, 1995), 54, 60–61; John Bukowczyk, *And My Children Did Not Know Me: A History of the Polish Americans* (Bloomington: Indiana University Press, 1987), 49, Stanislaus Blejwas, *The Polish Singers Alliance of America, 1888–1998* (Rochester: University of Rochester Press, 2005), 52. During the period of American neutrality, where one stood on the issue of support for the Central Powers or Russia was also affected by whether one supported Jósef Pilsudski and the PPS, which until 1916 was allied with the Central Powers, or Roman Dmowski and the National Democrats, which supported the Entente. Recruiting for the Polish Army in the United States was limited to those who were single and not American citizens. For more information, see Joseph Hapak, "The Polish Military Commission, 1917–1919," *Polish American Studies* 38, no. 2 (1981): 26–38. The Haller Army in France has not been particularly well studied, though published work includes Józef Sierociński, *Armja Polska we Francji: Dzieje Wojsk Generała Hallera na obczynie* (Warsaw: Nakł własnym, 1929); Paul S. Valasek, *Haller's Polish Army in France* (Chicago: Paul S. Valasek, 2006).

8. HSTAD RD 16021—Rep. PPB to RPA, Aug. 19, 1919; Klessmann, *Polnische Bergarbeiter*, 172–73. See also article 113 of the Versailles Treaty.

9. STAM RA 14051—Rep. PBB to RPA, July 19, 1919.

10. For an overview of the economic situation in the early Weimar period see Gerald Feldman, *The Great Disorder: Politics, Economics, and Society in the German Inflation, 1914–1924* (Oxford: Oxford University Press, 1997). Also useful is the work by Theo Balderston, *Economics and Politics in the Weimar Republic* (Cambridge: Cambridge University Press, 2002).

11. BBA Bestand 20, File 563—Reports Zeche Amalie and Helene on Arbeiterunruhen, May 1919; HSTAD RD 15975—Rep. Generalkommando VII. Armee, June 25, 1918; STAM RA 14051—Rep. PPB to RPA, July 19, 1919; Kulczycki, *Polish Coal Miners Union*, 159–82. For a complete understanding of the extent to which Polish activities were monitored, see reports in STAM Büro Kölpin, especially STAM Büro Kölpin 147.

12. Kulczycki, *Polish Coal Miners Union*, 183–84; HSTAD RD 16021—Rep. PPE to RPD on Krupp Works, Dec. 31, 1920; STAM RA 14051—PDB to RPA, Jan. 4, 1921, June 8, 1921.

13. There was also a plebiscite held in East Prussia, in which mostly Germans and Polish-speaking Masurians in the Ruhr were eligible to participate. However, this plebiscite did not arouse the same degree of discord, largely because the Masurians, ignoring attempts by Polish agents to persuade them to vote for Poland, overwhelmingly opted for Germany.

14. STAM RA 14051—Rep. PDB to RPA, Dec. 11, 1920; Feb. 22, 1921; March 16, 1921.

15. STAM RA 14051—Rep. PDB to RPA, Sept. 1, 1920; Dec. 30, 1920. In Bochum, the Police Director (Augustini) even went so far as to grant members of the Heimattreuer associations access to police files kept on leading Polish figures.

16. STAM RA 14051—Rep. Interior Ministry to RPA, Aug 20, 1920; Rep. LRD to RPA, Aug. 24, 1920; Rep. PDB to RPA, Aug. 24, 1920; Rep. PDB to RPA, Aug. 29, 1920.

17. HSTAD RD 16021—*Wiarus Polski*, Dec. 5, 1920; Rep. PPE to RPD, Dec. 4, 1920; HSTAD RD 15742—Rep. Polizei Revier Herne to PD Bochum, April 18, 1921.

18. STAM RA 14051–Appeal to Poles in Westphalia and the Rhineland, *Wiarus Polski*, Jan. 16, 1923, reprinted in the *Herner Zeitung*, Jan. 23, 1923; Kulczycki, *Polish Coal Miners Union*, 194. STAM RA 14514—Rep. Staatskommissar für öffentliche Ordnung, March 6, 1923; STAM RM VII, Nr. 35—Rep. MdI to RPM, May 17, 1923; Rep. PPR to RPM, June 20, 1923. For a history of the occupation see Conan Fischer, *The Ruhr Crisis, 1923–1924* (Oxford: Oxford University Press, 2003).

19. STAM RA 14051—Rep. Polizeiverwalter Dortmund to RPA Oct. 15, 1921; Rep. PDB to RPA, Oct. 31, 1921. A telling example of changes in attitudes can be seen in 1921, when the police chief in Dortmund asked the Minister President in Arnsberg if Poles could be expelled from Germany as soon as they revealed a nationalist outlook, noting that the Polish element in the Ruhr was a "pox upon the body of the German people." In response to this inquiry, the Minister President asked the police director in Bochum, who replied that while such an outcome would be desirable from a "German national standpoint," legally it could not be achieved because Poles were German citizens and that merely having a pro-Polish outlook could not justify expulsion.

20. HSTAD LA Essen 101—Rep. PPB to LR Essen, Sept. 10, 1918; Kulczycki, *Polish Coal Miners Union*, 2–3; Klessmann, *Polnische Bergarbeiter*, 152. For a history of the ZZP in Poland during the interwar period see Kotłowski, *Zjednoczenie Zawadowe Polskie*.

21. HSTAD LA Moers 395 Bd. 1—Rep. PV Hochemmerich to LR Moers, Nov. 11, 1918; STAM RA 14051—Rep. PPB to RPA, Nov. 4, 1919; STAM RA 14051—Reports PDB to RPA, Jan. 16, 1920, Feb. 13, 1920, Feb. 19, 1920; HSTAD RD 16021—Replies to MdI inquiry on Poles, Aug. 1920.

22. STAM Kreis Gelsenkirchen 52, Bd. 1—"Erlass der Minister des Innern," Dec. 6, 1921; "Merkblatt zu den . . . Abkommens über Staatsangehörigkeits- und Optionsfragen vom 30. August 1924."

23. Kulczycki, *Polish Coal Miners Union*, 218–19.

24. HSTAD RD 15379—"Nachrichten Blatt Münster," no. 41, Dec. 24, 1921; "Nachrichten Blatt Münster," no. 23, March 7, 1921.

25. Klessmann, *Polnische Bergarbeiter*, 161–66; HSTAD RD 15379—"Nachrichten Blatt Münster," no. 52, April 25, 1922; RD 15737—Rep. Polizeidirektor Bochum to OPW, April 6, 1922; May 17, 1922; Kulczycki, *Polish Coal Miners Union*, 222–31. For a history of the Polish migrant experience in France, see Janine Ponty, *Polonais méconnus: Histoire des travailleurs immigrés en France dans l'entre-deux-guerres* (Paris: Publications de la Sorbonne, 1988).

26. Kulczycki, *Polish Coal Miners Union*, 253; Klessmann, *Polnische Bergarbeiter*, 174.

27. For background into the early organization of Polish-language classes, see HSTAD RD 16021—Rep. PPB to RPA, Aug. 19, 1919; HSTAD RD 16020—Rep. PPB to RPA, Oct. 23, 1919; BBA Bestand 72, File 499—Rep. Abt. für Kirchen- und Schulwesen to LR Recklinghausen, Oct. 15, 1919. For 1921 and 1922 figures as reported by German officials, see Klessmann, *Polnische Bergarbeiter*, 253. For Polish estimates, see Henryk Chałupczak, *Szkolnictwo polskie w Niemczech, 1919–1939* (Lublin: Wydawnictwo Uniwersytetu Marii Curie Skłodowskiej, 1996), 156–61. In addition to language classes, Poles also continued to organize summertime trips to Poland for children between the ages of eight and fourteen. In 1932, for example, as many as 1,900 young Poles participated in a month-long visit to Poland. For further information, see HSTAD RD 17212—Rep. PP Duisburg-Hamborn to RPD, Aug. 4, 1931; Aug. 3, 1932.

28. Kulczycki, *Polish Coal Miners Union*, 240. For a complete history on the relationship between the Polish government and the Polish minority in Germany during the interwar period, see Henryk Chałupczak, *II Rzeczpospolita a mniejszość polska w Niemczeck* (Poznań: Instytut Zachodni, 1992).

29. For a complete history of Polish efforts to preserve ethnic unity in interwar German society, see Wojciech Wrzesiński, *Polski ruch narodowy w Niemczech, 1922–1939*, 3rd edition (Toruń: Wydawnictwo Adam Marszałek, 2005). For a history of the ZPwN see Helena Lehr and Edmund Osmańczyk, *Polacy spod znaku rodła* (Warsaw: Wydawnictwo Ministerstwa Obrony Narodowej, 1972); Klessmann, *Polnische Bergarbeiter*, 168–71.

30. Susanne Peters-Schildgen, *"Schmelztiegel" Ruhrgebiet: Die Geschichte der Zuwanderung am Beispiel Herne bis 1945* (Essen: Klartext, 1997), 291; Klessmann, *Polnische Bergarbeiter*, 179–81. For an analysis of the tribulations faced by Poles in the school system, see Ralf Karl Oenning, *Du da Mitti, polnische Farben: Sozialisationserfahrungen von Polen im Ruhrgebiet 1918 bis 1939* (Münster: Waxmann, 1991). For insight into the difficulties faced by Poles active in ethnic affairs during the Nazi period as well as the divisions among family members over "becoming German" or retaining attachments to Polish ethnic culture, see HSTAD Gestapo Düsseldorf 13818 and 66958—Files on Julian Kilinski; Gestapo Düsseldorf 32531—File on Joseph Kallus.

Nazi racial policy toward various Slavic peoples was never uniform, and in the Ruhr great pressure was placed on younger German nationals of ethnic Polish descent (that is, second- and third-generation Ruhr-Poles) to join the Hitler Youth. In certain ways the situation parallels what occurred to hundreds of thousands of Poles living in areas of western Poland incorporated into Germany after 1939 who were summarily placed on the German Volksliste and subsequently made eligible for service in the German army. For a discussion of Nazi policies toward East Europeans see John Connelly, "Nazis and Slavs: From Racial Theory to Racist Practice," *Central European History* 32, no. 1 (1999): 1–33.

31. Klessmann, *Polnische Bergarbeiter*, 182–86.

32. Donald Miller and Richard Sharpless, *The Kingdom of Coal* (Easton, Penn.: Canal History and Technology Press, 1998), 298–94; Blatz, *Democratic Miners*, 253–60; Dublin and Licht, *Face of Decline*, 40, 50–57.

33. Blatz, *Democratic Miners*, 261.

34. To better understand the decline of the anthracite industry over the course of the twentieth century and its social effects, see Dublin and Licht, *Face of Decline*.

35. *Scranton Republican*, April 2, 1919.

36. *Scranton Times*, May 2, 1919.

37. *Scranton Republican*, April 25, 1919

38. *Scranton Republican*, May 26, 1919, May 27, 1919; *Scranton Times*, May 26, 1919.

39. *Scranton Republican*, May 7, 1920

40. *Wall Street Journal*, Sept. 25, 1923.

41. AMM-*Coal Age*, Jan. 1, 1916.

42. Madison Grant, *The Passing of the Great Race; or, The Racial Basis of European History* (New York: Charles Scribner, 1916). For a further discussion of Grant and the Immigration Restriction League see Robert Zeidel, *Immigrants, Progressives, and Exclusion Politics: The Dillingham Commission, 1900–1927* (DeKalb: Northern Illinois Press, 2004), 23–24, 120, 124.

43. Zeidel, *Immigrants, Progressives, and Exclusion Politics*, 138; Pula, *Polish Americans*, 65; *Wall Street Journal*, Sept. 17, 1924. In terms of immigrants from the Western Hemisphere, only those persons from European dependencies in the Caribbean, Central, and South America were affected by the Quota Act of 1921 and National Origins Act of 1924. See *Wall Street Journal*, Sept. 17, 1924.

44. *Wall Street Journal*, July 10, 1923; *New York Times*, July 16, 1923.

45. *New York Times*, July 1, 1924; Pula, *Polish Americans*, 65.

46. *Scranton Republican*, May 26, 1919; Pula, *Polish Americans*, 61–62, 68.

47. For a history of the struggles Polish returnees from the United States faced in re-adapting to Polish society, see Adam Walaszek, *Reemigracja ze Stanów Zjednoczonych do Polski po I. wojnie światowej, 1919–1924* (Cracow: Nakl. Uniwersytetu Jagiellonskiego, 1983). For a condensed discussion, see Hieronim Kubiak, *The Polish National Catholic Church in the United States of America from 1897 to 1980* (Cracow: Nakl. Uniwersytetu Jagiellonskiego, 1983), 124; Pula, *Polish Americans*, 60, 68–69; Bukowczyk, *And My Children Did Not Know Me*, 66–67.

48. For an account of the role of American popular culture in the 1920s and 1930s on immigrant assimilation, see Lizbeth Cohen, *Making a New Deal:*

Industrial Workers in Chicago, 1919–1939 (New York: Cambridge University Press, 1990).

49. For a further discussion of the effects of the immigration restrictions on the cultural life of the Polish-American community, see James Pula, "'A Branch Cut off from Its Trunk': The Effects of Immigration Restriction on American Polonia," *Polish American Studies* 61, no. 1 (2004): 39–50.

50. Kubiak, *Polish National Catholic Church*, 124–25; Pula, *Polish Americans*, 73.

51. Bukowczyk, *And My Children Did Not Know Me*, 65–104.

Bibliography

Primary Sources

Archival Collections

Archiwum Państwowe Miasta Poznania i Województwa Poznańskiego
Bochum Bergbau Museum Archive
Catholic University of America Archives
Hauptstaatsarchiv Düsseldorf
Historical Society of Pennsylvania Archives
Pennsylvania Historical and Museum Commission
Staatsarchiv Münster
Stadtarchiv Bochum
Stadtarchiv Gelsenkirchen
Stadtarchiv Oberhausen

Newspapers and Periodicals

Arbeiter Zeitung
Der Bergknappe
Catholic Light (formerly *Diocesan Record*)
Coal Age
Deutsche Berg- und Hütten Arbeiter Zeitung
Diocesan Record (Scranton)
Dortmunder Zeitung
Emscher Zeitung
Essener Volkszeitung
Freeland Progress
Gazeta Robotnicza (Katowice)
Gelsenkirchen Zeitung
Harper's Weekly
Hazleton Daily Standard
Hazleton Sentinel
Herner Zeitung
Los Angeles Times
Ludensch-Generalanzeiger
Märkischer Sprecher

Narodowiec (Herne)
New York Times
Niederrheinische Volkszeitung
Orędownik
Philadelphia Public Ledger
Philadelphia Sun
Rheinisch-Westfälische Arbeiter Zeitung
Rheinisch-Westfälische Zeitung
Ruhrorter Zeitung
Scranton Republican
Scranton Times
Sokół (Posen)
Straż (Scranton)
Süddeutsche Zeitung
Tremonia (Dortmund)
United Mine Workers Journal (UMWJ)
Wall Street Journal
Westfälische Anzeiger
Wiarus Polski (Bochum)
Wilkes-Barre Record

Other Works

Adressbuch der Stadt Buer, 1910/1911.
Adressbuch der Stadt Gelsenkirchen, 1910.
Adressbuch der Stadt Osterfeld, 1921.
American Coal Foundation. "Coal: Ancient Gift Serving Modern Man." http://www.ket.org/Trips/Coal/AGSMM/agsmmtoc.html.
Anthracite Coal Strike Commission. *Report to the President on the Anthracite Coal Strike of May–Oct. 1902.* Washington, D.C.: Government Printing Office, 1903.
Bailey, Alice Ward. "A Bright Green Pole." *The Outlook* 76, no. 6 (1904): 368–77.
Balch, Emily. *Our Slavic Fellow Citizens.* New York: Charities Publication Committee, 1910.
Bernhard, Ludwig. *Das polnische Gemeinwesen im preussischen Staat: Die Polenfrage.* Leipzig: Duncker and Humblot, 1907.
Bischoff, Walter. *Das kleine Bergbaulexikon.* Essen: Verlag Glückauf, 1985.
Brandt, Hans Jürgen. *Die Polen und die Kirche im Ruhrgebiet.* Münster: Aschendorff, 1987.
Bredt, Joh. Victor. *Die Polenfrage im Ruhrkohlengebiet: Eine wirtschaftspolitische Studie.* Leipzig: Duncker and Humblot, 1909.
Diocese of Scranton. *Directory of the Diocese of Scranton,* 1990.
George, Henry, Jr. "What the Single Tax Is Doing." In *Great Leaders and National Issues of 1912.* New York: L. T. Myers, 1913.
Grant, Madison. *The Passing of the Great Race; or, The Racial Basis of European History.* New York: Charles Scribner, 1916.
Herkner, Heinrich. *Die Arbeiterfrage: Eine Einführung.* 2 vols. Berlin and Leipzig: de Gruyter, 1922.

Hössch, Otto. *Die dringendste Aufgabe der Polenpolitik*. Flugschriften des Alldeutschen Verbandes. Munich: I. F. Lehmanns Verlag, 1907.

Hue, Otto. *Die Bergarbeiter: Historische Darstellung der Bergarbeiter-Verhältnisse von der ältesten bis in die neue Zeit*. 2 vols. Stuttgart: Dietz Verlag, 1910, 1913.

Instytut Gospodarstwa Społecznego. *Pamiętniki chłopów*. 2 vols. Warsaw: Instytut Gospodarstwa Społecznego, 1935–36.

———. *Pamiętniki emigrantów: Stany Zjednoczone*. 2 vols. Warsaw: Książka i Wiedza, 1977.

Jankowski, Robert, ed. *The Growth of a Church: A Historical Documentation*. Scranton, Penn.: Straż Printers, 1965.

Johnson, E. S. "The Younger Generation." *American Magazine* 62, no. 5 (1906): 369–77.

Jones, Eliot. *The Anthracite Coal Combination in the United States*. Cambridge, Mass.: Harvard University Press, 1914.

Korson, George. *Minstrels of the Mine Patch: Songs and Stories of the Anthracite Industry*. Hatboro, Penn.: Folklore Associates, 1938.

Kruszka, Wacław. *A History of Poles in America to 1908*. 3 vols. Edited by James Pula. Washington, D.C.: Catholic University Press, 1993.

Lauck, W. Jett. *Comparison of Earnings and Wage Rates in the Anthracite and Bituminous Mines of Pennsylvania*. Washington, D.C., 1920.

———. *Irregularity of Employment in the Anthracite Industry*. Washington, D.C., 1920.

———. *Wholesale and Retail Prices of Anthracite Coal 1913 to 1920*. Washington, D.C., 1920.

Lengowski, Michał. *Mój Życiorys*. Olszytyn: Pojezierze, 1974.

Pamiętniki emigrantów, 1878–1958. Warsaw: Czytelnik, 1960.

Pennsylvania. Department of Mines. *Report of the Department of Mines of Pennsylvania*, Part I—Anthracite, 1903. Harrisburg: Wm. Stanley Ray, State Printer, 1904.

———. *Report of the Department of Mines of Pennsylvania*, Part I—Anthracite, 1904. Harrisburg: Wm. Stanley Ray, State Printer, 1905.

———. *Report of the Department of Mines of Pennsylvania*, Part I—Anthracite, 1905. Harrisburg: Wm. Stanley Ray, State Printer, 1906.

———. *Report of the Department of Mines of Pennsylvania*, Part 1—Anthracite, 1912. Harrisburg: Wm. Stanley Ray, State Printer, 1913.

———. *Report of the Department of Mines of Pennsylvania*, Part 1—Anthracite, 1914. Harrisburg: Wm. Stanley Ray, State Printer, 1915.

Pennsylvania. Inspector of Mines. *Reports of the Inspectors of Coal Mines of Pennsylvania, 1885*. Harrisburg: Edwin Meyers, 1886.

———. *Reports of the Inspectors of Coal Mines of Pennsylvania, 1896*. Harrisburg: Edwin Meyers, 1897.

Pennsylvania. State Legislature. *Laws of the General Assembly of the Commonwealth of Pennsylvania, passed at the Session of 1895*. Harrisburg: Edwin Meyers, 1897.

———. *Laws of the General Assembly of the Commonwealth of Pennsylvania, passed at the Session of 1897*. Harrisburg: Clarence Busch, 1899.

———. "Legislative Investigating Committee Report on Conditions Existing Among the Miners and those Employed in and about the Mines in the

Anthracite Coal Regions." *Journal of the Senate of the Commonwealth of Pennsylvania for the Session begun at Harrisburg of the 5th day of January 1897*, II. Harrisburg: Wm. Stanley Ray, State Printer, 1897.

Die Polen im rheinisch-westfälischen Steinkohlen-Bezirk. Published by Gau "Ruhr and Lippe" des Alldeutschen Verbandes. Munich: I. F. Lehmans Verlag, 1901.

Polish Falcons of America. "About Us—History." http://www.polishfalcons.org/aboutus/index.html.

Polish National Catholic Church. *Księga Pamiątkowa "33."* Scranton, Penn.: PNCC Press, 1930.

———. *Po Drodze Życia*. Scranton, Penn.: PNCC Press, 1923.

Polish Roman Catholic Union of America. "About PRCUA." http://www.prcua.org/about.htm.

"The Progress of the World." *American Monthly Review of Reviews* 26, no. 5 (1902): 515–35.

Publications of the Immigration Restriction League. No. 38. Boston, 1903.

Reymont, Ladislas St. *The Peasants*. 4 vols. Translated by Michael Dziewicki. New York: Knopf, 1925.

Rhone, Rosamond. "Anthracite Coal Mines and Mining." *American Monthly Review of Reviews* 26, no. 1 (1902): 54–63.

Roberts, Peter. *Anthracite Coal Communities*. New York: Macmillan, 1904.

———. *The Anthracite Coal Industry*. New York: Macmillan, 1901.

———. *Civics for Coming Americans*. New York: Young Men's Christian Association Press, 1912.

———. *English for Coming Americans Advanced Course: History, Geography, Government, Language Lessons*. New York: Young Men's Christian Association Press, 1917

———. *English for Coming Americans: A Rational System for Teaching English to Foreigners*. New York: Young Men's Christian Association Press, 1909.

———. *English for Foreigners*. Urbana: University of Illinois, 1914.

———. *The Problem of Americanization*. New York: Macmillan, 1920.

Schulze, Franz. *Die polnische Zuwanderung im Ruhrrevier und ihre Wirkung*. Munich: Josefs Druckerei, Bigge, 1909.

Smull's Legislative Hand Book and Manual of the State of Pennsylvania. Harrisburg: Harrisburg Publishing, 1907–15.

Thomas, William, and Florian Znaniecki. *The Polish Peasant in Europe and America*. 5 vols. Boston: G. Badger, 1918.

United Nations Department of Economic and Social Affairs. *World Economic and Social Survey: International Migration*. New York: United Nations Publishing Section, 2004.

United Nations Development Programme. *Human Development Report 2009: Overcoming Barriers: Human Mobility and Development*. Basingstoke, UK: Palgrave Macmillan, 2009.

"The United Nations on Levels and Trends of International Migration and Related Policies." *Population and Development Review* 29, no. 2 (2003): 335–40.

U.S. Bureau of the Census. *Census of Religious Bodies, 1936—Bulletin No. 30.* Washington, D.C.: Government Printing Office, 1940.

———. *Mines and Quarries, 1902.* Washington, D.C.: Government Printing Office, 1905.

———. *Seventh Census of United States, 1850—Population.* Washington, D.C.: Government Printing Office, 1853.

———. *Tenth Census of United States, 1880—Population.* Washington, D.C.: Government Printing Office, 1883.

———. *Eleventh Census of United States, 1890—Population.* Washington, D.C.: Government Printing Office, 1895.

———. *Twelfth Census of United States, 1900—Population.* Washington, D.C.: Government Printing Office, 1902.

———. *Thirteenth Census of United States, 1910—Population.* Washington, D.C.: Government Printing Office, 1913.

———. *Thirteenth Census of United States, 1910—Mines and Quarries 1909: General Report and Analysis,* vol. 11. Washington, D.C.: Government Printing Office, 1913.

———. *Fourteenth Census of the United States, 1920—Mines and Quarries,* vol. 11. Washington, D.C.: Government Printing Office, 1923.

U.S. Senate. "The Children of Immigrants in Schools—Scranton and Shenandoah, Pennsylvania." *Reports of the U.S. Senate Immigration Commission.* Vol. 33. Washington, D.C.: Government Printing Office, 1911.

———. "Immigrants in Industries—Part 19: Anthracite Coal Mining." *Reports of the U.S. Senate Immigration Commission.* Vol. 16. Washington, D.C.: Government Printing Office, 1911.

———. "Statements and Recommendations Submitted by Societies and Organizations Interested in the Subject of Immigration." *Reports of the U.S. Senate Immigration Commission.* Vol. 41. Washington, D.C.: Government. Printing Office, 1911.

Viebig, Clara. *Das schlafende Heer.* 1903. Reprint, Berlin: Egon Fleischel, 1910.

Wachowiak, Stanislaus. *Die Polen in Rheinland-Westfalen.* Leipzig: Robert Noske, 1916.

Wachowiak, Stanisław. *Czasy, które przeżyłem, 1890–1939.* Warsaw: Czytelnik, 1983

Warne, Frank. *The Slav Invasion and the Mine Workers.* Philadelphia: J. B. Lippincott, 1904.

Williams, Talcott. "A General View of the Coal Strike." *American Monthly Review of Reviews* 26, no. 1 (1902): 64–66.

Secondary Sources

Accursia, M. "Polish Miners in Luzerne County, Pennsylvania." *Polish American Studies* 3, no. 1 (1946): 5–12.

Alba, Richard. "Assimilation, Exclusion, or Neither?" In *Paths to Inclusion: The Integration of Migrants in the United States and in Germany,* edited by Peter H. Schuck and Rainer Münz. New York: Berghahn Books, 1998.

Alba, Richard, and Victor Nee. *Remaking the American Mainstream: Assimilation and Contemporary Immigration.* Cambridge, Mass.: Harvard University Press, 2003.

———. "Rethinking Assimilation Theory for a New Era of Immigration." *International Migration Review* 31, no. 4 (1997): 826–74.

Anderson, Margaret Lavinia. *Practicing Democracy: Elections and Political Culture in Imperial Germany.* Princeton, N.J.: Princeton University Press, 2000.

Aurand, Harold W. *From the Molly Maguires to the United Mine Workers.* Philadelphia: Temple University Press, 1971.

Bade, Klaus. *Auswanderer, Wanderarbeiter, Gastarbeiter: Bevolkerung, Arbeitsmarkt und Wanderung in Deutschland seit der Mitte des 19. Jahrhunderts.* 2 vols. Ostfildern: Scripta Mercaturae, 1984.

———. "German Emigration to the United States and Continental Immigration to Germany in the Late Nineteenth and Early Twentieth Centuries." *Central European History* 13, no. 4 (1980): 348–77.

———. "Immigration, Naturalization, and Ethno-National Traditions in Germany from the Citizenship Law of 1913 to the Law of 1999." In *Crossing Boundaries: German and American Experiences with the Exclusion and Inclusion of Minorities,* edited by Larry Jones. Oxford: Oxford University Press, 2001.

———. *Legal and Illegal Immigration into Europe: Experiences and Challenges.* Antwerp: Netherlands Institute for Advanced Study, 2003.

Bade, Klaus, and Michael Bommes. "Migration und politische Kultur im 'Nicht-Einwanderungsland.'" In *Migrationsreport 2000,* edited by Klaus Bade and Rainer Münz. Bonn: Bundeszentrale für politische Bildung, 2000.

Balderston, Theo. *Economics and Politics in the Weimar Republic.* Cambridge: Cambridge University Press, 2002.

Barendse, Michael A. *Social Expectations and Perception: The Case of the Slavic Anthracite Workers.* University Park: Pennsylvania State University Press, 1981.

Barrows, Susanna, and Robin Room, eds. *Drinking: Behavior and Belief in Modern History.* Berkeley: University of California Press, 1991.

Bendix, Reinhard. *Nation-Building and Citizenship: Studies of Our Changing Social Order.* 1964. Berkeley: University of California Press, 1977.

Biskupski, M. B. "Bishop Hodur, the Pilsudskiites, and Polonia Politics on the Eve of World War I: Documents and Commentary." *Polish National Catholic Church Studies* 7, no. 1 (1986): 39–52.

Blackbourn, David, and Geoff Eley. *The Peculiarities of German History: Bourgeois Society and Politics in Nineteenth-Century Germany.* Oxford: Oxford University Press, 1984.

Blanke, Richard. *Polish-Speaking Germans? Language and National Identity among the Masurians since 1871.* Cologne: Bohlau, 2001.

———. *Prussian Poland in the German Empire, 1871–1900.* Boulder, Colo.: East European Monographs, 1981.

Blatz, Perry K. *Democratic Miners: Work and Labor Relations in the Anthracite Coal Industry, 1875–1925.* Albany: State University of New York Press, 1994.

Blecking, Diethelm. *Die Geschichte der nationalpolnischen Turnverien Sokół im deutschen Reich, 1884–1939.* Dortmund: Forschungstelle Ostmitteleuropa, 1987.

———. "Polish Community before the First World War and Present-Day Turkish Community Formation—Some Thoughts of a Diachronistic Comparison." In

Irish and Polish Migration in Comparative Perspective, edited by John Belchem and Klaus Tenfelde. Essen: Klartext, 2003.

Blejwas, Stanislaus. "American Polonia and the School Strike in Wrzesnia." *Polish American Studies* 58, no. 2 (2001): 9–59.

———. *The Polish Singers Alliance of America, 1888–1998.* Rochester: University of Rochester Press, 2005.

———. "Polonia and Politics." In *Polish Americans and Their History: Community, Culture, and Politics,* edited by John Bukowczyk. Pittsburgh: University of Pittsburgh Press, 1996.

Blobaum, Robert. *Rewolucja: Russian Poland, 1904–1907.* Ithaca, N.Y.: Cornell University Press, 1995.

Bodnar, John. *Lives of Their Own: Blacks, Italians, and Poles in Pittsburgh, 1900–1960.* Urbana: University of Illinois Press, 1982.

———. *The Transplanted: A History of Immigrants in Urban America.* Bloomington: Indiana University Press, 1985.

Bosniak, Linda. *The Citizen and the Alien: Dilemmas of Contemporary Membership.* Princeton, N.J.: Princeton University Press, 2006.

Brody, David. *In Labor's Cause: Main Themes on the History of the American Worker.* New York: Oxford University Press, 1993.

Broehl, Wayne, Jr. *The Molly Maguires.* Cambridge, Mass.: Harvard University Press, 1964.

Broszat, Martin. *Zweihundert Jahre deutsche Polenpolitik.* Munich: Ehrenwirth, 1963.

Brożek, Andrzej. *Polish Americans, 1854–1939.* 1977. Reprint, Warsaw: Interpress, 1985.

Brubaker, Rogers. *Citizenship and Nationhood in France and Germany.* Cambridge, Mass.: Harvard University Press, 1992.

———. "The Return of Assimilation? Changing Perspectives on Immigration and Its Sequels in France, Germany, and the United States." *Ethnic and Racial Studies* 24, no. 4 (2001): 531–48.

Brüggemeier, Franz-Josef. *Leben vor Ort: Ruhrbergleute und Ruhrbergbau.* Munich: C. H. Beck, 1983.

Bukowczyk, John. *And My Children Did Not Know Me: A History of the Polish Americans.* Bloomington: Indiana University Press, 1987.

———, ed. *Polish Americans and their History: Community, Culture, and Politics.* Pittsburgh: University of Pittsburgh Press, 1996.

Buszek, Daniel. "Equality of Right: Polish American Bishops in the American Hierarchy?" *Polish American Studies* 62, no. 1 (2005): 5–28.

Castles, Stephen, and Mark J. Miller. *The Age of Migration: International Population Movements in the Modern World.* London: Macmillan, 1996.

Chadwick, Owen. *A History of the Popes, 1830–1914.* Oxford: Clarendon Press, 1998.

Chałupczak, Henryk. *II Rzeczpospolita a mniejszość polska w Niemczeck.* Poznań: Instytut Zachodni, 1992.

———. *Szkolnictwo polskie w Niemczech, 1919–1939.* Lublin: Wydawnictwo Uniwersytetu Marii Curie-Skłodowskiej, 1996.

Chickering, Roger. *We Men Who Feel Most German: A Cultural Study of the Pan German League.* Boston: Allen and Unwin, 1984.

Cinel, Dino. *The National Integration of Italian Return Migration, 1870–1929.* Cambridge, UK: Cambridge University Press, 1991.

Cohen, Lizbeth. *Making a New Deal: Industrial Workers in Chicago, 1919–1939.* New York: Cambridge University Press, 1990.

Connelly, John. "Nazis and Slavs: From Racial Theory to Racist Practice." *Central European History* 32, no. 1 (1999): 1–33.

Conzen, Kathleen. "Thomas and Znaniecki and the Historiography of American Integration." *Journal of American Ethnic History* 16, no. 1 (1996): 16–26.

Cyphers, Christopher J. *The National Civic Federation and the Making of a New Liberalism, 1900–1915.* Westport, Conn.: Greenwood, 2002.

Dahlmanna, Dittmarra, Alberta S. Kotowskiego, and Zbigniewa Karpusa, eds. *Schimanski, Kuzorra i inni: Polacy w Zagłębiu Ruhry 1870/71–1945.* Toruń: Wydawnictwo Adam Marszałek, 2006. [Bibliographic note: First author's name appears as Dittmar Dahlmann in the German version of this book.]

Dahrendorf, Ralf. *Society and Democracy in Germany.* London: Weidenfeld and Nicolson, 1968.

Daniels, Roger. *Coming to America: A History of Immigration and Ethnicity in American Life.* New York: Harper Collins, 1990.

Davies, Norman. *God's Playground: A History of Poland.* Vol. 2. Oxford: Clarendon Press, 1981.

Ditt, Karl, and Dagmar Kift. "Der Bergarbeiterstreik von 1889: Ein Testfall für die sozialpolitische Reformfähigkeit des Kaiserreichs." In *1889 Bergarbeiterschaft und Wilhelminische Gesellschaft,* edited by Karl Ditt and Dagmar Kift. Hagen: Linnepe, 1989.

Dolan, Jay P. *The American Catholic Experience: A History from Colonial Times to the Present.* New York: Doubleday, 1985.

Dublin, Thomas, and Walter Licht. *The Face of Decline: The Pennsylvania Anthracite Region in the Twentieth Century.* Ithaca, N.Y.: Cornell University Press, 2005.

Dubofsky, Melvyn, and Foster Rhea Dulles. *Labor in America: A History.* 6th ed. Wheeling, Ill.: Harlan Davidson, 1999.

Earley, James. *Envisioning Faith: The Pictorial History of the Diocese of Scranton.* Devon, Penn.: Cooke, 1994.

Eifert, Christian. "Coming to Terms with the State: Maternalist Politics and the Development of the Welfare State in Weimar Germany." *Central European History* 30, no. 1 (1997): 25–47.

Eley, Geoff, and Jan Palmowski, eds. *Citizenship and National Identity in Twentieth-Century Germany.* Stanford, Calif.: Stanford University Press, 2008.

Faist, Thomas. "Transnationalization in International Migration: Implications for the Study of Citizenship and Culture." *Ethnic and Racial Studies* 23, no. 3 (2000): 189–222.

———. *The Volume and Dynamics of International Migration.* Oxford: Oxford University Press, 2000.

Feldman, Gerald. *The Great Disorder: Politics, Economics, and Society in the German Inflation, 1914–1924.* Oxford: Oxford University Press, 1997.

Fischer, Conan. *The Ruhr Crisis, 1923–1924.* Oxford: Oxford University Press, 2003.

Foner, Nancy. *From Ellis Island to JFK: New York's Two Great Waves of Immigration.* New Haven, Conn.: Yale University Press, 2000.

Fox, Paul. *The Polish National Catholic Church.* Scranton, Penn.: PNCC Press, 1957.

Fuchs, Lawrence. *The American Kaleidoscope: Race, Ethnicity, and the Civic Culture.* Hanover, N.H.: University Press of New England, 1990.

Gallagher, John. *A Century of History: The Diocese of Scranton, 1868–1968.* Scranton, Penn.: Diocese of Scranton, 1968.

Galush, William. "Both Polish and Catholic: Immigrant Clergy in the American Catholic Church." *Catholic Historical Review* 70, no. 3 (1984): 407–27.

Gans, Herbert. "Second Generation Decline: Scenarios for the Economic and Ethnic Futures of Post-1965 Immigrants." *Ethnic and Racial Studies* 15, no. 2 (1992): 173–92.

Glazer, Nathan, and Daniel Patrick Moynihan. *Beyond the Melting Pot: The Negroes, Puerto Ricans, Jews, Italians, and Irish of New York City.* Cambridge, Mass.: MIT Press, 1963.

Gleason, Philip. "American Identity and Americanization." In *Concepts of Ethnicity,* edited by William Petersen, Michael Novak, and Philip Gleason. Cambridge, Mass.: Belknap Press of Harvard University Press, 1982.

Glenn, Evelyn Nakono. *Unequal Freedom: How Race and Gender Shaped American Citizenship and Labor.* Cambridge, Mass.: Harvard University Press, 2003.

Gordon, Milton. *Assimilation in American Life.* Oxford and New York: Oxford University Press, 1964.

Gosewinkel, Dieter. "Citizenship and Naturalization Politics in the Nineteenth and Twentieth Centuries." In *Challenging Ethnic Citizenship: German and Israeli Perspectives on Immigration,* edited by Daniel Levy and Yfaat Weiss. New York: Berghahn Books, 2002.

———. *Einbürgern und Ausschliessen: Die Nationalisierung der Staatsangehörigkeit vom Deutschen Bund bis zur Bundesrepublik Deutschland.* Göttingen: Vandenhoeck and Ruprecht, 2001.

Gowaskie, Joseph. "John Mitchell and the Anthracite Mine Workers: Leadership Conservatism and Rank-and-File Militancy." *Labor History* 27 (Winter 1985–86): 54–83.

Green, Simon. *The Politics of Exclusion: Institutions and Immigration Policy in Contemporary Germany.* Manchester: Manchester University Press, 2004.

Greene, Victor. "Poles." *Harvard Encyclopedia of American Ethnic Groups,* edited by Stephan Thernstrom. Cambridge, Mass.: Harvard University Press, 1980.

———. *A Singing Ambivalence: American Immigrants between Old World and New, 1830–1930.* Kent, Ohio: Kent State University Press, 2004.

———. *The Slavic Community on Strike: Immigrant Labor in Pennsylvania Anthracite.* Notre Dame, Ind.: University of Notre Dame Press, 1968.

Guarnizo, Luis Eduardo. "On the Political Participation of Transnational Migrants: Old Practices and New Trends." In *E Pluribus Unum? Contemporary and*

Historical Perspectives on Immigrant Political Incorporation, edited by Gary Gerstle and John Mollenkopf. New York: Russell Sage, 2001.

Habermas, Jürgen. "Anerkennungskämpfe im demokratischen Rechtsstaat." In *Multikulturalismus und die Politik der Anerkennung,* edited by Charles Taylor, Amy Gutman, and Jürgen Habermas. Frankfurt: S. Fischer, 1993.

———. *The Inclusion of the Other.* Edited by Ciaran Cronin and Pablo De Greiff. Cambridge, Mass.: MIT Press, 1998.

———. *Structural Transformation of the Public Sphere: An Inquiry into a Category of Bourgeois Society.* Cambridge, Mass.: MIT Press, 1989.

———. *The Theory of Communicative Action,* 2 vols. London: Heinemann, 1984/1987.

Hagen, William. *Germans, Poles, and Jews: The Nationality Conflict in the Prussian East, 1772–1914.* Chicago: University of Chicago Press, 1980.

Haiman, Mieczysław. *Polacy w Ameryce.* Chicago: Nakładem Polskiej Katolickiej Spółki Wydawniczej, 1930.

Handlin, Oscar. *The Uprooted: The Epic Story of the Great Migrations That Made the American People.* Boston: Little, Brown, 1951.

Hapak, Joseph. "The Polish Military Commission, 1917–1919." *Polish American Studies* 38, no. 2 (1981): 26–38.

Hickey, S. H. F. *Workers in Imperial Germany: The Miners of the Ruhr.* Oxford: Oxford University Press, 1985.

Hirschman, Charles. "America's Melting Pot Reconsidered." *Annual Review of Sociology* 9 (1983): 397–423.

Hobsbawm, Eric. "Identity Politics and the Left." *New Left Review* 1, no. 217 (1996): 38–47.

Hochstadt, Steve. *Mobility and Modernity: Migration in Germany, 1820–1989.* Ann Arbor: University of Michigan Press, 1999.

Hoerder, Dirk, ed. *Labor Migration in the Atlantic Economies: The European and North American Working Classes during the Period of Industrialization.* Westport, Conn.: Greenwood Press, 1985.

Holmes, Colin. *John Bull's Island: Immigration and British Society, 1871–1971.* Basingstoke, UK: Macmillan, 1988.

Holt, Sharon Ann. "Life and Labor of Coxe Miners." *Pennsylvania Legacies* 1, no. 1 (2001): 6–13.

Holtfrerich, Carl Ludwig. *Quantitative Wirtschaftsgeschichte des Ruhrkohlenbergbaus im 19. Jahrhundert.* Dortmund: Gesellschaft für Westfälische Wirtschaftsgeschichte, 1973.

Hunt, Lynn. *The Family Romance of the French Revolution.* Berkeley: University of California Press, 1992.

Ignatiev, Noel. *How the Irish Became White.* New York: Routledge, 1995.

Jones, Larry, ed. *Crossing Boundaries: German and American Experiences with the Exclusion and Inclusion of Minorities.* Oxford: Oxford University Press, 2001.

Jones, William. *Wales in America.* Scranton, Penn.: University of Scranton Press, 1997.

Joppke, Christian. "How Immigration is Changing Citizenship: A Comparative View." *Ethnic and Racial Studies* 22, no. 4 (1999): 644–47.

———. *Immigration and the Nation-State: The United States, Germany, and Great Britain.* Oxford: Oxford University Press, 1999.

Joppke, Christian, and Ewa Morawska. "Integrating Immigrants in Liberal Nation-States: Policies and Practices." In *Towards Assimilation and Citizenship: Immigrants in Liberal Nation-States,* edited by Christian Joppke and Ewa Morawska. Basingstoke, UK: Palgrave Macmillan, 2003.

Kenny, Kevin. *Making Sense of the Molly Maguires.* New York: Oxford University Press, 1998.

Kivisto, Peter. "Theorizing Transnational Immigration: A Critical Review of Current Efforts." *Ethnic and Racial Studies* 24, no. 4 (2001): 549–77

Klessmann, Christoph. *Polnische Bergarbeiter im Ruhrgebiet, 1870–1945: Soziale Integration und nationale Subkultur einer Minderheit in der deutschen Industriegesellschaft.* Göttingen: Vandenhoeck und Ruprecht, 1978.

Koch, Max J. *Die Arbeiterbewegung im Ruhrgebiet zur Zeit Wilhelms II.* Düsseldorf: Droste, 1954.

Koopmans, Ruud, and Paul Statham. "How National Citizenship Shapes Transnationalism: Migrant and Minority Claims-Making in Germany, Great Britain and the Netherlands." In *Toward Assimilation and Citizenship: Immigrants in Liberal Nation-States,* edited by Christian Joppke and Ewa Morawska. Basingstoke, UK: Palgrave Macmillan, 2003.

Kotłowski, Tadeusz. *Zjednoczenie Zawadowe Polskie: Zasięg wpływów i działalność społeczno-polityczna w latach 1918–1939.* Poznań: Uniwersytet im. Adama Mickiewicza, 1977.

Kozłowski, Jerzy. *Rozwój organizacji społeczno-narodowych wychodżstwa polskiego w Niemczech w latach 1870–1914.* Wrocław: Zakład Narodowy im. Ossolińskich, 1987.

Kroker, Evelyn, and Werner Kroker. *Solidarität aus Tradition: Die Knappen Verein im Ruhrgebiet.* Essen: C. H. Beck, 1988

Kubiak, Hieronim. *The Polish National Catholic Church in the United States of America from 1897 to 1980.* Cracow: Nakl. Uniwersytetu Jagiellonskiego, 1983.

Kula, Witold, Nina Assorodobraj-Kula, and Marcin Kula. *Writing Home: Immigrants in Brazil and the United States, 1890–1891.* Edited and translated by Josephine Wtulich. New York: Columbia University Press, 1986.

Kulczycki, John J. "The First Polish Clergymen in the Ruhr: Religion in Service of National Identity." In *States, Societies, Cultures: East and West: Essays in Honor of Jaroslaw Pelenski,* edited by Janusz Duzinkiewicz, Myroslav Popovych, Vladyslav Verstiuk, and Natalia Yakovenko. New York: Ross Publishing, 2004.

———. *The Foreign Worker and the German Labor Movement: Xenophobia and Solidarity in the Coal Fields of the Ruhr, 1871–1914.* Providence, R.I.: Berg, 1994.

———. *The Polish Coal Miners Union and the German Labor Movement in the Ruhr, 1902–1934.* Oxford: Berg, 1997.

————. "Polscy górnicy w Zagłębiu Ruhry." *Przegląd Polonijny* 13, no. 3 (1987): 21–26.

————. "Scapegoating the Foreign Worker." In *The Politics of Immigrant Workers: Labor Activism and Migration in the World Economy since 1830*, edited by Camille Guerin-Gonzales and Carl Strikwerda. New York: Holmes and Meier, 1993.

————. *School Strikes in Prussian Poland, 1901–1907: The Struggle over Bilingual Education*. Boulder, Colo.: East European Monographs, 1981.

Kymlicka, Will. *Multicultural Citizenship: A Liberal Theory of Minority Rights.* Oxford: Clarendon Press, 1995.

Lehr, Helena, and Edmund Osmańczyk. *Polacy spod znaku rodła.* Warsaw: Wydawnictwo Ministerstwa Obrony Narodowej, 1972.

Les, Barbara. *Kościół w procesie asymilacji Polonii amerykańskiej: Przemiany funkcji polonijnych instytucji i organizacji religijnych w środowisku Polonii chicagowskiej.* Wrocław: Zaklad Narodowy im. Ossolinskich, 1981.

Lister, Ruth. "Citizenship: Towards a Feminist Synthesis." *Feminist Review* 57, no. 1 (1997): 28–43.

Lopata, Helena Znaniecka. *Polish Americans.* New Brunswick, N.J.: Prentice Hall, 1994.

Lucassen, Leo. *The Immigrant Threat: The Integration of Old and New Migrants in Western Europe since 1850.* Urbana: University of Illinois Press, 2005.

————. "Old and New Migration in the Twentieth Century: A European Perspective." *Journal of American Ethnic History* 21, no. 4 (2002): 85–101.

Lucassen, Leo, David Feldman, and Jochen Oltmer, eds. *Paths of Integration: Migrants in Western Europe, 1880–2004.* Amsterdam: Amsterdam University Press, 2006.

Luhmann, Niklas. "Inklusion und Exklusion." In *Nationales Bewusstsein und kollektive Indentität: Studien zur Entwickelung des kollektiven Bewusstseins in der Neuzeit*, edited by Helmut Berding. Frankfurt a.M.: Suhrkamp, 1994.

Majewski, Karen. *Traitors and True Poles: Narrating a Polish-American Identity, 1880–1939.* Athens: Ohio University Press, 2003.

Marshall, T. H. *Citizenship and Social Class.* Cambridge, UK: Cambridge University Press, 1950.

Massey, Douglas. "The New Immigration and Ethnicity in the United States." *Population and Development Review* 21, no. 3 (1995): 631–52.

Matwiejczyk, Witold. *Katolickie towarzystwa robotników polskich w Zagłębiu Ruhry, 1871–1894.* Lublin: Towarzystwo Naukowe Katolickiego Uniwersytetu Lubelskiego, 1999.

————. "Mieędzy integracją kościelną a izolcją społeczną: Katolicy polscy w Zągłębiu Ruhry w latach 1871–1914." In *Schimanski, Kuzorra i inni: Polacy w Zagłębiu Ruhry 1870/71–1945*, edited by Dittmarra Dahlmanna, Alberta S. Kotowskiego, and Zbigniewa Karpusa. Toruń: Wydawnictwo Adam Marszałek, 2006.

Maynard, Theodore. *The Story of American Catholicism.* New York: Macmillan, 1942.

McCook, Brian. "Becoming Transnational: Continental and Transatlantic Polish Migration and Return Migration, 1870–1924." In *Relations among Internal, Continental, and Transatlantic Migration,* edited by Annemarie Steidl, Josef Ehmer, Stan Nadel, and Hermann Zeitlhofer. Göttingen: Vandenhoeck and Ruprecht Unipress, 2009.

———. "Divided Hearts: The Struggle between National Identity and Confessional Loyalty among Polish Catholics in the Ruhr, 1904–1914." *Polish Review* 47, no. 1 (2002): 67–96.

———. "Migration, Citizenship, and Polish Integration in the Ruhr Valley and Northeastern Pennsylvania, 1870–1924." *Bulletin of the German Historical Institute* 38, no. 1 (2006): 119–34.

———. "The Struggle for Polish Autonomy and the Question of Integration in the Ruhr and Northeastern Pennsylvania, 1880–1914." In *Towards a Comparative History of Coalfield Societies,* edited by Stefan Berger. Aldershot, UK: Ashgate, 2005.

Mertins, Günter. *Die Kulturlandschaft des westlichen Ruhrgebiets (Mühlheim-Oberhausen-Dinslaken).* Giessen: Wilhelm Schmitz Verlag, 1964.

Miller, Donald, and Richard Sharpless. *The Kingdom of Coal.* Easton, Penn.: Canal History and Technology Press, 1998.

Moch, Leslie Page. *Moving Europeans: Migration in Europe since 1650.* Bloomington: Indiana University Press, 2003.

Molenda, Jan. "The Role of Women in Polish Migration to the Rhine-Westphalia Industrial Region at the Beginning of the Twentieth Century." *Polish Review* 42, no. 3 (1997): 317–38.

Montgomery, David. *The Fall of the House of Labor: The Workplace, the State, and American Labor Activism, 1865–1925.* New York: Cambridge University Press, 1987.

Morawska, Ewa. "Disciplinary Agendas and Analytic Strategies of Research on Immigrant Transnationalism: Challenges of Interdisciplinary Knowledge." *International Migration Review* 37, no. 3 (2003): 611–40.

———. *For Bread with Butter: The Life-Worlds of East Central Europeans in Johnstown, Pennsylvania, 1890–1940.* Cambridge, UK: Cambridge University Press, 1985.

———. "Immigrants, Transnationalism, and Ethnicization: A Comparison of This Great Wave and the Last." In *E Pluribus Unum? Contemporary and Historical Perspectives on Immigrant Political Incorporation,* edited by Gary Gerstle and John Mollenkopf. New York: Russell Sage, 2001.

———. "In Defense of the Assimilation Model." *Journal of American Ethnic History* 13, no. 2 (1994): 76–87.

———. "Labor Migrations of Poles in the Atlantic World Economy, 1880–1914." *Comparative Studies in Society and History* 31, no. 2 (1989): 237–72.

Mosse, George L. *The Crisis of German Ideology: Intellectual Origins of the Third Reich.* 1964. New York: Schocken Books, 1981.

Murdzek, Benjamin. *Emigration in Polish Social-Political Thought, 1870–1914.* Boulder, Colo.: East European Monographs, 1977.

Murphy, Richard Charles. *Guestworkers in the German Reich: A Polish Community in Wilhelmine Germany.* Boulder, Colo.: East European Monographs, 1983.

Murzynowska, Krystyna. *Die polnische Erwerbsauswanderer im Ruhrgebiet während der Jahre 1880–1914.* Dortmund: Forschungsstelle Ostmitteleuropa, 1979.

Nadolny, Anastazy. "Problemy duszpasterstwa Polaków w Zągłębiu Ruhry na przykładzie losów księży Józefa Szotowskiego i Franciszka Lissa." In *Schimanski, Kuzorra i inni: Polacy w Zagłębiu Ruhry 1870/71–1945,* edited by Dittmarra Dahlmanna, Alberta S. Kotowskiego, and Zbigniewa Karpusa. Toruń: Wydawnictwo Adam Marszałek, 2006.

Noiriel, Gérard. *Le creuset français: Histoire de l'immigration, XIXe–XXe siècles.* Paris: Du Seuil, 1988.

———. "Immigration: Amnesia and Memory." *French Historical Studies* 19, no. 2 (1995): 367–80.

Oenning, Ralf Karl. *Du da Mitti, polnische Farben: Sozialisationserfahrungen von Polen im Ruhrgebiet 1918 bis 1939.* Münster: Waxmann, 1991.

Olzak, Susan. "Contemporary Ethnic Mobilization." *American Review of Sociology* 9, no. 1 (1983): 355–74.

Park, Robert. *Race and Culture.* Glencoe, Ill.: Free Press, 1950.

Pateman, Carole. "The Fraternal Social Contract." In *Civil Society and the State,* edited by John Keane. London: Verso, 1988.

———. "The Patriarchal Welfare State." In *Democracy and the Welfare State,* edited by Amy Gutman. Princeton, N.J.: Princeton University Press, 1988.

———. *The Sexual Contract.* Stanford, Calif.: Stanford University Press, 1988.

Pederson, Susan. *Family Dependence and the Origins of the Welfare State: Britain and France, 1914–1945.* Cambridge, UK: Cambridge University Press, 1993.

Peters-Schildgen, Susanne. *"Schmelztiegel" Ruhrgebiet: Die Geschichte der Zuwanderung am Beispiel Herne bis 1945.* Essen: Klartext, 1997.

Phelan, Craig. *Divided Loyalties: The Public and Private Life of Labor Leader John Mitchell.* Albany: State University of New York Press, 1994.

Pienkos, Donald. *One Hundred Years Young: A History of the Polish Falcons of America, 1887–1987.* Boulder, Colo.: East European Monographs, 1987.

———. *PNA: A Centennial History of the Polish National Alliance of the United States of North America.* Boulder, Colo.: East European Monographs, 1984.

Piore, Michael. *Birds of Passage: Migrant Labor and Industrial Societies.* Cambridge, UK: Cambridge University Press, 1979.

Ponty, Janine. *Polonais méconnus: Histoire des travailleurs immigrés en France dans l'entre-duex-guerres.* Paris: Publications de la Sorbonne, 1988.

Portes, Alejandro, Luis E. Guarnizo, and Patricia Landolt. "The Study of Transnationalism and the Promise of an Emergent Research Field." *Ethnic and Racial Studies* 22, no. 2 (1999): 217–37.

Portes, Alejandro, and Rubén G. Rumbaut. *Immigrant America: A Portrait.* Berkeley: University of California Press, 1996.

Portes, Alejandro, and Min Zhou. "The Second Generation: Segmented Assimilation and Its Variants." *Annals of the American Academy of Political and Social Science* 530 (November 1993): 74–96.

Powers, Madelon. *Faces Along the Bar: Lore and Order in the Workingman's Saloon, 1870–1920.* Chicago: University of Chicago Press, 1998.

Praszalowicz, Dorota. "Jewish, Polish, and German Migration from the Prussian Province of Posen/Poznań during the 19th Century." In *Irish and Polish Migration in Comparative Perspective,* edited by John Belchen and Klaus Tenfelde. Essen: Klartext, 2003.

Pula, James. "'A Branch Cut off from Its Trunk': The Effects of Immigration Restriction on American Polonia." *Polish American Studies* 61, no. 1 (2004): 39–50.

———. *Polish Americans: An Ethnic Community.* New York: Twayne, 1995.

Radzilowski, John. *The Eagle and the Cross: A History of the Polish Roman Catholic Union of America, 1873–2000.* Boulder, Colo.: East European Monographs, 2003.

Radzilowski, Thaddeus. "Family, Women, and Gender: The Polish Experience." In *Polish Americans and Their History: Community, Culture, and Politics,* edited by John Bukowczyk. Pittsburgh: University of Pittsburgh Press, 1996.

Ritter, Gerhard, and Klaus Tenfelde. *Arbeiter im Deutschen Kaiserreich, 1871 bis 1914.* Bonn: Dietz, 1992.

Roediger, David. *The Wages of Whiteness: Race and the Making of the American Working Class.* New York: Verso, 1991.

Rzepa, Krzysztof. *Socjaliści polscy w Niemczech do 1914 roku.* Warsaw: Książka i Wiedza, 1988.

Schäfer, Michael. *Heinrich Imbusch: Christlicher Gewerkschaftsführer und Widerstandskämpfer.* Munich: C. H. Beck, 1990.

Schiller, Nina Glick, Linda Basch, and Cristina Szanton Blanc. "Transnationalism: A New Analytic Framework for Understanding Migration," In *Towards a Transnational Perspective on Migration: Race, Class, Ethnicity, and Nationalism Reconsidered,* edited by Nina Glick Schiller, Linda Basch, and Cristina Szanton Blanc. New York: New York Academy of Sciences, 1992.

Schuck, Peter, and Rainer Münz, eds. *Paths to Inclusion: The Integration of Migrants in the United States and Germany.* New York: Berghahn Books, 1998.

Scott, Joan Wallach. "French Feminists and the Rights of 'Man': Olympe de Gouge's Declarations." *History Workshop Journal* 28, no. 1 (1989): 1–21.

Sierociński, Józef. *Armja Polska we Francji: Dzieje Wojsk Generała Hallera na obczyznie.* Warsaw: Nakł własnym, 1929.

Skocpol, Theda. *Protecting Soldiers and Mothers: The Political Origins of Social Policy in the United States.* Cambridge, Mass.: Harvard University Press, 1992.

Smith, Helmut Walser. *German Nationalism and Religious Conflict: Culture, Ideology, and Politics, 1870–1914.* Princeton, N.J.: Princeton University Press, 1995.

Smith, Michael, and Luis Guarnizo, eds. *Transnationalism from Below.* New Brunswick, N.J.: Transaction Publishers, 1998.

Smith, Robert. "Diasporic Memberships in Historical Perspective: Comparative Insights from the Mexican, Italian, and Polish Cases." *International Migration Review* 37, no. 3 (2003): 724–59.

Smith, Rogers M. *Civic Ideals: Conflicting Visions of Citizenship in U.S. History.* New Haven, Conn.: Yale University Press, 1997.

Soysal, Yasemin. *The Limits of Citizenship.* Chicago: University of Chicago Press, 1994.

Stasik, Florian. *Polska emigracja zarobkowa w Stanach Zjednoczonych Ameryki 1865–1914.* Warsaw: Państwowe Wydawnictwo Naukowe, 1985.

Stefanski, Valentina-Maria. *Zum Prozess der Emanzipation und Integration von Aussenseitern: Polnische Arbeitsmigranten im Ruhrgebiet.* Dortmund: Forschungsstelle Ostmitteleuropa, 1984.

Steidl, Annemarie. *Auf nach Wien! Die Mobilität des mitteleuropäischen Handwerks im 18. und 19. Jahrhundert am Beispiel der Haupt- und Residenzstadt Wien.* Munich: Oldenbourg, 2003.

Stern, Fritz. *The Failure of Illiberalism: Essays on the Political Culture of Modern Germany.* 1972. Reprint, New York: Columbia University Press, 1992.

Stolarik, M. Mark. *Immigration and Urbanization: The Slovak Experience, 1870–1918.* New York: AMS Press, 1989.

Strassberg, Barbara Les. "The Origins of the Polish National Catholic Church: The 'Polish National' Factor Reconsidered." *Polish National Catholic Church Studies* 7, no. 1 (1986): 25–39.

Święciochowski, Bolesław, ed. *Strajk szkolny we Wreśni w. 1901 r.* Września: Wrzesińskie Tow. Kulturalne i Muzeum Regionalne we Wreśni, 2001.

Tarapacki, Thomas. *Chasing the American Dream: Polish Americans and Sports.* New York: Hippocrene, 1995.

Tenfelde, Klaus. "The Herne Riots of 1899." In *The Social History of Politics: Critical Perspectives in West German Historical Writing since 1945,* edited by Georg Iggers. Dover, N.H.: Berg, 1985.

———. *Sozialgeschichte der Bergarbeiterschaft an der Ruhr im 19. Jahrhundert.* Bonn: Verlag Neue Gesellschaft, 1977.

Thomas, William, and Florian Znaniecki. *The Polish Peasant in Europe and America.* 5 vols. Boston: G. Badger, 1918.

Trzeciakowski, Lech. *Kulturkampf w zaborze pruskim.* Poznań: Wydawnictwo Poznańskie, 1970.

———. "The Prussian State and the Catholic Church in Prussian Poland, 1871–1914." *Slavic Review* 26, no. 4 (1967): 618–37.

Turner, George. "Ethnic Responses to the Lattimer Massacre." In *Hard Coal, Hard Times,* edited by David Salay. Scranton: Anthracite Museum Press, 1984.

———. "The Lattimer Massacre." *Proceedings of the Second Annual Conference on the History of Northeastern Pennsylvania* 2, no. 1 (1990): 1–15

Valasek, Paul S. *Haller's Polish Army in France.* Chicago: Paul S. Valasek, 2006.

Versteegh, Pien. "Glück Auf: The Polish Labor Movement in the United States and Germany, 1890–1914." *Polish American Studies* 62, no. 1 (2005): 53–66.

———. "'The Ties That Bind': The Role of Family and Ethnic Networks in the Settlement of Polish Migrants in Pennsylvania, 1890–1940." *History of the Family* 5, no. 1 (2000): 111–48.

Walaszek, Adam, ed. *Polska diaspora.* Cracow: Wydawnictwo Literackie, 2001.

———. *Reemigracja ze Stanów Zjednoczonych do Polski po I. wojnie światowej, 1919–1924.* Cracow: Nakl. Uniwersytetu Jagiellonskiego, 1983.

Waldinger, Roger, and David Fitzgerald. "Transnationalism in Question." *American Journal of Sociology* 109, no. 5 (2004): 1177–95.

Wallace, Les. *The Rhetoric of Anti-Catholicism: The American Protective Association, 1887–1911.* New York: Garland, 1990.

Walsh, William. *The United Mine Workers of America as an Economic and Social Force in the Anthracite Territory.* Washington, D.C.: Catholic University Press, 1931.

Weber, Eugen. *Peasants into Frenchmen: The Modernization of Rural France, 1870–1914.* Stanford, Calif.: Stanford University Press, 1976.

Wehler, Hans Ulrich. *Das Deutsche Kaiserreich.* Göttingen: Vandenhoeck and Ruprecht, 1973.

———. "Die Polen im Ruhrgebiet bis 1918." In *Moderne deutsche Sozialgeschichte,* edited by Hans Ulrich Wehler. Cologne: Kiepenheuer and Witsch, 1966.

Weisbrod, Bernd. "Arbeitgeberpolitik und Arbeitsbeziehungen im Ruhrbergbau: Vom 'Herr-im-Haus' zur Mitbestimmung." In *Arbeiter, Unternehmer und Staat im Bergbau: Industriellen Beziehungen im Internationalen Vergleich,* edited by Klaus Tenfelde and Gerald Feldman. Munich: C. H. Beck Verlag, 1989.

Wieczerzak, Joseph. "Bishop Francis Hodur and the Socialists: Associations and Disassociations," in *Bishop Francis Hodur: Biographical Essays,* edited by Joseph Wieczerzak. Boulder, Colo.: East European Monographs, 1998.

———. "Bishop Hodur and the Polish National Alliance (1896–1908): Re-viewing a Relationship." In *Bishop Francis Hodur: Biographical Essays,* edited by Joseph Wieczerzak. Boulder, Colo.: East European Monographs, 1998.

Włodarski, Stephen. *The Origin and Growth of the Polish National Catholic Church.* Scranton, Penn.: PNCC Press, 1974.

Wrzesiński, Wojciech. *Polski ruch narodowy w Niemczech, 1922–1939.* 3rd ed. Toruń: Wydawnictwo Adam Marszałek, 2005.

Wyman, Mark. *Round Trip to America: The Immigrants Return to Europe, 1880–1930.* Ithaca, N.Y.: Cornell University Press, 1993.

Wytrwal, Joseph A. *The Poles in America.* Minneapolis: Lerner, 1971.

Yancey, William L., Eugene P. Eriksen, and Richard N. Juliani. "Emergent Ethnicity: A Review and Reformulation." *American Sociological Review* 41, no. 3 (1976): 391–403.

Yuval-Davis, Nira. "Women, Citizenship and Difference." *Feminist Review* 57, no. 1 (1997): 4–27.

Zeidel, Robert. *Immigrants, Progressives, and Exclusion Politics: The Dillingham Commission, 1900–1927.* DeKalb: Northern Illinois Press, 2004.

Zhou, Min. "Segmented Assimilation: Issues, Controversies, and Recent Research on the New Second Generation." *International Migration Review* 31, no. 4 (1997): 975–1008.

Zolberg, Aristide. *A Nation by Design: Immigration Policy in the Fashioning of America.* New York: Russell Sage, 2006.

Index

Italicized page numbers refer to the appendix.